Normalization of U.S.-China Relations

An International History

Harvard East Asian Monographs 254

Normalization of U.S.-China Relations

An International History

Edited by

William C. Kirby, Robert S. Ross,

and Gong Li

Published by the Harvard University Asia Center
Distributed by Harvard University Press
Cambridge (Massachusetts) and London, 2005

© 2005 by the President and Fellows of Harvard College

Printed in the United States of America

The Harvard University Asia Center publishes a monograph series and, in coordination with the Fairbank Center for East Asian Research, the Korea Institute, the Reischauer Institute of Japanese Studies, and other faculties and institutes, administers research projects designed to further scholarly understanding of China, Japan, Vietnam, Korea, and other Asian countries. The Center also sponsors projects addressing multidisciplinary and regional issues in Asia.

Library of Congress Cataloging-in-Publication Data
Normalization of U.S.-China relations : an international history / edited by William C. Kirby, Robert S. Ross, and Gong Li.
     p. cm. -- (Harvard East Asian monographs ; 254)
    Includes bibliographical references and index.
    ISBN 0-674-01904-0 (cloth : alk. paper)
    1. United States--Foreign relations--China. 2. China--Foreign relations--United States.
I. Kirby, William C. II. Ross, Robert S., 1954- III. Gong, Li, 1952- IV. Series.
    E183.8.C5N66 2005
    327.7305109'047--dc22

                            2005028674

Index by Anne Holmes of EdIndex

∞ Printed on acid-free paper

Last figure below indicates year of this printing
15 14 13 12 11 10 09 08 07 06 05

Acknowledgments

The publication of this volume reflects the assistance and contributions of many friends and colleagues. The editors are grateful to Andrew Watson, who, as Representative of the Ford Foundation in China, recognized the importance of this project and provided generous support enabling continued collaboration between Chinese and American scholars on U.S.-China cold war cooperation. We also deeply appreciate the contribution of our many translators and editors, including Teresa J. Lawson, whose contributions are apparent on every page. Anne Holmes prepared the Index with her customary close attention to detail and accuracy.

Contents

Preface

GONG LI

This volume is the latest result of a collaborative research project between the Center of International Strategic Research of the Central Party School of the Chinese Communist Party and the Fairbank Center for East Asian Research at Harvard University. The contributors to this volume seek to advance our understanding of the many domestic and international factors behind the normalization of Sino-U.S. relations. Participants in this stage of the project included not only the scholars from China, the United States, Great Britain, and Canada who had contributed to earlier stages of the project but also scholars from Russia and Taiwan. Thus, during this stage of the collaboration, we have tried to develop a more comprehensive approach to the normalization of Sino-U.S. relations and offer a more multilateral perspective on bilateral Sino-U.S. relations.

The chapters in this book offer scholarly research and analysis on the process of normalization, based on archival materials and the recollections of participants in the negotiations leading to rapprochement and the establishment of diplomatic relations, from 1969 to 1979. They offer a window on the behind-the-scenes diplomacy and the dynamics of normalization. This volume also addresses strategic perspectives and decision making in Moscow and Taipei. Taken together, the chapters in this volume make it possible to understand the many factors that shaped the bilateral Sino-U.S. negotiations and the process by which Beijing and Washington eventually surmounted the various obstacles to cooperation and established the framework for normalization.

This volume builds on the work of previous stages of our collaboration. The Center of International Strategic Research and the Fairbank Center for East Asian Research began their scholarly partnership in 1995. The purpose was to utilize each other's advantages and to offer the latest and most authoritative scholarship based on the archival resources available in the two countries. This most recent stage of joint efforts began in 2000. We agreed to focus on "progress toward normalization of Sino-U.S. relations in 1969–79" and to examine four subtopics: relations in the period 1969–72; relations in the period 1973–79; the Soviet factor; and the influence of domestic politics on both sides of the Taiwan Strait.

The Chinese scholars participating in this project were Research Fellow Li Danhui of the Contemporary China Institute, Professor Gong Li of the Central Party School, Professor Wang Zhongchun of the University of National Defense, and Research Fellow Li Jie of the Party Literature Research Center. The scholars invited by the Fairbank Center to take part in this project were Professor Rosemary Foot of Oxford University, Professor Robert Accinelli of the University of Toronto, Professor Vitaly Kozyrev of Moscow State University, and Professor Jaw-ling Joanne Chang of the Institute of European and American Studies, Academica Sinica, Taiwan. The project organizers were Professors Gong Li, William C. Kirby of Harvard University, and Robert S. Ross of Boston College.

After extensive research, discussion, and writing, in January 2002 the authors held a research symposium in Beijing to discuss their papers. In addition to the project directors and the chapter authors, several former Chinese and American diplomats participated in the symposium. The American diplomats were Winston Lord, former ambassador to China; Stapleton Roy, former ambassador to China; Chas W. Freeman, former ambassador to Saudi Arabia; and Richard H. Solomon, former ambassador to the Philippines. Professor Erza F. Vogel, who had been director of the Fairbank Center for East Asian Research when this project first began, also joined the discussions. The former Chinese officials were Ambassadors Chai Zemin, Zhu Qizhen, Li Daoyu, and Li Fenglin and Consul General

Wang Li. Based on their personal experiences, these officials offered helpful comments on the chapter drafts and made valuable contributions to the quality of this volume.

The Chinese and foreign scholars engaged in a rich dialogue on the papers. Their discussion contributed to a greater understanding of U.S.-China relations, helped to clarify many issues, and reduced misunderstandings. There was a consensus that our research established that in order for Sino-U.S. relations to develop smoothly, realize common interests, and maximize cooperation, it was necessary to compromise on contradictory interests. Because China and the United States sought common ground while reserving their differences on important questions and forged successive compromises, Beijing and Washington improved relations and ultimately normalized relations in 1979, despite the prolonged role of the Taiwan factor as an obstacle to collaboration. There was also a consensus that the foreign policies of both countries were influenced, in different degrees, by domestic politics. The "Watergate" affair and partisan struggles in the United States restricted President Nixon's diplomatic flexibility during his second term as well as President Ford's foreign policy options, thus delaying the opening of relations with China. In China, the politics of the "cultural revolution," especially the political interference of the Lin Biao and Jiang Qing cliques, also influenced, in various degrees, Chinese policy toward the United States. Zhou Enlai and Deng Xiaoping, who were primarily responsible for managing Chinese policy toward the United States, were subject to intense political pressures and had to exercise considerable caution in foreign policy–making.

Because of different theoretical foundations, research methods, and archival materials, it was inevitable that differences developed. Discussion helped both sides consider issues from different angles and promoted research. Five areas in particular generated divergent viewpoints. First, some western scholars contended that in the 1970s Chinese policy was significantly affected by internal political instability, whereas Chinese scholars held that that the Politburo meeting of May 1971 had decided the fundamental principles of China's U.S. policy and, despite interference from politics, there was no significant change in this policy. These Chinese scholars argued that it was the United States, because of the number of presidents during the 1970s, that frequently changed its policy.

Second, western and Chinese scholars had different perspectives on Deng Xiaoping's foreign policy. Some western scholars observed the differences between Deng Xiaoping's speech to the UN General Assembly in 1974 and his U.S. policy in 1978 and concluded that he was not consistently in favor of U.S.-China cooperation. But Chinese scholars argued that prior to 1977 Deng was not the chief decision-maker regarding policy toward the United States; rather he was simply an implementer. Thus, the UN speech did not express his own perspective, and Deng's own policy toward the United Stares emerged only in the context of the later negotiations leading to diplomatic relations.

Third, some scholars argued that while seeking cooperation with China, the United States paid close attention to Taiwan's interests, in the hope of avoiding a reputation for "abandoning an old friend." But others observed that the U.S. government only belatedly notified Taiwan of Nixon's visit to China and of the normalization of relations, in contrast to France and Japan, which gave Taiwan ample notification of their intent to establish relations with China.

Fourth, on the issue of Chinese representation in the United Nations, some western scholars believed that both Beijing and Taipei adhered to the traditional attitude that it is "better to die in glory than live in dishonor," and thus each side rejected the two-China approach. The Chinese view at the symposium was that there was no cultural bias toward "dying in glory," and that the only price China paid was to postpone for one or two years the resumption of its legitimate seat in the United Nations. Some Chinese scholars also suggested that although the change in U.S. policy toward China in the early 1970s played a role in Mainland China's rejoining the United Nations, the process began in the 1950s, and that, had there not been the "cultural revolution" in the 1960s, it would have been completed several years earlier. They noted that by July 1971 the number of states having relations with the PRC exceeded that of states with relations with Taiwan. This meant that

Beijing's resumption of China's seat in the United Nations was inevitable. Once the United States recognized this trend, it adjusted its
policy.

Fifth, some western scholars criticized the stand taken by both
sides of the strait (including the Nationalist Party, or KMT, in
Taiwan before the 1990s) to persist in unification. Chinese scholars
explained that this reflected a common approach to legitimacy based
on a traditional Chinese cultural perspective and Confucian orthodoxy. They observed that Nationalist Party history books establish the legitimacy of Nationalist rule by portraying Chiang
Kai-shek as the successor to the Duke of Zhou. But Deng Xiaoping's
"one China, two systems" ideology broke with the traditional
"orthodoxy" regarding the sources of political legitimacy in China.

After the symposium on Sino-U.S. relations, the editors offered
detailed written comments and suggestions for revising the papers.
On the basis both of these comments and of the symposium discussion, the authors revised their papers. The chapters in this
volume thus reflect an extensive scholarly process, a truly collaborative project involving an international community of scholars.

The chapter by Li Danhui presents new perspectives and many
new archival materials. She examines the role of Vietnam in Chinese
policy toward the United States and analyzes how China, during the
many phases of normalization, adjusted its approach toward the
Vietnam-U.S. peace talks and its assistance to the Vietnamese resistance. Robert Accinelli's chapter complements Li Danhui's chapter.
His detailed research and extensive use of authoritative documents
explain how China and the United States made temporary compromises on the Taiwan issue problem from 1969 to 1972, as the two
sides began the rapprochement process.

Gong Li's chapter analyzes the changes in Chinese policy toward
the United States during normalization, especially the role of the
Taiwan factor. Rosemary Foot presents a distinctive perspective on
the role of the Taiwan problem after the publication of the "Shanghai Communiqué." She argues that the Nixon administration, in
prioritizing its strategic interests to emphasize U.S.-China relations
and normalization, was too ready to compromise key aspects of
Taiwan's diplomatic future.

Wang Zhongchun's chapter offers a military perspective on China's U.S. policy. His chapter analyzes the importance of the Soviet factor, particularly the growing Soviet threat to Chinese security from 1969 on, in the normalization of Sino-U.S. relations. Vitaly Kozyrev's participation in our collaborative project makes it possible to better understand the reaction of the former Soviet Union to the U.S.-China rapprochement and Moscow's policies toward China and the United States as attempts to undermine Sino-U.S. cooperation. His chapter provides an important global and regional analysis of Sino-U.S.-USSR interactions from 1969 to 1979.

Li Jie's chapter offers an in-depth and revealing discussion of the influence of China's domestic political situation on Sino-U.S. relations. He argues that after the re-emergence of Deng Xiaoping in Chinese domestic politics, especially after the reform and opening policy was launched in December 1978, Chinese domestic politics tended to support the development of Sino-U.S. relations. After the plenum, the urgent need for reform and opening superseded the need for unity with the United States to counter the Soviet Union and became the impetus for the rapid development of Sino-U.S. relations.

Joanne Chang's participation in the project brought a significant perspective to our research. Her chapter focuses on the interaction between U.S.-Taiwan relations and Sino-U.S. relations. Her analysis of Taiwan's response to three critical events in Sino-U.S. relations (the U.S. decision to cease its naval patrols of the Taiwan Strait, Taiwan's response to the posting of a representative of the PRC in the United States, and the normalization of Sino-U.S. relations) underscores the impact of growing Sino-U.S. cooperation on Taiwan and on U.S.-Taiwan relations from 1969 to 1978 and on the corresponding U.S. and Taiwan decision-making dynamics.

Although at this stage of our research there have been many breakthroughs and significant achievements, we are very aware that such a limited volume of academic research cannot definitively assess all the issues in Sino-U.S. relations during such a complex historical period. Chinese and Western scholars need to make further efforts to better understand the sources of U.S.-China cooperation.

I would like to express my appreciation to the Central Party School and to Harvard University for their support and assistance, which made it possible for this project to proceed so smoothly. I am also grateful to Professor Jiang Changbin, Professor Liu Jianfei, and Research Fellow Zhang Baijia for their considerable efforts on behalf of the project and for participating in the symposium discussions. I also thank my American colleagues, William C. Kirby and Robert S. Ross, for cooperating with me in the editorial work of this volume. I further thank the Ford Foundation for its financial support. Last of all, I thank all the contributors to this volume. Their academic efforts and their fine and exemplary scholarship make the study of Sino-U.S. relations more stimulating and productive.

Contributors

ROBERT ACCINELLI is Professor Emeritus in the Department of History at the University of Toronto. He is the author of *Crisis and Commitment: United States Policy Toward Taiwan, 1950–1955* (1996).

JAW-LING JOANNE CHANG is a member of the Institute of European and American Studies, Academica Sinica, and Deputy Representative of the Taipei Economic and Cultural Representative Office in the United States.

ROSEMARY FOOT is Professor of International Relations and the John Swire Senior Research Fellow in the International Relations of East Asia, St Antony's College, University of Oxford. In 1996 she was elected a Fellow of the British Academy. She is the author of several monographs and editor of collections, the most recent being *Rights Beyond Borders: The Global Community and the Struggle over Human Rights in China* (2000), *Human Rights and Counter-Terrorism in America's Asia Policy* (2004), and (co-edited with Barry Buzan) *Does China Matter? A Reassessment* (2005). Presently, her research focuses on human rights and security issues in the Asia-Pacific region and on Chinese perceptions of American hegemony.

GONG LI is Professor of International Relations and Vice Director of the International Strategic Research Center, Central Party School of the Chinese Communist Party. He received his Ph.D. from the Central Party School in 1991 and has published several books on Sino-American relations and Chinese foreign policy, including *Mao*

Zedong yu Meiguo: Mao Zedong dui Mei zhengce sixiang de guiji (Mao Zedong and the United States, 1999) and *Deng Xiaoping yu Meiguo* (Deng Xiaoping and the United States, 2004).

WILLIAM C. KIRBY is Dean of the Faculty of Arts and Sciences and Edith and Benjamin Geisinger Professor of History at Harvard University. His research focuses on China's economic and political development within an international context. Among his publications are *Germany and Republican China* (1984), *State and Economy in Republican China* (co-edited with Man-houng Lin, James Chin Shih, and David A. Pietz, 2000), and *Realms of Freedom in Modern China* (2004).

VITALY KOZYREV is Assistant Professor of History at the Institute of Asian and African Studies of Moscow State University. He is an expert on international conflicts in Asia, international relations in Eurasia, and China's economic history. He is editor and author of several books in Russian: *Revolution and Reforms in Contemporary China: The Search for a Developmental Paradigm, China in World War II,* and *State and Peasantry in Republican China.* In his numerous publications and conference papers, Kozyrev explores Sino-Russian energy cooperation, the Shanghai Cooperation Organization, Russia's policies in Central Asia, and recent trends in the development of Taiwan. He has taught courses at a variety of universities in Russia, the United States, China, and Taiwan. In addition, he has been an analyst for the Russian News Agency (RIAN) and a member of the "Kremlin Expert Network."

LI DANHUI is Senior Research Fellow at the Cold War International History Studies Center of East China Normal University and concurrently Professor in the School of International Relations, Peking University. Her research focuses on cold war international history with an emphasis on postwar Sino-Soviet relations. She is the editor of *Zhongguo yu Yinduzhina zhanzheng* (China and the Indochina wars, 2000) and editor in chief of *Beijing yu Mosike: cong lianmeng zouxiang duikang* (Beijing and Moscow: from alliance to confrontation, 2002).

LI JIE is Research Professor and Vice Director of the Department for Research on Party Documents, Central Committee of the Chinese Communist Party. His most recent book is *Mao Zedong yu xin Zhongguo de neizheng waijiao* (Mao Zedong and the politics and diplomacy of New China, 2003).

ROBERT S. Ross is Professor of Political Science at Boston College; Associate, John King Fairbank Center for East Asian Research, Harvard University; and Senior Advisor, Security Studies Program, Massachusetts Institute of Technology. His current research focuses on Chinese security policy and U.S.-China relations, especially the Chinese use of force and deterrence in East Asia. Among his recent publications is *Re-examining the Cold War: U.S.-China Diplomacy, 1954–1973* (co-edited with Jiang Changbin, 2001).

SENIOR COLONEL WANG ZHONGCHUN is Professor and Deputy Director of the Training and Research Division for Foreign Officer Students, National Defense University, China. He obtained the Ph.D. degree in International Relations from the Central Party School of the Chinese Communist Party. His current research focuses on Sino-U.S. relations, particularly in the security field. He is, among other titles, a co-editor (with Pan Zhenqiang and Xia Liping) of *Guoji caijun yu junbei kongzhi* (International disarmament and arms control, 1996), co-author (with Wen Zhonghua) of *Busan de he yinyun—he wuqi yu he zhanlue: cong zuotian dao mingtian* (Nuclear weapons and nuclear strategies: from yesterday to tomorrow, 2000), and co-author (with Xia Liping) of *Meiguo de he liliang yu he zhanlue* (The nuclear arsenal and nuclear strategy of the United States, 1995), as well as numerous academic papers.

Normalization of U.S.-China Relations

An International History

Introduction

WILLIAM C. KIRBY, ROBERT S. ROSS,

AND GONG LI

Relations between China and the United States have been of central importance to both countries in and beyond the era of the cold war. The history of U.S.-China relations over the past half-century—the subject of heated debates by scholars of both countries—may now be addressed more dispassionately on the basis of newly available archival materials, memoirs, and oral histories on both sides of the Pacific.

This book is a product of the evolution of Chinese-American relations. It is a collaborative enterprise of the Chinese and American scholarly communities. It offers the first multinational, multi-archival review of the history of Chinese-American conflict and cooperation in the 1970s. The book builds on earlier collaborations, for it is the second English-language volume in a series of joint research projects between the Institute of International Strategic Research at China's Central Party School and the John King Fairbank Center for East Asian Research at Harvard.[1] The overall project began in 1995, just as new documentation on the U.S.-China conflict following the Korean War was becoming available to scholars in both China and the United States. The time had arrived for diplomatic historians and specialists in international relations to reassess the U.S.-China relationship from 1954 to 1972. The first two volumes in the project thus covered U.S. and Chinese policy on such critical issues as the Taiwan Strait crises, the war in Vietnam, and the diplomacy of U.S.-China rapprochement. These volumes also examined the domestic sources of U.S.-China conflict and of the 1972 rapprochement, including the role of elites and of domestic political instability in each country.

As the first collaborative volumes neared completion, the ongoing process of declassification of documents in the United States and of expanding access to Chinese documents made possible a conference, as well as this volume, on the "diplomatic revolution" of the 1970s, which captured the world's attention with President Nixon's visit to China in 1972 and culminated in the normalization of U.S.-China diplomatic relations in 1979. The result is, we believe, a strong set of essays on the era that gave birth to contemporary Chinese-American relations. It is distinguished from other studies by its use of newly available historical materials; by the fact that it is the result of a truly international conference of scholars from and beyond both the United States and China, with participants from the PRC, Taiwan, the United States, Canada, Great Britain, and Russia; and by the fact that the conference papers were discussed by historical figures: former ambassadors and other senior officials who were themselves part of this history.

This volume follows, but goes beyond, the format of the previous volumes. Participants were selected both for their knowledge of U.S.-China relations and for their research experience in using recently available archival materials. Chinese scholars were invited to write papers on Chinese foreign policy, and Western scholars were invited to write on the United States' China policy. But Sino-American relations have never been a purely bilateral affair, and to appreciate the broader, international and cross-strait arenas that were part of the diplomatic scene, it was essential to study Chinese-American relations from the vantage points of Moscow, Taipei, and Hanoi.

The authors presented their research at a conference in Beijing in January 2002, hosted by the Central Party School. The papers were then critiqued not only by all the paper writers but above all by historical actors: former senior U.S. and Chinese diplomats active in U.S.-China relations during the 1970s. Former U.S. diplomats Chas Freeman, Winston Lord, Stapleton Roy, and Richard Solomon were joined by their Chinese counterparts Chai Zemin, Li Daoyu, Li Fenglin, Wang Li, and Zhu Qizhen. In addition, the conference benefited from the participation of Chinese and American scholars who served as discussants. The Chinese discussants were Jiang Changbin, Liu Jianfei, Shi Yinhong, Tao Wenzhao, and Zhang Baijia. The American discussants were Steven Goldstein and Ezra Vogel. The result was a stimulating set of discussions on history, as viewed from the archive and as remembered from personal experience. The final papers are much richer because of the contributions and critiques of our diplomats and the other discussants.

What are the central findings of this book? The research in this volume underscores that the main foreign policy actors in U.S.-China relations were motivated primarily by pragmatic attention to their respective country's national security objectives. On the Chinese side, normalization of U.S.-China relations was instrumental to Beijing's effort to enhance its security vis-à-vis the Soviet Union. Mao Zedong, despite his ideological opposition to "imperialism" and because of his growing understanding of Soviet power, saw the tactical necessity for compromising with the Americans in order to promote Chinese security. During the early post-Mao era, when Deng Xiaoping assumed authority over policymaking, China's interest in promoting development through foreign trade and investment joined with its national security interests, including Chinese efforts to contend with Soviet-Vietnamese cooperation in Indochina, to encourage further Chinese efforts to normalize relations with the United States. Wang Zhongchun's chapter shows just how thoroughly military-strategic determinations were at the heart of Chinese-American relations.

But Beijing consistently balanced its interest in normalization of relations with its interest in compelling the United States to terminate official relations with Taiwan. From 1969 to 1979, Beijing never wavered from its insistence that following normalization any U.S. presence in Taiwan must be unambiguously unofficial. Chinese leaders understood that any compromise on this principle would jeopardize the eventual unification of Taiwan with the mainland as well as the political legitimacy of the PRC's leadership, party, and state.

As Li Danhui's chapter suggests, China also developed its Vietnam policy in the context of its interest in developing strategic cooperation with the United States. During the early stages of U.S.-China rapprochement, Beijing understood that the U.S. involvement in the war in Vietnam was an obstacle to normalization of U.S.-China relations. It thus manipulated its economic and military assistance to Vietnam to promote Vietnamese willingness to negotiate an early peace agreement with the United States. Only later, when Beijing developed confidence in U.S.-China relations and sought to resist greater Soviet influence in Indochina did it resume its full aid program for Hanoi.

The United States was equally motivated by national security concerns to normalize U.S.-China relations. The Nixon and Ford administrations' preoccupation with Vietnam and with a potential "post-Vietnam" political vulnerability to Soviet power created the U.S. security interest in normalization. Although the early Carter administration was reluctant to acknowledge the importance of U.S.-China relations to American security, by mid-1978 it, too, was pursuing normalization of U.S.-China relations for its contribution to U.S. security vis-à-vis the Soviet Union.

Like China, the United States considered its policy on U.S.-China relations in the context of its relationship with Taiwan. While pursuing cooperation with Beijing, Presidents Nixon, Ford, and Carter sought to maximize the United States' post-normalization political relationship with Taiwan. The United States was not necessarily opposed to mainland-Taiwan unification, but its concern about the political ramifications of "abandoning" Taiwan—and the implications of this for Asian, global, and domestic U.S. politics—constrained its negotiating flexibility.

In the end, of course, the United States acquiesced to China's demand that it sever all official contact with Taiwan. Was this inevitable? Although U.S. negotiators believed that they had made the minimal concessions necessary to achieve normalization, there is no consensus among this volume's authors that the content of the normalization agreement was a foregone conclusion.

Gong Li and Robert Accinelli, relying on both U.S. and Chinese diplomatic documents, concur that Chinese leaders consistently opposed official U.S.-Taiwan contacts following normalization and would not have agreed to normalization on any other terms. Both Mao Zedong and Deng Xiaoping were adamant that no vestige of official relations between the United States and Taiwan could remain. Moreover, Accinelli argues that the Carter administration negotiated a favorable agreement, insofar as it obtained China's agreement to normalize relations despite the U.S. insistence that Washington would continue to sell weaponry to Taiwan.

Rosemary Foot suggests, however, that the game was given away much earlier. She argues that the archives of the Nixon and Ford administrations reveal Henry Kissinger's repeated readiness to agree secretly to China's demands for normalization very early in the relationship. She argues that although such secret pledges may have been necessary to secure Chinese willingness to receive Richard Nixon in Beijing, such premature commitments to U.S. concessions constrained the Carter administration's negotiating flexibility and undermined its ability to negotiate Chinese acceptance of the posting of State Department officials to a U.S. liaison office in Taipei. Because such U.S. demands amounted to policy "reversals," Washington could not effectively counter Chinese opposition. Nixon's and Kissinger's excessive readiness to placate Chinese concerns thus predetermined a critical aspect of the Carter administration's negotiations with China over normalization.

Despite Chinese and U.S. leaders' preoccupation with national security interests, throughout the cold war domestic politics was a constant factor in policymaking in both Beijing and Washington. In the 1960s, particularly at the height of the "Cultural Revolution," Chinese domestic politics was a more important factor in U.S-China relations than U.S. domestic politics. This may still have been the case in the early 1970s, when China teetered on the edge of civil war before the resolution of the Lin Biao affair. (It was noted during the conference that, had the Americans known how unstable the political situation was in 1971, they would never have risked a presidential visit. Ignorance may have its benefits in foreign affairs.) But from 1974 on, U.S. domestic politics would prove as, if not more, important to the relationship than Chinese domestic politics. Although both President Nixon and President Ford understood the significance of normalization for U.S. security and hoped to achieve a normalization agreement with Beijing, their respective political interests compelled them to prolong the process. The Watergate scandal undermined Nixon's domestic political authority and his flexibility to follow through on his secret commitment to break diplomatic relations with Taiwan and establish relations with Beijing in his second term. When Gerald Ford became president after Nixon's resignation, the 1976 presidential campaign dominated Ford's policy agenda, and he, too, avoided the potential controversy of a normalization agreement with Beijing. Since Nixon and Ford expected high domestic costs should they make the compromises necessary for normalization, they placed their domestic political interests ahead of the country's foreign policy interests.

In China, domestic political disputes did not determine foreign policy, but foreign policy played a critical role in the course of succession politics among Mao's subordinates. From 1969 until mid-1976, Mao Zedong controlled both domestic politics and Chinese foreign policy. Whereas in the 1960s he had allowed his domestic ideological objectives to shape his security policy, in the 1970s the necessity for strategic cooperation with the United States pushed his domestic objectives to the background in China's U.S. policy. But as Li Jie's detailed and informative chapter shows, China's U.S. policy was a critical factor in the contest for power among Defense Minister Lin Biao, Mao's wife Jiang Qing, and Premier Zhou Enlai. First Lin maneuvered for advantage over Zhou by opposing U.S.-China cooperation, and then Jiang Qing tried to weaken Zhou with charges that he was too eager to normalize relations with the United States. But Mao's support for Zhou, his constant focus on Chinese security interests, and his ideological contempt for the Soviet Union prevented China's succession politics from destabilizing U.S.-China relations. Following Mao's death in September 1976, Deng Xiaoping not only quickly established authority over China's foreign policy and maintained Mao's strategy of alignment with the United States but also ousted opposition leaders who had resisted U.S.-China cooperation. This further minimized the role of domestic politics in China's U.S. policy.

The chapters on Taiwan and the Soviet Union reveal the different impact of the U.S.-China rapprochement on each country. Joanne Chang's research underscores how completely Taiwan's dependence on the United States for its security constrained its diplomacy. Although Taipei frequently considered various policy options in response to developments in U.S. policy toward China, including a counteroffensive in U.S. domestic politics and opening a political relationship with the Soviet Union, in the end Taiwan could be little more than a passive observer of U.S. diplomacy, compelled to react to events rather than try to forestall them. The risk to Taiwan of alienating the United States was simply too high, and it could only hope that Washington would not sacrifice Taiwan in the interest of great power cooperation.

Vitaly Kozyrev's paper shows that the Soviet Union, by contrast, frequently took the diplomatic initiative to try to persuade the United States to forsake anti-Soviet security cooperation with China. Such initiatives included discussions of military cooperation against China's nuclear program, manipulation of the U.S.-Soviet nuclear arms control negotiations, and various diplomatic warnings to U.S. statesmen. In the end, however, despite its superpower capabilities, Moscow was no more effective than Taipei in shaping U.S. policy toward China. Other than the brief period at the beginning of the Carter administration when Secretary of State Cyrus Vance deferred improved relations with Beijing in order to facilitate arms control cooperation with Moscow, Soviet power encouraged rather than deterred U.S.-China cooperation. Moreover, the early Carter interlude reflected not so much successful Soviet foreign policy as Carter's and Vance's own *a priori* conceptions of the prospects for détente and of U.S. strategic priorities.

There still remain many unanswered questions about U.S.-China relations during this period. We know very little about Mao's decision to remove Deng Xiaoping from the leadership in the period from November 1975 to April 1976 and its relationship to Chinese foreign policy. Similarly, we know little about the interplay between domestic politics and foreign policy during the period immediately after Mao's death, when Hua Guofeng was China's titular leader and Deng was maneuvering to return to power. And despite the excellent research on Deng's role in the normalization process, we know precious little about the role of other Chinese leaders in Chinese policymaking and possible sources of support and opposition to Deng's policy. We look forward to the day when the archives of all of China's foreign policy–making bureaucracies are fully open and when these questions can be addressed. A first and very important step in this process is the recent Chinese decision to open the Foreign Ministry archives to scholars from all countries.

On the American side, there are still many unanswered questions regarding the Carter administration's China policy, including President Carter's understanding of the role of China in U.S. security policy, his decision to grant greater authority to Zbigniew Brzezinski in China policy, and his planning for U.S.-Taiwan relations in the post-normalization era. As the U.S. government widens access to the Carter administration archives, we are confident that scholars from many countries will be able to address these questions.

There still is much work to be done on the history of U.S.-China relations during the crucial decade of the 1970s. We hope that the cooperation between the Central Party School and Harvard University and the scholarship in this volume encourage the further study of U.S.-China relations in both China and the United States. We are especially grateful to Jiang Changbin for his strong leadership since the inception of our project and to Liu Jianfei, whose tireless efforts helped to bring this book to publication. Equally important, we are very pleased and honored that this volume has been published under our joint sponsorship, and we look forward to future collaborative projects between Chinese and American scholars.

and that Nixon and Kissinger made significant private concessions to the PRC. The materials also permit a close analysis of the strategy pursued by the White House to manage the issue domestically and internationally. The new sources likewise provide a fresh view of the State Department's underappreciated contribution to the initiative and the White House's management of the volatile issue of Chinese representation in the United Nations.

The key objective of the Taiwan strategy employed by Nixon and Kissinger was to arrive at a modus vivendi with the PRC without provoking damaging domestic opposition or destabilizing either the U.S.-ROC relationship or internal order on Taiwan. They wanted an accommodation that deferred a final resolution of differences over Taiwan and cleared the path for a strategic relationship with China. In pursuing a modus vivendi, they needed to avoid creating a crisis of confidence with the Nationalist regime or inciting domestic accusations of betraying a loyal ally. A rift with Taiwan or a domestic blowup would jeopardize the opening to China. On the home front, Nixon and Kissinger were particularly solicitous of the views of right-wing conservatives in the Republican party, who were avid supporters of the Nationalist regime.

Adding to the potential hazards of a misstep on the Taiwan issue was that a perceived retreat from the commitment to the ROC's security could undermine American credibility. Maintaining credibility in the eyes of friends and foes alike was a key concept in U.S. foreign policy during the cold war, one deeply embedded in Nixon's and Kissinger's outlook on world affairs.[2]

Although Nixon and Kissinger wanted to remove the Taiwan issue as a stumbling block to accord with the Chinese, they also believed that the issue could work to the U.S. advantage. Since the United States was the greatest barrier to the PRC's control of Taiwan, the Chinese had an incentive to improve relations with Washington. In addition, the two leaders hoped that concessions regarding the American military presence on Taiwan would motivate the Chinese to lean on their North Vietnamese allies to negotiate an acceptable settlement of the conflict in Indochina.

Secrecy and deception were essential features of Nixon's and Kissinger's Taiwan strategy, as they were of their entire China ini-

tiative. Relying on the White House–centered policymaking appa-
ratus set up at the start of the Nixon presidency, the two men
conducted secret negotiations with the Chinese without involving
the national security bureaucracy or the State Department. At the
same time, secrecy enabled them to protect their China initiative
from unwanted domestic and international complications. In their
confidential negotiations, Nixon and Kissinger offered unilateral
assurances to the Chinese regarding the Taiwan issue and the normalization of U.S.-PRC relations. These secret understandings were
a crucial component of the Taiwan modus vivendi finalized during
the president's visit to China in February 1972. They went well
beyond the public position on the issue taken by the United States
in the Shanghai Communiqué. Maintaining the distinction between
the secret and the public sides of the modus vivendi was central to
the Nixon-Kissinger Taiwan strategy. As the president remarked to
Premier Zhou Enlai during his stay in Beijing, the difficulty was
"not in what we are going to do, the problem is what we are going to
say [publicly] about it. . . . [My] record shows I always do more than
I can say, once I have made the decision as to the direction of our
policy."[3]

A Taiwan strategy first began to take shape in early 1970 when
the United States and China resumed ambassadorial talks in Warsaw
after a hiatus of several years. Nixon had previously let Beijing
know through secret third-party contacts and various conciliatory
gestures that he wanted to improve relations. A significant signal
conveyed privately through Pakistani authorities in October 1969
was that the United States was ending the permanent naval patrol of
the Taiwan Strait initiated at the start of the Korean War and then
routinely carried out by two specially designated U.S. destroyers.
To ensure that Beijing did not miss this important signal, the Central Intelligence Agency also passed along the information to a secret
contact in Hong Kong. An intelligence report in early January 1970
indicated that the Chinese were aware of the change and "that they
saw this as a modification of U.S. policy in the Taiwan Strait area."[4]

The ending of the naval patrol had symbolic but no real military
significance. The termination was intended, as Kissinger informed a
Pakistani official, to remove an "irritant" in Sino-American rela-

tions but not to imply a lessening of the American commitment to Taiwan's defense.[5] Moreover, the Navy continued intermittent patrols with vessels from the Seventh Fleet. Chiang Kai-shek withdrew a protest over the end of the permanent patrol after being assured that the U.S. Navy was not letting its guard down in the Strait.[6]

The reactivation of the Warsaw talks opened the first direct dialogue between the United States and China during Nixon's presidency. At this early point in the China initiative, Nixon and Kissinger had not yet assumed exclusive control of the operation. As a result, the State Department was involved, along with the White House, in determining a suitable approach at the renewed talks. In his memoirs, Kissinger unfavorably compares the State Department's cautious and traditional approach to the bold and innovative one preferred by him and the president.[7] His self-serving account misrepresents and undervalues the department's contribution to the talks and the development of a Taiwan strategy.

The first substantive session of the revived talks took place on January 20, 1970. In advance of this session, the State Department prepared a guidance for Ambassador Walter Stoessel, the U.S. representative at the talks, with exact instructions for his discussions with his Chinese counterpart, Lei Yang. Emphasizing "a new beginning" in Sino-U.S. relations, the guidance included an unprecedented offer to send a special American representative to Beijing or have a Chinese representative come to Washington. The guidance also contained, along with a reaffirmation of U.S. diplomatic and military ties with the ROC, three new formulations on the Taiwan issue. State Department Asian experts understood the significance of this issue to the Chinese. The language of the formulations, as one of them later recalled, was intended to find favor with the Chinese "without, ultimately, giving away the store so far that it would be totally unacceptable on Taiwan or on the [Capitol] Hill."[8] The new formulations stated that the United States would not stand in the way of a peaceful settlement of Taiwan's status by Beijing and Taipei; would not support offensive military action from Taiwan against the mainland; and "hoped" to reduce the American military presence on Taiwan as "peace and stability in Asia grow."[9]

Stoessel was guardedly optimistic in his report to the State Department on the meeting. Lei Yang had been receptive to ongoing U.S.-PRC discussions, either at the ambassadorial talks or at a higher level. His opening statement, focusing on the Taiwan issue, had been free of ideological polemics while reiterating the basic Chinese position. In a noteworthy departure, he had refrained from demanding immediate and unconditional American withdrawal from Nationalist-controlled territory or from insisting that the PRC alone would decide whether to use peaceful or forceful means to "liberate" Taiwan.[10]

Encouraged by Lei Yang's "most interesting and inviting presentation," Kissinger advised the president that they now had to consider "what we want from them [the Chinese], and what we would give in return." The Chinese were focusing on Taiwan, "an area in which they want something from us." Whether they would compromise on this issue in order to reach an understanding with the United States was uncertain. They were certainly aware that U.S. concessions on the issue could disrupt Washington's relations with Taipei. Kissinger speculated that the Chinese might prove amenable to an interim settlement that did not require the United States to sacrifice the Nationalist government. He cautioned that "we will need to move most carefully [on the Taiwan issue] to avoid giving them a windfall by upsetting the present stability on Taiwan."[11]

Kissinger's reflections contained the germ of a Taiwan strategy aimed at achieving a modus vivendi. The State Department's guidance for the January 20 meeting, which the president had approved, also pointed in the same direction by indicating a readiness to show at least some flexibility on the Taiwan issue in the interest of improved relations with China.

In preparing for a second Warsaw meeting on February 20, State Department Asian experts drafted another guidance along with a strategy paper outlining their preferred course of action at the ambassadorial talks. Secretary of State William Rogers forwarded both documents to the White House with his own memorandum of support. Rogers and his colleagues favored a go-slow approach in order to determine if the Chinese were genuinely interested in better relations or simply wanted the appearance of more amiable relations to give Moscow pause. Before advancing to high-level talks, the department wanted to test Chinese intentions at the Warsaw talks. An initial test would be to determine whether the Chinese would join in finding a way to set aside the Taiwan issue so as to lend momentum to improved relations and to proceed with discussion of other bilateral issues.

The strategy paper posited that putting the Taiwan issue on the "back burner" required a formula "which is sufficiently vague and ambiguous to leave us both [Chinese and Americans] free to do what we wish"; this would give the "Chinese 'face' to move on to discuss other matters" and leave "basically unaltered" the U.S. relationship with Taipei. Arriving at such a formula would not be easy. Beijing would want an acknowledgment from the United States that the Taiwan problem was an "internal" Chinese matter, that it did not envisage an independent Taiwan, and that it intended to reduce its military presence on the island. For its part, Washington would want an assurance that the PRC would not attack Taiwan.

The strategy paper identified "two essential questions" requiring a decision by Washington if the Warsaw negotiations showed promise. The first related to the status of Taiwan. Contrary to the claims by both Beijing and Taipei that Taiwan was part of China, the United States had since the Korean War maintained that the island's status was "undetermined." For the United States to acknowledge that Taiwan was part of China would foreclose the option of a formal separation of the island from the mainland. It would also "prejudice" the ability of the United States to sustain its diplomatic and defense commitment to the Nationalist government. As State Department analysts recognized, maintaining that Taiwan's status was "undetermined" made it easier to justify the U.S. relationship with the ROC without appearing to intervene in Chinese internal affairs. As an initial negotiating position, the paper recommended trying to blur this issue while granting that the relationship between Taiwan and the China mainland was "one to be decided by those directly involved."

The second question related to the U.S. military presence on Taiwan. Since 1964 the number of American military personnel on the island had soared from 1,000 to 10,000, mainly because of the

Indochina conflict. The strategy paper, as an initial negotiating position, recommended informing the Chinese that the United States intended to reduce these forces and then follow this with some symbolic removals.[12]

The White House did not share the State Department's reluctance to move quickly to high-level discussions. Scornful of the department's bureaucracy and encouraged by back-channel signaling from Beijing (which Foggy Bottom knew nothing about), Nixon and Kissinger were eager to press ahead to such consultations. At the president's request, the department revised its guidance for the February 20 meeting to reflect a more upbeat attitude toward high-level talks. Apart from this change, Nixon found the guidance "generally excellent and in keeping with the philosophy he desires for the talks."[13]

The treatment of the Taiwan issue in the revised guidance was entirely the product of the State Department. The guidance expressed the hope that the talks might enable the two sides to reach "some meeting of the minds" on an issue that was a "major obstacle" to better relations. Discussion of this issue would, however, have to proceed simultaneously with consideration of the entire range of problems between the two countries. The guidance reiterated the earlier formulation favoring a peaceful settlement of the Taiwan question by the two disputing parties but contained a more definitive version of the formulation on a reduced U.S. military presence on Taiwan. The revised formulation stated the "intention" (rather than just the "hope") to reduce U.S. military facilities on the island "as tensions in the area diminish." Implicit in the formulation was a connection between force reductions on Taiwan and an end to the war in Indochina along with more satisfactory relations between the United States and the PRC. The guidance also included a proposal for a joint declaration incorporating an affirmation of the "Five Principles of Peaceful Coexistence." These principles had been a fixture of Chinese diplomacy since the mid-1950s but had not been unconditionally embraced by the United States, despite their compatibility with the UN Charter.[14]

A breakthrough took place at the February 20 session, when Lei Yang declared the PRC's willingness to receive a high-level

American envoy in Beijing. He insisted, however, that settlement of the Taiwan issue had to precede any fundamental improvement in Sino-American relations or the resolution of "secondary" differences. He made plain that a "two Chinas" or "one China, one Taiwan" settlement was unacceptable. In what Stoessel interpreted as a hint of flexibility, however, Lei Yang noted that the PRC realized that an effort was needed to create the right conditions for a resolution of the issue.[15]

Buoyed by the outcome of the second Warsaw session, Nixon and Kissinger wanted to seize the opportunity for a high-level meeting. The State Department preferred to probe Chinese intentions further and find some common ground before risking an encounter in the full glare of domestic and international publicity. In the end, the White House agreed on a compromise.[16] The guidance for the next session responded positively to the Chinese offer but also laid out six principles as a basis for a high-level meeting. The principles, whose purpose was to gauge the flexibility of the Chinese and the chances for a successful outcome from a high-level parley, were basically a restatement of positions already advanced at the talks on the initiative of the State Department. In response to Chinese concerns, the guidance also stated that the United States had no intention of imposing a "two China" or "one China, one Taiwan" solution of the Taiwan problem. The guidance reaffirmed the U.S. objective of "gradually reduc[ing] the limited military presence on Taiwan as tensions in the Far East and the Taiwan area diminish."[17]

The Chinese cancellation of the next scheduled session of the talks following the American incursion into Cambodia ended the prospect for an immediate high-level meeting in Beijing. The cancellation gave Nixon and Kissinger the opportunity to take full operational control of China policy, permitting them to shunt aside the State Department (except on the issue of Chinese representation in the United Nations) and pursue the China initiative through personal, secret diplomacy. The Warsaw talks never resumed.[18] Nonetheless, the two sessions in early 1970 represented an important way station on the road to Sino-American reconciliation. The talks generated a positive atmosphere and enabled both sides to show a willingness to move beyond polemics and to explore ways to end their hostile relationship. The talks also unmistakably confirmed that the Taiwan issue remained the main source of Sino-American conflict.

In the *White House Years*, Kissinger was dismissive of the State Department's preoccupation during the talks with traditional "pet projects" such as the Taiwan issue.[19] Yet he and the president never expressed reservations about the department's approach to this issue. Indeed, in their own future dealings with the Chinese they would adopt elements of that approach. They would search for a modus vivendi that would permit the two sides to put the issue aside without resolving fundamental differences while improving their overall relationship and carrying on consultations on a broad agenda. They would offer assurances to the Chinese about U.S. intentions toward Taiwan (including a number inspired by State Department guidances during the Warsaw talks) while attempting to secure from the Chinese a commitment to seek a peaceful solution of the Taiwan question. They would maintain the linkage between U.S. force reductions on Taiwan and the lessening of regional tensions, including the Indochina conflict. Furthermore, the State Department's hesitancy to move immediately to an attention-grabbing high-level public meeting in Beijing without more preliminary discussion was understandable. Kissinger was to make two trips to Beijing in 1971 to prepare for Nixon's visit early the next year.

In early December 1970 a message from Zhou Enlai conveyed to the White House by the Pakistani ambassador revived the prospect for a high-level meeting. The message invited a presidential envoy to Beijing to discuss the "subject of the vacation of Chinese territories called Taiwan."[20] In late October, Nixon had used back-channels through Pakistan and Romania to broach the possibility of secret high-level talks. At that time, he had told Romanian president Nicolae Ceausescu that the United States could not start by establishing diplomatic relations with the PRC; that was a "a step for later on." A beginning had be made through talks, preferably outside formal channels.[21]

In his memoirs, Kissinger downplayed Zhou Enlai's stated purpose for a high-level meeting, asserting that top Chinese leaders

"would not associate themselves with any invitation patently inca-
pable of fulfillment." The United States could clearly not consent to
an agenda restricted only to discussion of its departure from Taiwan.
Underlying the invitation, in his view, was a "deeper imperative" involving the security of China.[22] Whatever the "deeper imperative"
motivating Chinese leaders, Taiwan remained a major concern for
them. This was evident from their back-channel communications
with the White House over the next six months on an agenda for
the contemplated high-level talks.

In a reply in mid-December to the Chinese invitation, the White
House welcomed the possibility of a high-level meeting in Beijing
but proposed expanding the agenda beyond the Taiwan issue to
"encompass other steps designed to improve relations and reduce
tensions." The White House message also stated that the United
States would reduce its military presence "in the region of East Asia
and the Pacific as tensions in this region diminish."[23] Kissinger, in
presenting the message to the Pakistani ambassador for transmission
to Beijing, observed that it "would not be difficult to comply with
the Chinese request for withdrawing American forces from Taiwan" because these forces were involved in logistics and training
missions. Kissinger may have intended this comment to reach the
ears of Chinese leaders.[24]

The White House message was not delivered to Beijing until
January 15. Meanwhile, another message arrived from Zhou Enlai
on January 11 through the Romanian channel; it once again tied the
visit of a high-level envoy to the Chinese capital to the Taiwan issue.
In an unexpected step, the Chinese premier for the first time
broached a visit by the president himself.[25]

A third message from Zhou Enlai arrived on April 27 in reply to
the White House's mid-December missive. The message came only a
few weeks after the widely publicized visit of the U.S. table tennis
team to Beijing at the invitation of the Chinese. This message put
the emphasis on American military withdrawal, the one aspect of
the Taiwan issue that Nixon had chosen to mention in his own
message. The Chinese response, which once again proposed a
presidential visit to Beijing, greatly encouraged the president and his
national security advisor.[26] Kissinger believed that the Chinese de-

termination to recover Taiwan, not just their worries about the Soviet threat, would spur them to engage in high-level talks aimed at Sino-American reconciliation. "They [the Chinese] cannot trick us out of Taiwan," he told the president. "They have to have a fundamental understanding."[27]

The White House reply, sent on May 10, rested on the assumption that Beijing had too much at stake in holding a high-level meeting to reject a broadened agenda as long as Taiwan was included. The reply stressed the importance that Nixon attached to "normalizing relations" between the United States and China and his readiness to travel to Beijing for a meeting with PRC leaders at which "each side would be free to raise the issue of principal concern to it." The message also proposed that Kissinger travel to Beijing for a preliminary secret meeting.[28]

Late the next month, a response from Zhou Enlai cleared away the agenda problem, marking a critical advance in the China initiative. The Chinese bent to the American requirement for a broadened agenda. Mao extended a welcoming hand to Nixon to come to Beijing for direct conversations "in which each side would be free to raise the principal issue of concern to it." At the same time, the message asserted that "the first question to be settled is the crucial issue between China and the United States which is the question of the concrete way of the withdrawal of all U.S. Armed Forces from Taiwan and [the] Taiwan Straits area." While placing Taiwan at the top of their agenda, the Chinese once more narrowed the issue to the removal of American forces.[29]

In the weeks following this breakthrough, Kissinger prepared for a secret preliminary trip to Beijing as the president's envoy. He and a small number of National Security Council (NSC) staff assisting him had available several major policy papers on China produced at the president's request by the Interdepartmental Group for East Asia and Pacific Affairs, which was attached to the NSC. National Security Study Memorandum (NSSM) 106, "United States China Policy," was completed in mid-February 1971, and NSSM 124, "Next Steps Toward the People's Republic of China," was finished near the end of May. Written without knowledge of the White House's secret communications with Beijing, the papers nonetheless provided valuable information and analysis. Their purpose was to formulate and assess policy options rather than to recommend specific courses of action. Both papers devoted considerable attention to the Taiwan issue. Both started with the assumption that the United States, in seeking to build relations with the PRC, would maintain its existing diplomatic relationship with, and security commitment to, the Nationalist government. The papers exposed a sharp difference within the national security bureaucracy over the reduction of U.S. military forces on the Nationalist bastion.

In discussing China policy options, NSSM 106 examined a number of subjects directly related to Taiwan. One was the question of Taiwan's future status. Although the official U.S. position was that the island's status was undetermined, Washington had informed the PRC during the Warsaw talks the previous year that it was willing to accept a peaceful resolution by the parties directly concerned. NSSM 106 speculated that the PRC would not be satisfied with this assurance (despite its implication that the United States would accept the peaceful incorporation of Taiwan into the mainland government) but would instead insist on an acknowledgment that Taiwan was part of China. For the Nationalist government, too, the one-China principle was sacred. Taipei's claim to be the legal government of China was the basis of its domestic and international legitimacy. NSSM 106 pointed out that the current U.S. position with respect to this claim of legal sovereignty over China was ambiguous. For at least the past five years, Washington had abstained from public statements recognizing the ROC as the legal government of China, but it had also avoided challenging the Nationalist government's claim to that status. Washington did recognize the Nationalist government as legitimately exercising sovereignty over Taiwan and dealt with it as the de facto government of the territory it controlled.

However much Beijing might covet Taiwan, NSSM 106 stressed that for the foreseeable future the vast majority of native Taiwanese, as well as many mainlander refugees, would oppose any settlement placing them under the PRC's control. Indeed, better-educated and politically alert Taiwanese strongly favored eventual independence. Although no organized independence movement existed on the is-

land, pro-independence sentiment could grow more politically as-
sertive if the independence alternative were foreclosed by either the
Nationalist government or the United States. In any case, the trend
on Taiwan ever since the Japanese annexation had been in the direction of separation. Moreover, the "practical effect" of many
American programs and policies over two decades, in combination
with the island's outstanding economic success, had been to create
the potential for Taiwan's "continued viability separate from the
mainland," as long as it was secure from external attack.

NSSM 106 affirmed the strategic importance of Taiwan to the
United States. Because of the island's geographic location on
China's southeastern flank and its central position in the island
chain extending from Japan to Southeast Asia, it occupied "an important position for U.S. regional support and communication
operations and intelligence activities." Moreover, the Nationalist
armed forces held in place opposite Taiwan a large part of the
Chinese Communist armed forces, which might otherwise be diverted elsewhere. Of the approximately 9,000 U.S. military personnel on the island, half had been deployed there since 1965 in
support of operations in Vietnam and elsewhere in the region. The
only military unit with attack capability was a small detachment of
jet fighters. Other units had advisory, contingency, communications, logistics, and intelligence responsibilities. A "significant portion" of American intelligence on China came from collaboration
with the Nationalist government.

The section of NSSM 106 dealing with the U.S. military presence
on Taiwan revealed a clash of viewpoints between the Department
of Defense and other parts of the national security bureaucracy.
Along with other participants in the study, Pentagon planners
agreed that the size and character of the U.S. military presence could
have "an important bearing on whether we can persuade Peking to
set aside the Taiwan issue and permit an improvement in our relations." Pentagon planners were opposed, however, to unilateral reductions as an inducement for better relations; instead, they wanted
reductions to take place only on a quid pro quo basis as the Chinese
offered concrete evidence of their good intentions. All the participants in the NSSM 106 study were in accord that during the eight-

year period covered by their policy review the United States would have to retain quick and easy access to bases and facilities on Taiwan, regardless of the level of the U.S. military presence.[30]

Whereas NSSM 106 concentrated on broad policy goals and options, NSSM 124 examined specific short-term measures to construct relations with China. The measures were clustered into three groups ranging from the modest to the bold, with each group posing progressively greater problems in relations with the Soviet Union, Japan, and Taiwan. Among the most risky measures relating to Taiwan were two later adopted by the White House: a proposal for a joint renunciation-of-force agreement with the PRC and a significant cutback in American forces on Taiwan. None of the boldest measures was considered sufficiently provocative to the Guomindang leadership to cause a break in relations or jeopardize basic U.S. diplomatic and security objectives with respect to Taiwan. Such measures could, nevertheless, severely strain the relationship with Taipei, even to the point of a major crisis, and could undermine the credibility of the United States as an ally among other nations.[31]

Nixon and Kissinger needed no reminder of the Nationalists' sensitivity to any weakening of American support or softening of the U.S. posture toward the mainland regime. Early in his term, Nixon had reversed a decision to seek diplomatic relations with the Mongolian People's Republic after Chiang Kai-shek vociferously objected.[32] In the following months, as the Nixon administration publicly signaled its desire to reduce tensions with the PRC, Taipei grew increasingly uneasy. Visits to Taiwan by Secretary Rogers in August 1969 and by Vice President Spiro Agnew in January and August 1970 were intended in part to allay fears that the administration's developing China initiative would erode Washington's support for its Nationalist ally.[33] A strong note from Chiang Kai-shek protesting certain positions taken by the U.S. representative at the Warsaw talks called forth a soothing letter from the president containing a personal assurance that the U.S. commitment to the defense of Taiwan remained firm, as did his own desire for friendship and cooperation with the Nationalist government.[34] In late August 1970, the administration rolled out the red carpet during a four-day official visit to Washington by Vice Premier Chiang

Ching-kuo, Chiang Kai-shek's son and heir apparent. In meetings with Chiang Ching-kuo, both the secretary of state and the president offered assurances that the administration's pursuit of better relations with the mainland would not affect its security commitment to, or close association with, the Nationalist government. "I will never sell you down the river," Nixon told the vice premier.[35]

Public statements affirming the ties between the United States and Taiwan also accompanied the opening to China. Such statements were directed at audiences not only in Taiwan and other foreign countries but also at home. When Nixon took office, American opinion increasingly favored a more positive policy toward the PRC. Yet public skepticism of China remained high, as did endorsement of the U.S. diplomatic and defense relationship with Taiwan.[36] Sympathy and support for Taiwan were especially intense among conservative opinion leaders and politicians. Although the once-powerful China lobby of the 1950s had largely faded away, vocal remnants were still active. Given the state of domestic opinion, Nixon could not afford to appear to sacrifice Taiwan for the sake of rapprochement with the PRC. He was particularly anxious about right-wingers in his own party. Despite his anticommunist credentials, he did not consider himself invulnerable to criticism from this quarter. As he moved toward reconciliation with China and détente with the Soviet Union, he was determined to avoid a right-wing backlash.[37]

The cloak of secrecy that concealed their dealings with Beijing gave Nixon and Kissinger more room to maneuver, free from unwanted intrusions from the national security bureaucracy, the Nationalist government, or domestic opinion. Before Kissinger set off on his first secret trip to Beijing in early July 1971, he and his staff authored a collection of briefing papers, which were presented to the president under Kissinger's name. The papers, among other things, laid out American and Chinese objectives for a Mao-Nixon summit and U.S. negotiating positions on a wide range of issues, including Taiwan.

In examining American and Chinese objectives, Kissinger calculated that even though both sides wanted a summit, the Chinese perhaps wanted it more. For the United States, the benefits of a summit were more closely balanced with costs; one cost was a severe strain in relations with the Nationalist government. Kissinger's goal in Beijing would be to use the "Chinese desire for a summit to construct a framework for the meeting that will serve our objectives—improving relations, relaxing tensions in Asia, getting the Chinese to influence Hanoi on an Indochina settlement, having a balanced impact on the Soviet Union, and minimizing the adverse impact on the GRC [Government of the Republic of China] and our other allies."

Although expecting the Chinese to highlight the Taiwan issue, Kissinger did not anticipate that they would demand an immediate solution or exclude discussion of other matters at the summit. His objective would be to craft a "Sino-U.S. modus vivendi on the Taiwan situation which will permit our relations to Peking to develop while we at the same time retain our diplomatic ties and mutual defense treaty with the ROC."[38] He would stress the absence of any major conflict between U.S. and PRC national interests, apart from Taiwan. He would emphasize that the Nixon administration wanted to "disassemble" the barriers to U.S.-PRC relations erected by the United States as a result of the Korean War. However much the Chinese might feel that the United States was "interfering" in Taiwan, they should understand that the United States could not easily set aside a relationship with the Nationalist government developed over many years and involving "strong emotional considerations as well as political considerations." The PRC could not ask the United States "to open a relationship with it by an act of unconscionable betrayal of the long-standing U.S.-ROC relationship, that is, by immediately severing all ties with the ROC." While taking a "principled" approach to the Taiwan issue, Kissinger hoped to make a modus vivendi more attractive by moving closer to the Chinese positions on the questions of the future status of Taiwan and the American military presence.[39]

In the *White House Years*, Kissinger quickly passes over the Taiwan issue in his account of the July talks in Beijing, claiming that it was "mentioned only briefly during the first session."[40] The transcripts of his conversations with Zhou Enlai reveal, however, that this was far from the case. Not only was Taiwan a major topic of discussion, but Kissinger stretched the limits of his conception of a suitable modus vivendi.

Zhou Enlai made plain that the Taiwan issue was "crucial" and that "normalization of relations" between China and the United States meant establishing full diplomatic relations. Zhou insisted that to implement such relations the United States would have to satisfy four requirements: recognize Taiwan as an inalienable part of China and a province of China; recognize the PRC as the only legitimate government of China; withdraw all its armed forces and military installations from the area of Taiwan and the Taiwan Strait within a limited time period; and consider its defense treaty with the Taiwan regime invalid. Kissinger was taken aback by Zhou's emphasis on establishing diplomatic relations. Previous back-channel communications with Beijing had led him to anticipate that the Chinese premier would concentrate on removing the American military presence. Instead, Zhou went straight to the core—the Taiwan issue. Without making diplomatic relations an "absolute" precondition for a summit, he maintained that the presidential visit ought to set this objective as the desired direction.[41]

Kissinger went a long way toward meeting Chinese expectations. In a move with great significance for the China initiative, he held out the prospect of diplomatic relations during the first half of Nixon's second term. Once the two sides had agreed on a "fundamental course" in their relationship, he told Zhou, "then we will know that [diplomatic relations] will happen and then the only issue remaining is 'when.'" Although the president's visit would have "tremendous symbolic significance because it would make clear that normal relations were inevitable," the final step toward normalization would have to await Nixon's re-election.[42]

Whether Kissinger had discussed this scenario for the future path of Sino-American relations with Nixon is unknown. In any event, the president offered no objection after his national security advisor returned to Washington. Indeed, the prospect of establishing diplomatic relations with the PRC during his second term became a critical element in his and Kissinger's Taiwan strategy. How they intended to achieve this objective, given the stringent requirements set forth by Zhou Enlai, is uncertain. What was undeniable was that they saw a modus vivendi on Taiwan as a prelude to a fundamental transformation of the U.S.-PRC relationship.

The July talks touched on other aspects of the Taiwan issue. With regard to Taiwan's future status, Kissinger offered assurances that the United States did not advocate a "two China" or "one China, one Taiwan" solution and would accept any peaceful resolution devised by the concerned parties. When Zhou objected to a recent statement by a State Department spokesman that the legal status of Taiwan was "undetermined," Kissinger pointedly remarked (to "considerable laughter from the Chinese side") that the spokesman had not repeated the statement. In effect, Kissinger implied that the United States would no longer publicly maintain that Taiwan's status was unsettled, although he stopped short of actually repudiating this position. When Zhou probed the American attitude toward the Taiwan independence movement, Kissinger declared that the United States did not and would not support the movement.[43] Although no organized independence movement existed on Taiwan, Taiwanese independence activists were agitating for that cause in other countries, including the United States.[44]

Among the inducements Kissinger offered to ease the way for accommodation on the Taiwan issue was a reduction of the U.S. military presence on the Nationalist redoubt. He informed Zhou that the president was prepared to withdraw all units unrelated to Taiwan's defense (about two-thirds of U.S. forces on the island) "within a specified brief period of time after the ending of the war in Indochina" and to start reducing the other units "as our relations improve." This disclosure made explicit the linkage first established during the Warsaw talks between force reduction and the relaxation of "tensions" in East Asia, including the hostilities in Indochina. Kissinger undoubtedly hoped that the lure of force reduction would motivate the Chinese to assist the Nixon administration to achieve an honorable exit from the conflict in Southeast Asia. He and Zhou did not, however, strike a deal, not even tacitly, to trade force reduction on Taiwan for Chinese diplomatic help with Hanoi.[45] By linking force reductions after the Indochina War to improved

U.S.-Chinese relations, Kissinger also offered a carrot for Chinese cooperativeness on other issues, including the peaceful unification of Taiwan.

Chinese fears about Japanese ambitions in East Asia surfaced during the discussion of force reductions. Zhou expressed apprehension that, as American units pulled out, Japan might attempt to replace the United States as the military protector of the Nationalists. Adding to his other assurances about U.S. intentions toward Taiwan, Kissinger pledged that the United States would firmly oppose any Japanese military presence on the island.[46]

On his last day in Beijing, Kissinger mentioned to Zhou that Nixon would be willing during his visit to enter into a formal agreement for the mutual renunciation of force. A State Department paper, commissioned by Kissinger in March, had concluded that such an agreement would encounter opposition from the Nationalist government but would serve to symbolize improved U.S.-PRC relations. The Chinese themselves had offered a similar agreement to the United States during the ambassadorial talks in 1955. The State Department felt that an agreement of this kind might, without mentioning the Taiwan question, nonetheless encourage Beijing to pursue a peaceful solution, since it would be politically difficult to employ force against the Nationalist stronghold after signing such a declaration.[47] Zhou was cool to Kissinger's suggestion. When Kissinger expressed hope for a peaceful settlement of the Taiwan question, Zhou merely replied, "We are doing our best to do so." Sticking to longstanding Chinese policy, the premier refused to renounce the use of force to bring Taiwan within the PRC's fold.[48] Kissinger did not press Zhou on this point.

Before leaving Beijing, Kissinger tangled with the Chinese over the language of the joint communiqué announcing his talks with Zhou Enlai as well as Nixon's visit to China the next year. Kissinger rejected the initial Chinese draft stating that the purpose of the president's visit was to discuss Taiwan as a preliminary to normalization of relations. This draft was too politically loaded and skewed toward the Taiwan issue to gain his approval. A second Chinese draft, which he accepted with minor changes, omitted any mention of Taiwan and stated that the purpose of the high-level meeting was to "seek the normalization of relations between the two countries and also to exchange views on questions of concern to the two sides."[49] Kissinger recognized that "normalization of relations" meant the establishment of full diplomatic relations, a goal that he himself had set for the president's second term.

In a rapturous report on his Beijing talks, Kissinger told the president that "we have laid the ground work for you and Mao to turn a page in history." Yet there could be "no illusions" about future progress. The Chinese would be "tough before and during the summit on the question of Taiwan and other major issues." They were, in his view, "deeply ideological, close to fanatic in the intensity of their beliefs," while also possessing an "inward security" that allowed them, "within the framework of their principles, to be meticulous and reliable in dealing with others."

The process now set in motion between the United States and China would, Kissinger predicted, "send enormous shock waves around the world." Among its effects would be a "violent upheaval in Taiwan." In dealing with the impact on Taiwan, "we can hope for little more than damage limitation" by affirming the diplomatic and defense commitment "even while it becomes evident that we foresee a political evolution over the coming years." Elsewhere in the report, Kissinger was more specific about the kind of "political evolution" he had in mind. He informed the president that although Zhou Enlai had conceded that U.S. recognition of the PRC was not a precondition for the summit, he did want Nixon's visit "to set recognition as the *ultimate* [emphasis in original] direction of our policy." The premier had accepted Kissinger's position that "some time would be required, i.e., well into your second term."[50]

In a brief televised announcement on July 15, Nixon stunned his fellow Americans and the rest of the world with the news of Kissinger's secret Beijing talks and his own planned visit the next year. His quest of a "new relationship" with the PRC, he pledged, "will not be at the expense of our old friends." "Old friends" unmistakably included Taiwan.[51] Because of the secrecy that shrouded the contents of the July talks, Nixon and Kissinger could pursue their private Taiwan strategy with the Chinese without triggering an eruption at home or turmoil on Taiwan. Knowledge of what had transpired in Beijing was highly restricted. It is not clear that Secretary Rogers was fully informed (he had been told of Kissinger's secret mission only after Kissinger had left for Beijing).[52]

The American public greeted the news of the president's planned trip to China with wary approval. Polls showed that a substantial majority of Americans favored the visit yet remained distrustful of Chinese Communist intentions. A majority (50 percent) disagreed with the view that it had been "wrong to 'sell-out' Nationalist China in this way," but a minority (27 percent) endorsed this sentiment.[53] Although some anticommunist conservatives were suspicious or disapproved of Nixon's China gambit, there was no concerted right-wing opposition. The fact that prominent Republican conservatives such as Arizona Senator Barry Goldwater and California Governor Ronald Reagan lined up behind the president reduced the threat of a right-wing backlash.[54] Reagan even agreed to go to Taipei as the president's special representative to ease Chiang Kai-shek's anxieties about Nixon's China trip.[55]

The announcement of Nixon's journey to the Chinese mainland shook the government and people of Taiwan. The Nationalist government immediately registered a stern official protest, and newspaper commentary reflected "shock, anger, and bitterness."[56] The White House and State Department moved quickly to pacify Taipei. Both Rogers and Kissinger told Nationalist Ambassador James Shen that no secret agreements had been reached during the Beijing talks and that the United States would stand by its security treaty.[57] In a personal message to Chiang Kai-shek, Nixon acknowledged that the steps he had taken were "disturbing to the Republic of China" but offered assurances that they did not detract from the ties of friendship and the alliance between their two governments.[58]

In a memorandum to Nixon, Rogers predicted that the Nationalist government, despite "feelings of shock and betrayal," would not incite or tolerate an anti-American campaign among its citizens. Realizing that its primary interest was "its continued existence as a viable entity on Taiwan," the government would probably recognize that it could not "afford the luxury of giving complete vent to its true feelings." Virulent anti-Americanism would seriously harm the island's economy, unsettle a population long accustomed to relying on the United States for its security, and weaken political and popular support in the United States. In the immediate future, Taipei was likely to try to "walk a fine line," reacting with enough vigor to the China opening to "preserve face and hopefully deter further U.S. movements toward Peking" while simultaneously avoiding damaging extremism. Rogers also saw little chance that the shock of the Nixon announcement would set off a political upheaval challenging Nationalist rule. All in all, the secretary of state's memorandum argued that the China initiative could proceed without precipitating a crisis of confidence with the Nationalist government or destabilizing the island.[59] The memorandum accurately predicted the disturbed but relatively restrained reaction on Taiwan as the rapprochement unfolded in the coming months.

In the months before Kissinger's second trip to Beijing in late October, he and the president had to cope with the knotty issue of Chinese representation in the United Nations. The issue presented a difficult test for their Taiwan strategy and their entire China initiative. For nearly twenty years, the United States had annually mobilized resistance to the PRC's admission to the United Nations, utilizing procedural devices to ensure that the Republic of China rather than its mainland foe occupied the China seat in the world organization. Since 1961 the procedural device had taken the form of declaring the issue of changing Chinese representation an "important question resolution," which required a two-thirds vote of approval. The United States had also led the yearly opposition to an Albanian resolution giving the China seat to the PRC. By 1970 a shift in voting patterns in the General Assembly on the Chinese representation issue had become evident; this shift favored the PRC's entry and boded ill for the continuing success of Washington's strategy.[60]

NSSM 107, a national security study of the representation issue completed in January 1971, predicted that the existing strategy would end in defeat either that year or the next. The study conceded that defeat on these terms did have advantages: it would lay to rest the troublesome representation issue and increase the prospects for better relations with the PRC while still permitting the United

States to remain faithful to the ROC (which preferred the existing strategy to any alternative reflecting a "two Chinas" position). Yet the study warned that the United States would be widely viewed as "wrong-headed, static, inflexible, and unrealistic" if it chose to go down to defeat with the existing strategy; this would strike a major blow to the nation's international prestige and generate unwelcome domestic consequences.

The most promising alternative that NSSM 107 envisioned was a dual-representation formula permitting the PRC to enter the United Nations while preventing the ROC's expulsion. Such a formula stood a good chance of winning majority support in the General Assembly and would be seen both at home and abroad as realistic and forward-looking. In the UN debates on the representation issue in recent years, the United States had placed more emphasis on arguing against the ROC's ouster than against admitting the PRC. The most serious liability of a dual-representation formula, however, was that its "two China" implications were unpalatable to both Beijing and Taipei.[61]

On August 2, shortly after Nixon's startling revelation about his China trip, Secretary Rogers publicly unveiled a new approach to the representation issue.[62] The secretary's announcement of U.S. support for dual representation followed several months of internal deliberations within the Nixon administration, and it came only a few months before the General Assembly was expected to hold its annual vote on the issue. Kissinger presents an unreliable account in his memoirs of his and Nixon's role in shaping the new approach. He claims that he and the president were less than keen about the dual-representation formula, because it "was bound to raise havoc with our relations with Peking and even to some extent Taipei" and would, in any event, only delay Beijing's entry for a year or two. He and Nixon therefore preferred to stick to the existing strategy, even if doomed. In the end, they deferred to Rogers and his State Department colleagues, who had been left in charge of the UN aspect of China policy and who favored dual representation.[63]

The documentary record now available shows not only that Nixon and Kissinger were actively involved in defining the dual-representation approach but also that they employed secret diplomacy to ensure that it did not run afoul of Chiang Kai-shek or upset the budding relationship with Beijing. Far from being dubious about dual representation, Kissinger recommended it to the president in a memorandum on March 20 as the only method offering the "realistic prospect for preventing Taipei's expulsion, not just for a year or so, but for the foreseeable future." To enhance the appeal of dual representation for UN members, he favored tying it to the principle of universality as a guide to UN membership. As additional protection for Taiwan, he suggested modifying the important question resolution to require a two-thirds vote to expel Taipei. The combination of dual representation and a modified important question resolution would permit Beijing's entry by a majority vote but would raise the bar for the ejection of Taiwan. Nothing would stand in the way of Beijing's entry except its "own insistence that it will not come in until it can set its own terms," a position that Kissinger anticipated would not garner much sympathy among UN members. With Nixon's ever-present concerns about the domestic dimension of China policy in mind, Kissinger presented evidence from public opinion studies indicating a "sharp change" over the past five years in public opposition to UN membership for Beijing.[64]

Although Kissinger was convinced that his approach stood the best chance of keeping Taiwan in the United Nations for an extended period, he was acutely aware that this ploy was unworkable unless Chiang Kai-shek went along. In early April, he obtained Nixon's approval to send retired veteran diplomat Robert Murphy, now a corporate executive, on a secret mission to Taipei to consult with the Generalissimo about this approach.[65]

Nixon's approval of the Murphy mission is understandable. The existing UN strategy spelled certain defeat—a defeat that would besmirch American prestige, damage his own reputation for foreign policy leadership, and invite domestic criticism for following a sterile, unviable course ending in Taiwan's expulsion. The defeat could very well rebound against his Taiwan strategy and his entire China initiative. Further, the president appears to have found persuasive Kissinger's argument that his approach might succeed in keeping Taiwan in the United Nations for the foreseeable future. This would help to sustain the Nationalist government's interna-

tional role and its confidence in its American ally's reliability as he
and his national security advisor constructed a strategic partnership
with Beijing. It would also prevent the domestic fallout from Taiwan's exclusion. The State Department, which knew about the
Murphy mission, also favored a new approach based on dual representation.[66]

The Murphy mission turned out to be a comedy of errors. The
president's emissary failed to give Chiang an accurate description
of Kissinger's approach (he did not convey the distinction between
the existing and the modified important question resolutions).
Far worse, he assured the Generalissimo that under the dual-
representation arrangement the ROC government would retain its
place on the Security Council. Although Chiang seemed surpris-
ingly willing to keep an open mind about dual representation, he
warned that the ROC would leave the United Nations if deprived of
its Security Council seat.[67] Murphy ought to have known from his
preparatory briefings that the United States could not guarantee
that Taipei would keep its Security Council seat and that, furthermore, a dual-representation resolution stipulating that would
almost certainly fail. Rather than immediately clarifying Chiang's
misconception about the Security Council seat, Nixon chose to let
the matter ride, apparently hoping that later developments would
demonstrate to the Nationalist president that his insistence on
keeping the seat was self-defeating.[68]

Kissinger's secret trip to Beijing in July gave him an opportunity
to gauge the reaction of Chinese leaders to the prospective new U.S.
position on the representation issue. He admitted to the president
that consulting with the Chinese was an "unorthodox course";
nonetheless, the Chinese needed to understand that the Nixon
administration could not support the PRC's admission at the expense of Taiwan's membership and that Washington was at least
taking their views into consideration.[69] Kissinger and the president
were under no illusion that the Chinese would approve the new
approach. The best that could be hoped was that the Chinese would
not let differences over the representation issue stand in the way of
improved relations.

Kissinger had reason to feel relieved when he mentioned the possible new U.S. stand to Zhou Enlai. The premier, while predictably rejecting the new approach and insisting on the restoration of China's rights in the United Nations, downplayed the importance and urgency of the representation issue. He assured Kissinger that "we won't pay much attention to it [the new approach]" if the United States were to adopt it. When Kissinger later suggested that China mute its rhetoric on the issue, Zhou smilingly agreed.[70] In the months before the decisive UN vote on the issue in October, China did tone down its rhetoric, earning the gratitude of the White House.[71]

Kissinger's July trip removed any anxiety that the representation issue would chill the warming relationship with Beijing. It also jolted Taipei into a decision on dual representation. After the Murphy mission, the State Department had consulted with Japan and NATO allies about the proposed new approach and also engaged in further discussions with Nationalist officials.[72] In early July, Rogers informed Nixon that the department's best current estimate was that a dual-representation resolution could win by a majority of five to seven votes, but only after intensive lobbying and only if the resolution stated that the Security Council seat should go to Beijing.[73] Not long after Nixon's surprise July 15 announcement, Nationalist Foreign Minister Chow Shu-kai informed Washington that his government would "understand" if the United States proposed a dual-representation resolution, inasmuch as the United States and other nations, especially Japan, were willing to sponsor a modified important question resolution to protect the ROC's position in the world body. The Nationalist government still drew the line, however, at U.S. support for Beijing's occupation of the Security Council seat.[74]

In late July, the State Department received the go-ahead from the president to publicize the new U.S. stand on representation. This stand mirrored the basic approach first advanced by Kissinger to the president five months earlier. Nixon wanted to open the door for Beijing's entry into the United Nations but without "double-crossing Taiwan."[75] In his August 2 announcement, Secretary

Rogers tried to remove the two-China implications from dual representation, stating that such an arrangement need not prejudice either Beijing's or Taipei's "claims to be the sole government of China and the representative of all the people of China." He also disclosed that the United States was prepared to have UN members decide who should hold the seat in the Security Council. Informed beforehand of the announcement, Taipei indicated a reluctant willingness to live with this stance on the disposition of the seat.[76]

Over the next month, the State Department tried to line up cosponsors among important Asian allies for a dual-representation resolution that remained silent on the occupancy of the Security Council seat. When this effort failed, the president approved a recommendation from Rogers to revise the resolution to recommend that the PRC hold the seat.[77] Despite an incensed official protest from Taipei, Rogers was hopeful that the Nationalist government would restrict itself to pro forma public opposition to the representation resolution while working behind the scenes for its passage. Warned that without such tacit support the dual-representation resolution would fail and the ROC would risk expulsion from the world organization, Taipei did consent to provide discreet assistance.[78]

In the period before the decisive UN vote on the representation issue, the State Department and the UN mission engaged in an intensive campaign to preserve a UN seat for Taipei—all to no avail. On October 25, the modified important question resolution failed by four votes, prompting the ROC delegation's withdrawal from the General Assembly. The Assembly then overwhelmingly approved an Albanian resolution expelling the ROC and admitting the PRC. The dual-representation resolution never came to a vote.[79]

Kissinger received news of the UN votes as he departed from Beijing after his second set of preliminary talks. He had gone to China over the strenuous objection of Rogers, who had learned of the trip only a few days before its announcement. The secretary feared that the timing of the trip would make it harder to save Taiwan's seat. So, too, did Nationalist officials.[80] In a memorandum to Nixon on October 12, before Kissinger left for Beijing, Rogers estimated the chances for success in the United Nations as "just a little less than even."[81]

In his memoirs Kissinger contends that he could not have postponed the trip and that, in any case, he did not believe that it would decisively affect the vote, which came a week earlier than expected.[82] Whatever Kissinger's calculations, his trip was undeniably ill timed from the standpoint of winning the pending UN vote. Down to the final count, the UN mission believed that it had the votes to win.[83] It is probable that Kissinger's presence in Beijing during the climactic debate helped tipped the balance against the U.S. position. Yet what was ultimately critical in determining the outcome was the widespread desire among UN members to end the PRC's exclusion from the world body and their recognition of a sea change in U.S.-PRC relations. In this context, saving the ROC's seat was less important than ensuring the PRC's admission. In the aftermath of the vote, State Department intelligence analysts concluded that most UN members, including those who voted with the United States, welcomed the PRC's entry; despite considerable sympathy for the ROC, its expulsion was "not generally regarded as a matter of deep or disturbing significance."[84]

The UN action represented a temporary setback for Nixon's and Kissinger's Taiwan strategy. They had hoped that the new approach on the representation issue would permit them to carry on their prized relationship with the PRC while preserving the ROC's seat for the foreseeable future. In actuality, their China initiative worked against their objective of keeping their Taiwan ally in the United Nations. Nevertheless, the two men appeared committed to this objective to the very end. The president privately lent a hand in trying to corral votes to protect the ROC seat.[85] While in Beijing, Kissinger told Zhou Enlai that defeat of the Albanian resolution would best serve the president's quest for Sino-American reconciliation. Pointing out that in a recent public opinion poll 62 percent of the American public opposed the expulsion of Taiwan, Kissinger expressed anxiety that the double shock of Nixon's July 15 announcement and Taiwan's ejection would provide critics of the president's China initiative a "rallying point."[86]

Kissinger's worries were not unfounded. The reaction in Congress to Taiwan's ouster was bitter and relatively widespread.[87] The reaction of Republican right-wingers particularly troubled Nixon. Upon learning that Ronald Reagan and conservative Republican Senator James Buckley of New York were irate over the UN decision, he immediately took action to calm them. He felt that to "keep the right wing on track" he needed to make clear that he had "fought the China battle as hard as he could" and that the blame for Taiwan's expulsion lay within the United Nations, not with him.[88] Despite the evident displeasure in some quarters, the UN defeat did not derail the China initiative domestically.

Neither did the defeat impair Washington's basic relations with Taipei or destabilize Taiwan. Nationalist officials did not blame Washington for the defeat. Despite some public ill feeling on Taiwan against the United States, there were no major anti-American displays. The State Department noted that the Nationalist government's "restrained and realistic actions in the wake of the UN defeat have had a calming effect."[89] The UN vote did accelerate the international political isolation of the Nationalist government. Yet, according to State Department intelligence analysts, the ROC government had already turned its attention to this problem before the UN reversal and was moving in the direction of making economic growth (a central element in the island's viability and stability) its primary objective. The government was therefore expanding efforts to maintain informal economic connections with countries recognizing Beijing. At the same time, Taipei still counted on the U.S. defense commitment.[90]

The purpose of Kissinger's October trip to Beijing was to sustain the momentum of the China initiative and make additional preparations to ensure a successful presidential visit. Kissinger's briefing book indicated that the Chinese were expected to make normalization and Taiwan major topics for discussion. They might want the president to endorse normalization in a way that implied that the United States was withdrawing support from Taiwan and no longer considered it a "valid international entity." They also might want to pin the president down formally to "a fixed and fairly brief time-table" for the withdrawal of U.S. forces from Taiwan. (Nixon wrote "no" next to each of these possible Chinese gambits in his copy of the briefing book.) The Chinese would, in any event, want the president himself to repeat the assurances relating to Taiwan given by Kissinger during his last visit as well as his national security advisor's promise about "addressing the political status of Taiwan within the first half of his second term."

The briefing book contained no new concessions on Taiwan but did counsel caution in dealing with the issue. Kissinger was to avoid committing the president to a formal stand on either normalization or troop withdrawals "which would have the effect of letting the political evolution of Taiwan get out of hand and move so fast that we lose any initiative which we now exercise." The White House, in other words, wanted to eschew any formal statement that would deprive it of influence over the pace and direction of Taiwan's "political evolution." The briefing book also underlined the need to avoid putting any more strain on the U.S.-ROC relationship than was "absolutely necessary" or giving the "appearance of selling out an ally." Overall, Kissinger was to keep his description of what the president would say and do regarding the Taiwan issue and normalization within the general limits of what he had told Zhou Enlai in July.[91]

The exchanges on these two topics between Kissinger and Zhou Enlai in October covered much the same ground as in July. Kissinger reaffirmed his earlier assurances about U.S. intentions toward Taiwan and confirmed that the president was prepared to move toward normalization. In an appeal for understanding from the Chinese, he observed that the United States would not find it easy to "make the changes that we have outlined to you," partly because of the long-established relationship with Taiwan and partly because of "many elements in the U.S. who are violently opposed to the policy that we are pursuing and who will be even more opposed as it begins to unwind." The White House's task would be less difficult, he told Zhou, if Beijing declared its readiness to settle the Taiwan question peacefully. The premier was no more willing to guarantee a peaceful resolution than he had been in July.

As in July, Zhou Enlai exhibited uneasiness about the Taiwan independence movement and Japanese designs on Taiwan. When he told Kissinger that his concerns about the latter extended to economic and political inroads, not just a military presence, the national security advisor replied that it was not "American policy to let Taiwan become a subsidiary state of Japan." Zhou also returned to the subject of the U.S. position on the legal status of Taiwan. Kissinger, as he had in his previous visit, assured him that U.S. spokesmen would no longer declare that the island's status was undetermined but again stopped short of an outright rejection of this position. He did state that the United States would "encourage a peaceful solution [of the Taiwan question] within the framework of one China." In effect, Kissinger espoused the idea of one China achieved through peaceful means while maintaining some degree of ambiguity on the legal status issue (at least in public) so as not to prejudice the international legitimacy of the mutual security pact with Taiwan. He may also have wanted to maintain a measure of public ambiguity on the legal status issue so as not to appear to foreclose the option of the permanent separation of Taiwan from the mainland, for fear that this could provoke a negative reaction from pro-Taiwan conservatives or the indigenous majority on Taiwan.[92]

In another exchange with Zhou, Kissinger appeared to suggest that the complete withdrawal of U.S. forces from Taiwan and the termination of the mutual security treaty would occur only after the peaceful unification of Taiwan. If his remarks were intended to prod Zhou to abjure forceful unification, they fell on deaf ears. Zhou reminded Kissinger that a total military withdrawal and abrogation of the defense treaty were necessary to establish diplomatic relations.[93] The Chinese conditions for diplomatic relations left no room for a continuing U.S. military presence or security commitment that might serve as a deterrent against forceful unification.

Among Kissinger's assignments during his second Beijing trip was to negotiate a joint communiqué for Nixon's own visit. These negotiations, which he and Zhou Enlai personally conducted, proved more time-consuming and demanding than he had expected. At the start, the American and Chinese draft communiqués were radically different in structure, tone, and content. The negotiations consumed most of five meetings lasting eleven hours during the final two and a half days of Kissinger's six-day stay. After going through seven drafts, he and Zhou settled on a tentative communiqué. Their hardest problem was to find mutually agreeable language for the American statement on the Taiwan issue. They devoted more time to this part of the communiqué than any other, and it was the only section left unresolved.[94]

For Kissinger, negotiating the language of this section involved giving the Chinese a sense of progress on the issue while trying as far as possible to protect the White House against accusations from domestic critics and the Nationalist government of having "sold out" Taiwan. The communiqué would present the public face of the Taiwan modus vivendi while concealing the private understandings he had offered the Chinese. Critical to the White House's Taiwan strategy was the need to preserve the distinction between public and secret undertakings on the Taiwan issue. As Kissinger told Zhou Enlai, "we [Nixon and Kissinger] could do more than we can say" on the issue.[95] During his conversations with Zhou in both July and October, he impressed on him the difficulties with domestic opinion and Taiwan that Nixon was encountering in pursuing his China initiative.

At their concluding negotiating session on the communiqué, Kissinger remarked to Zhou that "the Prime Minister seeks clarity, and I am trying to achieve ambiguity."[96] His observation pinpointed the nub of their differences over the language of the U.S. statement on Taiwan. These differences came to a head over formulations relating to the framework for the resolution of the Taiwan question and to the U.S. military presence. On the Taiwan question, what the Chinese sought at the outset was a U.S. pledge to encourage peaceful negotiations by Chinese on both sides of the Taiwan Strait within a one-China framework as well as to refrain from activities aimed at severing Taiwan from China.[97] This formulation was much too revealing of his private undertakings to the Chinese to be acceptable to Kissinger. After an exchange of drafts, Zhou Enlai finally accepted a partial formulation advanced by Kissinger: "The U.S. side declared: The United States acknowledges that all Chinese on either side of the Taiwan Straits maintain there is but one China and that Taiwan is a province of China. The United States does not challenge that position." Except for two minor changes in wording, this language would later appear in the Shanghai Communiqué. Its adoption represented a significant Chinese concession to Kissinger's preference for ambiguity. The formulation said nothing about the U.S. position on pro-Taiwan independence activities and avoided acceptance of the position that Taiwan was part of China. In a concession to the Chinese, Kissinger agreed that the United States would not "challenge" (rather than merely "take note of" as in the initial U.S. draft) the one-China position held by Chinese on both sides of the Strait. The agreed language contained no reference to the American interest in a peaceful settlement.[98]

On the issue of the American military presence, the first formulation presented by the Chinese committed the United States to a total and unconditional removal of troops and installations following the withdrawal of its forces from Indochina. The draft communiqué Kissinger brought to Beijing did not even mention military reductions on Taiwan.[99] Kissinger and Zhou narrowed this gap during their long hours of negotiation but failed to reach agreement. Stretching beyond his instructions, Kissinger did take a major step toward satisfying the Chinese. In the final negotiating session, he provisionally put forward a formulation accepting the "ultimate objective" of the withdrawal of U.S. forces and their progressive reduction "as tensions diminish." This was his first acceptance of the principle of total (though conditional) withdrawal of American forces. Although Zhou rejected this formulation, it contained key elements that would surface again in the Shanghai Communiqué.[100]

In his post-Beijing report to Nixon, Kissinger acknowledged that Taiwan remained the "single most difficult issue" between the two sides. Yet momentum toward accommodation had continued. Zhou Enlai had shown patience and restraint while adhering to fundamental principles. A modus vivendi on the Taiwan issue would depend on "China's willingness to accept our thesis that we can do more than we can say, that to push the process too fast and too explicitly would wreck the whole fabric of our China initiative." Although Zhou understood this dilemma, he himself had to show tangible progress on the issue to his own domestic and international audiences. Kissinger predicted that it would "prove difficult and painful to close the remaining gap" on the Taiwan issue, but he believed that this was doable.[101]

By the time that President Nixon set off on his journey to Beijing in February 1972, a modus vivendi on Taiwan was within reach. To make it happen, the American statement on Taiwan in the joint communiqué would have to satisfy the Chinese by signifying a meaningful advance toward their goal of regaining their lost territory but would also have to accommodate the White House's domestic and international imperatives. In addition, Mao and his associates would have to be willing to trust the reliability of the White House's secret assurances, particularly that Nixon would be reelected and proceed toward normalization during his second term.

The briefing book Kissinger and his aides prepared for Nixon included a detailed paper on the Taiwan issue. The paper alerted him that the issue would be at the top of the agenda and that Chinese leaders, for their own domestic purposes, had to have "something from your visit to show progress in 'liberating' Taiwan and destroying the ROC." Therefore, "movement on Taiwan as the prime U.S-PRC issue is again required, and is a prerequisite to some of our needs." For his part, Nixon had to address the issue "with flexibility and frankness," while making Chinese leaders "understand that they cannot press U.S. too hard or expect too much."[102]

Before the president's departure, Kissinger forwarded to him a second briefing book prepared in the State Department. The officers responsible for this briefing book, despite having been shut out of Kissinger's secret dealings with the Chinese, produced papers that were "substantively consistent," Kissinger told the president, with those prepared within the White House. In their Taiwan paper, State Department analysts recommended setting as the goal for the president's visit "an interim arrangement or a setting aside of the issue acceptable to both sides" that would remove the issue as the major obstacle to normalization but without seriously impairing the credibility of American commitments. On the U.S. side, such an interim agreement could include a phased withdrawal of all U.S. forces from Taiwan, a public statement of willingness to accept any peaceful settlement negotiated by Beijing and Taipei, and a private assurance barring official encouragement or assistance for any movement aiming at Taiwan's independence or permanent separation from the mainland. On the PRC side, an agreement would involve a renunciation of the use of force in the Taiwan area and a public acknowledgment that resolving the Taiwan problem would be a lengthy process and that the "PRC would take into account the economic and social differences stemming from Taiwan's long separation." The State Department analysts maintained that such undertakings by the Chinese would alleviate public concerns in the U.S. about a "sudden or violent change in Taiwan's status."[103]

The official party accompanying Nixon to China included Secretary Rogers, who was not privy to Kissinger's discussions with Zhou Enlai in October. Rogers had, however, seen the unfinalized U.S. statement on Taiwan in the draft communiqué brought back by Kissinger, and he had later sent Nixon his own proposed statement.[104] Not long before the presidential party left for Beijing, Rogers also transmitted to the president a paper recommending an "evolutionary policy" toward Taiwan. The paper outlined a series of possible U.S. actions over the following eighteen months that would help remove Taiwan as the "basic stumbling block" in relations with the PRC while preserving close ties with Taipei and avoiding "the major risk of contributing to profound destabilization on Taiwan." Rogers contended that over the long term an "evolutionary policy" would leave Taiwan with the option either of peaceful integration with the mainland or permanent separation. He intimated that he personally preferred the second outcome, speculating that over time Beijing might come to accept separation as a fait accompli.[105] In passing along Rogers's paper to Nixon, Kissinger took exception to the view that Beijing might eventually reconcile itself to Taiwan's separation.[106]

Nixon went to Beijing with his sights set on a diplomatic and political triumph. He wanted to launch the Sino-American rapprochement in dramatic fashion and garner political credit for himself in a presidential election year. The White House organized the visit for maximum publicity, and Nixon prepared thoroughly for his private talks with Chinese leaders.[107]

Nixon knew full well that no substantive issue was more critical to the success of his journey than Taiwan. Shortly after his arrival in the Chinese capital, he and Kissinger met with Mao and Zhou Enlai. While symbolically significant, the meeting consisted mostly of light repartee and banter. Nixon did specifically mention Taiwan as one of the issues he was prepared to discuss during his stay. Mao's only mention of Taiwan was a casual observation about name-calling by the two Chinese sides in the cross-Strait dispute.[108]

Taiwan was a major topic at two of the meetings that Nixon and Kissinger had with Zhou Enlai. At the first session, the day after his arrival, Nixon personally endorsed five "principles" that would guide U.S. actions on the issue: (1) "There is one China, and Taiwan is part of China," and the United States would no longer assert that the status of Taiwan was undetermined; (2) the United States did not and would not support any Taiwan independence movement; (3) the United States would discourage Japan from "moving into" Taiwan or backing Taiwanese independence; (4) the United States would embrace any peaceful resolution of the Taiwan question and would not support a military return to the mainland by the government on Taiwan; and (5) the United States would seek the normalization of U.S.-PRC relations within the framework of the preceding principles. Nixon's "principles" reiterated assurances already given by Kissinger. The president then confirmed that two-thirds of the American forces on Taiwan would be removed after the Indochina War with the rest to follow as progress occurred toward peaceful resolution of the Taiwan problem. This arrangement was intended to preserve some leverage in dealing with the Chinese on the issue of peaceful unification.

In explaining his position on Taiwan, Nixon stressed that political hazards at home limited public revelation of his private views and intentions. He warned of the danger from a potential domestic alliance joining the pro-Taiwan far right with the "pro-Soviet left and the pro-Indian left" (to which Kissinger added "the pro-Japanese group"). He could not give such a coalition an opening to charge that he had "sold Taiwan down the river." It was essential therefore to find language on this issue for the joint communiqué that would meet Chinese needs "yet does not stir up the animals so much that they gang up on Taiwan and thereby torpedo our initiative."

Zhou Enlai offered his own assurances to the president. Having already waited over twenty years to regain Taiwan, he said, China could "wait a few more years." Moreover, the PRC would not build military or nuclear bases on the island.[109]

At another meeting two days later, Zhou expressed a "hope" that the "liberation" of Taiwan could be realized in Nixon's next term. The PRC would not ask the United States to remove Chiang Kai-shek. "We will take care of that ourselves," he said. When Nixon added "peacefully," Zhou replied, "Yes, we have self-confidence." The premier gave assurance that Chinese forces would not engage in military confrontation with U.S. forces while they remained on Taiwan.

No doubt to Zhou's gratification, Nixon informed him that his goals were to remove all U.S. forces from the island as well as to normalize relations with the PRC by the end of his second term. Not only did the president personally confirm that he wanted to establish diplomatic relations before he left office, but for the first time he set a timetable for a complete U.S. military withdrawal. He did not, as in his first meeting with Zhou, tie a final military withdrawal to peaceful settlement of the Taiwan question. Whether or not this apparent decoupling was intentional, the fact remains that Nixon was no more prepared than Kissinger to press the Chinese to accept the principle of peaceful unification. The best that the two were able to obtain during the various talks culminating in the rapprochement were private assurances that insofar as possible the Chinese would strive for a peaceful settlement.

In explaining his goals for his second term to Zhou, Nixon stressed that it was essential that he be able to deny the existence of any "secret deals" on Taiwan after his return to Washington. He would also need "running room" in the joint communiqué's language on Taiwan to carry forward his plans.[110] The communiqué language delineating the American position on Taiwan was still a bone of contention when the presidential entourage arrived in Beijing. Early in 1972, Kissinger's deputy, Brigadier General Alexander Haig, Jr., had presented Zhou Enlai with another formulation during a trip to Beijing to finalize technical arrangements for Nixon's visit. From the Chinese standpoint, this formulation was less satisfactory than the one that Kissinger had provisionally put forward in October; unlike Kissinger's formulation, it did not set forth the "ultimate objective" of American military withdrawal.[111]

The negotiation of the final text of the communiqué during Nixon's visit was left in the hands of Kissinger and Vice Minister of Foreign Affairs Qiao Guanhua, a longtime associate of Zhou Enlai. Their negotiations occupied a total of 24 hours in four late-night sessions. Kissinger repeatedly pleaded domestic necessity to justify the need for Chinese adaptability.

The most protracted discussions took place over the U.S. statement on Taiwan. The two sides had difficulty in agreeing on suitable language to express the U.S. positions on the peaceful resolution of the Taiwan question and on military withdrawal from Taiwan. The Chinese wanted the United States to indicate only its "hope" for a peaceful solution of the Taiwan question, whereas the Americans insisted on stronger language. The final text read that the U.S. "reaffirms its interest in the peaceful settlement of the Taiwan question by the Chinese themselves." From the American viewpoint, "reaffirms its interest" implied an ongoing concern and commitment. The Chinese also wanted to tie a peaceful solution explicitly to a one-China position but gave way on this point. On the military evacuation issue, they pressed for a commitment to total and unconditional withdrawal, whereas the Americans favored language providing only for a conditional phased reduction. The final text affirmed the "ultimate objective" of the United States to withdraw all its military forces and installations but linked this objective to the "prospect" of a peaceful solution of the Taiwan question. The text further stipulated that "in the meantime" the United States would "progressively reduce" these forces and installations "as the tension in the area diminishes." This artfully devised compromise established total military withdrawal as a final objective and provided for phased reduction while making both of these eventualities conditional. The phrase "as tension in the area diminishes" contained an implied linkage between phased reduction, on one hand, and an end to the Indochina conflict, a peaceful resolution of the Taiwan question, and progress in Sino-American relations, on the other.[112]

In coming to terms on the Taiwan statement, Kissinger (who had consulted with Nixon throughout the negotiations) and Qiao Guanhua cleared the way for Mao and the Politburo to put their imprimatur on the entire joint communiqué. Kissinger, to his chagrin, had to convene another session with Qiao Guanhua after the document's approval but before its public release. He was compelled to do so to address points raised by Secretary Rogers and Assistant Secretary for East Asian Affairs Marshall Green, neither of whom had seen the entire communiqué until after its approval. The drafting of the communiqué was the work of Kissinger together with Winston Lord, his special assistant on the NSC, and John H. Holdridge, a career Foreign Service officer and the NSC's senior staff member for East Asia. Although they had drawn on ideas from the State Department in preparing the communiqué, the department was excluded from the actual drafting.[113] In reviewing the approved text, Assistant Secretary Green noticed that it affirmed U.S. treaty obligations to a number of Asian allies without mentioning the security pact with Taiwan. This omission would have riled the Nationalist government and caused political trouble at home. When told of the omission, Qiao Guanhua flatly refused to allow any mention of the Taiwan defense treaty in the document. Kissinger therefore dropped the passage referring to specific Asian defense commitments. With Qiao's approval, he made a discreet reference to the Taiwan treaty during a press conference in Shanghai after the release of the communiqué.[114]

Kissinger also apologetically presented to Qiao a number of changes proposed by Rogers in the language of the communiqué, including the painstakingly crafted Taiwan statement. The secretary, who was angered by his exclusion from the meeting with Mao and the communiqué negotiations, was less than enthusiastic about Kissinger's handiwork. Qiao unequivocally rejected all the proposed changes in the Taiwan statement, but after another late-night session the Chinese did consent to other changes in the communiqué. Although Rogers was dissatisfied with this outcome, he obediently fell into line when Nixon directed him and the

State Department to give "100 percent" support to the communiqué.[115]

The final version of the communiqué, issued in Shanghai at the conclusion of Nixon's visit, soon became a symbol and touchstone of the Sino-American rapprochement. The communiqué indicated that the two sides, despite persistent if narrowing differences over Taiwan, had agreed to subordinate the issue to the pursuit of common interests. Yet the document evaded and concealed as much as it revealed about the Taiwan modus vivendi. The Chinese, in stating their own position on the issue, refrained from denouncing the Taiwan defense treaty or specifying their conditions for "normalization of relations" (a phrase that appeared four times in the document without definition). The American statement did not mention the secret assurances given by Nixon and Kissinger. Nonetheless, the statement signified a departure from past hard-line positions on the Taiwan issue. It could be read as tacitly suggesting that the United States had retreated from its previous position that the status of Taiwan was "undetermined." It supported, even if conditionally, a phased reduction of American forces and the "ultimate objective" of a complete U.S. military withdrawal. The statement could be interpreted as implicitly expressing a "one China, but not now" stance.

"One China, but not now" was in fact the policy premise underlying the secret assurances. Taken together, they indicated American support for a peaceful solution of the Taiwan question by the disputants themselves within the framework of the one-China principle. They also pointed to a total U.S. military withdrawal and the establishment of U.S.-PRC diplomatic relations by the end of Nixon's second term, eventualities that would measurably enhance China's chances of rejoining Taiwan to the mainland. All these considerations entered into that part of the Taiwan modus vivendi hidden from public scrutiny. Without the secret U.S. commitments, it is unlikely that the Americans and Chinese could have arrived at a modus vivendi, and without such an accommodation, the process of Sino-American reconciliation would have been thrown into doubt. The Taiwan modus vivendi was an essential component of the rapprochement sealed during Nixon's February 1972 visit.

On returning to Washington, Nixon set about putting his own interpretation on the Shanghai Communiqué so as to steer public opinion in a favorable direction. In a homecoming address at Andrews Air Force base, he asserted that he had made "no secret deals of any kind" in Beijing or sacrificed a U.S. commitment to any country.[116] The president and Kissinger, either separately or together, conducted briefings for the cabinet, White House staff, congressional leaders, and journalists in which they underscored the accomplishments of the trip and the merits of the communiqué. They offered assurances that the new association with China did not compromise the basic commitment to Taiwan.[117] As usual, Nixon fretted most about the reaction of conservatives. After returning to Washington, Kissinger immediately phoned Reagan and Goldwater, both of whom promised their support so long as the president did not deviate from the Taiwan commitment.[118]

Nixon and Kissinger had reason to be satisfied with the overall domestic reaction to the China trip and the Shanghai Communiqué. In Congress as well as among the press and public, Nixon's actions were well received. Only a small number of politicians and editorial writers complained that the president had let Taiwan down. Although a few right-wing journals accused him of betraying an ally, there was no conservative backlash against the China initiative.[119] Late in March, Nixon advised a State Department official to "play down Taiwan" in a forthcoming appearance on a nationally televised press interview program "since the heat had died down on this issue and there was no sense in reigniting it."[120]

Besides tending to the domestic front, the White House took action to cushion the blow to Taiwan from the outcome of Nixon's trip. Assistant Secretary Green and NSC staff member Holdridge were dispatched directly from China to reassure government leaders in Taiwan and other U.S. friends and allies in East Asia that their interests had not been sacrificed.[121] Soon after their return from China, Nixon, Kissinger, and Rogers met separately with ROC Ambassador James Shen to offer similar reassurances. They denied the existence of secret arrangements with the Chinese, affirmed U.S. treaty commitments to Taiwan, and advised Taipei against creating the public impression of tense relations with Washington.[122] A report to the president in late March indicated that Taipei had "drawn back" from its initial shock over the communiqué, yet was "still highly apprehensive of our long-term intentions."[123]

In addition to comforting words, U.S. diplomatic and military assistance was employed to bolster Taipei's confidence in Washington. The United States was instrumental in preserving Taiwan's position in international financial institutions and urged some countries that had severed diplomatic relations with Taipei to retain cultural and commercial ties.[124] American officials turned a deaf ear, however, to Taipei's requests for assistance in deterring Japan from establishing diplomatic relations with the PRC. During another trip to China in June 1972, Kissinger told Zhou Enlai that the United States favored the normalization of Sino-Japanese relations and was encouraging Japanese leaders in this direction.[125] The establishment of diplomatic relations between Tokyo and Beijing in September 1972 was yet another blow to Taiwan, although the latter's important economic connections with Japan remained intact.

The United States also continued to look after Taiwan's defensive military needs. In October 1972, the president sanctioned the sale of two World War II–type submarines to Taiwan, the first such vessels acquired by the ROC navy; however, a restriction limited their use to anti–submarine warfare training. In connection with a massive military resupply program for South Vietnam in the fall of 1972, the United States agreed to temporarily deploy two squadrons of F-4 Phantom jets on Taiwan in exchange for Taipei's transfer of 45 F-5A aircraft to the South Vietnamese air force. In January 1973, the Nixon administration gave final approval to an agreement for the joint assembly and production of short-range fighter aircraft on Taiwan.[126]

Despite the unsettling impact on Taiwan, Nixon's China trip and the Shanghai Communiqué did not precipitate either a rift between Taipei and Washington or internal disorder within the Guomindang bulwark. The Nationalist government, bent on Taiwan's survival, continued to cultivate amicable relations with the United States, its indispensable military protector and its only major friend after the defection of Japan. It continued efforts to fashion a more flexible, pragmatic foreign policy that placed priority on Taiwan's economic well-being while continuing to reject negotiations with Beijing and to uphold its political claims on the mainland. The Nationalist regime under the leadership of Chiang Ching-kuo (who became premier in 1972) remained firmly in command, although it now had to contend with heightened aspirations for political reform.[127] As Nixon completed his first term, Kissinger reported to him that Taipei was "now largely resigned to the prospect of slow improvement in U.S.-PRC relations" but was carefully watching the pace of this improvement for signs of lessened U.S. support. Moreover, the prospects for internal stability over the short term were favorable, and the mainlander leadership was enlarging somewhat the role of the politically marginalized Taiwanese majority in national politics.[128]

In the aftermath of Nixon's China trip, Washington and Beijing temporarily put the Taiwan issue on the shelf. Before leaving once again for China in February 1973, Kissinger informed the president that the PRC had taken a "more relaxed view" of the issue over the past six months or so. Chinese officials had not commented on the sale of submarines or the deployment of U.S. Phantom jets.[129] Nixon, having won re-election in a landslide and concluded a peace settlement in Vietnam, intended to make good on his pledge to seek normalization during his second term. While in Beijing, Kissinger told Zhou Enlai that "we are prepared to proceed as rapidly with the specific steps toward normalization as the PRC may be prepared to take." He and the Chinese premier agreed to establish liaison offices in each other's capitals to further the goal of normalization.[130]

That goal would elude the United States and China for almost six more years and would ultimately be attained by a different set of American and Chinese leaders. Even so, the drawing together of the two bitter adversaries during the critical 1969–72 period was a historic achievement, which set in motion the quest for normalization and placed Sino-American relations on a more amicable footing. The Nixon-Kissinger Taiwan strategy helped to make this breakthrough possible; indeed, without an accommodation on Taiwan the rapprochement would likely have been stillborn. Together with Chinese leaders, Nixon and Kissinger crafted a modus vivendi that significantly narrowed differences over this crucial issue, overcame the most daunting obstacle to improved relations, and opened the vista for eventual normalization.

In setting their sights on reconciliation and normalization of relations with the People's Republic of China, Nixon and Kissinger were prepared to alter the United States' relationship with its longtime ally on Taiwan radically. No previous administration had envisioned such a striking reversal of relations with the two rival Chinese governments. Relying on secrecy and repeated assurances of continuing support for Taiwan, Nixon and Kissinger avoided a breach with the Nationalist regime or upheaval on the island. At the same time, as Joanne Chang demonstrates in her chapter in this volume, Taiwan quickly rose to the challenges posed by the developing U.S.-PRC nexus after 1971. The Nationalist leadership headed by Chiang Ching-kuo took steps to ensure Taiwan's stability, strength, and security in a new and uncertain international environment. Even as Washington distanced itself from Taiwan in the period leading up to the final severance of official ties in 1979, Taipei strove to maintain and reinforce its many American connections.

To bring about the modus vivendi on Taiwan, Nixon and Kissinger offered a set of secret unilateral assurances to the Chinese going beyond the more guarded and conditional language on the Taiwan issue in the Shanghai Communiqué. Whether Nixon and Kissinger may have given away too much on the issue during the secret talks is a question worth asking, as Rosemary Foot suggests in her contribution to this volume. A definitive answer would require a more complete understanding of Chinese decision making at that time. Nonetheless, given the crucial importance the Chinese leadership attached to this issue, it is hard to see how a modus vivendi could have materialized in the absence of significant American concessions addressing well-known Chinese positions and concerns.[131] It is also arguable that Nixon and Kissinger could have negotiated more forcefully to obtain a Chinese commitment to a peaceful resolution of the Taiwan unification question. However, it is important to recall that the Chinese had since the 1950s refused to rule out the use of force to settle the Taiwan question, that they held fast to this stance throughout the negotiations concerning normalization under three presidents in the 1970s, and that this remains the PRC's position to this day.

Although the Taiwan modus vivendi opened the road to normalization, it left to the future the formidable problem of reaching an agreement on full diplomatic relations. The conditions for normalization Zhou Enlai set down during Kissinger's first visit to Beijing required a rupture of the U.S.-Taiwan diplomatic and security relationship. If Nixon had been able to press forward with normalization during a full second term unencumbered by Watergate, he would have had to deal with the problem of an adverse reaction at home and on Taiwan from any agreement that appeared to "sell out" the longtime ally. The dual public-secret character of the Nixon-Kissinger strategy covered up contradictions between public expectations and secret assurances that would have been extremely difficult to reconcile in a way acceptable to domestic audiences and Taiwan as well as to the Chinese. There is no evidence that Nixon and Kissinger gave focused attention to this problem prior to 1973, despite the secret pledge to move toward establishing diplomatic relations before the conclusion of the president's second term. In the end, Nixon was unable to keep this pledge during his abbreviated second term. Neither could Gerald Ford achieve normalization during his short tenure in the Oval Office. Kissinger, who carried forward negotiations with the Chinese from 1973 to 1976, was unable to find a formulation for normalization that satisfied American needs and Chinese requirements. By the time Jimmy Carter took office, relations between Washington and Beijing had fallen into a slump. Chinese disenchantment stemming from the stalemate over normalization contributed to this downturn, as did mounting opposition from Republican right-wingers to the pursuit of strengthened U.S.-PRC relations at the expense of Taiwan. Final agreement on normalization was reached only after the Carter administration finally met the conditions that Zhou Enlai had first laid down in July 1971. Even then, in arriving at an agreement, the two sides left unresolved the sticky issue of American arms sales to Taiwan.

The reliance on secrecy and personalized diplomacy that characterized Nixon's and Kissinger's dealings with the Chinese as they pursued rapprochement carried forward into the prolonged normalization discussions after 1973. This operating style had obvious benefits in conducting highly sensitive interchanges with Beijing but meant that the American public and Congress were inadequately prepared for the sharp break with Taiwan required by the normalization agreement eventually reached by the Carter administration. Reflecting concerns about the administration's secretiveness and about future relations with Taiwan, Congress on its own initiative and over Chinese protests included provisions in the 1979 Taiwan Relations Act affirming a strong American interest in maintaining Taiwan's security.

In the more than two decades since the United States and China established full diplomatic relations, the issue of Taiwan has persisted as a point of disagreement and friction. Today, it is the most difficult and prominent problem facing the two sides. Yet, it is well to keep in mind that, despite occasional flare-ups, the two nations have managed the issue peacefully, in part by opting for interim accommodation in the absence of a permanent solution. The underlying concept behind the modus vivendi that facilitated the Sino-American rapprochement between 1969 and 1972 was that there existed a mutual interest in "agreeing to disagree" on some fundamental issues until the time was right for a final resolution. Adherence to this concept has become an enduring feature of the relationship between Washington and Beijing.

TWO

China's Domestic Politics
and the Normalization of Sino-U.S.
Relations, 1969–1979

LI JIE

The end of the 1960s and the beginning of the 1970s witnessed significant changes in China's domestic political situation and foreign policy unprecedented in the history of the People's Republic of China. Domestically, the nation's highest leadership was engulfed in political uncertainty, as elites positioned themselves in preparation for the post-Mao era. Moreover, in 1971, the "September 13 Incident"—the death of Mao's heir presumptive, Vice Chairman Lin Biao, in a plane crash in Mongolia as he tried to flee to the Soviet Union—opened the way for unprecedented challenges to the theory and practice of the Cultural Revolution. Internationally, as the period began, China's foreign policy was directed against both the United States and the Soviet Union, but the 1969 Zhenbao Island incident, when Soviet and Chinese forces clashed, forced significant adjustments in China's foreign policy.

The publication of the Shanghai Communiqué in 1972 caused a sensation in western countries, but Sino-U.S. relations did not develop as rapidly as many observers had expected. Rather, relations wavered between a gradual thaw and dramatic progress. Complicating the development of better relations was conflict in China's domestic politics. The favorable outcome of this conflict cleared the way for the establishment of diplomatic relations, but the process took a decade, with many twists and turns, and the conclusion often appeared uncertain. China's dramatic internal situation was puzzling and frequently difficult to understand.

Containment of the Lin Biao and Jiang Qing Cliques, 1969 to mid-1973

Between 1969 and 1973, China remained in the throes of the Cultural Revolution. Domestic instability was heightened by the political struggles among Chairman Mao's lieutenants as they prepared for the succession to Mao's leadership. Coinciding with this domestic instability were the first steps in the normalization of U.S.-China relations. Chairman Mao, concerned about the increasing security threat posed by the Soviet Union, focused on the prospects for U.S. cooperation and the normalization of diplomatic relations. In the context of China's changing international security environment, Mao both responded to and managed the political struggle among his lieutenants so as to support his emerging policy toward the United States. Throughout this period, there was close interaction between Chinese politics and U.S.-China relations.

DOMESTIC POLITICS AND FIRST CONTACTS
WITH THE UNITED STATES

The Ninth Congress of the Chinese Communist Party (CCP) convened in April 1969. The Lin Biao and Jiang Qing cliques, which had developed during the Cultural Revolution, were officially given high positions in the Central Committee.[1] The Lin Biao clique reached the pinnacle of its power during this period.

At the time, it appeared that domestic order had been restored. In fact, however, China remained under the control of the ultra-left ideology espoused by these two cliques. To maintain their influence, the ultra-left forces needed tense relations with the United States and the Soviet Union and continuing disorder in China's politics.

Meanwhile, Mao Zedong attempted to counter these influences. In internal politics, Mao wanted the forthcoming Fourth National People's Congress to proceed smoothly, and he hoped to restore order by consolidating the results of the Cultural Revolution. He also wanted to weaken the role in the state played by Lin Biao's clique. This would leave him free to deal with the Soviet threat and the constraints on China's freedom of action imposed by both superpowers.

During this period, Mao Zedong increasingly warned of the threat of war. In early April 1969, he observed: "As to the problem of world war, there are only two possibilities; one is that war will lead to revolution, and the other is that revolution will check war."[2] On April 28, speaking to the First Plenary Session of the Ninth Congress, Mao predicted two alternatives, either local fighting or all-out war: "Local fighting would be fought along the border, [but] if a full-scale war is to be fought, I am of the opinion that we should withdraw a little and leave some space for them [the Soviets]."[3] To the proposed "Slogans Celebrating the Twentieth Anniversary of the Founding of the People's Republic of China" submitted by Zhou Enlai, Mao added a new Article 22: "Unite, people of the whole world, to counter a war of invasion launched by any imperialist or social-imperialist, especially any war of invasion using atomic bombs as weapons. If such a war should happen, the people of the whole world should annihilate the invaders with revolutionary war. We should be prepared from now on."[4]

In substance, Mao's calls to prepare for war were aimed at stabilizing China's domestic situation. In the same April 28 speech, he emphasized unity: "The aim of uniting is to strive for bigger victory."[5] The most troublesome problems at the time were the ongoing factional fighting and local conflicts. On August 28 of the same year, Mao Zedong approved and distributed an order of the Central Committee: "With a formidable enemy standing before us, all the army and the people should unite as one man, to oppose the enemy jointly." He requested an unconditional stop to the factional hostilities.

In foreign policy, Mao Zedong tried to keep the situation under control and to prevent Sino-Soviet relations from deteriorating. After the Sino-Soviet clash at Zhenbao Island on March 2, 1969, Mao immediately articulated the principle of "justified, favorable, and moderate." Starting the night of March 21, the Soviet side asked several times for direct telephone contacts with Mao. Soviet embassy officials in China also made several visits to the Chinese Foreign Ministry, stating that, on the order of the president of the Soviet Union's Conference of Ministers, they had some messages to pass to the Chinese side. Learning of these efforts, Mao directed the Chinese Foreign Ministry to be "prepared to undertake diplomatic negotiations."[6]

To Chairman Mao, domestic order and international stability were related. Among his important efforts were instructions to several of China's highest-ranking marshals to study the international situation. On the afternoon of February 19, 1969, Mao Zedong called together the members of the Central Cultural Revolution Team and four marshals, led by Chen Yi. He asked them to study the international situation and appointed Chen Yi head of the team, with Marshals Xu Xiangqian, Nie Rongzhen, and Ye Jianying participating. He sensed that the international situation was changing, and he asked them to pay attention to those states that China had neglected in the past when studying the international situation.[7]

On February 24, 1969, Nie Rongzhen received a telephone call from Chen Yi, reporting on the results of the February 19 meeting at Mao Zedong's residence, at which Mao had ordered them to study the international situation and advise the central leadership.[8] The four marshals then met on March 1, 5, 8, and 16 in the Ziguang Pavilion in the leadership compound, Zhongnanhai. Their analysis was reported in a document entitled "To See the Zhenbao Island Tree from the Forest of the World." After the Ninth Party Congress, the marshals again met several times, in Wuchen Hall in Zhongnanhai, starting on June 7. On July 11, they submitted "A Preliminary Estimate of the War Situation" to Mao Zedong and Zhou Enlai. They concluded that the contradictions between China and the Soviet Union were more serious than those between China and the United States and that the contradictions between the United States and the Soviet Union were more serious than those between China and Soviet Union. In their view, this made an anti-Chinese war unlikely. Their analysis provided support for Mao's decision to seek détente with the United States.

However, the Lin Biao and Jiang Qing cliques wanted neither a relaxation of tensions between China and the United States nor a restoration of domestic political order. If these took place, those cadres who had been removed in the Cultural Revolution would be returned to office and Zhou Enlai's role in the domestic political order would be strengthened.

Thus, as China and the United States began to make contact and gradually normalize relations, the domestic political situation was polarized between two camps. In this context, on the advice of Zhou Enlai, Ye Jianying, and others, Mao Zedong more actively promoted normalization of Sino-U.S. relations for national security and domestic political reasons. The Lin Biao and Jiang Qing cliques sought to contain this effort and attacked those who favored such policies.

In a typical example, as the four marshals were appraising the international situation, Lin Biao and his supporters were preparing their own assessment of the international situation. They continued to insist that war was inevitable. In June 1969, the administrative group of the Military Commission of the CCP Central Committee, presided over by Lin's subordinate and chief of the General Staff Huang Yongsheng, held a symposium. Based on Lin Biao's argument that we should "watch, check, and realize everything with a view to fighting a war," the symposium advocated a major defense buildup. Carrying out this program would seriously interfere with the goals of the Outline of the Fourth Five-Year Plan then being drafted under the guidance of Zhou Enlai.[9] On October 18, Lin Biao, in a move kept secret from Mao Zedong and others, issued through Huang Yongsheng "An Emergency Order on the Strengthening of War Preparedness to Prevent the Enemy from Making a Sudden Attack" (Order No. 1, from Vice Chairman Lin). This order was intended to mobilize the People's Liberation Army (PLA) into a state of emergency preparedness. This serious step was unprecedented. On October 19, Lin Biao informed Mao of his action. Mao immediately said, "Burn it [the mobilization order]."[10] These events indicate that while Lin Biao continued to work carefully under the banner of realizing Mao Zedong's directives and to show deference to Mao's leadership, his strategic ideas were quite different from those of Mao.

Lin Biao's attitude toward the decision of the CCP Central Committee to normalize relations with the United States was always ambiguous. Mao later remarked to President Nixon that Lin Biao opposed that decision: "A faction in our party was against our communicating with you; in the end, they went to a foreign country by plane." In a reference to Lin's death, Mao further commented: "America has the best information-gathering work. The second best is that of Japan. As to the Soviet Union, it can only dig up the corpses."[11]

THE SEPTEMBER 13 INCIDENT

The new contacts between China and the United States brought Mao Zedong and Zhou Enlai closer, consolidating Zhou's position in the political hierarchy. Meanwhile, Mao was engaged in a struggle with Lin Biao and his followers over questions of revision of the state constitution and the establishment of the post of a president of the state. The Lin Biao clique hoped to consolidate its uncertain position during the Fourth National People's Congress. The result of the struggle was the defeat of the Lin Biao clique.

The September 13 Incident in 1971 was a turning point in the fortunes of the ultra-left forces led by the Lin Biao clique. Following the exposure and criticism of Lin Biao and his followers, a great number of old cadres were politically rehabilitated, and Zhou Enlai assumed responsibility for the daily work of the central government, with support from Mao Zedong. This in turn forced the Jiang Qing clique to retrench. This trend, along with the support of Ye Jianying, strengthened Zhou's leadership in foreign affairs.

On November 8, 1971, with Zhou Enlai in attendance, Mao received members of the Chinese delegation to the twenty-sixth session of the United Nations General Assembly. When Fu Hao, the chief of the General Office of the Foreign Ministry and the general secretary of the delegation, was introduced, Zhou Enlai deliberately mentioned to Mao that Fu Hao had signed the "ninety-one-men big-character poster." (In the spring of 1968, a group of cadres in the Foreign Ministry had signed a big-character poster in support of Chen Yi, who was being persecuted by ultra-left forces in the Foreign Ministry; the petition was called the "ninety-one-men poster.")

Mao Zedong took this opportunity to declare publicly that he agreed with their action. Mao's declaration resulted in the rehabilitation of a group of cadres who had been persecuted in the Cultural Revolution for supporting Vice Premier Chen Yi, and they were able to resume their work.[12]

Even so, Jiang Qing and her supporters still sought every opportunity to hinder the normalization of Sino-U.S. relations. They knew that normalization of relations was Mao's highest priority, and missteps by Zhou Enlai, Ye Jianying, and others would cause Mao Zedong to lose confidence in them.

From January 3 to 10, 1972, Alexander Haig, deputy assistant for national security affairs, and an advance party visited China to make preparations for President Nixon's upcoming visit. On January 4 and 5, Zhou Enlai held a preparatory meeting of officials who were to talk with Haig and his group about certain technical problems concerning Nixon's visit raised by the American side. Zhou and Haig had agreed in principle to relay to the United States a television broadcast of Nixon's visit via a U.S. satellite. Jiang Qing conveyed her opposition to this decision through Yu Huiyong, who was in charge of the Cultural Revolution Group of the State Council. In response, Zhou emphasized that, to preserve China's state sovereignty, China would buy the communications satellite and then rent it to the United States. He criticized the argument made by Jiang Qing and others that Beijing should not "propagandize" for Nixon by relaying the television coverage of his visit.[13]

On January 6, Zhou Enlai and Ye Jianying briefed Mao Zedong. Mao used this meeting to back Zhou Enlai and the pragmatic forces in the Chinese leadership. He pointed out that there had in fact been no "February adverse current," a reference to the leftists' charge that certain Chinese leaders were trying to reverse the Cultural Revolution. When Mao was told that the four marshals predicted that there would not be a war, he ordered talk of imminent war to cease and told Zhou and Ye to pass this instruction along to Chen Yi.[14]

That evening, Marshal Chen Yi passed away. His analysis of the international situation had contributed significantly to the easing of Sino-U.S. tensions. On January 10, Mao Zedong, in a departure from his usual practice, attended the memorial service. He told those at the service that the problem of Deng Xiaoping was one of contradiction among the people. This paved the way for Deng's eventual return to office.

Due to Mao Zedong's support of Zhou Enlai, Ye Jianying, and others, the efforts of the Jiang Qing clique to sabotage normalization, although they posed some difficulties for Zhou and the other pragmatists, did not impede overall progress toward that goal.

THE STRENGTHENING OF
THE PRAGMATIC FORCES

During this period, the domestic situation in China interacted with the Sino-U.S. relationship, both as cause and as effect. National security was the main consideration behind China's decision to improve relations with the United States, but changes in China's diplomacy, away from leftist emotionalism and toward pragmatism, also had an important impact. The publication of the Shanghai Communiqué in February 1972 signified that national security had become the most important factor in diplomatic strategy. This change occurred at a time when the domestic forces for pragmatism were rapidly increasing in strength, and the Shanghai Communiqué in turn reinforced those pragmatic forces.

A crucial factor in this period was Mao Zedong's full support, in both the domestic and the foreign policy areas, for Zhou Enlai, who was in charge of the day-to-day work of the party and government. Mao's backing served to contain, temporarily, the ultra-leftist tendencies that had erupted since the Cultural Revolution. In addition, the pragmatic forces criticized during the Cultural Revolution began to reassemble.

These trends contributed in various ways to Sino-U.S. rapprochement. First, as Lin Biao's supporters were being ousted from their party and military positions, the rehabilitation of a large number of old cadres, especially foreign affairs experts, began. Second, along with the gradual stabilization of internal order, economic construction resumed. The gateways to the country, closed for so long, were opened again, and the Chinese people began to learn more about the outside world. Calls for accelerating the development of the economy and expanding international ties became louder and louder. Following the visits to China of Henry Kissinger and President Nixon and with the expansion of reporting on the United States in Chinese newspapers, people's views on America changed greatly. Previously viewed as China's "number one enemy," it was now seen as a powerful friend. Third, after the Tenth National Party Congress in 1973, Deng Xiaoping gradually resumed power and took charge of the routine work of the party, the government, and the army. His re-emergence contributed greatly to domestic stability and the improvement of Sino-U.S. relations.

Under these circumstances, the political and social climate favored the smooth development of Sino-U.S. relations. Aversion to ultra-leftism and the yearning for stability became popular sentiments, and Beijing was able to eliminate various unfavorable domestic factors. In this context, on June 19–23, 1972, Henry Kissinger visited China for the fourth time and communicated to Zhou Enlai the status of the U.S.-Soviet talks on limiting strategic weapons. On the day that Kissinger left China, Zhou reported to the last session of the full membership of the Central Rectification Meeting to Criticize Lin Biao. His comments centered around a criticism of a Taiwan publication and were entitled "The Truth about the Rumor-mongering Publication by the Kuomintang (KMT) of the So-called 'Announcement of Wu Hao.'" Zhou used the opportunity to rebut Jiang Qing's charges that there were political problems in his personal history.

Soon after Kissinger left Beijing, Mao Zedong, in the company of Zhou Enlai, received the prime minister of Sri Lanka. Mao spoke about the influence on China's foreign policy of the "leftists" and said that "the one who stood behind them is gone now; his name was Lin Biao."[15] Zhou Enlai and others who sought to eliminate the influence of the ultra-leftists soon followed up on this signal from Mao. On August 1 and 2, Zhou, in a long report to a Foreign Affairs Work Conference, suggested that Lin Biao had encouraged an ultra-leftist trend of thought in foreign affairs.

To eliminate the interference of ultra-leftism in diplomatic work and to consolidate the results of China's new diplomacy, the International Department of the CCP Central Committee and the Foreign Ministry, at the suggestion of Zhou Enlai, prepared to convene a Foreign Affairs Work Conference. On November 28, the report of the two bodies to Zhou Enlai and the Central Committee of the CCP proposed a thorough criticism of the ultra-leftist thought of the Lin Biao clique and its divergence from current circumstances in foreign affairs. On November 30, Zhou indicated that he would consent to this proposal.

But, contrary to the expectation of Zhou Enlai and others, Zhang Chunqiao and Jiang Qing rejected this formulation. They insisted that the Lin Biao clique was not "ultra-left" but "left in form but right in essence." On December 3, the two departments, following up on a discussion in the Politburo the day before, removed the section of the report that recommended criticism of the "ultra-left trend of thought and anarchism"; the report was then submitted to Mao Zedong for approval.[16] Clearly there were still many obstructions to the total elimination of interference with China's foreign policy by the ultra-leftists.

On February 15–19, 1973, Kissinger made his fifth visit to China. Zhou Enlai's six meetings with Kissinger focused on the Taiwan issue and Sino-U.S. relations. The two countries declared in a joint statement that

the proper time has come to accelerate the normalization of their relationship. For this purpose, both sides have agreed to expand their contacts in various fields. They have drawn up a concrete program to expand commercial, scientific and cultural intercourse. To accelerate such a process and to improve their contacts, it is agreed that each side will set up a Liaison Office in the capital of the other side in the near future.[17]

On February 17, Mao Zedong met with Kissinger and introduced the strategy of a global "horizontal line" to counter hegemony jointly. The Chinese side held high hopes for the Sino-U.S. relationship.[18]

In addition to pressure from Jiang Qing and others, Zhou Enlai also suffered from a severe illness. What worried him most was who would assume his responsibility for day-to-day management of party and government work, should he become too weak to work. On March 3, 1973, Zhou wrote to Mao Zedong to report several discussions in the Politburo recommending that Deng Xiaoping resume his party activities and return to the post of vice premier. Mao approved, and on March 10, the Central Committee of the Chinese

Communist Party issued a "Decision on Deng Xiaoping's Resumption of Party Activities and the Post of Vice Premier of the State Council." On March 29, at the suggestion of Mao Zedong, Zhou presided over a meeting of the Politburo and announced that Deng would participate in the work of the administrative group of the State Council and in external activities in the capacity of vice premier and that he would attend Politburo meetings, as a nonvoting member, to discuss important policies.[19] This was a crucial step in putting Deng Xiaoping in charge of all the work of the central government. While being treated for illness at the health facility at Yuquanshan in Beijing, Zhou held several long talks with Deng Xiaoping in preparation for his resumption of office.

On May 1, 1973, China and the United States established liaison offices in each other's capitals. Huang Hua and David Bruce became the chiefs of the respective liaison offices. Following this promising step in diplomatic normalization, Sino-U.S. relations stagnated, in part because of renewed turbulence and uncertainty in Chinese domestic politics.

Domestic Political Uncertainty, July 1973–1977

From mid-1973 through 1977, the main impact of China's domestic political situation on the Sino-U.S. relationship was interference from the ultra-leftists. At the same time, there was a crisis in decision making at the highest levels, because Mao Zedong was seriously ill. This created great uncertainty in China's domestic politics and in its diplomacy.

THE "NEW INFORMATION" INCIDENT

On June 16, 1973, Mao Zedong discussed with Zhou Enlai the drafting of the political report for the Tenth CCP Congress. Mao suggested that the report should point out the characteristics of the era.[20] Shortly thereafter, Leonid Brezhnev visited the United States to sign the "Basic Principles of Negotiations on Strategic Arms Limitation" and the Agreement Between the United States of America and Union of Soviet Socialist Republics on the Prevention of Nuclear War. China was extremely concerned about the relaxation of tensions between the United States and the Soviet Union and its implications for Sino-U.S. relations. On June 25, Zhou Enlai met with David Bruce and expressed China's apprehensions about the two agreements. "The Soviet leader's visit to the United States leaves the impression," the premier remarked, "that the two great powers will dominate the world."[21] The next day, when Mao Zedong read the minutes of the interview, he said, "Now that we are taking a firm stand, Bruce will be comfortable."[22]

At the suggestion of Zhou Enlai, the Foreign Ministry prepared a report entitled "A Preliminary View on the Talks Between Nixon and Brezhnev" for publication in *New Information*. The report called the U.S.-Soviet negotiations "deceptive" and claimed that they indicated that "the United States and the Soviet Union would like to dominate the world."[23]

Mao Zedong seriously criticized this report, stating that it was in contradiction to his ideas. He believed that Zhou Enlai and the Foreign Ministry were overly fearful of U.S.-Soviet collusion and its impact on Chinese security. On July 3, Zhou Enlai, learning of Mao's criticism from Wang Hairong, then assistant foreign minister in charge of protocol, wrote a letter to Foreign Ministry personnel. Among other things, he said, "I bear the main responsibility for this mistake. . . . I hope you will take this as a lesson. You should keep up the initiative of studying, and you may ask me to convene a short meeting to exchange ideas. Do not think I am too busy and I would only think of what is important and leave what is unimportant aside. We should learn Chairman Mao's way of working."[24]

On July 4, Mao again criticized the article: "Recently, there has been something unsatisfactory in the work of the Foreign Ministry. I always say 'great turbulence and great reorganization,' but the Foreign Ministry says suddenly 'great deception and dominance.' It pays attention to what is superficial only, and not to what is substantial." Mao's criticism continued: "They do not discuss what is important, but submit to me what is unimportant. If they do not change their ways, they are headed for revisionism. When that happens, do not say I did not warn you beforehand."[25]

Mao Zedong's criticisms of the Foreign Ministry did not directly mention Zhou Enlai, who was in charge of the Foreign Ministry.

But because Mao stated his criticisms to Zhang Chunqiao and Wang Hongwen, allies of Jiang Qing, and used the phrase "headed for revisionism," he placed Zhou Enlai in a difficult political position. Moreover, Mao's statement created considerable uncertainty throughout the political elite, because the Chinese leadership was in the midst of preparing for the Tenth Party Congress, which would determine important personnel appointments.

The next day, Mao Zedong, on reading Zhou Enlai's July 3 letter to Foreign Ministry personnel, commented: "This chronic and stubborn disease is widespread, not just the affliction of a specific person. You should study how to correct it."[26] By this, Mao Zedong meant that his two previous criticisms had not been directed specifically at Zhou Enlai or other specific individuals. The mild expression, "you should study how to correct it," indicated that there was no question of Zhou stepping down; it was only a matter of making a "correction."

That same day, July 5, Zhou Enlai presided over a Politburo meeting. Zhang Chunqiao reported Mao's July 4 criticisms. Zhou Enlai then briefed the meeting on Mao Zedong's comments on the Foreign Ministry since late June and confessed his own errors. Based on Mao's views of international problems, the meeting suggested some revisions in the report to the Tenth Party Congress concerning the international situation and China's task.

Zhou Enlai then immediately summoned a group of Foreign Ministry personnel to draft a new article critical of the *New Information* article. On July 15, he submitted the draft article to Mao Zedong for examination, along with a letter saying that, "as to self-criticism of the mistakes, I will submit another report." Mao read the article the same day and crossed out the word "severely" in the comment that Zhou's mistakes had been "severely criticized" by the CCP Central Committee; he also said Zhou "need not write the self-criticism."[27] Although Mao had treated the article in *New Information* relatively lightly and had indicated that he was not prepared to remove Zhou from office, it was nonetheless a serious warning to Zhou and other pragmatic leaders.

During this period, Mao was greatly interested in the long struggle between the Confucianists and the Legalists in Chinese

history; he talked with Jiang Qing and others about it many times.[28]
On August 5, at a Politburo meeting presided over by Zhou Enlai,
Jiang Qing reported on Mao Zedong's comments about this struggle.
She read a poem written by Mao, called "Lessons Learned from 'On
Feudalism,' Submitted for Criticism by Comrade Guo Moruo." She
wanted to use Mao's criticism of Confucius to weaken Zhou Enlai
and asked that the poem be included in the Political Report of the
Tenth Congress. Zhou tried to oppose Jiang Qing in a roundabout
way. He said that it would take time to understand Mao's poem
fully and that it was not necessary to publish it immediately.
Nonetheless, more and more articles critical of Confucius and Con-
fucianism were published in the Chinese media; these were in fact
thinly veiled attacks on the "modern-day Confucius," Zhou Enlai.

On August 20, Mao Zedong gave, in principle, his consent for the
draft Political Report of the Tenth Congress, prepared under Zhou
Enlai's leadership. This was the first time that Zhou had made a
political report to a party congress on behalf of the Central Committee. This served as Mao's confirmation of his intention that
Zhou was to continue to be in charge of the routine work of the
central government after the Tenth Congress.

The Tenth Congress of the CCP met August 23–28, 1973. Many
pragmatists, including Deng Xiaoping, were rehabilitated and elected
to the leadership. At the same time, however, Jiang Qing and her
followers were also re-elected to the central leadership. Of particular
significance was Wang Hongwen's election as vice chairman of the
party, a position second only to that of Zhou Enlai. He had become
Mao's apparent successor as CCP chairman, and his promotion en-
hanced the power of the Jiang Qing clique.

ZHOU ENLAI IS CRITICIZED AGAIN

As the political situation in China was undergoing these subtle
changes, Henry Kissinger, who was now both secretary of state and
national security advisor, made his sixth visit to China on November 10–14, 1973. Zhou Enlai held talks with Kissinger on November
11, 12, 13, and 14. Zhou was very cautious in these talks, so as not to
give the Jiang Qing clique a pretext to impede the improvement of
Sino-U.S. relations.

Kissinger and Zhou discussed the establishment of a hotline between the two countries and the provision by the United States to China of a satellite system. Both sides were interested in establishing strategic coordination. The statement released on November 14 noted the importance of strengthening consultations at "authoritative levels and exchanging views on problems of concern to both sides."[29]

On November 17, Mao Zedong reviewed the meetings between Zhou Enlai and Kissinger and concluded that Zhou had made mistakes. He met with Zhou and criticized his comments. He suggested that the Politburo meet to discuss his opinions. Mao warned Zhou not to be deceived by the Americans:

They want to clutch at a straw to save their lives. You should be careful of America. We tend to be "left" when struggling with them and "right" when cooperating with them. I am of the opinion that, basically, we should do nothing with them. By this, I mean, we should not form a military alliance with America. Now we have imported too much [help] from America. But I gave consent to it; I was the chief culprit. This time, the chief culprit in colluding with America is also me.[30]

Later, when talking about the meetings between Zhou and Kissinger, Mao said that the United States is a " protective umbrella," and Washington is "lending an umbrella to us."[31]

That evening, Zhou Enlai presided over a Politburo meeting and reported on his meetings with Kissinger and conveyed Mao Zedong's comments. Jiang Qing went on the attack, charging Zhou with "right capitulationism." Despite his well-known patience, Zhou was forced to argue with Jiang Qing.[32]

This conflict with Jiang Qing placed Zhou Enlai in a dilemma. On one hand, he had to admit his mistake to Mao Zedong. On the other hand, he had to struggle with Jiang Qing and her supporters. The next day, November 18, Zhou wrote two letters to Mao, reporting on the Politburo meeting and conceding that he had not "done well enough" in the most recent Sino-U.S. talks.[33] Even before this incident, Jiang Qing and others had been interfering in Chinese foreign policy making and attacking Zhou's foreign policy to undercut his position in the leadership. On November 13, 1973, Jiang had suggested that her followers Zhang Chunqiao and Yao

Wenyuan be among those who received the *Bulletin of Foreign Affairs Activities* (edited by the Chinese People's Association for Friendship with Foreign Countries). Accordingly, Zhou Enlai instructed the Foreign Ministry that "starting today, the *Bulletin of Foreign Affairs Activities* should be sent to the Chairman, all members of the Politburo in Beijing, and all relevant departments, commissions, and groups. Please give notice to the association to comply with this directive."[34] On November 18, in a discussion of the invitation extended to two Turkish musicians to visit China, Jiang Qing had argued that China should "receive fewer or no theater troupes from capitalist countries." Together with Zhang Chunqiao and Yao Wenyuan, she sponsored a movement "to criticize the spread of capitalist . . . music" in Beijing, Tianjin, Shanghai, and other places. The Foreign Ministry was forced to cancel the visit.

Mao Zedong's criticism of Zhou's handling of the Sino-U.S. talks increased the political pressure on Zhou. From November 21 to early December, the Politburo, at Mao Zedong's suggestion, held meetings to criticize Zhou Enlai and Ye Jianying. At the meetings, Zhou engaged in self-criticisms, but Jiang Qing, Yao Wenyuan, and others were not satisfied. They argued that this was the "eleventh struggle between two lines," that Zhou Enlai was the "chief of the incorrect line," and that he "could not wait" to replace Mao Zedong.[35] After the meeting, Jiang Qing urged Mao Zedong to appoint herself and Yao Wenyuan as standing members of the Politburo.[36]

Although Mao had severely criticized Zhou Enlai, he did not intend to pull him down. On December 9, he met with Zhou and with Wang Hongwen. He said that the criticism meetings had been good, except for some incorrect statements, including the statement about "the eleventh struggle between two lines." Mao thought that Jiang Qing "should not say this, and in reality it is not so." The other incorrect statement was that the premier "could not wait." He said that it was not the premier who could not wait to succeed Mao as party leader, but Jiang Qing. Mao indicated that he would reject the request to appoint Jiang Qing and Yao Wenyuan as standing members of the Politburo.[37]

Nevertheless, it was obvious to everyone in the Chinese leadership that Mao was dissatisfied with Zhou's handling of the day-to-
day work of the central government. On December 12, 1973, Mao
presided over a Politburo meeting. He criticized "the Politburo
[because it] does not discuss political affairs" and "the Military Affairs Commission [because it] does not discuss military affairs." He
said, "If you do not make corrections, I will convene a meeting. Let
everyone come here." But Mao also suggested that Deng Xiaoping
should participate in the work of the Military Affairs Commission.[38] Two days later, on December 14, he nominated Deng to be a
member of the Politburo and the chief of the General Staff and to
participate in the leading work of the Military Affairs Commission.[39] Mao seemed dissatisfied with Zhou Enlai, and he had placed
his hopes on Deng Xiaoping.

THE RISE AND FALL OF DENG XIAOPING

In early 1974, the Jiang Qing clique used the Criticism of Lin Biao
and Confucius Campaign to create obstacles to Sino-U.S. relations,
and it attempted to exploit the "Snail Incident" to reverse the diplomatic work led by Zhou Enlai.

In December 1973, the Fourth Department of Machine-Building
Industry sent an investigation group to visit the Corning Company
in the United States. The Corning Company presented the Chinese
delegation with a glass snail as a souvenir. This trivial event would
become a foreign affairs incident that required the intervention of
the Politburo. On February 10, 1974, Jiang Qing gave a speech to the
Fourth Machine-Building Department, charging the investigation
group with "worshipping and having blind faith in anything
foreign." She urged the department to stop its import plans, to return the souvenir, and to make a protest to the U.S. Liaison Office
in China.

Zhou Enlai understood that he was Jiang Qing's real target, and
he acted cautiously. Before responding to Jiang's criticism, he asked
the Foreign Ministry to make a serious investigation. On February
21, the Foreign Ministry submitted "A Report on the Snail Presented by Americans as a Souvenir." The report concluded that
there was no ill intention on the American side, and it recom-

mended that the souvenir not be returned and China should open a dialogue with the Corning Company.

Zhou Enlai accepted the report and passed it along to Mao Zedong for approval. At the time, Mao was becoming increasingly dissatisfied with Jiang Qing and other leftists for using the Criticize Lin Biao and Confucius Movement to attack veteran cadres, and he endorsed Zhou's report. Zhou then convened a Politburo meeting on this incident and ordered that Jiang's speech to the Fourth Machine-Building Department be withheld from distribution and that copies already in circulation should be recalled immediately.[40]

During this period, Deng Xiaoping gradually assumed responsibility for foreign policy, including Sino-U.S. relations. Jiang Qing and other leftists opposed this trend. On March 20, 1974, Mao named Deng to lead the Chinese delegation to the Sixth United Nations Special Session and instructed the Foreign Ministry to record this decision in the appropriate reports. Jiang Qing and her supporters opposed this decision. On March 25, Mao sent a message to Zhou Enlai, again suggesting that Deng Xiaoping attend the United Nations special session, but he added that if the Politburo did not agree with his suggestion, it could be dropped. On March 26, at a Politburo meeting, all the participants except for Jiang Qing agreed to the selection of Deng Xiaoping. Learning of this, Mao warned Jiang Qing: "Deng Xiaoping goes abroad at my suggestion. You had better not object."[41] Under pressure, Jiang Qing was forced to back down.

It was clear that Mao Zedong wanted Deng Xiaoping to succeed Zhou Enlai as the person managing foreign affairs, but Jiang Qing and her supporters coveted diplomatic power and would not accept this. Under the circumstances, Deng could do little in foreign affairs. China's many domestic problems required all his energy. At the same time, the domestic situations in both the United States and China prevented Deng from making breakthroughs in the Sino-U.S. relationship, which could have helped to consolidate his domestic position. For these reasons, Deng's attention had to be devoted solely to domestic problems.

In this period, Mao's ideas guided Deng Xiaoping's approach to foreign affairs. The basis of diplomatic strategy was Mao Zedong's view of the world as divided into the first, second, and third worlds; it was Deng who expounded the main points of this idea. Second, analysis of the international situation was based on Mao's predictions that "there will be turbulence in the world" and that "the rising wind forebodes the coming storm." In this view, the threat of world war came mainly from the Soviet Union, and the United States was strategically on the defensive. In particular, the Soviet Union wanted to gain a year-round outlet to the sea through the Indian subcontinent. Third, the Taiwan problem was the key to normalization of Sino-U.S. relations, and in Mao's view, the only way to solve the problem was the Japanese way, that is, the United States must recognize that "there is only one China, not two Chinas, and not one and one-half Chinas."[42]

Even though Deng was following Mao's guidance, Jiang Qing used his foreign policy activities to attack him. This was a critical period for preparations for the Fourth National People's Congress and the debate over who would be named to powerful positions. Jiang Qing opposed the re-emergence of the pragmatists under Deng Xiaoping, which would pose a serious threat to her clique. The struggle between the two sides erupted in the "*Fengqing* Incident."

The *Fengqing* was a Chinese-made oceangoing freighter. On the eve of China's National Day in 1974, it returned to the port of Shanghai from Romania. Wang Hongwen, then in charge of work in the Central Committee, criticized the Ministry of Communications for not granting approval for the freighter to go to sea earlier and said that this delay had been caused by the ministry's "blind faith and worship of anything foreign"; this amounted to a "national betrayal." On October 14, Jiang Qing made a written comment on the incident and used it as a pretext to criticize the State Council. On October 17, she and her allies attacked Deng Xiaoping during a meeting of the Politburo. After the meeting, she sent Wang Hongwen to Changsha to see Chairman Mao and indict Deng Xiaoping.

On October 18, Wang Hongwen told Mao Zedong that because of the *Fengqing* issue, Jiang Qing and Deng Xiaoping were engaged in a bitter quarrel. Deng Xiaoping persisted in his old saying, "To buy a ship is better than to build a ship, and to rent a ship is better than to buy a ship." Jiang said that Deng's posture reflected his efforts to influence the coming decision on the appointment of the chief of the General Staff. The political situation in Beijing, Wang said, was now similar to that at the 1959 Lushan Conference.[43] Although Premier Zhou was seriously ill, he spent his days talking with Deng Xiaoping, Ye Jianying, and Li Xiannian, among others. They communicated with one another so frequently that it was clear they were considering personnel decisions in preparation for the Fourth National People's Congress. Mao Zedong criticized Wang Hongwen for carping about these activities, saying that "you should talk with them face to face if you have different opinions; you should not do it like this. You should unite with Deng Xiaoping." He advised Wang to talk more with Zhou Enlai and Ye Jianying and not to work with Jiang Qing.[44]

On October 19, Jiang Qing asked Wang Hairong and Tang Wensheng (who were to accompany Deng Xiaoping as he escorted the prime minister of Denmark to meet Chairman Mao at Changsha) to report to Mao on the problem of "worship and blind confidence in anything foreign." Learning of this, Zhou Enlai asked to see Wang Hairong and Tang Wensheng; he warned them that this was a plot to criticize Deng Xiaoping and that Deng had been restraining himself for a long time.[45]

On October 20, after listening to the report by Wang Hairong and Tang Wensheng in Changsha, Mao Zedong indicated the *Fengqing* issue was "a trifle" and said that even though Li Xiannian had taken care of it, Jiang Qing still wanted to "make a noise" about it. He asked Wang and Tang to pass a message along to Zhou Enlai: "You are still the premier. The preparation work for the Fourth National People's Congress and personnel arrangements should be under the leadership of the premier and Wang Hongwen, but they should consult with all sides." He once again nominated Deng Xiaoping to be the first vice premier of the State Council and chief of the General Staff.[46]

On November 12, Deng Xiaoping reported to Chairman Mao in Changsha on the debate in the Politburo meeting on October 17. Deng told Mao that he considered the political situation in the

Politburo abnormal. He also mentioned his quarrel with Jiang Qing. Mao supported Deng and said of Jiang Qing that "she forces her opinion on others. I am not happy with this either."[47]

From December 23 to 27, Zhou Enlai and Wang Hongwen reported to Mao Zedong in Changsha on preparations for the Fourth National People's Congress. Mao criticized Jiang Qing as ambitious and reiterated his nomination of Deng Xiaoping as the first vice premier of the State Council, vice president of the Central Military Commission, and chief of the General Staff. He also agreed with Zhou's suggestion to name Deng vice president of the CCP Central Committee and a standing member of the Politburo. He again affirmed that Zhou was still the premier and that, following the Fourth National People's Congress, Deng was to be in charge of the work of the State Council.[48]

Because Mao Zedong tilted toward Deng Xiaoping during this period, the assignment of personnel to party and government positions, in preparation for the Second Plenary Session of the Tenth Congress of the Communist Party of China and the Fourth National People's Congress, was finally settled. This created the necessary conditions for the full rehabilitation of Deng Xiaoping in 1975. Nonetheless, China's political situation remained unstable, and Deng was especially cautious in the sensitive and thorny field of diplomacy.

Meanwhile, in the United States on August 9, 1974, Nixon resigned and Gerald Ford succeeded to the presidency. Ford was necessarily a weak president. Internationally, the United States had disentangled itself from the Vietnam War, and it had achieved some measure of détente with the Soviet Union. This decreased pressure on the United States to improve its relationship with China, and Washington was no longer as anxious to resolve the Taiwan issue and normalize relations. Ford, however, wanted to know China's current thinking on normalization and the strategic environment, and he sent Henry Kissinger on his seventh visit to China.

Deng Xiaoping held five talks with Kissinger between November 26 and November 28. In advance of these talks, on November 12, Deng asked Mao Zedong for negotiating instructions. Deng reported that because the world believed that the Sino-U.S. relationship had cooled, Kissinger wanted to demonstrate that the relationship was stable and that the main item on his agenda was still the Taiwan issue. Mao replied, "At this time, we don't need to take Taiwan. He wants us to promise not to use force, but we will not do that. On the contrary, they owe us something. Let the U.S.-Chiang treaty stand; the problem can be solved when there are great changes in the world."[49] This attitude was called "to await changes with a cold attitude." Ultimately, however, the breakthrough in the Sino-U.S. relationship would require not only "great changes in the world" but also great changes in China.

Jiang Qing continued to interfere in Chinese diplomacy. At the end of 1974, a complaint was made to Mao Zedong against the chief of the Chinese Liaison Office in the United States, Huang Zhen. The issue was settled only after a personal investigation by Zhou Enlai. But in summer 1975, pressure from the clique forced Huang Zhen to offer his resignation. Deng Xiaoping, however, delayed making a decision, on the pretext that he needed Huang to make preparations for President Ford's visit to China at the end of the year. During Ford's visit to China, the matter was settled when Mao Zedong personally asked Huang to stay in his post for one or two more years.[50]

On December 1–5, 1975, President Ford visited China. Although the visit did not solve any substantial problems and did not set a timetable for normalization, it provided an opportunity for summit-level talks in which the two sides could express their principal positions. This was helpful following the leadership change in the United States.

At the end of 1975, the movement "to criticize Deng Xiaoping and beat back the rightist reversal of verdicts" began to sweep China. Mao Zedong again severely criticized Deng Xiaoping. The domestic political situation turned abruptly leftward. The ultra-leftists had gained the upper hand, dashing the hopes of the Chinese people for stable domestic and international political situations.

There were many reasons for this shift. One important reason was the crisis in decision making. Mao Zedong was seriously ill, and a successor had not been determined. His contacts with members of the leadership, including Deng Xiaoping and other leaders in charge of the day-to-day work of the central government, were curtailed. But the deeper reason for the leadership crisis was that since the Lin Biao incident, Mao Zedong himself had vacillated between the pragmatists and the ultra-leftists. If he favored the pragmatic side, this would negate the theoretical basis of the Cultural Revolution, an outcome he would not like to see. But he also yearned for restoration of order. This was his guiding thought when he put Zhou Enlai and Deng Xiaoping in charge of the day-to-day work of the central government. Mao's wavering enabled Jiang Qing and other leftists to attack Zhou Enlai and Deng Xiaoping. Following Zhou's death in January 1976, Deng was forced out of all his posts. This was a disaster for the domestic political situation, which had been improving, and for Sino-U.S. relations, which had been moving toward normalization.

Then, in September 1976, Mao Zedong passed away. In October, after the Jiang Qing clique was crushed, ultra-left influence evaporated, and the Cultural Revolution came to an end. This led to a new turning point in the Chinese political situation and the Sino-U.S. relationship.

Reform and Opening, 1977–January 1979

In July 1977, ten months after Chairman Mao Zedong died, the Third Plenary Session of the Tenth CCP Congress decided that Deng Xiaoping should resume his posts. This formed the basis for a crucial transformation in China's domestic and foreign policies.

DOMESTIC DYNAMICS OF THE OPENING
TO THE OUTSIDE WORLD

Support for eliminating the influence of the ultra-left ideology of the Jiang Qing clique was widespread, as was support for making domestic economic construction the highest priority of the party and the country, expanding openings to the outside world, and narrowing the gap between China and the developed countries. These trends created a domestic incentive for improving Sino-U.S. relations.

On May 12, 1977, Deng Xiaoping, speaking with the head of the Chinese Academy of Sciences, said:

In the past, we did not absorb advanced knowledge from foreign countries. The developed countries attach importance to scientific achievements. It is said that each day, some science news reaches the desks of the heads of other governments. The advanced result of scientific study is the result of human labor. Why not absorb these results? What is shameful about absorbing them? For our whole country to catch up and surpass the advanced countries of the world, scientific study is the prerequisite.[51]

Then, on September 14, Deng Xiaoping received a delegation from a Japanese opposition party, the New Freedom Club. He pointed out:

All advanced achievements are the result of the common efforts of human beings. Even the bourgeoisie understand this as common sense, so they are the ones who introduce anything advanced into the world. Japan, too, does this. To rely on oneself means to rely on one's own efforts and one's own resources, but it does not mean to refuse all advanced achievements of others.

He also remarked: "the international situation has undergone many changes; many old concepts and old formulas do not reflect reality, and past strategies are also not consistent with the current reality."[52] On September 29, Deng expressed to the British writer Han Suyin his urgent objective of raising China's level of scientific achievement:

In the 1960s, the gap between the scientific and technological levels of China and those of the rest of the world was not very big. However, in the late 1960s and the early 1970s, the scientific and technological levels of the rest of the world improved tremendously. All fields of science developed quickly. The improvement made in one year amounted to that of several years; we might even say the improvement made in one day amounted to that of several years. In 1975, I once said, China was fifty years behind Japan in science. At the time, I had wanted to pay more attention to scientific study, but, in the end, I could not do so, since I myself was under house arrest. If we do not take the newest scientific achievements as our starting points and create favorable conditions and try our best, I am afraid there is no hope for China.[53]

Within a few months, as Deng repeatedly emphasized the importance of introducing advanced science and technology, as well as business management practices, from the rest of the world, the calls within the party for reform and opening to the outside world became stronger. Against this background, the Third Plenary Session of the Eleventh Congress of the Communist Party of China, convened in December 1978, marking a historic turning point.

Deng Xiaoping also explained China's interest in improving relations with the United States from this perspective. In a meeting with the Norwegian foreign minister on March 25, 1978, he said "the United States has not put China on its agenda. A really clever politician should understand what position China is in. Strategically, we are decisive. We are clear that in order to realize the four modernizations, we need to cooperate with the western world."[54]

Ten days earlier, the Politburo had met to discuss a report proposing that China "introduce new technologies and import complete sets of equipment in 1978." During the meeting, Deng Xiaoping suggested the establishment of a leading group on the introduction to China of new technologies.

I agree [with the proposal] to set up such a group to introduce new technologies. It is certain that we should introduce new technologies. What is important is to make the most of the time. We should shorten the time between negotiation and import. If the time to introduce a project can be shortened by half a year, then we will benefit a lot. . . . In the negotiations, it does not matter if the price is a little bit higher. What is important is that the quality of the project be good and the technologies be advanced.[55]

On May 17, 1977, the Leading Group for the Introduction of New Technology was established in the State Council, with Yu Qiuli as head of the group and Gu Ming as the deputy leader. During this period, high officials of the State Council visited developed countries in the West to study their economic policies. The most important delegation was the China Government Economic Investigation Group, under the leadership of Vice Premier Gu Mu, which visited France, Switzerland, Belgium, Denmark, and the Federal Republic of Germany from May 2 to June 11, 1978. Before Gu departed China, Deng Xiaoping asked him to investigate "both what was good and what was bad," examining the other countries' modern industry and their economic management practices. "We should learn from the advances and good experiences of capitalism."[56] After returning to China, Gu Mu reported to the CCP Central Committee and the State Council that all western European countries had made use of foreign capital and introduced advanced technology during their economic takeoff periods and asked, "Why shouldn't we do so too?"[57] On June 30, the Politburo convened a special meeting to hear Gu's report.[58]

The call for opening China to the world reflected the widespread demands for social and economic development. Deng Xiaoping said in October 1978, "We sent many people out to see the world. It allowed more people to know what the world is like. We cannot develop if we close the door, stand still, refuse to make any progress, and become arrogant." "It is time," he declared, "for us to learn from the advanced countries in the world."[59]

From July 6 to September 9, 1978, the State Council convened to discuss basic policy issues. Gu Mu's report on his visit to Western Europe was printed and distributed to the State Council, and those in attendance studied it carefully. As recalled by Yu Guangyuan, at the time vice president of the Chinese Academy of Social Sciences, vice minister of the State Commission for Science and Technology, and a leading advisor to the top leadership: "This report made us realize that there are some very good systems in capitalist countries."[60] In his summary speech, Li Xiannian said, "The international situation is quite favorable to us; we should be ambitious enough and be able to use foreign advanced technology, equipment, capital, and organizational experience to accelerate our construction. We should not miss this rare opportunity. It would be several times quicker than groping for experience by ourselves behind a closed door."[61]

From September 5 to October 22, the National Planning Conference was convened in Beijing. The conference recommended that China abandon its closed-door policy and its rejection of technological exchanges with capitalist countries and actively begin introducing foreign advanced technology, using foreign capital, and bravely entering the international market.[62] In retrospect, it is clear that this recommendation resulted in China's merger into the international mainstream.

During this push for domestic reform and opening to the world, the Third Plenary Session of the Eleventh Congress of the Chinese Communist Party convened in December 1978. This meeting established the policy guidelines for the post-Mao era, thus inaugurating the new epoch of reform and opening to accelerate the socialist, modernized construction of China.

DENG'S NEW APPROACH TO SINO-U.S. RELATIONS AND THE TAIWAN ISSUE

The end of the Cultural Revolution, the new strategy of reform and opening up, and the elevation of Deng Xiaoping to the core of the second-generation leadership reflected the changes in China's domestic political situation of the late 1970s. These profound and historic changes also laid a new political foundation for the Sino-U.S. relationship.

At the initiative of Deng Xiaoping, the Communist Party of China reached an understanding: to achieve modernization, Beijing had to adopt a policy of reform and opening up, and it must learn from the West and introduce its advanced technologies and modern management methods to China. The United States was clearly the main source of advanced ideas and technology. Thus, the smooth normalization of relations had become a key component in China's opening to the world. The development of Sino-U.S. relations had never been so closely linked to the domestic political strategy. Normalization of Sino-U.S. relations was now necessary not only for maintaining national security in the cold war but also for implementing the strategy of reform and opening up. The main elements of this new strategy were:

> Domestic reform and opening to the outside world should be a long-term national policy, and the development of Sino-U.S. relations was inherently necessary to these policies;

> The purpose of establishing diplomatic relations with the United States was to create an international environment favorable to domestic construction and reform and opening up;

The Taiwan problem was the key to the Sino-U.S. relationship, and therefore Beijing must find a new way to solve the Taiwan problem while continuing to insist on the principle of "one China."

Thus, domestic policy encouraged China to adopt a more flexible Taiwan policy.[63]

On January 20, 1977, Jimmy Carter became president of the United States. Soon after taking office, on February 8, he received Huang Zhen, the chief of the Chinese Liaison Office. Carter stated that "the Shanghai Communiqué guides my policy toward the People's Republic, and the aim of our policy is the normalization of the U.S.-China relationship." But for some time, Carter did not make development of U.S.-China relations a priority; instead, he focused on détente with the Soviet Union.

At the suggestion of U.S. National Security Advisor Zbigniew Brzezinski, President Carter advanced a planned visit to China by Secretary of State Cyrus Vance, from November to August 1977, suggesting that the Carter administration might be placing a higher priority on its policy toward China. When Vance visited China on August 22–26, 1977, the key issue on the agenda was still Taiwan. Vance proposed that following normalization, China would guarantee that U.S.-Taiwan commerce, investment, tourism, scientific exchanges, and other nongovernmental relationships would continue as before and that China would allow U.S. officials to continue to stay in Taiwan in an "unofficial" status. In addition, Vance said that the U.S. government would make a declaration of its concerns about Taiwan and its interest in encouraging the Chinese people to solve the Taiwan problem peacefully and that Washington expected that the Chinese government would not oppose this declaration.

On August 24, Deng Xiaoping rejected Vance's proposal, reiterating Chinese opposition to the "reverse liaison office" proposal. He said that the Taiwan issue must be solved in accordance with China's "three principles": abolition of the U.S. treaty with Taiwan, withdrawal of U.S. troops from Taiwan, and the severing of U.S. diplomatic relations with the Taiwan government. It had to be "the Japanese way." Deng said frankly that even the Japanese approach was a "concession" from China. He added:

We declare our stand because there will be, in the course of improving the Sino-U.S. relation, a more suitable time for us to deal with the problem of Taiwan. There will be more common ground for us to deal with global strategy. But we do wish that there be no misunderstanding that the Chinese will put off solving the Taiwan problem indefinitely.[64]

After Vance returned to the United States, one news report suggested that China had been somewhat flexible on the Taiwan issue. In response, in meeting with the Board of Directors of the Associated Press, Deng bluntly pointed out that "the one outcome of Vance's visit to China was he came to China. This is the first time your American administration sent a high official to visit China. But the plan [he proposed] for establishing diplomatic relations between the US and China was a step backward."[65]

At the end of 1977, Leonard Woodcock, the chief of the U.S. Liaison Office in China, asked to meet with Foreign Minister Huang Hua. Woodcock merely offered an elaboration of Vance's August proposal. Huang Hua reiterated the principal positions of the Chinese government and said that the two sides could talk again once the United States had put forward a new proposal.

Deng Xiaoping, making every effort to promote reform and opening, was very concerned about the normalization of Sino-U.S. relations. But he also knew that, in dealing with the Americans, it was important to be patient. On January 7, 1978, he received a delegation of members of the U.S. Congress. Talking about the Taiwan problem, he remarked: "Flexibility means we can wait." He also said:

It takes two hands to solve the Taiwan problem. Neither of the two methods should be excluded. We will try our best to solve the problem peacefully, with our right hand, and maybe we must exert more energy with the right hand. But if that does not work, we may have to use our left hand; that means the military way. It is impossible for us to be flexible on this question.[66]

Although the prospects for breaking the deadlock in Sino-U.S. relations were slim, Deng Xiaoping was full of confidence. On February 16, 1978, in a meeting with U.S. Senator Henry Jackson, Deng said:

We would like to introduce the advanced technologies and experiences of the world. Not only would we send people to the United States, but we would also send people to other advanced countries to make inspections. There are many countries who would like to cooperate with us. If the normalization of the Sino-U.S. relations could come early, the speed of the development of the Sino-U.S. commerce would be faster. [But] the U.S. government has not put the normalization of the Sino-U.S. relation on the agenda.

Deng added that "if President Carter would like to visit China, we heartily welcome him. But it would not be reciprocal, that means the Chinese leaders would not go to Washington because there is an 'embassy' of the KMT." He also suggested that he might visit the United States, once relations had been normalized: if "President Hua Guofeng has no time to go, I would like to go to Washington first."[67]

SIMULTANEOUS ESTABLISHMENT OF DIPLOMATIC RELATIONS AND OF REFORM AND OPENING

Deng Xiaoping was rewarded for his patience. In April 1978, in response to the pro-Soviet coup d'état in Afghanistan, the U.S. government became determined to establish diplomatic relations with China as a means of seeking a favorable position in its negotiations with the Soviet Union. It began to make preparations for a visit to China by National Security Advisor Zbigniew Brzezinski.

Brzezinski visited China from May 20 to May 23, 1978, bringing with him the good news that President Carter was determined to promote the development of Sino-U.S. relations. Deng responded positively. Speaking with foreign reporters, he said that "it took only one second for China to . . . sign the Sino-Japan Treaty of Peace and Friendship, and it may need only two seconds to realize the normalization of Sino-U.S. relations."[68]

The Chinese and U.S. sides decided that negotiations on the establishment of diplomatic relations would begin on July 5. The Chinese representative would be Foreign Minister Huang Hua and the U.S. representative would be Leonard Woodcock, chief of the U.S. Liaison Office in China. There were six talks in all. On October 30, after a period of fruitless negotiations, Brzezinski asked to speak with Chai Zemin, chief of the Chinese Liaison Office in the United States. He expressed President Carter's hope that the two sides could accelerate the process of normalization of relations. Chai Zemin recalled that

Brzezinski summoned me for an interview, saying now was the best time to solve the Sino-U.S. relationship. If it was not solved right now, the question would be put off to the autumn of 1979 when the Congress would be in session, and the focus of the session would be the U.S. relationship with the Soviet Union. I passed his words back home, and it is possible that my report made China have a sense of urgency to resolve the issue."[69]

Three days later, on November 2, during the fifth round of Sino-U.S. negotiations in Beijing, the U.S. side put forward a draft joint communiqué for the establishment of diplomatic relations.

Deng Xiaoping read Chai Zemin's report of his talk with Brzezinski and on the same day was informed of the results of the fifth round of negotiations. When Deng saw that the United States intended to accelerate normalization, he grasped the opportunity. On November 2, 1978, he spoke to the Politburo. After reading the report of the talk between Brzezinski and Chai Zemin and the request for instructions from the Foreign Ministry regarding the fifth round of talks between Huang Hua and Woodcock, he said: "It appears that the U.S. side wishes to accelerate normalization. We should seize the opportunity. Of course, we do not need to go ahead of an agreement between the United States and the Soviet Union on the second phase on the limitation of strategic weapons." Deng emphasized that Beijing's interest in improving the Chinese economy encouraged acceleration of normalization with the United States. Of course, he said, "we should not abandon our principles. We may discuss the topics raised by the U.S. side, and we should not slam the door during the discussions. It is in our favor if normalization is realized early."[70]

On November 27, Deng Xiaoping convened another Politburo meeting. He emphasized the importance of not missing this opportunity to normalize relations and issued crucial instructions on dealing with specific problems. He also gave approval to the Foreign Ministry's suggestions for the sixth round of talks with Woodcock.[71] Then, on November 29, in a meeting with Japanese visitors, Deng said:

Now I have a wish, that is, to go to Washington. I don't know whether it can be realized. Americans always ask why I have not gone to Washington. How could I go when there is a Taiwan "embassy"? Chinese leaders can go there when the Sino-U.S. relations are normalized. This all depends on the determination of the U.S. government and President Carter. So long as the leaders of the two countries stand on a higher level and solve the problem as a political problem, it would be easier to reach agreement. We notice both the U.S. government and people do have such a wish. To us, we wish the quicker the better.[72]

It is significant that China published Deng's comments just before the key sixth round of talks with Woodcock on December 4.

On November 28, in a talk with an American friend, A. T. Steele, Deng acknowledged that "the social system of Taiwan is, of course, different from our social system" and that after unification China would "take this reality into consideration." He maintained that "the title 'Republic of China' will have to be abolished. [Taiwan] could be a local government. It could retain its capitalist system."[73] This is the embryo of what later became the "one state, two systems" policy.

Deng Xiaoping spoke with Woodcock four times during the last phase of the negotiations. Deng's highly pragmatic spirit enabled the two sides to circumvent the major obstacles in Sino-U.S. relations and thus finally opened the way to normalization. In this phase of the negotiations, the most sensitive question was the sale of U.S. weapons to Taiwan. Deng avoided quibbling over this issue in order to promote China's strategic and domestic objectives. He made no concessions on principles but left room for later negotiations. The arms sales issue would thus be raised again during President Reagan's term of office, when it led to the publication of the August 17 Communiqué in 1982.

In January 1979, Deng Xiaoping visited the United States. His visit caused a sensation in the United States. This was history's best reward to an old man who had personally opened the door for the normalization of Sino-U.S. relations.

At the same critical moment that Deng Xiaoping was promoting the establishment of diplomatic relations between China and the United States, he was also playing an important role in promoting the smooth convening of the Third Plenary Session of the Eleventh Party Congress. These two episodes had a far-reaching influence on China's future development and laid the foundation for Deng's historic role as the chief designer of China's policies of reform and opening.

Conclusion

The normalization of relations opened a new page both in Sino-U.S. relations and in China's reform and opening. In the thirty years since publication of the Sino-U.S. Shanghai Communiqué, the human race has entered into a new century. From this period of history, we may draw several conclusions. First, a stable political situation in China is crucial to the healthy development of the Sino-U.S. relationship. Without stability, there can be no continuity in policies, let alone advancement. Thus, stability is overwhelmingly important, both to the domestic development of China and to the development of the Sino-U.S. relationship. Any action damaging China's domestic stability would endanger Sino-U.S. relations.

Second, China's reform, opening, and modernization promoted the development of Sino-U.S. relations. For China, the road to modernization is the socialist road with Chinese characteristics. It follows neither the Soviet nor the Western model. But it cannot succeed without introducing scientific and technological advances and administrative techniques from the West. It must merge into the mainstream of economic globalization. From this, we may conclude that the healthy development of Sino-U.S. relations is most critical to China's reform and opening. Although the Sino-U.S. relationship has sometimes experienced heightened tension (such as it did for a period of time after 1989), to create a favorable international environment for China's continuing reform, opening up, and modernization, China requires a healthy Sino-U.S. relationship.

Third, dealing with the Taiwan problem on the basis of the "one China" principle is critical to the healthy development of the

Sino-U.S. relationship. The Taiwan issue remains the biggest obstacle and most sensitive question between the two countries. Apart from the Taiwan issue, however, the common interests between the two countries in international affairs far exceed their differences. This is a special bilateral relationship that needs thoughtful and focused attention. Internationally, the Sino-U.S. relationship is decisive. Thus, the leaders of both countries should deal with the Taiwan problem from a strategic viewpoint, with wisdom and courage. They should not act on impulse. The difficult yet successful journey from the Shanghai Communiqué to the establishment of diplomatic relations reflects the value of this approach.

Fourth, the mechanism of dialogue between the two countries' leaders, first developed in the process of negotiating the Shanghai Communiqué, is a reliable way to maintain relations in difficult situations. The relationship between China and the United States can never be completely smooth. However, the thirty years since the Shanghai Communiqué show that there has always been a way to avert danger and to promote relations to a new level even when troubles and obstacles appeared. The most important element in stable Sino-U.S. relations, besides the common strategic interests of both countries, is direct dialogue between the leaders of the two countries. This mechanism was part of the process that led to President Nixon's 1972 visit to China. Establishment of diplomatic relations between the two countries reflected this process—discussions between Deng Xiaoping and Woodcock at critical moments were in effect direct dialogues between Deng Xiaoping and the highest authority of the United States. Moreover, the deterioration of Sino-U.S. relations in 1989, the tensions in the relationship caused by the Taiwan issue in 1996, the U.S. bombing of the Chinese embassy in Belgrade, and the collision of Chinese and U.S. aircraft in 2001 were solved by this mechanism of direct dialogue between the leaders of the two countries. Problems in Sino-U.S. relations are to be expected; the most dangerous situation would be to underrate or dismiss the mechanism of direct dialogue between the leaders of the two countries.

THREE

Prizes Won, Opportunities Lost

The U.S. Normalization of Relations with

China, 1972–1979

ROSEMARY FOOT

The broad outlines of the U.S. negotiations with China leading to the establishment of diplomatic relations on January 1, 1979, have been well known for some time. With the publication of several important memoirs[1] as well as scholarly and journalistic analyses,[2] the highs and the lows of that seven-year period have already been delineated. The most productive periods in relations occurred between July 1971 and the spring of 1973 and again between May and December 1978. Particularly delicate and difficult moments were experienced in the summer and fall of 1973 and again in October 1975, when Secretary of State Henry Kissinger tried in vain to negotiate a joint communiqué for President Ford's projected visit.[3] Undoubtedly, a coincidence of strategic interest associated with Soviet power and purpose was a major factor in promoting normalization, but this was never sufficient to propel the parties either easily or swiftly over all the hurdles in their path. Disagreements over the global and regional implications of heightened Soviet power and the methods for best dealing with it, together with domestic political environments that hobbled several individuals at the highest levels of the American and Chinese governments, ensured that the negotiations would be drawn out. And although the Soviet factor may have brought the two parties together, the centerpiece of the negotiations involved Taiwan—an issue that required sensitivity from both parties.

This chapter begins with reflections on some of the main contextual points in the moves from a U.S. rapprochement with China in February 1972 to full diplomatic relations in January 1979. The major part of the analysis, however, focuses on the details of the negotiating process and the methods chosen to resolve the matter of Taiwan—the issue that America was frequently informed was "one of fundamental principle" for China. As Kissinger told President Nixon in October 1971, Zhou Enlai "has made it clear that there will be no normal relations until this problem is resolved."[4] Undoubtedly, the commencement and completion of normalization were major achievements of the Nixon and Carter administrations and have promoted global order. Despite the securing of this major prize, however, the specifics of the negotiations over Taiwan's future, the legacy of statements made at earlier stages in the negotiations, the tendency to use obscure or ambiguous language at certain points, and a reluctance to test how much leverage U.S. negotiators could bring to bear undercut the effectiveness of the United States' negotiating efforts.[5] What resulted was an agreement on Taiwan that was incomplete in several respects, probably fell shorter of America's aims than needed to be the case, and in the past ten years or more has led to dangerous periods of friction in the Sino-American relationship. Chinese and U.S. official views converged around a focal point in the second half of 1978 sufficient to form the basis for establishing diplomatic relations. But, as has long been argued, to maintain cooperation, such a point of convergence has to be underpinned by a deeper understanding and acceptance of the spirit of any agreement, and that aspect was missing from the terms arrived at in mid-December 1978.[6] Premier Zhou Enlai gave voice to an idea close to this in February 1972 when he stated to President Nixon: "In view of the current interests of our two countries . . . we may find common ground. But this common ground must be truly reliable. It should not be a structure built upon sand, because that structure will not be able to stand."[7]

There were three main issues to resolve involving Taiwan: the status of U.S. relations with Taiwan after the normalization of its relations with the PRC (this involved the acceptance and implementation of the "Japan formula," explained below); the U.S. sale of defensive weapons to the island and the time period connected with such sales; and Chinese guarantees that it would abjure the use of force in effecting unification. On the basis of an examination of the negotiating record between 1971 and 1978, it appears that an acceptable outcome for U.S. administrations with respect to these three core issues was: (1) the retention of an official or semi-official relationship with Taiwan, such as the maintenance of a liaison office or a consulate in Taipei; (2) a Chinese statement that the Taiwan question would be resolved peacefully; and (3) Chinese acceptance that U.S. arms sales to Taiwan would continue after the termination of the U.S.-ROC defense treaty and until there had been a peaceful resolution of the issue. These three positions were interconnected in the negotiations and in reality,[8] but for analytical clarity they are dealt with separately in later sections of this chapter.

Of importance to our broader understanding of the complexity of these negotiations are various constraining factors. Domestic politics, for example, intervened in distinct ways in that U.S. officials believed that other policy goals or electoral outcomes could be affected adversely by an agreement that appeared to sell out a long-time Asian ally. There were also time-related costs: electoral politics ruled out certain periods when agreement might have been sought, and one consequence of holding brief, high-level talks at regular intervals often meant that U.S. officials were framing joint communiqués and press statements under considerable time pressure. The negotiating game was repetitive since it lasted several years. American officials, especially Kissinger, wanted to build a reputation with the Chinese for being reliable interlocutors; hence, it was difficult for a new U.S. administration to introduce novel negotiating positions even though it might have found previous stances inadequate. Adding to the complications was another aspect that related to the U.S. reputation: that of reliable alliance partner, an especially important perception to maintain for other Asian states such as South Korea and Japan, particularly after the fall of Saigon in the spring of 1975.[9] Thus, both domestic and international audiences influenced the course of these negotiations, as is detailed in the next section.

The Path to Normalization:
The Negotiating Environment

The U.S. interest in rapprochement with China stemmed from its understanding that such a move would help it to recover a pivotal role in the global system. A more productive relationship with China would complicate the Soviet Union's strategic landscape, inducing more cooperative relations between the two superpowers. Such a policy would also bring the administration more into line with western allied and U.S. public attitudes—save those of the Republican right. More immediately, it would compensate for the U.S. failure to prevail in the war in Vietnam: Washington would have lost a battle but, with China on its side, would be seen to be winning the war against its major communist adversary.[10] Chinese leaders, too, had come to perceive Moscow as a primary enemy whose hegemonic and expansionist tendencies needed to be contained or reduced. The Shanghai Communiqué signed in February 1972 recorded a joint opposition to hegemony in the Asia-Pacific region, and the Communiqué on the Establishment of Diplomatic Relations (January 1, 1979) repeated that sentiment. At the close of Kissinger's November 1973 visit to Beijing, the two sides went further and extended joint opposition beyond the Asian region to the rest of the world.

This is not to claim that the Soviet factor was enough to paper over all the differences between the two states. Kissinger as national security advisor and later as secretary of state could not convince Chinese leaders that different U.S. and Chinese approaches toward the Soviet Union did not matter much: their assessments of the threat that Moscow posed were identical, he labored unsuccessfully to propose, and that was the crucial point. As Steven Goldstein has put it, Kissinger took every opportunity to deepen the anti-Soviet ties between China and the United States and to create a "virtual alliance."[11] During his February 1973 visit, as part of this quest, he wooed and flattered Chinese leaders: "We speak to no other country as frankly and as openly as we do to you." He also offered a security guarantee: "We will never knowingly cooperate in an attack on China." By November of that year, he was implying that the Soviets had a plan to attack Chinese nuclear installations, and stated that, if a Sino-Soviet war became prolonged, the United States "could be helpful by supplying equipment and other services." He even offered to shorten China's period of vulnerability through the provision of an early warning system via a "hotline between [U.S.] satellites and Beijing by which we could transmit information to you in a matter of minutes."[12] Zhou Enlai stated that he would study the proposal, apparently fearful that it would prove impossible to implement the scheme in "a manner so that no one feels we are allies."[13]

In the end, it seems that this particular suggestion was not taken further. Li Jie's chapter in this volume is particularly helpful for understanding why: Mao criticized Zhou for even considering strategic coordination with the United States, and Jiang Qing leaped at the opportunity this criticism provided to try to undermine Zhou's position. Overall, the Chinese retained their suspicion both of Chinese leaders (other than Mao) that might get too close to the United States and of American motives. Many of their senior political figures believed that Washington's ultimate goal was to enhance its leverage over the Soviet Union at the expense of China's future security.[14]

Despite numerous contacts between 1973 and 1977, little real progress toward the normalization of relations occurred during this period. All that could be offered were actions intended to give an illusion of progress (notably a reduction in U.S. military personnel on Taiwan and the repeal in 1974 of the January 1955 congressional resolution on the defense of Taiwan).[15] International and domestic developments constrained U.S. policy choices. Nixon's embroilment in the Watergate crisis and eventually his forced resignation, while it puzzled and dismayed the Chinese, rendered forward movement impossible on the U.S. side. His unelected replacement, Gerald Ford, had little room politically to strike a compromise agreement. Indeed, his political leeway narrowed still further once he decided to contest the 1976 presidential election. Ford's senior political advisors had tried unsuccessfully to dissuade him from going to China at the end of 1975, pointing out that Nixon had already gathered all the political mileage that could be gained from such a trip and that it would be better if the vice president or secretary of state made the visit instead.[16] Thus, they were not surprised when, during the election campaign, Republican challenger Ronald Reagan not only criticized Ford for visiting Beijing and not Taiwan in December 1975 but also focused strongly on the argument that normalization of relations with Beijing should not come at the expense of ties with Taiwan.[17]

The arrangements for the summit itself caused Ford and Kissinger much grief. Kissinger found in October 1975 that the Chinese were not going to agree to a joint communiqué at the end of the visit, which prompted the administration to shorten the length of time Ford would stay in the PRC and to add Indonesia and the Philippines to his itinerary.[18] Before and after the trip, Ford had to dampen expectations and took pains to explain to congressional leaders, among others, that the summit had been designed to "sustain" relations, not to advance them.[19]

While Ford and his party were in Beijing, Chinese leaders stepped up their rhetoric. Setting out a view of the world wholly at odds with that of the United States, Deng proclaimed during his banquet speech that there was "great disorder under heaven," a situation that he described as "excellent." He also appreciated that the "basic contradictions in the world are sharpening daily. The factors for both revolution and war are clearly increasing."[20] In the private discussions, the Chinese also deepened their criticism of détente, labeling it "appeasement"; Mao dismissed the president's proposals for joint efforts against Moscow as "just talk."[21] The few crumbs of comfort that Ford might have enjoyed came when, in a meeting with Deng at which the Chinese leader stated that China was more experienced in dealing with the Soviets than was the United States, the president pointed out: "I think it would be helpful in this frank talk with you if you could indicate the various places and ways—whether in Southeast Asia, the Middle East, or Africa—what your country is doing to meet this challenge so we can better un-

derstand how we can act in parallel."[22] Deng admitted that the
Chinese had prepared themselves for attack, and otherwise could
only "fire some empty cannons." On the Chinese side, it was mostly
just talk, it seems.

Domestic political constraints were much heavier, or at least
personally threatening, for Chinese leaders during this period than
they were for their counterparts in Washington. As Li Jie details in
his chapter in this volume, not only did "ultra-left forces" in China
put Zhou under severe pressure, but Deng could do nothing to
consolidate Sino-U.S. ties between 1974 and 1977 because of the attacks on him by the so-called Gang of Four. Mao regularly shifted
his allegiances between the pragmatic and the more radical elements
in the leadership, reinforcing the pragmatists' sense that it was un-
wise to take significant steps to improve relations with the United
States. Mao's and Zhou's deaths in 1976 gave free rein for a while
to the Gang of Four, leading once again to Deng's removal from
power. However, their period of dominance was short-lived, and
they were arrested in October 1976 under the leadership of Hua
Guofeng. American officials, especially Richard Solomon, charted
as best they could the varying fortunes of different individuals over
this turbulent period and hoped and waited for the political situation to stabilize.[23] Kissinger, who always displayed respect and ad-
miration when describing his conversations with Mao and especially
with the urbane Zhou, was far less enamored of the Chinese leaders
emerging in these years. As he said to the Australian prime minister
in July 1976, the Chinese "would like to get the U.S. into a posture
of irreconcilable hostility with the USSR and then they would
mobilize the Third World against both powers. Their policy is
becoming more transparent with the lower level of competency in
the Chinese leadership since Chou's death."[24]

International events also imposed their own constraints on forward U.S. movement toward normalization. In the wake of the
collapse of the Saigon regime in April 1975, U.S. leaders believed that
U.S. credibility as an alliance partner had come under closer international and domestic scrutiny. For Kissinger, it "created a context
where any major change in our relationship with Taiwan which
implied abandonment of yet another ally would be unacceptable."

Ford could not avoid reaffirming U.S. commitments to Taiwan, as well as to other U.S. treaty allies in Asia, at a press conference in May 1975.[25] The relationship with Taiwan had symbolic value in the mid-1970s in its ability to show that the United States would be steadfast in its commitments. Squaring that with a Chinese leadership that had distanced itself from the United States since late 1973 and had toughened its stance on the conditions for normalization would render forward progress impossible until 1978.

Progress finally occurred when four things were in place: on the PRC side, heightened Chinese fears of the Soviet Union in the context of Moscow's deepening relationship with a unified Vietnamese government, and Deng Xiaoping's dominance of decision making. Finally—at the end of 1978—Deng Xiaoping had managed to consolidate his position and policy line, affording the opportunity for U.S.-China negotiations to get back on track. As Gong Li puts it in his chapter, Deng had two primary concerns: one was the deterioration of China's relations with Vietnam and his belief that it needed to be "taught a lesson"; second, he wanted to act on the consensus he had established behind his position that China needed desperately to develop and modernize its economy—with the United States a major factor in securing that objective. On the U.S. side was President Carter's decision finally to put less faith in the policy of détente in light of Moscow's perceived expansionist behavior. This shifted power into the hands of Carter's national security advisor, Zbigniew Brzezinski, and away from that of the secretary of state, Cyrus Vance, who had been giving priority to the relationship with Moscow. Unlike Vance, Brzezinski was more than ready to pressure Moscow by normalizing relations with Beijing. (Or as Carter less flatteringly put it to Brzezinski: "Zbig. You have a tendency to exalt the PRC issue" [above all other foreign policy questions].)[26]

The prospects for normalizing U.S.-China relations had not looked promising in the early stages of the Carter administration. During Carter's first meeting with Huang Zhen, head of the liaison office in Washington, in February 1977, there was no meeting of minds either on Taiwan or on the Soviet Union. Carter pledged adherence to the Shanghai Communiqué and confirmed a "longstanding hope and expectation that [Taiwan] can be settled in peaceful ways." Huang repeated that the matter was an internal affair and that it would be "good" if it could be solved peacefully. However, he added, "since we see a bunch of counterrevolutionaries on the island, it seems there is no other way than by force." With regard to the Soviet Union, Carter stressed that he had a responsibility to negotiate with Moscow on issues of importance to the maintenance of world peace. Huang described such negotiations as a chimera: the Soviets, he averred, "bully the soft but are afraid of the tough. Quite often they do not mean what they say. They talk disarmament but do the opposite."[27]

Secretary of State Vance's visit to Beijing in August 1977, if anything, set matters further back because he proposed continuing official links between Taiwan and the United States after the normalization of relations. Deng Xiaoping described this proposal as unacceptable and a "retreat" on past promises. Vance's emphasis on the importance of strategic nuclear arms negotiations with Moscow—especially the signature of the SALT II agreement—also cut no ice. As far as the Chinese were concerned, Moscow was "on the offensive" and Washington "on the defensive." Vance found the claim absurd: "There can be no question but that we have devastating power, both to deter and to respond. In addition to our military strength, we have economic strength that is unparalleled in the world. We have great political power and the will to use that power. We have the support of the American people for what we do. No one should make the mistake of underestimating our strength."[28]

By March 1978, however, President Carter had decided to modify the administration's priorities and give increased weight to the wider benefits that might be derived from normalizing ties with China. Once he gave Brzezinski permission to visit China at an early date, the negotiations entered into their final stages. During the national security advisor's visit to Beijing in May 1978, he informed the assembled Chinese leaders on several occasions that President Carter had made up his mind to normalize ties. Deeper exploration of the Taiwan issue commenced, with only one aspect of it at that point fully agreed: the United States would withdraw its proposal for maintaining official contacts with the Taiwan authorities. As Vance spelled out in a June 1978 cable to Leonard Woodcock—then head of the U.S. liaison office in Beijing and charged with conducting and bringing the negotiations to a successful close—there were four main issues for the U.S. administration: "(1) the nature of the post-normalization American presence on Taiwan; (2) our statements on the occasion of normalization; (3) American trade with Taiwan after normalization; and (4) a Joint Communique and the modalities of normalization."[29]

As with the question of the form of contacts with Taiwan after normalization—whether official or unofficial—the persuasiveness of the U.S. case was undercut by the positions adopted in the Nixon and Ford eras. Although at the time these positions may have been designed to ensure future flexibility in the negotiations and to prevent domestic political attacks on the evolving China policy, during this last phase of the bargaining they more often caused difficulties for U.S. officials. Similarly, when Beijing officials heard statements that could be interpreted as showing a lack of consistency in the U.S. position, the Chinese seized upon them, prompting a U.S. retreat. Finally, a U.S. tendency to engage in verbal acrobatics that succeeded only in dizzying the spectators rather than clarifying U.S. objectives as the two sides edged closer to agreement resulted in a messy end to the negotiations and differing interpretations as to what had actually been agreed. I first explain why the Carter administration felt constrained to reverse itself on the form of future relations with Taiwan between the short period of Vance's visit in August 1977 and Woodcock's return to Beijing in November of that year. Subsequent sections deal with the second and third issues mentioned in Vance's June 1978 cable to Woodcock.

The Political Status of Taiwan

From the time of the rapprochement with China, U.S. officials claimed to be in search of means that would allow retention of as close a relationship as possible with Taiwan while improving relations with Beijing. At the time, the 1972 Shanghai Communiqué was depicted as a clever device for ensuring that U.S.-China relations made progress while not compromising either side's position on the status of Taiwan: "The United States *acknowledges* that all Chinese on either side of the Taiwan Strait maintain there is but one China and that Taiwan is part of China." It went on: "The United States Government *does not challenge* that position" (italics added).[30] This qualified and deliberately ambiguous language, as U.S. lawyers pointed out at the time, implied that the United States did not accept, but only acknowledged, the Chinese position that Taiwan was a part of China and that which government represented China was yet to be determined.[31]

However, that ambiguity was undermined by other secret pledges that Nixon made during his Beijing summit, pledges that tilted the U.S. administration toward recognition of the Beijing government as the true representative of China and that suggested Taiwan's status had indeed been tacitly decided in the PRC's favor. As the president put it in his handwritten notes for his first private meeting with Zhou Enlai, the "status of Taiwan is determined."[32] At the meeting itself, he stated that his government accepted the principle of one China and that Taiwan was a part of China, would not support a Taiwan independence movement, would use its influence to ensure that neither Japan nor other third parties would move to fill the vacuum created by U.S. withdrawal from the island, would support any peaceful resolution of the Taiwan issue worked out between the two sides, and would progressively reduce its military presence on the island as the Indochina war drew to a close and in response to movement toward a peaceful resolution of the Taiwan issue. Finally, Nixon stated that he would work to ensure full normalization of U.S.-PRC relations during his expected second term in office.[33] Kissinger repeated these secret pledges during his February 1973 visit to Beijing, further bolstering the idea that the government to be recognized and to rule Taiwan was indeed the one that currently resided in Beijing.

Kissinger's February 1973 visit was consequential in shaping future negotiations over Taiwan in other ways. In February the national security advisor committed his government "in the next two years to move to something like the Japanese solution," adding "but we have not worked this out." He also pledged: "After 1974 we want to work toward full normalization and full diplomatic relations with the People's Republic of China before the middle of 1976."[34] When Japan established diplomatic relations with China in 1972, it had closed its embassy in Taipei and substituted a private, non-governmental office to facilitate the continuation of trade and cultural relations.[35] Having made reference to this form of future relationship between the United States and Taiwan, U.S. officials later found it difficult to build a case for something more substantial in their future ties with Taiwan. The testing of these waters became even more problematic once the nongovernmental aspect of the "Japan formula" came to be projected as essential by all senior Chinese leaders from Mao on down, and as part of what the Chinese described as their three principles for normalization: namely, severance of U.S.-Taiwan diplomatic relations, abrogation of the U.S.-Taiwan Mutual Defense Treaty, and withdrawal of all American forces from the island.

These three principles were stated in the first of the contacts with Kissinger in July 1971, but Mao's most authoritative statement in support specifically of the Japan formula as a basis for normalization of relations came during his meeting with Kissinger in November 1973—that is, after several meetings had already taken place with U.S. officials.[36] Despite Mao's remarks, in late 1973 Kissinger still believed that all doors were not closed on this agenda item, and he had taken great heart from Zhou's statements on Taiwan during those November meetings. As he had explained the U.S. predicament to the Chinese premier: "We cannot go faster than the schedule which I gave you if it is on the Japan formula. However, if we could find a formula which is more flexible, as long as we understand that we will end up there, we are prepared to establish diplomatic relations sooner."[37] Kissinger was sure that he had got this point across and that a solution was in the making: in discussions on the phrasing of the joint communiqué, Zhou had said "in the Taiwan portion there will be nothing new in the reiteration in your statement. On the Chinese side there is a new sentence." That new sentence read: "The Chinese side reiterated that the normalization of relations between China and the United States can be realized only on the basis of confirming the principle of one China." Kissinger believed that this meant that in practice viable, potentially

official, ties with Taiwan could continue, perhaps via the transformation of the U.S. embassy in Taipei into a consulate general.[38]
As he replied to Zhou: "I have understood this. And it gives us the
possibility of talking with you concretely."[39]

However, those concrete discussions did not occur. Kissinger's
embroilment in Middle Eastern diplomacy as well as the Watergate
crisis prevented his focusing on the implications of the potentially
new language on Taiwan, much to the frustration of Winston Lord,
Richard Solomon, and Arthur Hummel.[40] Significant, too, was an
apparent hardening of the line in Beijing and signs that Zhou's
flexibility had come under scrutiny and attack, plain to analysts
such as Solomon beginning in February 1974. By April 1974, it
seemed that the "new flexibility" on Taiwan—if it existed at all—was
dead. Zhou's "new sentence on Taiwan" was decidedly opaque. A
conversation between Kissinger and Qiao Guanhua in April 1974
seemed to put a stop to the matter. At a dinner party that Kissinger
gave in New York for Deng Xiaoping and Qiao, the latter pointedly
stated: "I participated in the drafting of the [November] communiqué and in the drafting of this language [on Taiwan]. The normalization of our relations can only be on the basis of the Japanese
pattern. No other pattern is possible."[41]

Kissinger, however, was not yet ready to concede defeat. During
his next visit, in November 1974, he scrambled to recover lost
ground on the level of America's post-normalization ties with
Taiwan. As he said to Deng, the U.S. position was "different from
the situation of Japan, or for that matter from the situation of any
other country with which [the Chinese] have normalized relations,"
first because of the formal U.S.-ROC defense relationship, and
second because of the pro-Taiwan lobby in the United States. What
the Secretary of State wanted was a "Japan model plus": that is, the
Japan formula but with the added variation of a liaison office in
Taiwan, as well as the embassy in Beijing. Deng would not coun-
tenance that suggestion. All it represented to him was a reversal of
the current arrangement and an indication that the United States
wanted a one China and one Taiwan policy.[42] Mao's November 1973
reference to the Japan formula provided the immutable guidelines

and refuge for other Chinese officials too weak politically to be able to offer anything more.

The subsequent Ford administration failed to keep up the pressure on this issue, retreating once again into terminology that suggested indecision rather than a negotiating stance that had to be taken seriously. During Ford's meeting with Deng, the president promised that, after the election, he would "be in a position to move much more specifically to the normalization of relations, along the model perhaps of the Japanese arrangement." Deng leaped on this statement, interpreting it in ways that reflected Chinese preferences: "We have taken note of Mr. President's well-intentioned words, that under suitable conditions, you will be prepared to solve the Taiwan issue according to the Japanese formula."[43] Under Carter, there was a final attempt to stiffen the U.S. position, using as an opening the fact that the U.S. government had not yet explicitly responded to Deng's rejection of an official element in the relationship with Taiwan after normalization.[44] Carter instructed Vance to take up the question during his August 1977 visit, requesting the new secretary of state to try to elicit "flexibility from them on the Taiwan issue in the context of full diplomatic relations with Peking" and more generally to seek to generate some reciprocity in the relationship.[45]

Vance's statement in Beijing in support of a Japan-plus arrangement was both long and determined. The new secretary of state elaborated on Kissinger's 1974 arguments, stating that the "nature and extent" of the U.S. involvement in Taiwan were "different from that of any other country. Taking into account our laws, administrative practices, and public and congressional views, we have concluded that *totally*, and I underscore *totally*, private arrangements are not practicable for us." Although he claimed that the office to be set up in this manner would "*not* be diplomatic in character and would *not* perform diplomatic functions," nor would it fly flags or display a government seal, Chinese leaders remained unconvinced. As Deng put it: "You want an Embassy that does not have a sign on its door. No matter what you call it by name or whether you can fly your flag on it—in the final analysis it is the reversal of the existing Liaison Office, switching the Liaison Office to Taiwan."[46] As for reciprocity, since the United States owed a debt to China, reciprocity should not figure in this issue.[47] Carter administration officials quickly concluded that Chinese leaders would not budge, even though Brzezinski tried to make something of Ford's use of the word "perhaps" before the former president's reference to the Japan formula in December 1975.[48] Room for maneuver was minimal: U.S. officials, in their earlier acceptance of the PRC as the government of China, reference to the Japanese formula for establishing relations, including its clear nongovernmental components, and probable acknowledgment of U.S. debts owed to China over Taiwan, had undermined the case for more substantial U.S. relations with Taiwan after establishment of diplomatic relations with Beijing. A brief possibility for something more *might* have been there in the 1971–73 period, given China's desire for a rapprochement at that time, but after November 1973, China's position had begun to harden, and factional politics inside China seem to have prevented detailed consideration of anything other than nonofficial contacts with the Taiwanese authorities.

Arms Sales to Taiwan

As early as 1973, U.S. officials had been working on the assumption that some arrangement would have to be found that would permit U.S. arms sales to continue after normalization of relations with the PRC. The argument ran that continuation of sales would help Taiwan continue to feel secure in an era when the Mutual Security Treaty had lapsed and would also help to dampen U.S. domestic criticism of the administration's treatment of a loyal ally. Important, too, to the matter of future Taiwanese security was a Chinese commitment to the "peaceful resolution" of the Taiwan issue (see below), which mid-ranking officials believed should be linked in the "negotiating process to agreement on a residual program of sales of American military equipment (i.e., the more forthcoming a statement from the Chinese, the more limited our sales program might be)."[49] But, as with the consideration of the level of post-normalization ties with Taiwan, the Carter administration also discovered that the future sale of armaments was another issue that—although it might have been discussed at middle levels within the U.S. government—had never been addressed "systematically among ourselves or with the Chinese."[50] Neither had the matter been used as a form of leverage in the negotiations in ways that some officials had been suggesting. In Carter's instructions to Vance prior to his August 1977 visit, the president attempted to remedy some of that neglect: "Leave no doubt in the minds of Chinese leaders that we intend to preserve Taiwan's access to sources of defense equipment." Crucially, however, he added: "though I assume you will wish to broach this subject in a rounded fashion."[51]

The record of Vance's first meeting with Chinese Foreign Minister Huang Hua shows how "rounded" that could be: probably in the belief that a direct reference to arms sales would be too much for the Chinese to take, the secretary of state relied on the Beijing leadership picking up on what was omitted from his statement rather than allowing it to digest a direct reference to the matter of continuing post-normalization arms sales. In his section on security, Vance noted the U.S. desire to retain the credibility of its alliance structure as well as domestic support for a changed relationship with Taiwan. If the defense treaty were to terminate, the United States should "not be placed in the position of appearing to jeopardize stability." Vance went on to remind Huang that for twenty years the United States had had "extensive military ties with Taiwan," which included the treaty and U.S. armed forces, together with the "provision of grant military assistance, military credits, and extensive arms sales, and joint military exercises." Vance noted that U.S. armed forces on Taiwan had been steadily drawn down since 1972, that grant military assistance had been eliminated, and military credits and volume and types of military equipment reduced and controlled. Vance summed up the post-normalization position: "the Treaty would lapse, all U.S. military installations, advisors and other forces would be withdrawn, and all military credits would come to an end."[52] From this statement, the Chinese were expected to deduce that arms sales would continue.

Huang Hua's response the next day was harsh, charging the United States with an unwillingness to give up its privileges, pointing up that the U.S. debt to China was getting heavier, and that all this was evidence of a U.S. willingness to delay the normalization process.[53] However, neither he nor Deng in a meeting later that day made direct reference to U.S. arms sales. Brzezinski in a memorandum to the president found this omission significant and encouraging.[54] Others were not so sure: National Security Council officials Michael Armacost and Michel Oksenberg referred to the matter in March 1978 as possibly "more than [the Chinese] are willing to accept."[55] Brzezinski's May visit provided a useful opportunity to find out; more so than with Vance in August 1977, the method chosen was elliptical in the extreme. As Brzezinski put it, "During the historically transitional period the maintenance of full range of commercial relations with Taiwan would provide the necessary flexibility during the phase of accommodation to a new reality in the course of which eventually one China will become a reality," a statement that was repeated in somewhat less convoluted but still indirect form to Hua Guofeng the following day.[56]

Explanations offered in Washington, however, did tend to be somewhat clearer. When Han Xu, acting director of the PRC's Liaison Office in Washington, complained about a report of U.S. sales of F4s to Taiwan in June 1978, Brzezinski reminded him that the U.S. willingness to normalize relations did "not preclude the maintenance of full economic relations with the people on Taiwan." He went on: "There is bound to be a historically transitional phase in our relations with Taiwan in which the maintenance of economic and social relations will have to continue, given the historical legacies we are trying to overcome."[57] Richard Holbrooke, deputy national security advisor, was more direct with Han in September, stating that on entering "this period of historical transition following normalization, it will be of critical importance for the US to maintain a full range of commercial relations with Taiwan. . . . Sale of defensive military equipment would continue only in this context."[58] When Carter greeted Han's replacement, Chai Zemin, in Washington later that month, he told him that trade with Taiwan would continue after normalization, "including the restrained sale of some very carefully selected defensive arms." Han's reply to Holbrooke was perhaps stronger than the newly installed Chai's to Carter. Han stated emphatically that "the Chinese side can not agree to it" and that such actions would "only raise obstacles to the normalization of relations between the two countries," whereas Chai stated that such sales would "not be in conformity with the spirit of the Shanghai Communique."[59] China's foreign minister tried to toughen the language in a meeting with his American counterpart in October. On this occasion, Huang stated that arms sales not only contravened the spirit of the Shanghai Communiqué but also showed that the United States had not yet made up its mind with regard to normalization.[60]

These discussions formed the background to the negotiations being conducted by Leonard Woodcock in Beijing. Ambassador Woodcock believed that November 1978 represented the critical time: he had completed his presentations on the three basic issues and submitted a draft communiqué. The Chinese were particularly responsive at that point, he thought, because the establishment of relations "would give a major boost to their present outward-looking diplomacy as well as to their ambitious economic development plans," an assessment borne out in Gong Li's chapter in this volume. But Woodcock cautioned that major hurdles were still to be overcome.[61] In Woodcock's next set of instructions, the questions that Huang Hua had raised in the previous, fifth negotiating session, were answered: Washington confirmed that the interim period during which it would be "altering its relations with Taiwan" would last "no longer than one year." Huang had also asked what would be the nature of the "commercial, cultural, and other relations" that the United States would maintain with Taiwan. Among other things, Woodcock was to respond that there would continue to be the "restrained sale of carefully selected defensive arms."[62] By December 4, China's acting foreign minister (Huang had become ill), Han Nianlong, gave Beijing's reactions. Han recorded his government's "emphatic objection to the U.S. expressed intention of continuing its arms sales to Taiwan after normalization."[63] This was read in Washington as an indication that the Chinese would object but would not allow continuing arms sales to prevent normalization of relations.[64]

Woodcock's next meeting with Deng, on December 13, was a particularly crucial one because the two sides now considered themselves ready to work on the final terms of the agreement and joint communiqué that would announce the establishment of diplomatic relations. The report of the discussions showed, however, that the matter of the defense treaty and arms sales continued to remain somewhat confused. Deng stated that over the course of the one year in which the treaty would become invalid he hoped that the United States would "refrain from selling weapons to Taiwan." In this event, his government could agree that the word "terminate" rather than "abrogate" would be used in the communiqué when referring to the defense treaty. Woodcock sought further clarification of Deng's position: "Is it that the Chinese side will accept the word 'terminate' if it were accompanied by an agreement on the U.S. side not to sell arms?" Deng confirmed that that was so, for if the United States continued to sell defense equipment it would appear that the treaty was—in practical terms—still in effect. What was left unclear, however, was what both sides understood as likely to happen after 1979. Woodcock thought that Deng was solely concerned about how the U.S. president would respond to journalists' questions about future arms sales and that the Chinese leader fully understood that, in practice, arms sales would continue after 1979.[65] Washington was not so sure, given the obscurity of the language on this point in the telegrams Woodcock sent from Beijing and Deng's failure to respond directly to the matter of arms sales after the one-year moratorium.

Thus, new instructions were relayed to Woodcock. He was to seek another meeting with Deng, lay out the U.S. position, and ensure that Deng understood that Taiwan would be able to continue purchasing military equipment after December 31, 1979.[66] At the ensuing meeting, and although it is impossible to be absolutely categorical on this, the signs were that Deng had *not* fully understood U.S. intentions. On the contrary, he stated his understanding that Han's statement on December 4—the "emphatic objection" to arms sales—had represented China's last word on the matter. Deng was not alone in his misperception. Ambassador Chai in Washington in a discussion with Brzezinski on December 15 also made plain his expectation that arms sales would cease. As Chai said: "I have already obtained the information that on this issue the U.S. has already said that it will not sell weapons to Taiwan." If the two officials had been referring only to the one-year moratorium, then Brzezinski would not have had to correct Chai. In response to Brezinski's reiteration of the U.S. intention to continue sales after the one-year moratorium, Chai reminded the national security advisor that "this problem all along has been a major difficulty." In Beijing, Deng also recorded his dismay, telling Woodcock: "To be clear, in essence it means that the U.S. will still carry out the terms of the mutual defense treaty with Taiwan no matter what form it takes."[67]

Deng's suggested way around what seems to have been an unexpected obstacle was to leave it open for future negotiations. He also requested several times that Carter make no mention of post-1979 arms sales after diplomatic relations were established: the president should "evade this question"; otherwise, the fact of normalization would be reduced in significance. But Woodcock rightly informed him of the impossibility of dodging such an inquiry: if questioned on this issue, the president would be forced to respond in the affirmative. (Moreover, such a response was vitally important to the Carter administration's attempts to defuse domestic criticism of his China policy, especially in the event of attacks on administration failures to provide full guarantees for Taiwan's future security.) Deng seemed nonplussed and asked what could be done about the matter on the eve of such a historic announcement. The U.S. ambassador persuaded Deng that, provided normalization took place on schedule, over time the American people would come to support unification.[68] In this way, the problem would solve itself. Although probably not anticipated at the time, the problem has shown no signs of resolving itself; rather, it remains a central point of tension in U.S.-China relations to this day.

Peaceful Transition

Arms sales to Taiwan were closely connected to the U.S. desire to ensure a peaceful resolution of the Taiwan unification question, and, as noted above, some of Kissinger's staff believed that he should have related the level and duration of such sales to Beijing's language on peaceful unification. However, the Chinese leadership, when confronted in 1978 with the certainty of future U.S. sales, argued that their effect would be to make a peaceful transition less likely. As Deng said to Woodcock in December 1978, continuing arms sales "would prevent China from taking any rational formula to have a dialogue with Taiwan to solve the problem of unification . . . [and] in that case Chiang Ching-kuo would be extremely cocky. . . . His tail would stick up 10,000 meters. If that is the case, then a peaceful solution of the Taiwan issue would be impossible and the last alternative would be the use of force."[69]

The U.S. desire to get the Chinese to renounce the use of force against Taiwan had been a factor in U.S.-Chinese negotiations since the 1955 ambassadorial talks in Geneva. In 1971, members of the State Department had argued that the United States should use the withdrawal of its troops on Taiwan as a bargaining tool in exchange for a Chinese commitment to resolve the Taiwan issue only by peaceful means.[70] During Kissinger's first visit in July, he stated his hope that the issue would be solved peacefully, to which Zhou replied: "We are doing our best to do so." However, as with the later question of arms sales, Kissinger did not explicitly make the matter part of a bargaining strategy.[71] During his October visit, Kissinger did make an attempt to develop some linkage between the two ideas, stating that the Mutual Defense Treaty would lapse once Taiwan and China had peacefully united and confirming that the United States would not insist "on maintaining an American presence or military installations on Taiwan after unification of China by peaceful negotiation [had] been achieved." But his further comments showed his reluctance to attempt to impose any conditions at all: Kissinger moved from a statement that, in the absence of a peaceful settlement, it would be "easier for us to withdraw our military presence in stages . . . than to abrogate the Treaty" to one which promised that, whether or not China declared its willingness to settle the Taiwan issue by peaceful means, "we will continue in the direction which I indicated" toward the normalization of relations.[72]

Such a statement started to unravel the connection between, on one hand, troop withdrawals and abrogation of the defense treaty and, on the other, a Chinese commitment to peaceful transition before the full normalization of relations. The 1972 Shanghai Communiqué was meant to sustain the linkage in its reaffirmation of a U.S. interest in the "peaceful settlement of the Taiwan question by the Chinese themselves": "With this prospect in mind, [the U.S. government] affirms the ultimate objective of the withdrawal of all U.S. forces and military installations from Taiwan." The United States also promised, in reference to Indochina: "In the meantime, it will progressively reduce its forces and military installations on Taiwan as the tension in the area diminishes." However, as with Kissinger's remarks in 1971, the private promise made in 1972 to establish diplomatic relations before the end of Nixon's second term reinforced this sense that the statement of peaceful intent was not a major stumbling block. The tenor of the negotiations in 1972 bolstered an understanding that what mattered most was a form of words that satisfied both the Chinese and U.S. sides. Indeed, as the negotiations progressed, U.S. officials began to place primary emphasis on an agreement that China not directly oppose a U.S. statement—to be made at the time of normalization—that would make clear U.S. concern with the peaceful resolution of the Taiwan issue, rather than on the need for the Chinese themselves to make some reassuring remarks.

In 1971 and 1972, there were a sufficient number of statements from the Chinese side to give the Nixon administration some hope that Beijing would adopt peaceful means to effect unification. In 1973, however, that possibility seemed to recede into the background. Mao set the tone for this in November when he stated—on one hand—that Beijing could do without Taiwan for "one hundred years," but—on the other—that he did "not believe in a peaceful transition." Having needled Zhou at this point in asking him whether he believed in a peaceful solution, Mao went on: the Chinese on Taiwan "are a bunch of counterrevolutionaries. How could they cooperate with us?"[73]

Once Mao had chosen this phrasing, parts of it reappeared in a number of different statements. Qiao Guanhua told Kissinger in October 1974, "As Chairman Mao said, the main idea is that we don't believe in the possibility of a peaceful transition . . . the possibility for a smooth transition in our relations with Taiwan is very small."[74] Deng said to Ford in December 1975: "We do not believe in peaceful transition" with the "huge bunch of counter-revolutionaries over there."[75] The Chinese made perhaps one of the strongest statements to Senator Mansfield in October 1976 when Vice Minister Wang Hairong told "Chinese Mike" that the "butchers on Taiwan will not lay down their knives of their own accord. Therefore, we do not believe in a peaceful transition and we base ourselves on a footing to fight. As to when we shall liberate Taiwan, that is purely our internal affair and no other country has the right to interfere."[76] President Carter received a similar blast in February 1977 in a meeting with Ambassador Huang Zhen in Washington. When Carter stressed the need to solve the Taiwan issue peacefully, Huang took cover under Mao's formulation of 1973: "Since we see a bunch of counterrevolutionaries on the island, it seems there is no other way than by force."[77] By this point, of course, U.S. forces on the island had been reduced from about 10,000 in 1972 to 1,250 by 1977,[78] and the Chinese had made plain their three principles for normalization of relations.

Thus, by the time of Vance's visit in August 1977, the U.S. position on peaceful transition, as explained in Carter's letter to the secretary of state, had become the more modest goal of requiring "tacit or explicit assurances that Peking will not publicly contradict expressions of our expectation that the Taiwan problem will be resolved peacefully."[79] The matter of continuing arms sales was to carry the weight of more material guarantees for Taiwan's peaceful future; the U.S. public statement, as explained to Huang Hua, if the Chinese did not contradict it, was to help ensure "domestic acceptance" of diplomatic relations with the PRC. The Chinese foreign minister repeated the "bunch of counterrevolutionaries" formulation in his reply, and his expectation that "fighting is inevitable." However, Deng was somewhat more conciliatory during his meeting with the U.S. secretary of state. While reiterating that Taiwan was entirely China's internal affair, he also stated that China was "prepared to seek peaceful means. . . . But we do not exclude the forceful liberation of Taiwan under military means."[80]

During Brzezinski's visit, the two sides again took up this matter of a U.S. statement, to which the Chinese would implicitly acquiesce. In response to Brzezinski's expressed desire to find a formula to express these sentiments, Deng refused to give a commitment to resolve the Taiwan issue peacefully, but did suggest that the United States could express its "hopes and expectations and we will state our views." Brzezinski pressed that such a statement not be in direct contradiction of the U.S. one, but at that point Deng would not give that reassurance: "I think each side is free to state its views without any constraint."[81]

Acting Foreign Minister Han's authoritative statement of December 4 contained the breakthrough. In it, Han confirmed that the Chinese accepted the U.S. need "to say something to the people of the United States" and, in that instance, his government would "refrain from raising objections to statements by U.S. government leaders expressing their hope to see a peaceful solution of the Taiwan issue." The Chinese would reiterate, however, that the "way of bringing Taiwan back to the embrace of the motherland and reunifying the country is wholly a Chinese internal affair."[82]

As the next weeks and months were to make abundantly clear, that unilateral, uncontradicted U.S. statement of hope for Taiwan's peaceful future and the continuation of arms sales to the island for defensive purposes were not enough to stem the tide of domestic criticism of the terms of the agreement the Carter administration had made with the PRC.[83] Nor has the matter of continuing arms sales receded as an issue; it continues to bedevil U.S.-China relations. The 1982 U.S.-China communiqué on U.S. arms sales accepted the Chinese position of December 1978 that this matter had not been "settled in the course of negotiations between the two countries on establishing diplomatic relations." The lack of clarity over the issue in the 1970s could be seen as a clever U.S. device to avoid Chinese embarrassment on such a sensitive question, and the continuation of arms sales has indeed compensated for the U.S. failure to obtain an official Chinese statement in 1978 on peaceful intent toward Taiwan. However, that same failure to spell out U.S. demands also played into Chinese hands, reinforcing its projection of the United States as an untrustworthy negotiator whose debts to China were increasing rather than diminishing.

Conclusion

Large global and regional issues were always at stake in the U.S. decision to normalize relations with China. Alongside the antici-pated benefits for the U.S. relationship with the former Soviet Union and an expected improvement in the prospects for peace in the East Asian region, there was also the matter of underpinning China's constructive engagement with international society. China needed to be brought in to support some of the central international institutions that had been constructed in the post–World War II period. Given China's size and potential power, its closer associa-tion with the international community would boost claims that a consensus among states existed in areas such as arms control, trading relations, and prohibition of the use of force except in self-defense, among other areas. Moreover, the United States' China policy had long lost the levels of domestic and international support that would allow it to be seen as legitimate and credible.[84] This "thirty year anomaly" as Carter described it had to be brought to an end.

Despite the significance of this achievement, the United States' singular concentration on this larger goal placed constraints on its attempts to use the leverage that its position of support for Beijing gave Washington, especially in the initial phase of the rapproche-ment and during the endgame of the negotiations. Pursuit of some of these larger global aims prompted U.S. officials to give too much away at too early a stage of the negotiating process. Moreover, Nixon's and Kissinger's preference for secrecy and centralization of policymaking prevented full consideration of a detailed bargaining strategy. Unlike some of his associates, for example, Kissinger ap-peared unwilling to try to link the various negotiating positions or to seek to impose conditions on the Chinese. By 1972, full nor-malization had been promised, and some reference had been made to the Japanese formula as the basis for the establishment of dip-lomatic relations with the PRC. A Chinese statement on peaceful resolution of the Taiwan issue quickly became decoupled from the matter of U.S. troop withdrawal from the island as well as from the termination of the defense treaty. Neither was the matter of future U.S. arms sales directly linked to the terms of a Chinese statement of peaceful intent with respect to unification.

Whether the United States could have achieved something closer to its preferred outcome is difficult to determine conclusively. Many would argue that it was not possible to achieve more with respect to such a crucial issue for the Chinese as Taiwan: the PRC would simply have refused to negotiate. But this neglects the fact that, by 1969, Mao and others in the Chinese leadership had concluded that the Soviet Union was a larger threat to China than was the United States, and that in 1971 they were willing to embark on a truly dramatic reversal in policy and invite their former primary enemy and Taiwan's formal ally to their country. Again, in 1978, the Chinese under Deng's leadership were ready—even eager—to strike a deal because of concerns about the closeness of Soviet-Vietnamese ties and Deng's determination to undertake the modernization and economic development of China. Thus, there might have been more flexibility in their position than U.S. officials believed at the time. Three factors seemed in particular to assist Chinese toughness during the negotiations over Taiwan: (1) the apparent eagerness shown during the Nixon/Kissinger era to normalize relations as soon as U.S. domestic politics permitted, which made it difficult to strengthen U.S. negotiating stances at later stages; (2) the long-term avoidance of some of the thornier issues, which contributed to the loss of certain negotiating opportunities; and (3) the U.S. reluctance to use its bargaining leverage to achieve a package agreement. The misunderstanding over future arms sales has also played a role in deepening Chinese mistrust of U.S. intentions. Taiwan maintains its separate existence—an outcome that many in the United States and Taiwan and in other parts of the world find preferable in the twenty-first century. But this was not the outcome planned when negotiations were undertaken between 1971 and 1978. The assumption then was that, over a reasonably short space of time, unification would occur, and the problem of Taiwan would disappear.

FOUR

The Difficult Path to Diplomatic Relations

China's U.S. Policy, 1972–1978

GONG LI

The historic Shanghai Communiqué of February 1972 declared that the door between China and the United States was open. Nonetheless, there were still serious differences between the two countries on the most important problem in the relationship—the Taiwan issue. A complex process of overcoming difficulties and setbacks would take place before relations between the two countries could be normalized. This chapter explores how China's leaders, against a background of continuing changes in the international situation between 1972 and 1978, assessed their national interests and formulated policies toward the United States. It focuses particularly on their handling of the Taiwan issue, the greatest obstacle to normalization, and their hard negotiations and unremitting efforts to establish diplomatic relations with the United States.

The Evaluation of the
CCP Central Committee

After Premier Zhou Enlai and President Richard Nixon signed the Shanghai Communiqué, the Central Committee of the Chinese Communist Party assessed the results of the China-U.S. summit and considered the task of normalizing relations between the two countries. On March 3, 1972, Zhou Enlai explained the meaning of the Shanghai Communiqué to leading cadres of various units of the central state organs, stressing issues of principle and flexibility:

In the seventeen years before Nixon's visit, we persisted with two principles. One is to practice the Five Principles of Peaceful Coexistence between China and the United States.[1] The other is to insist on the withdrawal of U.S. troops from Taiwan and the Taiwan Strait. This would amount to overthrowing the U.S.-Chiang Treaty and permitting the Chinese people themselves to solve the problem of Taiwan. When Nixon came to power, the situation had changed, and times have also changed. If we continue to adhere to principles only and do not practice flexibility, we cannot progress.[2]

On March 5, 1972, Zhou Enlai submitted for Mao Zedong's approval a draft memorandum on the Shanghai Communiqué to be circulated to all diplomatic missions.[3] The draft requested that diplomatic missions

be cautious when making statements, not say anything too extreme, and especially to avoid propagandizing the Shanghai Communiqué as a Chinese victory and an American failure. We should not take the initiative, but neither should we avoid contact with U.S. officials in foreign countries. We should adopt an attitude that is neither haughty nor humble, neither too cold nor too enthusiastic. Our attitude should be polite, natural, and at ease.

Beijing adopted this line for two reasons. First, the agreement had not yet been implemented, and for that reason the results of the meeting should not be exaggerated.[4] Second, China needed to keep a low profile, to avoid giving conservatives in the United States an excuse to accuse Nixon of making excessive concessions; this might work against the results of the China-U.S. talks. Mao Zedong said, "This draft is a good one." He requested "some minor revisions and supplements" and then approved its circulation to domestic institutions.[5]

Therefore on March 7, 1972, the Central Committee issued a "restricted notice" (circulation was restricted to the provincial levels and above of the government). This document included a detailed explanation of the Shanghai Communiqué and China's new policy toward the United States. The notice confirmed that Mao Zedong's invitation to Nixon had played an important part in "exploiting contradictions, dividing enemies, and strengthening ourselves." On the other hand, it reminded high party officials to pay attention to the nuances of the wording of statements on important issues in the Shanghai Communiqué and to the limits of progress in the China-U.S. relationship. For example, it pointed out that in the section of the communiqué dealing with shared ideas and views between the two sides, the wording was "should," "prepared," and "hope." China had insisted on such wording to show there were significant differences in the fundamental positions of the two sides. The notice thus pointed out that the major points of agreement had not been put into practice yet and that whether and to what extent the United States would keep its word remained to be seen.

On the Taiwan issue, the United States had declared that it would "gradually withdraw its troops as tensions in the region relaxed." The notice pointed out that the "region" meant all of East Asia. The Chinese leaders wanted to make clear that the U.S. concern was not limited to Taiwan. Rather, the key to the relaxation of tensions in the Far East lay in Vietnam and the whole of Indochina. China consistently and fully supported the positions of all the Indochinese forces opposing the U.S. presence in the region. Unless the United States stopped its invasion, tensions in the Far East would not ease and China would continue to support the Indochinese people in their fight; this would affect normalization. Regarding the overall development of China-U.S. relations, the notice pointed out: "The communiqué only sets down principles on the intercourse of people and commerce between the two countries. Nongovernmental contacts will gradually increase; Americans will come to China, and our people will visit the United States. Nongovernmental commercial circles will also make contact."[6]

The notice indicated the views of the CCP Central Committee on the state of relations with the United States: first, the improvement of China-U.S. relations would help China exploit the U.S.-USSR contradiction and improve China's international environment; second, China had to remain attentive to the implementation of the communiqué—the summit meeting was only the first step, and how the communiqué was realized was more important than the mere fact of the agreement itself; third, certain significant issues, such as Taiwan, Vietnam, and Indochina, remained unresolved; fourth, attitudes toward the resumption and development of China-U.S. relations should be positive but cautious. The notice improved the understanding of leading cadres of Chinese foreign policy. Central and provincial organizations adjusted their policies accordingly and set out to resume and promote official and civil relations with the United States.

Resumption and Expansion of Bilateral Exchanges

The first concrete sign of China's new policy was the initiation of official contact between China and the United States in Paris. On March 13, 1972, what had been the "Paris secret channel" became an open channel of communication between the United States and China.[7] On that day, Huang Zhen, the Chinese ambassador to France, and Arthur K. Watson, the American ambassador to France, held their first official meeting. From then until February 1973, there were 53 contacts between the two sides.[8] In the absence of formal diplomatic relations, these meetings in Paris allowed a systematic exchange of views and contacts and promoted commerce and exchanges of visits.

Besides the regular meetings between the ambassadors in Paris, China and the United States initiated strategic dialogues at other authoritative levels. The most important of these contacts were the visits to China by Henry Kissinger, who served as the special envoy of the American president, for discussions with Chinese leaders on key issues in the bilateral relationship.[9] U.S. contacts with China through the Chinese delegation to the United Nations in New York also became more frequent.[10]

Nongovernmental exchanges also developed as China and the United States made strong efforts to engage each other. On April 12, 1972, China's table tennis team visited the United States for two weeks. After that, a Chinese medical delegation, a delegation of scientists, and the Shenyang Acrobatic Troupe paid visits to the United States. Although these three delegations were nongovernmental, their visits reflected the Chinese leaders' intention to develop relations with the United States. For example, the Chinese table tennis group was the first official PRC delegation to visit the United States. Zhou Enlai personally named Zhuang Zedong to head the delegation,[11] and he received all members of the group before they left for the United States. He encouraged them to do their utmost to promote mutual understanding between the two countries. All these delegations were received by the United States with unusual ceremony. President Nixon's personal meetings with them show that the U.S. government also attached considerable importance to the development of China-U.S. relations.

Meanwhile, more and more Americans were visiting China. Leaders of both U.S. political parties from the Senate and the House of Representatives visited China at the invitation of the Chinese Institute of Foreign Affairs in April and June 1972, and Zhou Enlai received them. Physicians of the American Medical Association and a delegation of computer scientists also joined in the wave of visitors to China that summer. On July 29, 1972, the Xinhua News Agency, the China News Picture Institute, and the Associated Press agency of the United States reached an agreement to exchange news and photographs. This was the first such official exchange in this area in 22 years.

During this period, trade between the two countries improved significantly.[12] The rate of increase exceeded expectations. According to U.S. statistics, total commerce between China and the United States in 1971 was only $4.9 million; U.S. imports from China dominated this trade, and U.S. exports to China were practically nil. But by 1972, the value of Chinese exports to the United States reached $32.3 million, and the United States exported $60.2 million worth of goods to China. Thus, the total trade between the two countries jumped to nearly $92.5 million.[13] One factor contributing to the growth of trade was that, after both sides relaxed restrictions, representatives of U.S. corporations attended the spring and autumn Export Commodity Fairs held in Guangzhou. In 1973, leading U.S. businesses established the National Council for US-China Trade. In strictly economic terms, the amount of trade was not great, and its influence on the economies of both countries was limited. However, since China had never had much international commerce, increased trade contributed to the promotion of normalization of relations between the two countries.

Acceleration of Normalization from a Strategic Viewpoint

In January 1973, the signing of the Paris Peace Accords established that the United States was determined to withdraw from Indochina. This removed a great obstacle to normalization.[14] Nixon promised to solve the second obstacle, the Taiwan issue, during his second term of office.[15] In February 1973, three months after Nixon was re-elected president with an overwhelming majority, he sent Kissinger to China with a specific plan for normalizing relations.

On February 16, 1973, Kissinger spoke with Zhou Enlai in Beijing. He proposed the improvement of China-U.S. relations in two stages. In the first stage, each country would set up a liaison office in the other's capital; this office would not have the status of an official embassy or government organization, but it would enjoy diplomatic privileges and would carry out the responsibilities of an embassy. In the second stage, full relations between China and the United States would be established. The United States intended, said Kissinger, to accomplish both stages during Nixon's second term of office. Zhou Enlai responded that "in the process of practicing these steps, we may talk again, and either we may realize it ahead of schedule, or we may put off normalization."[16] Both sides agreed that, because of the gradual reduction of differences between China and the United States, "now is the proper time to accelerate normalization"; to realize this, the two sides decided "to extend contacts in various fields."[17] They agreed to a program to expand commerce and exchanges in science, culture, and other fields.

The most important step in this process was the establishment of the liaison offices.[18] The Chinese view was that a Chinese liaison office in the United States would "help extend the influence of China among the American people."[19] The status of these offices would be much higher than that of commercial organizations. Although the staff of the offices would not officially be diplomats, the two sides agreed that they would enjoy diplomatic immunity and related privileges.

While China's relationship with the United States was improving, its relations with the Soviet Union were deteriorating. The Soviet Union increased its troops along the China-USSR border, from 21 divisions in 1969 to 33 divisions in 1971 to 45 divisions by 1973.[20] Mao Zedong was paying renewed attention to the complicated international situation. His strategy was to exploit the contradictions between the United States and the Soviet Union and to form an international antihegemony front to counter the Soviet Union.

On February 17, 1973, during a meeting with Henry Kissinger, Mao Zedong proposed "drawing a horizontal line" around the Soviet Union. To check Soviet expansion, Mao advised the United States to strengthen its relations with Europe and Japan and not to neglect the Soviet threat. "We hope you will cooperate with Europe and Japan. You may quarrel with them on some matters, but should cooperate on important matters." Only a year earlier, China had expressed vigilant opposition to the United States' "imperialist" promotion of Japanese militarism. But just one year after Nixon's visit to China—after the U.S.-China agreement on antihegemony in the Shanghai Communiqué and the realization of normal diplomatic relations with Japan—the Chinese leadership had fundamentally changed its view on Japan. Now, it pragmatically treated Japan as an important force in the struggle against hegemony. For these reasons, Mao Zedong urged the United States to strengthen its relations with Japan. Because of the increasing Soviet threat, Mao Zedong believed it was necessary to isolate the Soviet Union. He said to Kissinger, "we should draw a horizontal line through the United States, Japan, China, Pakistan, Iran, Turkey and Europe" to form an international united front against the Soviet Union.[21]

Although China did not cease criticizing the United States, it stressed that "we should distinguish the major and minor targets" and keep in mind that "the focal point of attack and exposure should be the revisionism of the Soviet Union." Chinese leaders concluded that improving relations with the United States while adhering to certain basic principles would be "favorable to the struggle with Soviet revisionism."[22]

Thus, China and the United States had successfully resumed contacts and were trying to eliminate obstacles to strategic cooperation and normalization of relations. The Chinese side stepped up preparations for the liaison office in the United States. At the suggestion of the Foreign Ministry and with the approval of Mao Zedong, Zhou Enlai nominated Huang Zhen, an experienced diplomat, as the chief of China's liaison office in the United States and Han Xu as its deputy chief.[23] These nominations were officially announced through the Xinhua News Agency on March 29, 1973. Huang Zhen and Han Xu, as envoys in Washington, and Huang Hua, as China's chief representative to the UN Security Council in New York, formed a very high level and highly qualified delegation; their appointments indicated the importance Chinese leaders attached to diplomacy with the United States. As Mao Zedong told Huang Zhen, "The liaison office in the United States is higher in status than an embassy."[24]

The Chinese and U.S. liaison offices began operation on May 1, 1973. On May 18, Zhou Enlai received David Bruce, chief of the U.S. liaison office in China. Zhou argued that the United States should take greater steps to promote normalization. "We spent a long time formulating the China-U.S. Shanghai Communiqué. [Now] we should promote the realization of those common points."[25]

Mao Zedong defended the close contacts between China and the United States and criticized various public comments, both domestic and foreign, on China's new strategic focus on the United States and on China's U.S. policy. Speaking to Zhang Chunqiao and Wang Hongwen on July 4, 1973, he criticized the saying "In making revolution, there should be no compromise" and defended the improvement in relations. "You had better," Mao said, "discuss whether the focus [of Chinese policy] should be on the east or on the west. I think it should be more or less on the west. Others want to go there, but you . . . try to delay them." Mao observed that many critics insist on ideological rigidity: "There should be no compromise in making revolution. No compromise under any condition. Is this Marxism? We have twice made compromises with Chiang Kai-shek. The U.S. president wanted to come to China. He was welcome. He sat here talking for an hour."

In this discussion with Zhang Chunqiao and Wang Hongwen, Mao Zedong indicated that he wanted to promote an "all-around" diplomatic strategy that included better relations not only with the United States but also with Europe and Japan: "I am the person who colludes with the wicked, such as U.S. imperialism, Japan, West Germany, and England." He quoted Lenin to reinforce his view: "Lenin said more than once, when you face a robber, either you are killed or you hand him your pistol and your automobile. He favored handing over the pistol and automobile, until the day when you will have a chance to wipe out the robber and take back your pistol and your automobile."[26] Mao also pointed out that the strategic focus of the United States was not on the East but on Europe. Thus, he argued, China could make some compromises with the United States and other western countries to expand China's room to maneuver.

Between August 24 and August 28, 1973, the Tenth National Congress of the CCP convened and, among other subjects, heard reports on the progress of normalization. Zhou Enlai's political report cited the words of Lenin that Mao had quoted to Zhang Chunqiao and Wang Hongwen to justify the improvement of relations with the United States. Rather than follow the Soviet saying "Join a gang and divide the spoils," China's approach to the United States was "a necessary compromise" by a "revolutionary country." In talking about the two superpowers' competition for hegemony, the political report of the Tenth Congress described the Soviet Union as the most dangerous enemy, both of China and of other states. Zhou Enlai said that "the Soviet Union is making a feint to the east and attacking the west, strengthening its fight in Europe and expanding to the Mediterranean Sea, the Indian Ocean, and any other place it can lay its hands on." Zhou reported that "the struggle for hegemony between the United States and Soviet Union is the source of unrest in the world," but he also condemned the Soviet Union more severely than the United States.[27] The wording of the political report was relatively mild whenever it mentioned the United States, and its tone was strikingly moderate when referring to the U.S. threat. Zhou Enlai even acknowledged that China-U.S.

relations had shown some improvement.[28] The report and Zhou Enlai's words reveal that China had adopted Mao Zedong's strategy of improving relations with the United States to counter China's number-one enemy, Soviet "social-imperialism."[29]

In order to practice Mao's strategy of "drawing a horizontal line," in addition to improving substantive bilateral relations with the United States, China undertook a more extensive and systematic strategic dialogue with the United States on international affairs. This was a distinctive feature of China-U.S. relations at the time. Because they did not have diplomatic relations, the two sides could not build confidence and reach a consensus through formal agreements. Rather, they depended on personal dialogues on the world situation between leaders and a sharing of common views. Thus, frequent talks between high-level officials were especially significant in promoting international cooperation.

One important dialogue was the long discussion between Mao Zedong and Henry Kissinger, recently appointed U.S. secretary of state, on November 12, 1973. Mao spoke of the Soviet Union, not the United States, as China's main enemy. He warned Kissinger that the Soviet Union "intends to seize Europe, Asia, and even the northern part of Africa." But Mao also saw "a contradiction between its ambition and its capability." As for the Soviet threat to the east, which the United States suggested, Mao said: "If the Soviet Union wants to attack China, it would hesitate to do so unless the United States were to agree and [first] allow it [the USSR] to occupy the Middle East and Europe. Only under such circumstances could it move its troops to the east, and it would have to increase its force to one million troops or more." Mao Zedong thus conveyed to the United States his understanding that, at least in the near term, Soviet strategic forces were focused on competing with the United States for Europe and the Middle East, not on attacking China.

Kissinger understood Mao Zedong's point, but he resisted the notion that the United States would "leave Europe and the Middle East to the Soviet Union." He agreed with Mao that "if Europe, Japan, and the United States stand together and if we work together in the Middle East, in those places that Chairman Mao has indicated, we would be able to reduce the possibility of an attack on China." Mao pointed out that Chinese forces' "containment" of some Soviet troops, for example, Soviet troops stationed in Mongolia, "is favorable to you, to Europe, and to the Middle East." Mao's main point was that the real danger lay not in the military strength of the Soviet Union but in its potential victims' failure to understand its aggressive intentions; this lulled them into letting down their guard.

Of the Taiwan issue, Mao Zedong said that the United States should "separate the relationship between the United States and China from that between China and Taiwan. If the United States would simply break off diplomatic relations with Taiwan, then the United States and China might solve the problem of the establishment of diplomatic relations . . . , in just the way that Japan did."[30] He continued: "As to our relationship with Taiwan, it is complicated." He cautioned that the United States should not think that

the world will never change. Why should we hurry so much? Taiwan is only a small island with only about 10 million people. It would be all right for China not to have Taiwan in the Republic now. That might take 100 years. As to the relationship with the United States, [however,] I think it does not need to take so long.

Mao pointed out that "we have established diplomatic relations with the Soviet Union, and with India too, even though our relations with them are not very good! They are not as good as our relations with the United States. So this is not a very important problem on the whole," in contrast with "international issues," which, Mao said, are the "important problems."[31]

In short, Mao was saying, the problem of Taiwan was insignificant compared with other international problems. Such a strategic, farsighted view formed the foundation on which China would develop relations with the United States. Mao Zedong's talk with Kissinger covered a wide range of subjects, in line both with China's immediate and with its long-term aims. This meeting laid an important foundation for the long-term and steady development of relations between China and the United States. Although the normalization process experienced many twists and turns, the relationship remained on the strategic level set by Mao Zedong's talk with Kissinger.

A Complicated Situation:
Twists, Turns, and Stagnation

In 1974, relations between China and the United States encountered unexpected setbacks. The Watergate incident weakened President Nixon's political position, rendering him powerless to make a breakthrough in U.S.-China relations. At around the same time, China's domestic situation also took a turn for the worse. Zhou Enlai encountered reverses in his effort to correct the "mistakes of the left." In addition, China increased its criticism of U.S. efforts to promote U.S.-Soviet détente.

China still pursued its "horizontal line" strategy toward U.S.-China relations, trying its best to maintain close relations with the United States to counter the Soviet Union and to prevent the United States from retreating from the principles on normalization agreed earlier. At the same time, China intentionally adopted a posture of indifference to normalization to show its dissatisfaction with U.S. policies; this caused the United States some concern.

For a brief period, neither head of the liaison offices was present in the capital of the other side. But Washington urged the resumption of contacts via the liaison offices, and David Bruce returned to Beijing and Huang Zhen to Washington. The United States also requested a meeting with Vice Premier Deng Xiaoping, who was then attending the Sixth Special Session of the UN General Assembly in New York. Mao Zedong decided that Deng Xiaoping should not go to Washington but instead meet with Henry Kissinger in New York. Deng and Kissinger met on April 14, 1974, and discussed normalization of China-U.S. relations. Kissinger parried Deng's query on Taiwan by saying that the United States was studying how to realize the idea of "one China" but had not been able to find a way to do so. Deng responded with a touch of sarcasm that China wished to solve the question quickly but was not especially worried about it.[32]

Soon after, Deng Xiaoping expressed dissatisfaction with the United States in a discussion with Zulfikar Ali Bhutto, the premier of Pakistan. The key to the normalization of relations between China and the United States, Deng said, was the Taiwan issue. "The

United States says that it needs to find a way out, but we do not need to. The right way is the way that has been adopted by Japan, that is, to confirm that there is only one China, not two Chinas, nor one and a half Chinas."[33] The "Japan formula" referred to Japan's decision to establish diplomatic relations with China while retaining only nongovernmental, unofficial exchanges with Taiwan.

In August 1974, Nixon resigned because of the Watergate affair. After becoming president, Gerald Ford frequently expressed his intentions of honoring the principles of the Shanghai Communiqué and affirmed that the new U.S.-China relationship founded on the basis of those principles "corresponds to important and objective interests of both sides."[34]

China responded actively to Ford's commitment to U.S.-China cooperation. On September 5, 1974, Deng Xiaoping received a delegation of members of the U.S. Congress. In his remarks, he said:

We have taken notice of President Ford's statements that the United States will continue the policy favoring the development of relations between the two countries as initiated by President Nixon. China has not changed its principles and policies toward the United States. We believe the relationship between the two countries can be developed on the basis of the Shanghai Communiqué.[35]

George Bush, the new chief of the U.S. Liaison Office in China, flew to Beijing on October 21, 1974. Referring to the Taiwan issue and its implications for normalization of relations, he said, "As to the urgency of the matter and whether we should accelerate [resolution of] it, I think there is considerable room for us to decide according to our own concerns. The United States is in no hurry in this matter." But he also said that the United States would like to see continuing improvement in China-U.S. relations: "This is my aim."[36] Deng Xiaoping responded in a November 2 meeting with Bush: "Both sides have agreed to move along the lines set by the Shanghai Communiqué." He said that on the basis of the Shanghai Communiqué, "it should always be possible to find a way to solve problems. We may wait if the conditions are not ripe. We have taken notice of President Ford's emphasis on continuity in U.S. policy toward China."[37]

On October 25, 1974, President Ford signed an act passed in Congress repealing the 1955 "Formosa Resolution," which had authorized the president to assist in the defense of Taiwan and the Penghu islands against mainland China.[38] However, the United States took no additional important steps to improve relations. On the contrary, an important aspect of President Ford's policy toward China was to delay action on the Taiwan issue, thus maintaining the status quo in relations.

In November 1974, Secretary of State Kissinger visited China again. By this time, he had lost his enthusiasm for normalization. Because Zhou Enlai was hospitalized with cancer, Deng Xiaoping served as China's main representative in the talks. Kissinger raised many issues. He said that the United States' relations with Taiwan differed from those of other countries, particularly because, first, the United States had signed a "mutual defense treaty" with Taiwan and, second, because of the strong pro-Taiwan lobby in the United States. Thus, although the United States would like to normalize relations according to the "Japanese formula," Kissinger said that it would have to set up a liaison office in Taiwan. He also said that although the United States would withdraw its troops from Taiwan, it had not found an appropriate way to settle the problem of its defense treaty with Taiwan. He hoped that China would publicly declare its intention to solve the Taiwan issue by peaceful means, thus removing the need for the United States to aid in Taiwan's defense. The United States had changed its stand on the Taiwan issue significantly, backing away from what had been promised by Nixon.

Deng Xiaoping reacted forcefully and directly: "In essence this is not, in fact, the Japanese formula, but 'one China, one Taiwan.' It is nothing more than a 'reverse liaison office.'"[39] China could not accept this proposal. As to the defense treaty between Taiwan and the United States, Deng Xiaoping insisted that it must be abolished. After the United States broke diplomatic relations with Taiwan, terminated the defense treaty, and withdrew its troops, the Chinese people would resolve the Taiwan issue on their own. Deng also insisted that the solution of the Taiwan problem was an internal Chinese affair.[40] The only achievement of Kissinger's visit was an agreement that President Ford would visit China in December 1975.

Because of the two countries' great differences on the Taiwan issue, the normalization of relations stagnated. Meanwhile the Ford administration, under pressure from domestic political forces, strengthened its relationship with Taiwan. When Chiang Kai-shek passed away on April 5, 1975, at 87 years of age, the United States intended to send the secretary of agriculture to attend the funeral. But once this intention became public, it aroused domestic controversy. Taiwan protested that it would be an insult to Chiang Kai-shek if anyone of lesser rank than Vice President Nelson Rockefeller or Secretary of State Kissinger were sent to attend the funeral, pointing out that the vice president had attended the recent funeral of King Faisal of Saudi Arabia.[41] Especially severe criticism came from Senator Barry Goldwater and conservative Republicans. Therefore, President Ford instead named Vice President Rockefeller to lead a nine-person delegation to attend the funeral of Chiang Kai-shek. This was an important compromise because Rockefeller was the first senior U.S. official to visit Taiwan in an official capacity since the improvement of China-U.S. relations began in the early 1970s. It also served to reassure Taiwan that the United States would not abandon it, at a time when Taiwan had begun to lose confidence in the United States.

On May 6, 1975, President Ford, in a press conference, reiterated that the United States would keep its commitments to its "allies," mentioning Taiwan specifically: "The commitment to Taiwan—including the security treaty which stipulates that America is to defend this island—is one of the things helping to keep the peace in the Pacific."[42] In response, China's government lodged a protest with the United States. However, Taiwan was quite satisfied; its spokesman said that such "timely assurance indicates the United States has not neglected the importance of this region."[43]

These policies of the Ford administration dimmed the prospects for normalization. China saw any action aimed at strengthening U.S. ties with Taiwan as a step toward "two Chinas," or "one China, one Taiwan." On June 2, 1975, Deng Xiaoping received a delegation from the American Society of Newspaper Editors. He reaffirmed China's strong position: "We cannot accept 'two Chinas,' 'one and a half China,' or 'one China, one Taiwan'; neither can we accept any other version of this position. We know that there are proposals intended to turn the Taiwan embassy in the United States into a liaison office. This, too, would be unacceptable. We cannot consider it."[44]

President Ford took no further steps toward normalization of relations. However, to win votes in the 1976 presidential election, he tried to use Sino-U.S. relations to press the Soviet Union to make concessions and break the deadlock in the U.S.-Soviet strategic arms talks. Ford sent Kissinger to Beijing in October 1975 to make preparations for his December visit to China. Mao Zedong believed that Ford and Kissinger were wrong to deny that the Soviet Union's focus was Europe and that they exaggerated the Soviet threat to China. In his view, the United States was trying to alarm China with the Soviet threat and was offering advanced technology and military aid to entice China to assist the United States in its strategy toward the Soviet Union. Ford also wanted to use his forthcoming visit to China to pressure the Soviet Union, but because Ford was worried that China would not cooperate and that his visit would be fruitless or even result in setbacks, he sent Kissinger to China for the eighth time to make preparations for the summit. Ford wanted to suggest continuing momentum in China-U.S. relations by reaching a superficial agreement on exchanges of commerce and personnel and by issuing a joint statement that could be used for propaganda.

Mao Zedong decided to exploit the contradictions between the United States and the Soviet Union and implement his "horizontal line" strategy. He emphasized that Soviet strategy was to feint to the east and attack in the west. China's attitude toward Ford's visit was: we welcome you if you want to come; we may reach an agreement, but we do not care if no agreement is reached; we will not accept American military aid; and we will reiterate China's three principles for the normalization of relations between the two countries—the United States must abolish its treaty with Taiwan, must withdraw its troops, and must break off diplomatic relations with Taiwan.[45]

Relying on Mao's views, Deng Xiaoping held four talks with Secretary of State Kissinger on October 20–22, 1975. The main topics were the preparations for President Ford's visit, the international situation and strategy, and bilateral relations. Deng told Kissinger:

"Chairman Mao has repeatedly emphasized that although there are certainly bilateral problems between China and the United States, international problems are more important. The United States and China will be able to see clearly and coordinate in certain fields only if we treat international problems politically."[46]

On November 12, Deng met with Mao Zedong to discuss China's reception of President Ford during his visit to Beijing. Deng told Mao that world opinion was that Sino-U.S. relations had cooled and explained that Kissinger hoped President Ford's visit to China would leave the impression that "the Sino-U.S. relationship is good." Thus, the issue for the summit was the Taiwan issue. Mao instructed Deng that it would be best if China did not try to recover Taiwan at that time. He understood that the United States did not want China to use force and he affirmed that China would not use force, observing that the U.S.-Taiwan treaty still existed. He advised Deng that China would just wait until there was great change in the world, and at that time China could solve the problem.[47]

President Ford arrived in Beijing on December 1, 1975, and met with Mao Zedong the next day. Mao stated his ideas about the international situation and criticized the United States once again for retreating from its policy of cooperation. Ford suggested that the two sides "reach an agreement that we will work together for our common aims. You will exert pressure from the east, and we will exert pressure from the west." Mao Zedong answered, "That is a gentlemen's agreement."[48]

Deng Xiaoping held three talks with President Ford on December 2–4. The U.S. side made no mention of the "reverse liaison office" plan. Ford indicated, however, that because of domestic constraints, he could not consider normalization of China-U.S. relations in accordance with the "Japanese formula" before winning the 1976 presidential election. Deng responded:

We take notice of the president's good-faith intention to solve the Taiwan issue in accordance with the Japanese formula under appropriate conditions. That is, when we normalize our bilateral relations, the United States must practice the three principles of "breaking off diplomatic relations, withdrawing troops, and abolishing the mutual defense treaty," as we have said. The "Japanese formula" means you may continue existing economic and commercial relations, but that other questions concerning Taiwan must be solved as internal affairs of China.

However, Ford again emphasized that "we expect any problems between your government and Taiwan to be solved peacefully." Deng would make no concession on this point and reiterated: "As to how these problems are solved, that is China's internal affair, to be decided by China."[49]

The normalization agenda was delayed because the Chinese and American sides made no substantial progress on the Taiwan issue and because the Chinese side had not set a timetable. But Deng Xiaoping still thought it was necessary for the two countries to continue high-level contacts. He said to Ford:

It is natural that there are many differences between our two countries because of differences in our social systems, but this does not prevent us from looking for common points and ways to develop our relationship on the basis of the Shanghai Communiqué. Both sides may exchange ideas thoroughly; it does not matter if there are differences or even quarrels.[50]

Because Chinese and American leaders took the long view of the Sino-U.S. relationship, they were able to maintain relations at the strategic level, despite the changes in U.S. policy that prevented resolution of the Taiwan issue and progress toward normalization of relations.

New Opportunity and Renewed Probing

In 1976, there were several sudden changes in the Chinese political arena. In January Zhou Enlai passed away, and in April Mao again dismissed Deng Xiaoping from his leadership positions. Then in September, Mao himself died. During this period, the normalization of China-U.S. relations was placed to the side as Chinese leaders sorted out the succession to Mao Zedong. Finally, in 1977, Deng Xiaoping re-emerged in China's political arena and the difficult task of breaking the deadlock over normalization necessarily fell on his shoulders. Now, however, Deng Xiaoping held more power and had become the main architect of China's policy toward the United States.

China's bottom line on the normalization of China-U.S. relations was still adherence to the "three principles." On July 4, 1977, Vice Premier Li Xiannian, when meeting with former U.S. chief of naval operations Admiral Elmo Zumwalt (ret.), reiterated the "three principles": "To realize the normalization of China-U.S. relations, the U.S. government must break off diplomatic relations with Taiwan, must withdraw its troops from Taiwan, and must abolish the mutual defense treaty with Taiwan. Normalization is not acceptable unless all three conditions are fulfilled."[51]

To resume progress toward normalization, President Jimmy Carter sent Secretary of State Cyrus Vance on an exploratory trip to China in August 1977. Meeting on August 23 with Foreign Minister Huang Hua, Vance suggested that the United States was prepared to recognize China as the only legal government, but, after the establishment of diplomatic relations, the two sides must agree that U.S. officials could continue to stay in Taiwan. Vance further stated that the United States would openly declare that it favored a peaceful solution of the Taiwan issue and that it hoped China would not negate such a declaration or make any declaration of intention to liberate Taiwan by force.[52]

Viewed from the Chinese side, Vance's proposal was a substantial step backward, because it indirectly sought a tacit Chinese promise not to use force against Taiwan and because "allowing American officials to continue to stay in Taiwan" amounted to the "reverse liaison office" plan that China had already rejected. Vance's suggestion that the U.S. and Chinese liaison offices be upgraded to embassies and the "embassies" between the United States and Taiwan be demoted to liaison offices was far from what China had sought.

In a meeting with Vance on August 24, Deng Xiaoping presented the Chinese response:

We have said many times that to realize normalization of relations between China and the United States there are three conditions: abolish the treaty, withdraw the troops, and break off diplomatic relations, in accordance with the Japanese formula. To speak frankly, the Japanese formula is a concession on our part. We have also said many times that we Chinese are patient. If you Americans need Taiwan, we may wait. It is now up to the United States to decide. When Secretary of State Kissinger visited China two years ago, I said that problems should be solved in a clear-cut way, not sloppily. As to the liberation of Taiwan, it is the internal affair of China. We are prepared to solve the Taiwan problem peacefully after the establishment of diplomatic relations between China and the United States, on the basis of the three conditions, without interference from the United States. But we do not exclude the possibility of solving the problem militarily and by force. On the Taiwan problem, you should not pay attention to how much money you have invested and how much property you have in Taiwan and how old your friendship is; rather, you should pay attention to our national feeling.[53]

Although no agreement was reached on Taiwan issue, it was helpful for each side to know the other's bottom line. Deng Xiaoping's firm insistence on the three conditions, in particular, served to dispel the American government's impractical illusion that China would eventually make greater concessions on the problem of Taiwan.

However, after Vance left Beijing, some U.S. correspondents published reports that the White House believed that Vance had discovered some Chinese "flexibility" on the conditions for normalization and that Vance's visit had resulted in some "progress."[54] The Chinese side was gravely concerned about these erroneous reports, because Chinese leaders were unwilling to be accused of backing down on matters of principle. China reacted quickly. On September 6, 1977, in a meeting in Beijing with the Board of Directors of the Associated Press, Deng Xiaoping firmly denied that Vance's visit had made "progress" toward normalization. He pointed out that Vance's proposal was a "retreat" and that China was

against the establishment of liaison offices. The American government agreed to the three conditions proposed by us: withdrawal of troops, abolition of the [defense] agreement, and breaking off of the diplomatic relation. But still the United States wants to set up a corresponding institution in Taiwan. So we want to reiterate our original stand for the normalization of the Sino-US relation. The problem of Taiwan is our internal problem. When and in what way the problem is to be solved is a problem for Chinese. Foreigners have no right to interfere.[55]

At the end of 1977, Leonard Woodcock, chief of the U.S. Liaison Office to China, explained Vance's plan for normalization of relations to Huang Hua. After listening to the Vance proposal, the

Chinese foreign minister explained that China and the United States could discuss normalization once the United States had offered a new proposal.

On January 7, 1978, Deng Xiaoping, in a meeting with a visiting delegation of U.S. congressmen, pointed out:

How to solve the Taiwan problem is our own business; it is impossible for us to declare that we will not use force. What I can say is that after the realization of the normalization of Sino-U.S. relations, we can consider the reality of Taiwan when we solve the Taiwan problem. We will try to solve the problem peacefully. But as Chairman Mao said to Kissinger in 1973, we Chinese, like you Americans, have two hands only. To solve the Taiwan problem requires two hands. No hand could be excluded. We will solve the problem peacefully by the right hand, [but] it may take more force. If that does not work, we will have to use the left hand, that is, military means. There cannot be any flexibility [on this question]. As to flexibility, to wait is the flexibility.[56]

Four days later, Deng Xiaoping met with a delegation from the Japanese Diet and pointed out once more that "Vance's visit was a step backward. America is trying to play a 'China card' and a 'Taiwan card.' This is intolerable."[57] Given the unpleasant atmosphere, normalization was again delayed.

Finally, in the spring of 1978, a turning point occurred. Because of the U.S.-Soviet relationship, the United States chose to "play the China card" again, and President Carter sent his national security advisor, Zbigniew Brzezinski, to China. Carter instructed Brzezinski to focus on the U.S.-China strategic relationship and normalization of relations. President Carter expressed his determination to push the negotiations forward and to eliminate the obstacles to normalization.[58] Lacking prior knowledge of these instructions, Chinese policymakers expected little from Brzezinski's visit to China.

On May 20, 1978, Brzezinski arrived in Beijing. He held substantial talks with Foreign Minister Huang Hua and with Deng Xiaoping. He stated that the U.S.-China relationship was the key link in the United States' global policy and that the U.S. government was determined to normalize relations with China and was willing to accept China's three conditions. He also stated that the

United States hoped, but would not make it a condition of normalization, that China would not publicly take issue with the United States when it declared its expectation that the Taiwan issue would be solved peacefully. This declaration and China's public silence would lessen domestic political objections to normalization in the United States.[59]

Deng Xiaoping responded to Brzezinski's presentation with a mixture of appreciation and skepticism:

I am glad to have heard the message from President Carter. The viewpoints of both sides on this problem are definite. The question is how to make a decision. The problem can be solved if President Carter is determined. We can sign an official document of normalization of relations any time. In the past, we had said, "How could we not be concerned about and anxious to solve the problem of the unity of our own country?" We are anxious to solve the problem sooner rather than later. On this problem, we have always insisted on the three conditions. . . . All three of these conditions concern the Taiwan issue. Because they are related to sovereignty, we cannot accept anything else.[60]

Negotiation and Breakthrough

Deng Xiaoping and other Chinese leaders were greatly interested in Brzezinski's message. Shortly thereafter, the two sides decided to hold secret talks in Beijing, which began on July 5, 1978. The Chinese representative was Foreign Minister Huang Hua;[61] the U.S. representative was Leonard Woodcock.

The negotiators on the Chinese side were under the direct guidance of Deng Xiaoping, who followed the progress of the negotiations closely and gave specific directions on both principles and tactics. In the first meeting, on July 5, Woodcock proposed four topics for discussion: (1) the form and nature of the U.S. presence in Taiwan after normalization; (2) the U.S. declaration stressing its expectation of a peaceful solution of the Taiwan problem; (3) U.S. commercial relations with Taiwan after normalization; and (4) the specific form of the communiqué and the establishment of diplomatic relations.[62] The American side suggested one meeting every two weeks, with each meeting devoted to one of the four issues; when understanding was reached on one problem, the two sides

would go on to the next problem. Woodcock further requested that
the talks be kept secret.

Huang Hua explained the Chinese position on the establishment
of diplomatic relations and proposed the topic of their next meeting.
Since the main obstacle to normalization was the Taiwan issue, he
requested that the U.S. side put forward specific proposals for satisfying the three conditions of the Chinese side, as well as its ideas
on the joint communiqué declaring normalization of relations. This
would allow the Chinese side to make a comprehensive and detailed
study.[63]

On July 9, 1978, in a meeting with a delegation of visiting U.S.
congressmen, Deng Xiaoping expressed his belief that normalization could be accelerated.

The twists and turns of Vance's visit to China are over. We hope that
Carter will take a more active attitude toward the normalization of the
Sino-US relations. Our stand on the Taiwan problem is clear; it concerns
the problem of unification and sovereignty of the state. The Chinese
government cannot go against the will of the Chinese people. If the United
States steps away from the Taiwan problem, we can solve the problem by
ourselves.[64]

Because of the considerable distance between the positions of the
two sides, there was not much progress at the third and fourth
meetings. At this time, the intention of the Chinese side was to
discern the United States' bottom line and to make decisions accordingly. Besides the secret talks in Beijing, Brzezinski also held
several talks with Han Xu and Chai Zemin, successive chiefs of the
Chinese Liaison Office in Washington, in an attempt to clarify each
side's thinking.

The key issue in the negotiations was the U.S. relationship with
Taiwan after the establishment of diplomatic relations. The fundamental positions of the Chinese side were the following. First, the
problem of Taiwan was the key obstacle to normalization, and this
problem was caused by the U.S. military presence on Taiwan,
which is Chinese territory, and this constituted interference by the
United States in the internal affairs of China. Therefore, it was up to
the United States to solve the question. Second, an essential

condition of normalization was that the United States comply with China's three principles by breaking off diplomatic relations with Taiwan, withdrawing its troops from Taiwan, and abolishing the U.S.-Taiwan treaty. Third, after normalization, the United States could maintain nongovernmental relations with Taiwan and establish nongovernmental organizations in Taiwan, but it should not continue to sell weapons to Taiwan. Fourth, the liberation of Taiwan was an internal Chinese affair, and other countries had no right to interfere.[65]

The United States made counterproposals on several points. It sought to keep the right to sell weapons to Taiwan after ending diplomatic relations; it wanted to give Taiwan a one-year notice of its intent to "terminate" the Mutual Defense Treaty, thus abiding by the terms of the treaty rather than abruptly "abolishing" the treaty; it also sought China's agreement to solve the Taiwan problem peacefully. On September 19, President Carter met with Chai Zemin and said that if the two U.S. positions—continued "restrained sale . . . of very carefully selected defensive arms" to Taiwan, and a declaration of the U.S. "expectation that the Taiwan problem would be solved peacefully"—could be solved satisfactorily, "there would be no other obstacles to the normalization of relations between the United States and China."[66] On October 30, Brzezinski indicated to Chai Zemin that Carter hoped to accelerate the negotiations and suggested December 1978 or January 1979 as a date for normalization of relations.

In the fifth meeting in Beijing, held on November 2, the U.S. side put forward a draft joint communiqué with sixteen articles. Deng Xiaoping, after analyzing in detail the progress of the China-U.S. talks, was now determined to step up the pace. On November 2, 1978, in a meeting of the CCP Politburo, Deng said

I have read the [memo on the] talk between Brzezinski and Chai Zemin and the request for instruction submitted by the Foreign Ministry on the fifth round of discussions with Woodcock. It appears that the American side wishes to accelerate normalization. We should seize the opportunity. Of course, we do not need to go ahead of an agreement between the United States and the Soviet Union on the second phase on the limitation of strategic weapons. We should accelerate normalization; we should even [accelerate] economic normalization. But of course we should not abandon our principles. We may discuss the issues rasied by the U.S. side, and we should not slam the door shut during the discussions.[67]

On November 27, Deng Xiaoping summoned the personnel concerned with U.S.-China relations and said to them: "The most important thing is not to miss the chance."[68]

Deng Xiaoping exploited every opportunity to send messages to the United States and to explain China's policy toward Taiwan. On November 28, in an interview with an American friend named A. T. Steele, Deng Xiaoping said:

The focus of the China-U.S. relationship may not be the three conditions. The U.S. side wants China to undertake not to liberate Taiwan by force, but this China will not accept. The furthest we can go is to adopt the Japanese formula. The United States may continue to invest in Taiwan and may continue to maintain its economic interests. We have said many times that, given the premise that Taiwan is to be returned to China and the unity of the motherland realized, we will take into consideration the reality of Taiwan to solve the question of Taiwan. The social system of Taiwan is, of course, different from our social system. In solving the problem of Taiwan, we will take this reality into consideration.[69]

At this time, new developments in China's domestic and international environments required that Chinese leaders grasp the chance to make an early decision. China was considering a limited punitive counterattack against Vietnam for its incessant provocations along the border and its aggression against Cambodia. Meanwhile, from November 10 to December 15, 1978, the CCP Central Committee held a work conference in Beijing to discuss Deng Xiaoping's suggestion that the focus of the party's work should be shifted to economic construction and modernization. Although the problem of establishing diplomatic relations between the two countries had not been submitted to the conference for discussion, Deng Xiaoping considered normalization of relations in the context of his domestic economic agenda. Talking to Chinese leaders about the establishment of diplomatic relations between China and the United States, he emphasized that "this really concerns the overall situation."[70] Thus, these international and domestic factors contributed to the Chinese leadership's determination to achieve normalization as soon as possible.

On December 1, 1978, the standing committee of the Politburo convened a meeting attended by the first secretaries of a number of provinces and the commanders of military regions, and Deng Xiaoping summarized for them the recent deliberations of the standing committee of the Politburo. The first thing he discussed was the establishment of diplomatic relations with the United States.

On December 4, Han Nianlong, in the sixth round of talks in Beijing, put forward a six-point program. First, he explained, the Taiwan issue was the key obstruction to the normalization. On this question the United States, not China, was the "debtor," meaning that "it is up to the United States to solve the problem." Second, China welcomed Carter's statement to Chai Zemin that the United States would like to act in accordance with the three conditions; that position should be expressed in the joint communiqué. Third, China proposed to solve the problem once and for all rather than agree to an interim solution. Appointment of ambassadors and establishment of embassies could only be made once the United States satisfied the three conditions within a limited period of time. Fourth, after normalization, interactions between the United States and Taiwan could follow the example of the Japanese formula. Fifth, China unequivocally could not agree to continued U.S. weapons sales to Taiwan after normalization. Finally, the timing and the means of the solution to the Taiwan problems were internal affairs, and other countries had no right to interfere; this could not be a topic for negotiation. Although the United States might make a statement expressing its expectation of a peaceful solution of the Taiwan problem, the Chinese side would also make a statement.[71]

Woodcock responded positively to Han Nianlong's presentation. He insisted, however, that the United States must be able to sell limited amounts of selected defensive weaponry to Taiwan, on the condition that it would not endanger the prospects for peace in the region or regions around China.

At a critical moment in the negotiations, Deng Xiaoping held four talks with Leonard Woodcock on December 13, 14, and 15, 1978.

Before the talks, Deng Xiaoping read the Foreign Ministry report on the negotiations and issued an instruction on the Taiwan issue. He pointed out that "we should make clear that the United States may express its intention that the issue be solved by peaceful means. But we should similarly express that when and in what way to solve the problem of returning Taiwan to the motherland is our own business."[72]

In the December 13 discussion, Woodcock indicated that, first, the U.S. side would affirm that there was only one China and that the People's Republic of China was the only legal government of China. Second, he said, after the publication of the communiqué, the United States would immediately terminate diplomatic relations with Taiwan, withdraw American troops and close installations within four months, and give notice to Taiwan of its intention to terminate the defense treaty. Third, Woodcock said that nongovernmental relations would be maintained between the people of the United States and of Taiwan. Fourth, commercial and cultural exchanges would be maintained between the people of the United States and of Taiwan. Fifth, the United States would declare its expectation of a peaceful solution of the Taiwan problem and hoped that the Chinese side would not publicly object to this declaration.[73] He subsequently presented a new draft joint communiqué and suggested that on January 1, 1979, the two sides publish the communiqué announcing the establishment of diplomatic relations and issue various other statements. He also proposed that on March 1 they could exchange ambassadors and set up embassies. The U.S. side also hoped to reach agreement on a date for a visit by a Chinese leader to the United States.

In response, Deng Xiaoping basically agreed to the new draft joint communiqué suggested by U.S. side but insisted that the draft should reiterate the antihegemony clause from the Shanghai Communiqué to emphasize its importance in U.S.-China relations. He agreed to publication of the communiqué and other statements on January 1, 1979. He also responded to the U.S. statement in the draft of the joint communiqué that the Taiwan-U.S. defense treaty would be terminated after one year rather than end upon the establishment of Sino-U.S. diplomatic relations. Deng asked: "I have read the communiqué drafted by the United States and also the record of Kissinger's discussion with Chai Zemin. Since the Taiwan-U.S. treaty will come to an end after one year, then it is still in force for one year?" He suggested that in the year before the treaty terminated, the United States should not sell weapons to Taiwan. He hoped Woodcock could understand the sensitivity of U.S. arms sales to Taiwan: "The weapons sales to Taiwan will damage the peaceful unification of China. If the United States sells a large amount of weapons to Taiwan, Jiang Jingguo would be proud, and this only would increase the danger of conflict."[74]

On the afternoon of December 14, Woodcock, on Washington's order, requested another meeting with Deng Xiaoping. Woodcock suggested publishing the normalization communiqué simultaneously at 10:00 A.M. on December 16, 1978, Beijing time, and 9:00 P.M. on December 15, Washington time, to reduce the possibility that news of normalization would leak before the official announcement. He also suggested that Deng Xiaoping visit the United States starting on January 29, 30, or 31, 1979. Deng agreed to change the date of the announcement and to begin his visit to the United States on January 29.

At 9:00 P.M. the same day, Woodcock again asked to speak with Deng Xiaoping, to respond to China's demands from the previous meeting. The United States agreed to include the "antihegemony" statement in the communiqué and not to include the proposed phrase "terminate the U.S.-Taiwan Treaty one year later."

On December 15, Woodcock asked to see Deng Xiaoping again. He requested a clarification from Deng regarding the arms sales issue, specifically whether China accepted that the United States would respond to reporters' questions on arms sales by saying Washington would sell certain classes of weapons to Taiwan after 1979. Deng Xiaoping disagreed with U.S. insistence that it could sell weapons to Taiwan following normalization. He said that if President Carter did make such a public statement, the Chinese side would express its own view immediately. For now, said Deng Xiaoping, both sides had better avoid talking about it; instead, "both sides will talk about it later." He reiterated, however, that if the United States continues to sell weapons to Taiwan, in the long run this will pose an obstacle to the peaceful return of Taiwan to the motherland and would thus ultimately lead to resolution of the problem by use of force. In realizing the peaceful unification of China, the United States could contribute much, and at least it should not play the opposite role.[75]

Woodcock promised to report these statements to Washington immediately. Deng Xiaoping further expressed the hope that "the United States would be prudent in its relations with Taiwan after the establishment of diplomatic relations between the two countries and would not put pressure on China, which might prevent it from taking the most reasonable way to solve the Taiwan problem peacefully."[76]

Both sides made concessions during the negotiations. The Chinese side had at first insisted on abolition of the U.S.-Taiwan Mutual Defense Treaty when diplomatic relations were established, but later, taking into consideration the difficulties on the U.S. side, it agreed that the United States could "terminate" the treaty one year later. The U.S. side, for its part, at first wanted to make a unilateral declaration expressing its hope that the Taiwan issue could be solved peacefully and wanted the Chinese side to refrain from publicly disputing the statement. Later in the negotiations, however, at the suggestion of Deng Xiaoping, it was decided that each side would express its own position. China pointed out in its unilateral statement that "the way to solve the problem of the return of Taiwan to the motherland and the unity of the country is totally an internal affair of China."[77] But in many instances Chinese leaders also expressed the position that China would be willing to use peaceful means to solve the problem of Taiwan.[78]

On the difficult question of U.S. arms sales to Taiwan, the two sides decided to postpone settlement of their differences. China reserved the right to raise the question later, and the United States believed that the atmosphere would be more favorable for discussing this question after normalization. The United States also agreed not to sell weapons to Taiwan during the final year of the U.S.-Taiwan Mutual Defense Treaty. Thus, both sides agreed on the farsighted attitude that this question should not influence the timetable for normalization of relations between the two countries.

Conclusion

The negotiations on the establishment of diplomatic relations between China and the United States succeeded because of mutual efforts based on common interests. As agreed, China and the United States published the Joint Communiqué on the Establishment of Diplomatic Relations between the United States and the People's Republic of China on December 16, 1978 (December 15 in the United States), formally declaring that the People's Republic of China and the United States of America had decided to recognize each other starting January 1, 1979, and to establish diplomatic relations.[79]

On the Chinese side, Deng Xiaoping played a decisive role. Once he assumed leadership in the post-Mao era, China was prepared to move forward. The normalization of relations meant the expansion of the international united front to counter hegemony.[80] Hence, normalization consolidated the foundation of China's foreign policy. This played an important role in checking the expansionism of the Soviet Union and the regional hegemony of Vietnam in Indochina. It also made an active contribution to maintaining and strengthening world peace and stability. The bilateral relationship between China and the United States also entered a new phase. The restoration of direct ties between the two countries resulted in an unprecedented development of political, economic, scientific, technical, and even military exchanges and cooperation. This trend provided China with a beneficial international environment for establishing Deng's domestic policy of economic construction and modernization.

At the same time, the normalization agreement won for the United States the time and space to strengthen its national power as it sought to contain Soviet power. In this context, President Carter's re-evaluation of U.S. policy toward the Soviet Union played a key role in the normalization process.

Ultimately, Beijing and Washington succeeded in ending thirty years of diplomatic estrangement by focusing not on ideology but on interests. Mutual accommodation served mutual security. The normalization of relations played a significant role not only in Chinese economic and political development but also in Chinese and American security policies.[81] Normalization may have required

ten years of probing and negotiation because of the complex interplay of international and domestic factors in both countries. But
despite the obstacles and the frequent disagreements, strong leadership in both countries led to success.

FIVE

The Soviet Factor in Sino-American Normalization, 1969–1979

WANG ZHONGCHUN

In the late 1960s, after twenty years of antagonism and confrontation, the People's Republic of China and the United States began a process of reconciliation and normalization. The most significant change in Sino-American relations since World War II resulted from the pursuit of shared strategic goals and an adjustment of both countries' policies.

At the February 1972 summit meeting, during Nixon's historic visit to China, the two countries signed the Shanghai Communiqué, which signaled the ending of the split between the two nations and the beginning of normalization. However, relations did not develop as both countries had hoped; instead a stalemate of several years' duration ensued. In mid-1978, China and the United States finally began to step up the pace of the negotiations, and on December 16, 1978, they signed the Joint Communiqué on the Establishment of Diplomatic Relations; full, formal relations were established on January 1, 1979.

For much of the decade prior to the Shanghai Communiqué, however, Sino-American normalization negotiations had stalled, mainly because of the two countries' divergent assessments of Soviet strategy and intentions and their different Soviet policies. It is these elements that are the subject of this chapter.

Concentration of Soviet
Forces on the Chinese Border, 1969–1972

Beginning in the late 1950s, China and the USSR ceased to be strategic allies and became adversaries. The eventual breakup grew out of a tortuous history of disputes, conflicts, and accommodations. However, a clear line through this complex course can be charted by viewing it from a military perspective.

The decline in military cooperation between China and the Soviet Union started in 1959, when the Soviet Union unilaterally terminated an October 1957 agreement promising to supply China with new military technologies, including materials for producing an atomic bomb.[1] Thereafter, the two communist parties and the two countries increasingly engaged in ideological polemics, and armed conflicts broke out repeatedly on their previously peaceful border. Starting in 1960, the Soviet frontier forces frequently challenged the status quo along the border. They pushed their patrol lines into Chinese territory, built military installations on Chinese territory, and installed monitoring sites on Chinese territory. They interfered with the normal passage and activities of the people along the border, beat up and kidnapped Chinese citizens living in the border areas, and prevented Chinese frontier forces from carrying out their own normal patrols.[2] Of particular concern to China was the great increase in Soviet military forces along the border.

CHINA REDIRECTS ITS
MILITARY STRATEGY

In China, a revision of military strategy is always a direct reflection of the strategic considerations and decisions of its highest leader. Before the escalation of Sino-Soviet conflict, guided by Mao Zedong's strategy of "leaning to one side," China had issued new military guidelines in March 1956 and February 1960.[3] Although these two guidelines differed in their emphases on equipment and doctrine, they were alike in their concern for the security of China's eastern and southeastern coastal areas and in identifying the United

States as China's main potential adversary and the Soviet Union as China's primary strategic ally.

However, the situation began to change in the mid-1960s. In 1964, China became aware of a Soviet military buildup along the Sino-Soviet borders and the presence of well-equipped mechanized Soviet troops in Mongolia.[4] In July 1964, Mao Zedong first formally raised the issue of preparing for a potential defensive war against the Soviet Union. During a meeting of the Politburo of the CCP Central Committee in July 1964, Mao said: "Don't just pay attention to the east and not to the north; don't just pay attention to imperialism and not to revisionism."[5] In August, China reshaped its overall strategy for national defense.

China refocused its attention on its eleven inland provinces located south of the Great Wall and west of the Peking-Guangzhou railway.[6] These would form its strategic rear area. It also began to adjust its military strategy. From September to November 1964, the Headquarters of the General Staff assigned a panel to make a reconnaissance of the important regions in north, northeast, and northwest China, paying particular attention to the routes used by Soviet troops to launch attacks on Japanese forces during World War II and to Japanese fortifications in those areas. During April and May 1965, the Military Commission of the CCP Central Committee convened meetings to redesign strategic battle plans. It decided to strengthen the national defense works in the "Three Norths"—China's northern, northeastern, and northwestern regions—which, along with the southeastern region, were identified as China's main strategic regions.[7]

At this time, the Chinese leadership's intention was to maintain stability on the northern borders. It did not want to provoke a border conflict with the Soviet Union while China was involved in indirect military conflicts with the United States through its support of North Vietnam. Although China was becoming more alert to Soviet military threats and had begun to make significant changes in its military strategy and national defense arrangements, it still viewed the U.S. military threat as equal to the Soviet threat.

THE SOVIET THREAT BECOMES
CHINA'S HIGHEST PRIORITY

In the late 1960s, however, China's security on its northern front continued to deteriorate as the Soviet Union multiplied its troops on the Sino-Soviet and Sino-Mongolian borders. According to reports from China's military departments, the number of Soviet infantry divisions in the region east of the Ural Mountains soared from approximately 10 in the early 1960s to 54 by the early 1970s. Soviet armed forces stationed there totaled 1.18 million troops, or 27 percent of the total Soviet force.[8] Although Soviet armed forces in this region were not solely directed against China,[9] Moscow continued to station more and more troops east of the Ural Mountains, including the Far East, the Lake Baikal region, Siberia, Central Asia, and Mongolia. It also continued to strengthen its Pacific naval fleet. These trends presented serious military threats to China.

From a strategic perspective, the Sino-Soviet and Sino-Mongolian borders consisted of a 12,000-kilometer (approximately 7,500 miles) stretch, along which the Soviet Union could assemble massive numbers of troops to launch multidirectional assaults against Chinese territory. Historically, during the Far East campaigns of 1945, Soviet mechanized troops had conducted decisive large-scale pincer attacks against Japanese troops in these areas near China, annihilating nearly one million Japanese troops.

Chinese military leaders were particularly anxious about a huge salient that posed a military threat from three directions—from the north, northeast, and northwest—to China's central northern border territory. These borders were adjacent to Mongolia, whose Treaty of Friendship, Cooperation, and Mutual Assistance with the Soviet Union was tantamount to a military alliance. The distance from Eren Hot City on the Sino-Mongolian border to Beijing is only about 560 km, via the Chinese city of Zhangjiakou.[10] Soviet doctrine held that its army groups could extend for more than 700 km in depth within ten to fourteen days. Soviet first echelons equipped with tanks and armored vehicles could, even without auxiliary fuel tanks, go more than 725 km across the salient regions, where much of the terrain is level enough to be accessible to mechanized troops with tanks. Mao Zedong reportedly characterized Mongolia, where the Soviet troops were stationed, as "a fist behind China's back."[11]

China's suspicions about Soviet strategic purposes deepened when, on August 20, 1968, the Soviet Union occupied Czechoslovakia. Three days later, Chinese Premier Zhou Enlai strongly condemned the Soviet invasion and charged that the Soviet Union had degenerated into "socialist imperialism."[12]

The military threat to China from the USSR became more imminent. On March 2, 1969, patrols of the Chinese and Soviet frontier forces engaged in an armed confrontation on a small island called Zhenbao Island by China, in the Wusuli (Ussuri) River, which forms part of the Sino-Soviet boundary between northeastern China and eastern Siberia. Starting in 1968, patrols by the border troops of both sides had clashed frequently, sometimes fighting with each other, sometimes firing into the air. On March 2, 1969, Chinese and Soviet frontier forces began fighting on Zhenbao Island and the frozen river course on both sides of the island. In the days that followed, the armed confrontation escalated to small-scale fighting.[13] The Soviet frontier force used over 50 armored vehicles and tanks, more than 110 infantryman, and 36 aircraft (although none dropped any bombs); it fired 10,000 artillery shells. The front of the artillery attack was ten kilometers wide with a depth of seven kilometers. During the most intensive fighting, on March 15, Mao Zedong warned that China must prepare for war: "Now that we are faced with a formidable foe, we must undertake mobilization and preparation."[14] Contemplating a possible Soviet invasion, Mao said plainly: "We must get ready for war."[15]

A few days after the March 17, 1969, ceasefire on Zhenbao Island, Soviet leaders Leonid Brezhnev and Alexei Kosygin asked to talk with Chinese leaders Mao Zedong and Zhou Enlai, using the high-frequency direct telephone hotlines. However, China refused the request for consultations. It responded with a memorandum to the chargé d'affaires *ad interim* of the Soviet embassy in Beijing, stating that, in view of the current relations between China and the USSR, communication by telephone was no longer appropriate and that all further communications should be sent through formal diplomatic channels.[16]

A further cause of China's distrust of its former Soviet ally was its fear in the late 1960s and early 1970s that the Soviet Union might be planning an attack on China's nuclear facilities. Arkady Shevchenko, who had been a senior Soviet diplomat and UN undersecretary before he sought political asylum in the United States, later confirmed this in his account of behind-the-scenes discussions by the Soviet Union's highest leaders.[17] Western strategic analysts also reported that the Soviets had made plans for a surgical strike against Chinese nuclear facilities.[18] In a meeting on September 11, 1969, between the Chinese and Soviet premiers at the Beijing airport, Zhou Enlai gravely warned his counterpart Alexei Kosygin that, if the Soviets were to make such a strike, "this would be aggression and an act of war which China would oppose to the end." Kosygin did not deny the accusation.[19]

Soviet intercontinental missiles deployed deep in Soviet territory and Soviet medium-range missiles deployed closer to the border could reach any point in China. Soviet long-range bombers based in the Far East could make air strikes as far south as the Yangzi River region. The Soviet Pacific Fleet could execute blockade and landing operations from the Sea of Japan directly into the Yellow Sea and the East China Sea. Of particular concern to China were the Soviet Union's offensive war exercises aimed at China. These activities strained the situation along the border to the brink of war.

Facing this urgent strategic situation, with massive Soviet forces and a tense situation along the entire border, China concluded that the primary military threat originated in the north.[20] Therefore, China accelerated its military redeployments and readjusted its strategic emphasis to the Three Norths. It formed division-size garrisons in strategic positions in its north, northeast, and northwest regions and strengthened many frontier regiments responsible for frontier logistics and frontline defense. Several army corps dissolved in the 1950s were re-established. To plan for a potential Soviet surprise attack, the General Staff Department set up a Leading Team for Preventing Surprise Attacks from the Enemy. War zones were set up in the north, northeast, and northwest, with advance command posts on the potential main battlefronts. Throughout the 1970s, Chinese troops undertook extensive defensive exercises targeted toward a potential Soviet attack, practicing such skills as opposing attacks by tanks, fighters, and paratroopers and guarding against nuclear, chemical, and biological weapons. All of China's fighting troops were on alert.

In Mao's strategic thinking, at any one time China could only face a single main enemy militarily. Later he said to Zhou Enlai, "neither the United States nor China is able to fight on two sides at once. We may say that we can fight on two sides, or three, four, or even five sides, but in fact, we cannot fight on more than one side at a time."[21] These remarks reflected the strategic considerations that guided China's defense policy. By the end of the 1960s, the Three Norths region had replaced the eastern and southern regions as China's key strategic regions, and planning for a defensive war against the Soviet Union had become the highest priority in Chinese military strategy.

Given the Soviet military threat, Chinese leaders were undoubtedly wise to repair China's defenses along its northern borders, where since the mid-1960s there had been no effective defense for more than ten thousand kilometers. In hindsight, however, it is clear that China overestimated the threat from Soviet strategic intentions and offensive military preparations. Although, when relations worsened, the Soviet Union wanted to put military pressure on China, Moscow's strategic emphasis remained in Europe, and it never came close to preparing for a full-scale war against China. China's decision to prepare for a large-scale conflict with the Soviet Union resulted in part from the misperceptions of China's top leaders, including Mao himself, and in part from domestic political demands arising from the Cultural Revolution to combat revisionism and the view that the USSR was the "leader of revisionism." These two factors together pushed China to revise its military strategy.

CHINA ADJUSTS ITS U.S. POLICY

Even as the Soviet military threat was prompting China to revise its military strategy, U.S. efforts to retrench in East Asia and to improve relations with China provided Chinese leaders with an opportune moment for a strategic adjustment. The shift in China's strategic emphasis to its northern frontiers had the effect of pinning down a large fraction of the Soviet armed forces; this caused U.S. policymakers to recognize China's important role on the global chessboard and contributed to U.S. interest in improving relations. In the late 1960s, the United States was on the defensive against the Soviet Union in the struggle for hegemony. The United States' intention to withdraw from the Indochina war and scale down its presence throughout East Asia created the possibility for a reconciliation and an improvement in bilateral relations between China and the United States.

Chinese leaders paid keen attention to Richard Nixon's policy remarks, both before and after his election in 1968, looking for a possible adjustment in U.S. foreign policy. In October 1967, Nixon published "Asia After Vietnam" in the U.S. journal *Foreign Affairs*.[22] Mao Zedong and Zhou Enlai read the article attentively and ordered the relevant departments to study trends in U.S. foreign policy and strategic objectives closely.[23] On November 25, less than three weeks after Nixon's electoral victory and with Mao's approval, the Chinese chargé d'affaires *ad interim* in Poland sent a note to the U.S. ambassador to Poland, proposing the resumption of ambassadorial-level talks. Although nothing came of this proposal, the first steps had been taken by the Chinese side. In January 1969, again on Mao's instructions, China's key newspaper, *The People's Daily*, published the full text of Nixon's inaugural address,[24] in which Nixon had vaguely expressed the willingness of his administration to open a dialogue with China. In February 1969, Mao urged Vice Premier and Deputy Foreign Minister Marshal Chen Yi to lead a study group consisting of himself and three other senior military leaders—Marshals Ye Jianying, Xu Xiangqian, and Nie Rongzhen—to assess the international situation and China's foreign policy. Zhou Enlai gave them more detailed instructions: "Chairman Mao believes that since reality keeps changing, our subjective understanding should follow these changes. Thus our previous views and conclusions must be partly changed or even completely updated."[25]

Thus Mao and Zhou gave careful consideration to a new and significant strategy to prevent China from falling into a deteriorating security situation in which it could be attacked from two sides. Several months later, the four senior marshals completed their research report, "The Initial Evaluation of War Situations." They speculated that there were more contradictions between China and the Soviet Union than between China and the United States, and more contradictions between the United States and the Soviet Union than between China and the Soviet Union. They concluded that China and the United States should resume ambassadorial-level talks. Mao and Zhou praised their analysis and consented to their proposal.[26] Mao Zedong, assessing the strategic situation and seizing the moment, suggested that China's strategic principle must be that of "fighting the two hegemonic powers, with the emphasis being on the Soviet Union."[27]

In October 1969, Sino-Soviet boundary negotiations opened in Beijing,[28] according to an agreement that the Chinese and Soviet premiers had reached during a September 11, 1969, meeting at the Beijing airport.[29] Although there is no proof that the Chinese leaders decided to undertake such talks to promote a Sino-American rapprochement, just two months later China and the United States resumed the ambassadorial-level talks. The interconnections and interactions between these two sets of talks cannot be ignored.

During the next two to three years, through their public remarks and by various back channels, U.S. leaders conveyed that the United States wanted to improve relations and that Nixon hoped to visit China. Chinese leaders seized the moment to reshape policy toward the United States and began, cautiously and positively, to relax relations with the United States.

On October 1, 1970, Mao invited U.S. journalist Edgar Snow, then visiting China, to stand beside him on the rostrum in Tiananmen Square as he inspected the Chinese National Day parades. In addition to this public signal of China's positive attitude toward the improvement of relations with the United States, Mao also requested that Snow pass along a message to the United States: "If Nixon is willing to come to China, I am willing to have a talk with him. Whether the talk is successful or not, whether we have a quarrel or not, whether he joins in the talk as a traveler or as a president, any of these would be acceptable."[30] In early April 1971, Mao directed China's Table Tennis Association to issue a formal invitation to the U.S. table tennis team, then preparing to return home from Japan after the conclusion of the world table tennis championship. The U.S. team's subsequent visit to China opened the door to mutual visits between the two long-isolated peoples.

With these successful policy interactions between China and the United States, and after a series of secret and public, direct and indirect, tortuous but ultimately fruitful diplomatic contacts, relations between the two countries, frozen for twenty years, finally began to improve. During his formal visit to China in February 1972, President Nixon carried out a historic dialogue with Mao Zedong and Zhou Enlai. The two sides reached some strategic understandings and shared some common views. They signed the Shanghai Communiqué, in which they expressed their joint opposition to hegemonism.[31]

China's strategic adjustment of its policy toward the United States in the late 1960s and early 1970s reflected the interplay of international and domestic factors, but the most urgent impetus for China's policy adjustment was its need to lessen the military threat from the Soviet Union and to improve a dangerous security environment in which it could be attacked from two sides. Chairman Mao later said of this strategic consideration, "We should win over one of the two superpowers, because we cannot fight on both sides."[32]

China's "Line" Strategy and the United States

After the 1972 China-U.S. summit meeting in Beijing, China formulated the "horizontal line" strategy—that is, a strategic line of defense against the Soviet Union stretching from Japan to Europe to the United States—as the basis for its cooperation with the United States. Although joint opposition to the Soviet Union was acceptable to the United States, the two countries differed greatly in their tactics. The United States did not respond positively to the line strategy; instead, it promoted U.S.-Soviet détente following rapprochement with China. The Chinese side argued that U.S. fawning on the Soviet Union amounted to appeasement of Soviet global expansionism, and it warned that such a policy would undermine the common ground for China-U.S. relations. During this period, the U.S. policy of détente toward the Soviet Union became the main obstacle to improvement of China-U.S. relations.

INCREASING SOVIET MILITARY
PRESSURE ON CHINA

During the early period of Sino-American rapprochement, Soviet military power rapidly expanded, and its military pressure on China increased. The Soviet Union and the United States signed the first Strategic Arms Limitation Treaty (SALT I) in 1972, but by 1972 the Soviet nuclear arsenal of strategic weapons had increased nearly sevenfold during the previous decade, becoming roughly equal to the American nuclear arsenal. In conventional weapons, the Soviet Union not only increased its superiority over the United States in tanks, armor, cannons, and total military personnel, but also narrowed the gap between itself and the United States in naval and air forces. By the mid-1970s, the five branches of the Soviet armed services exceeded 4.3 million members.

What drew the Chinese leadership's particular attention was the continuing expansion of the Soviet nuclear arsenal. Moreover, the Soviets' forward-deployed armies, field group armies, and motorized infantry armies were equipped with SS-2 missiles (thin board), SS-1 missiles (SCUD), and Frog-7 tactical missiles, respectively, any of which could deliver nuclear warheads. The Soviet bomber force, equipped mainly with TU-22M long-range bombers, and its fighter forces, consisting largely of MiG 25 and MiG 27 fighter aircraft, strengthened steadily. The Soviet tank army deployed in the Far Eastern military areas, which had been outfitted with T-55 tanks, was re-equipped with the more advanced and more aggressive T-62 tank. Together these forces could mount a powerful air and ground assault. Furthermore, the Soviet Pacific Fleet was the strongest of the Soviet Navy's four fleets, with 162 main fighting vessels, having a gross tonnage of over 540,000 metric tons. Meanwhile, Soviet armed forces stationed in the Far East, the Lake Baikal region, and Mongolia frequently conducted offensive military exercises targeted toward China.

Confronted with this powerful military presence, China actively and cautiously made war preparations. Starting in 1972, the CCP Central Military Commission ordered that "instructions for fighting against tanks be passed down to the whole army." Individual soldiers, squads, ground forces, artillery units, armored forces, and air force squadrons actively engaged in exercises to prepare to fight against Soviet tanks. The Chinese army also established a considerable number of defensive installations designed to defend against Soviet tanks and armored troops, along the border in the "three norths" area, where Soviet forces might launch assaults. Civilian air-raid shelters and tunnel defense works were built in Beijing and in the large and middle-sized cities of the north and northeast.

On December 25, 1973, Mao called a meeting of certain Politburo members and the leaders of the Beijing, Shenyang, Ji'nan, and Wuhan military areas. He spoke to them of "getting ready to fight in a war." He warned that the Soviet Union could "send off its missiles as far as a few thousand kilometers and could destroy Beijing with just one hydrogen bomb. But," he added, "the Soviet Union has an embassy here, which would also be destroyed."[33] These remarks reflected the analysis and deep concern about the potential for war among China's top leaders.

THE LINE STRATEGY FOR STRATEGIC
COOPERATION AGAINST THE SOVIET UNION

Both China and the United States had a variety of motives, some of them shared, for rapprochement. To a large extent, China expected to take advantage of the rapprochement to strengthen the global counterweight against the Soviet Union. The main U.S. objectives were leverage over the Soviet Union in the SALT talks, China's assistance in resolving the Vietnam issue, and resolution of various other bilateral and multilateral issues. Primarily, the United States wanted to play the "China card" to counterbalance the Soviet Union. As Kissinger put it, the United States had to develop relations with China before it could go to Moscow.[34] On the other hand, the United States did not want Sino-American relations to develop so fast that they would offend the Soviet Union or harm the course of U.S.-Soviet détente.

Even before Richard Nixon's visit to China, the United States was actively seeking détente with the Soviet Union. In May 1972, just three months after the first U.S.-China summit meeting, Nixon went to Moscow, the first visit by a sitting U.S. president. This trip accommodated the Soviet Union's objective of reconciliation with the United States, in part to ease its suspicions of U.S.-China rapprochement. The Soviet leaders expressed their hope of "establishing not only healthy but friendly relations with the United States," and Nixon predicted that U.S.-Soviet relations would enter a new era. At the Moscow summit, the two leaders signed the Anti-Ballistic Missile (ABM) Treaty and the Strategic Arms Limitation Treaty. After Nixon's visit to Moscow, Kissinger commenced his "shuttle diplomacy" between Washington, Beijing, and Moscow.

China watched the U.S.-Soviet diplomatic contacts vigilantly. In the Chinese view, the decline in Sino-Soviet relations meant that the Soviet Union faced challenges from both east and west; in order to avoid fighting on two fronts, the Soviet Union would seek accommodation, even cooperation, with the United States. During this period, the Soviet Union floated the possibility of forming a coalition with the United States against China.[35] Although the United States did not accept this Soviet proposal, believing it did not further its own strategic interests, even limited U.S.-Soviet détente partly satisfied Soviet strategic needs; an inevitable result of détente was that China faced increased Soviet military pressure.

Chinese leaders wanted both to head off a reconciliation between the United States and the Soviet Union that would undermine China's national security and to alleviate Soviet military pressure on China's borders. Their tactics for achieving these goals were to identify shared strategic interests with the United States and, on that basis, steadily improve Sino-American relations. For Chinese leaders, the potential for joint opposition to the Soviet Union became the strategic basis for stable relations between China and the United States.

During a February 1973 meeting with Henry Kissinger, Mao introduced the horizontal line proposal for joint opposition to the Soviet Union. Mao first expressed his anxiety about the U.S.-Soviet rapprochement. He argued that at the beginning of the two world wars the western countries followed policies that "pushed Germany to attack Russia." Kissinger denied that the U.S. aim was to push Russia to attack China. Mao responded:

This is what I wish to talk with you about: Are you pushing West Germany to reach a reconciliation with Russia? And then pushing Russia to advance eastward? I suspect that the west is pursuing such a policy. The Russian advance eastward is directed mainly against China and Japan, and partly against the United States in the Pacific and Indian Oceans.

Mao then proposed that China and the United States should unite to counter the Soviet Union. He told Kissinger: "We were at odds before, but now our relationship is called 'friendship.' We start from our common needs, and so we should be hand in hand." Mao continued, "As long as we share common objectives, we shall do no harm to you; so you should not do any harm to us. Let us fight together against one animal" (a reference to the Soviet Union).

In this meeting, Mao for the first time explicitly proposed the horizontal line strategy against Soviet hegemonism. By this, he meant that "the United States, Japan, China, Pakistan, Iran, Turkey, and Europe should form an alliance along a line, that is, along a parallel on the globe."[36] The main aim of the strategy would be to unite to oppose Soviet expansionism. The United States was clearly the most important country in this alliance. In this sense, the line strategy was predominantly one of enlisting the help of the United States to oppose the Soviet Union.

In a further meeting with Kissinger in November 1973, Mao pointed out that "China has pinned down a large fraction of the Soviet army since the Soviet Union had begun stationing large numbers of troops in Mongolia." "This is," Mao noted, "favorable to the American situation in Europe and in the Middle East."[37] Mao revealed his hope that a visit to China by the U.S. secretary of defense would demonstrate to Soviet leaders that China and the United States would join to fight against the Soviet Union. The then–secretary of defense, James Schlesinger, was among those insisting on a hard line toward the Soviet Union. If Schlesinger visited China, Mao would arrange for him to visit north and northeast China.[38]

During this period, Mao also aired his proposals about how to implement the horizontal line strategy. This strategy was founded on his theory of the "Three Worlds": the Soviet Union and the United States, the two superpowers, belonged to the first world; the vast majority of developing countries in Asia, Africa, and Latin America belonged to the third world.[39] China's hope was to form an extensive international united front against hegemonism by building the horizontal coalition and linking its members into "a large expanse" around the globe. Another hope was to unite with and rely on the third world to win the support of the second world, the countries of Eastern and Western Europe, in order to isolate the two superpowers and to counter Soviet hegemonism and expansionism.

China's strategy of joint U.S.-China opposition to the Soviet Union was based on the fact that the protracted rivalry between the Soviet Union and the United States dominated international relations. Although the two countries engaged in frequent diplomatic exchanges and their relations had relaxed somewhat, this relaxation was temporary, relative, and conditional. In its scramble for global hegemony, the Soviet Union was aggressive and prone to risk-taking. The main threat to world peace was Soviet global expansionism and the gigantic Soviet military force. China and the United States shared a strategic interest because the Soviet Union was both the main global rival to the United States and the most immediate threat facing China. Based on this strategic consideration, China argued that the two countries, united to counter Soviet expansionism, could be an effective force.

SINO-AMERICAN RELATIONS AND
THE U.S.-SOVIET DÉTENTE

Unfortunately, the United States did not fully accept China's line strategy. Although Washington regarded the Soviet Union as the main threat to the United States, it maintained that Sino-American rapprochement had forced the Soviet Union into a more passive strategic position. As a result, the Soviet Union had to make concessions to the United States and to try to ease its relations with the western countries. If the United States could seize this opportunity to realize reconciliation with the Soviet Union, it could constrain Soviet expansionism. American policy, however, increased China's anxiety about possible U.S.-Soviet collaboration, because it would place the United States in a favorable position: both China and the Soviet Union would turn to the United States for security, which would enhance Washington's bargaining position. As Kissinger explained in a report to Nixon on March 2, 1973, if Washington carefully managed the U.S.-China relationship, "it should continue to pay us dividends—in relaxing tensions in Asia, in furthering relations with Moscow, and generally in building a structure of peace."[40] As Kissinger put it, compared to China's line strategy, the U.S. response to Soviet expansionism was not as direct or as heroic.[41] Mao explained it this way: "As to fighting against the Soviet Union, China does Shaolin boxing," which is a direct and powerful style, "while the United States is engaging in taijiquan," which is similar to shadowboxing, the opposite strategy of Shaolin.[42]

During this period, China's leaders gave the United States advice and criticism regarding détente with the Soviet Union. China maintained that the U.S.-Soviet rapprochement did not conceal the facts that both countries were scrambling for global hegemony and that the rivalry between them was the main dispute in the world. Although Soviet military deployment in East Asia posed a grave threat to China, Chinese leaders insisted that the strategic emphasis of both the United States and the Soviet Union remained in Europe.

Among his subordinates, Mao went further. He severely criticized the idea that the U.S.-Soviet collaboration outweighed their rivalry. In response to a report submitted by the Foreign Ministry, which stated that the United States and the Soviet Union intended to collaborate and dominate world affairs, Mao pointedly explained that this was an incorrect and a one-sided approach, which "judged from appearance and not from the essence of the matter." Mao disputed the view that "America's strategic emphasis has shifted eastward" because of American involvement in the Vietnam War.[43] In December 1973, Mao spoke to participants in a conference of the Central Military Commission: "I spoke with Kissinger for nearly two hours [in November 1973]. All the words I said to him can be summarized in one sentence: 'Take care! The Polar Bear is going to punish you. First, it will punish your Pacific Fleet, then in Europe, then in the Middle East.'"[44] Chinese leaders repeatedly urged the United States to be alert to a Soviet strategy of a feint to the east as it prepared to attack in the west and not to allow the Soviet Union to visit trouble upon China.

However, the United States continued to engage in double-dealing in the U.S.-Soviet-China triangle. It maintained high-level contacts with the Chinese side and engaged in U.S.-China normalization negotiations at the same time as it accelerated détente with the Soviet Union. In June 1973, Leonid Brezhnev paid a visit to the United States where he and Nixon signed the "Basic Principles of Negotiations on Strategic Arms Limitation."

During June and July 1974, Nixon visited the Soviet Union again, where he proclaimed "the beginning of a negotiation age." Brezhnev declared that "the last quarter-century of cold war will give way to a period of peaceful co-existence." If one compares high-level contacts and negotiations during this period, the U.S.-Soviet rapprochement was more substantial and of more practical significance to the United States than developments in Sino-U.S. relations.

China opposed the U.S.-Soviet Agreement for the Prevention of Nuclear War. It insisted that this agreement would not check the development of the Soviet nuclear arsenal; rather, it would lead only to a false sense of security. Chinese leaders were convinced that the U.S. policy of détente with the Soviet Union would inevitably result in greater Soviet military pressure on China. Thus, superpower détente interfered with U.S.-China cooperation.

In August 1974, Nixon was forced to resign due to the Watergate scandal, and Gerald Ford succeeded him as president. In November, Ford followed a visit to Japan and the Republic of Korea with a visit to the Soviet Union. In Vladivostok, Ford and Brezhnev signed a Joint Statement on Further Restriction of Aggressive Strategic Weapons (the framework for SALT II). In the following two years, the Ford administration continued to engage in détente with the Soviet Union and expected to make progress toward a SALT II treaty.

While the Ford administration engaged in high-level diplomacy with the Soviet Union, it also attempted to advance Sino-American relations. In December 1975, President Ford visited China and held talks with Mao and Deng Xiaoping. China asserted that the Ford administration was following "dual policies." With regard to Taiwan, the United States emphasized cooperation with the mainland while maintaining its governmental ties with Taiwan; with regard to China and the Soviet Union, it gave priority to its relationship with the Soviet Union, while maintaining high-level dialogues with China. In this context, Sino-American relations were left to stagnate.

Seizing a Strategic Opportunity, 1977–1979

From 1973 to 1977, the United States failed to respond positively to China's proposed line strategy and to its concern over Soviet attempts to enlist the United States in collaboration against China. However, Soviet attempts to unite with the United States in opposition to China ultimately failed, whereas China's line formulation laid the foundation for limited strategic cooperation between China and the United States over the long term.

In the middle and late 1970s, a major political transformation took place in China. In 1976, Zhou Enlai and Mao Zedong, the top Chinese leaders who had opened this chapter in Sino-American relations, died. The ultra-leftist "Gang of Four" was then ousted.[45] Deng Xiaoping's political position at the core of the new Chinese leadership was consolidated. At the same time, the U.S.-Soviet détente stalled because of unremitting Soviet global expansion. This trend strengthened common strategic interests between China and the United States and created an opportune moment for improvement of Sino-American relations. After the 1979 Soviet invasion of Afghanistan, it was clear that the Soviet Union would not be able to enlist the United States in opposition to China.

By the end of the 1970s, China and the United States had built a pattern of joint opposition to the Soviet Union. In this context, China sought to promote its horizontal line strategy and shape a new policy of reform and opening to the world, with economic growth as the central task. Thus, on one hand, China rejected Soviet attempts at reconciliation, while, on the other hand, it accelerated negotiations for establishing diplomatic relations with the United States after Washington adjusted its policy toward China. The result was that in 1979 the two countries finally normalized relations.

CHINA'S REJECTION OF RECONCILIATION
WITH THE SOVIET UNION

The Soviet Union's leaders and propaganda departments argued that Mao and the radicals within the Chinese Communist Party were primarily responsible for Chinese hostility toward the Soviet Union and that more moderate leaders opposed the policy of hostility toward the Soviet Union. The Soviet Union anticipated that, after the death of Mao and Zhou, China would undergo a political and diplomatic transformation beneficial to the Soviet Union. Mao's death and the subsequent collapse of the Gang of Four thus prompted Soviet efforts to resume friendly relations with China. First, the Soviet media ceased anti-Chinese propaganda. Second, after Mao's death, the Central Committee of the Soviet Communist Party sent a brief message of condolence to the CCP Central Committee and then dispatched First Deputy Premier Kyril T. Mazurov and Foreign Minister Andrei Gromyko to the Chinese embassy in Moscow to offer condolences. Then, in a congratulatory message to the Chinese government on the eve of China's National Day, the Soviet government expressed its wish to develop friendly relationships with China. In late November 1976, in his first public statement following Mao's death, Leonid Brezhnev appealed for reconciliation between the Soviet Union and China. And on November 5, in his address to a grand rally in Moscow celebrating the anniversary of the October Revolution, Soviet Politburo member Feodor Kulakov declared the suspension of friendly relations with China for nearly fifteen years "unreasonable and abnormal."

However, for a number of reasons China rejected the Soviet offer of reconciliation. First, Chinese leaders found it difficult to trust and accept Soviet expressions of reconciliation because of the long-standing antagonistic relationship and because of the Soviet Union's aggressive military deployments along the Sino-Soviet border, which remained unchanged. China insisted that improvements in Sino-Soviet relations depended on Soviet actions, not just declarations. Specifically, China insisted that the Soviet Union withdraw its troops from the Sino-Soviet borders and Mongolia, thus restoring the border peace that had existed before the 1960s.[46] A second consideration in Chinese policy was more strategic: China preferred to defer rapprochement with the Soviet Union if it hindered the improvement of Sino-American relations.[47] Therefore, China rejected the Soviet condolence message on Mao's death and refused to publish the message in any Chinese newspaper, citing the lack of formal relationships between the two communist parties. China also rejected Brezhnev's message of congratulation to Hua Guofeng, who, on October 27, 1976, took office as the chairman of the CCP Central Committee. On November 2, the Chinese government issued a formal statement reaffirming China's policy of opposing the hegemonism of the two superpowers.

After 1977, Sino-Soviet relations remained tense. The Soviet Union continued to equip troops stationed along the Sino-Soviet and Sino-Mongolian borders with more advanced weapons, and it began to deploy mobile SS-20 medium-range ballistic missiles (5,000-km range) along both sides of Trans-Siberian Railway. In April 1978, Brezhnev and Soviet Defense Minister Dmitri F. Ustinov watched as military exercises with live ammunition simulated armed conflict on the Sino-Soviet borders; the exercises took place at Khabarovsk, only 25 kilometers from the Sino-Soviet border. On August 1, 1978, the Chinese minister of national defense, Xu Xiangqian, published an article in the CCP journal *Red Flag* asserting that "the Soviet Union has stationed one million troops on the Sino-Soviet borders and in Mongolia, deployed aggressive weapons, strengthened the power of its Pacific Fleet, and continuously held military exercises targeted against our country."[48]

Simultaneously, the Soviet Union strengthened its military ties with Vietnam. It acquired the right to use the naval bases in Vietnam at Cam Ranh Bay, Da Nang, and elsewhere, and supported Vietnam in creating disturbances on China's southern borders. The Soviet Union also backed the Vietnamese invasion of Cambodia at the end of 1978. These events prompted China to accelerate its efforts to normalize relations with the United States.

POSITIVE CHANGES IN THE
UNITED STATES' CHINA POLICY

After President Carter entered the White House, China closely followed the foreign policy debates in the new administration. National Security Advisor Zbigniew Brzezinski argued for a hard-line policy toward the Soviet Union. The United States, he contended, "should attach more importance to China, because Sino-American relations would produce an immediate impact on U.S.-Soviet relations." In contrast, Secretary of State Cyrus Vance maintained that the United States should actively promote détente with the Soviet Union. He believed that détente was central to U.S. diplomacy and that Sino-American normalization must not harm the U.S.-Soviet relationship.[49] In the early days of the administration, President Carter hoped for an early resumption of the U.S.-Soviet negotiations on SALT II. Détente with the Soviet Union remained the clear priority of Carter's foreign policy in 1977.

Carter's Soviet policy was not, however, successful. To the contrary, beginning in the mid-1970s, the Soviet Union took advantage of the U.S. desire for détente to quicken its global expansion. In the SALT II talks, the Soviet Union rejected the proposals made by Secretary of State Vance during his visit to Moscow in March 1977 and accelerated its development and deployment of nuclear weapons. Tensions between the United States and the Soviet Union increased.

Sino-American relations also experienced setbacks. Because the Carter administration placed a higher priority on U.S.-Soviet détente, progress toward normalization was checked. At the same time, the Carter administration stressed protection of Taiwan's interests. This policy interfered with any effort to break the stalemate in Sino-American relations. In August 1977, Vance visited China and proposed a solution to the Taiwan issue. In his talks with Deng Xiaoping and Huang Hua, the foreign minister of China, he suggested that after the establishment of diplomatic relation between the United States and China, U.S. officials should be allowed to continue to stay in Taiwan under an "unofficial arrangement," in an office lacking the customary official markings or flags. The Chinese side flatly refused his formulation and denounced it as merely a "reverse liaison office," replicating the current situation in U.S.-China relations. During President Ford's December 1975 visit to China, Deng Xiaoping had pointed out that after the U.S. presidential elections in 1976, Ford would be in a more favorable position to formalize relations between the two nations and urged Ford to do so in accordance with the "Japan formula," whereby Japan fully severed official relations with Taiwan. Vance's proposal, by contrast, was unacceptable.[50] On September 6, in addressing a delegation from the board of directors of United Press International, Deng Xiaoping reiterated that Vance's visit represented a step backward in Sino-U.S. relations.[51]

In 1978, faced with more aggressive Soviet expansion around the world and an uncompromising Soviet position in the SALT talks, as well as stalled Sino-American relations, the Carter administration was forced to reconsider its foreign-policy priorities. In the middle of March 1978, Carter told Vice President Walter Mondale and Secretary of State Vance that he was rejecting Vance's proposal to send Mondale to China; Brzezinski would go instead.[52] The dispatch of Brzezinski signaled the Carter administration's intent to renew attempts to normalize Sino-American relations.

CHINA ACCELERATES NEGOTIATIONS
AND REALIZES SINO-U.S. NORMALIZATION

Long before these positive changes in the Carter administration's policy toward China, the Chinese side had become confident that Sino-American normalization would be realized through negotiations. On September 27, 1977, only a month after Vance's fruitless visit, Deng Xiaoping met with George Bush, the director of the U.S. Liaison Office in Beijing. Deng expressed his hope that the pace of the Sino-American normalization negotiations could be accelerated. Deng told Bush: "We have always said that the government, the Congress, and the leaders of the United States must view the Sino-American relationship from a long-term and political perspective. Don't be so diplomatic! Since China and the United States share much in common, we must strengthen our exchanges."[53] In November 1977 China invited Brzezinski to come for a visit.[54]

Brzezinski visited China in May 1978 and conveyed the message that the U.S. government regarded the Sino-American relationship as central to American global policy and that the two countries shared parallel, long-term strategic goals. The most important of these goals was opposition by both countries to efforts by any other country to establish regional or global hegemony. He acknowledged the U.S. determination to oppose the Soviet arms expansion and global expansion by proxy. Brzezinski also stated that the United States intended to achieve normalization of the Sino-American relationship and that, to this end, Washington was willing to accept China's three basic principles for normalization—that the United States sever diplomatic relations with Taiwan, that it abrogate the U.S.-Taiwan defense treaty, and that it withdraw all its troops from Taiwan.[55]

The Chinese side attached great importance to the positive message that Brzezinski conveyed during his visit and recognized this as an opportune moment. The Chinese leadership quickly responded: although China continued to emphasize its principled position that the Sino-U.S. normalization must be settled by means of the "Japanese formula" and that the Chinese side would make no commitment to refrain from using force to settle the Taiwan issue, it also expressed its willingness to resume talks on establishment of diplomatic relations. Moreover, the Chinese side stated that on the Taiwan issue, each side could raise issues it believed were important without restricting the other side's freedom to do the same.[56]

Talks on the establishment of diplomatic relations, which had remained stagnant for five years, finally scored positive advances. In July 1978, China and the United States reopened the normalization negotiations in Beijing. On September 19, President Carter met with the new director of China's Liaison Office in Washington, DC, Chai Zemin. He expressed U.S. acceptance of China's three principles for establishment of diplomatic relations. He also urged the Chinese side to understand U.S. positions on the sale of defensive weapons to Taiwan and its concerns for a peaceful settlement of the Taiwan issue. During a meeting with a Japanese journalist on October 25, Deng turned to the topic of establishment of diplomatic relations with the United States: "Sino-American relations will advance. This is a general trend." On October 30, the American side responded to his remarks: Brzezinski met with Chai Zemin in Washington and stressed that President Carter hoped to hasten the normalization talks. He pointed out that the next two months presented a golden opportunity for talks. On November 2, the fifth round of the talks on establishment of diplomatic relations was held in Beijing. The United States put forward a draft for a joint communiqué, and on the same day, Deng Xiaoping, just back from a visit to Japan, instructed the Foreign Ministry to "seize the opportunity." He said, "We should not abandon our principles. We may discuss the issues raised by the U.S. side." In particular, he stressed that China should "quicken the pace of the talks. . . . It will be to our advantage."[57] On November 27, in a meeting with American columnist Robert Novak, Deng Xiaoping stated that both Chinese and American leaders believed it was advantageous to seek normalization soon, "the sooner, the better," and that Sino-American normalization was of great significance for world peace, security, and stability.[58]

At 10:00 A.M. on December 16, 1978, in Beijing—9:00 P.M. on December 15 in Washington—China and the United States simultaneously publicized to the world their Joint Communiqué on Establishment of Diplomatic Relations Between the United States and the People's Republic of China. In January–February 1979, Deng Xiaoping paid an official visit to the United States. The Sino-American relationship had turned over a new leaf.

Perhaps it is no accident that even as the talks on establishment of diplomatic relations between China and the United States entered their final stage, between November 10 and December 15, 1978, the working conference of the CCP Central Committee and then the Third Plenary Session of the Eleventh Central Committee of the CCP were being held in Beijing. These two significant conferences determined China's future. Based on discussions at the Central Committee meeting, the Plenary Session made a historic decision to shift the party's working emphasis to economic construction and to adopt a policy of reform and opening to the outside world.

The U.S.-China relationship was not the main topic at either conference; however, the Standing Committee of the CCP Politburo convened a meeting of the first secretaries of some provinces and the commanders in chief of several large military areas. At this meeting, Deng Xiaoping informed them of some of the issues being considered at the meeting of the Standing Committee of the Politburo, including in particular the Sino-American talks on establishment of diplomatic relations.[59] From this, we can conclude that the success in the Sino-American normalization negotiations was associated with Chinese military strategy and changes in China's economic strategy.

Not long after Deng Xiaoping finished his February 1979 visit to the United States, China undertook a "war of self-defense" against Vietnam. Throughout the 1970s, China had seen the main war threat as coming from the Soviet Union, but its relations with Vietnam had steadily deteriorated. After Vietnam reached an agreement with the Soviet Union, it allowed the Soviet Union to build military bases on its territory, and Vietnam invaded Cambodia with Soviet support. These events demonstrated that Vietnam was becoming a serious military threat to China. China's aim in fighting Vietnamese troops was to safeguard peace and stability on its border, to seek a strategic balance in the Indochina region, and to counter Soviet "global hegemonism" and Vietnamese "regional hegemonism."[60]

By the late 1970s, the United States had come to understand that China and the United States shared common strategic interests in countering Soviet expansionism. This understanding was cemented when, at the end of 1979, more than 10,000 Soviet soldiers invaded Afghanistan, extending the Soviet military presence several hundred miles to the south. If the Soviet Union had succeeded in its southward strategy and obtained warm-water seaports on the Indian Ocean, its sphere of military influence would extend eastward as far as the Strait of Malacca and westward as far as the Strait of Hormuz. The Soviet Union could thus link its strategy in Asia and the Pacific with its strategy in Europe. After the Soviet invasion of Afghanistan, the United States actively began to seek military cooperation with China.

During 1980, Sino-U.S. military cooperation made significant progress. In early 1980, just after the Soviet invasion of Afghanistan, Deng Xiaoping met with Harold Brown, the first U.S. secretary of defense to visit China. Deng said, "China and the United States should do specific jobs together to maintain the world peace and to oppose Soviet hegemonism." Brown acknowledged the two countries' common strategic perspectives and urged that China and the United States "maintain close exchanges, maintain sharp vigilance to danger, and continue to strengthen ourselves, [so that] we will be able to deter any aggression which might cause global conflicts."[61] China and the United States soon exchanged functional military delegations. The U.S. Defense Department approved the sale of military equipment to China, including air-defense radar, long-range communications equipment, and advanced technologies for military aircraft. Under a secret agreement signed in 1979, the United States also built two observatories in Xinjiang province in China's northwest, adjacent to the Soviet Union. These two observatories were equipped by the U.S. side and manned by the Chinese side to monitor Soviet nuclear tests.[62]

Some Conclusions and Implications

From this history of Sino-American relations, we can draw six major conclusions. First, the Soviet military threat was the direct and basic impetus for China to talk to and seek a reconciliation with the United States. It is unimaginable that China would have abandoned the "leaning to one side" strategy completely and engaged in high-level talks with the United States—once deemed China's "fierce enemy"—without the deterioration of the Sino-Soviet relationship and the massing of Soviet troops on the Sino-Soviet-Mongolia border. The rapprochement between the United States and China alleviated to some degree China's perilous external security environment, especially the military pressure from the north. Once the Soviet Union became China's enemy, Moscow had to deal with challenges from both its eastern and western strategic sides and to deploy one-third of its armed force in its Far Eastern war zone. This greatly improved the U.S. strategic position. China thus played a unique and indispensable role in U.S. security policy.

Second, although China overestimated the Soviet threat, the Soviet military was undoubtedly far stronger than the Chinese military, and the deployment of Soviet forces in forward areas did pose a threat to China, which remained in the grip of the political turmoil of the Cultural Revolution. China's leaders understood that the Soviet strategic focus was on Europe and that Moscow had yet to develop sufficient military deployments to wage war against China. However, the massed Soviet troops could launch a surprise attack against Beijing and the Chinese heartland from Mongolia. Thus China erred on the side of caution, preferring to overestimate the Soviet military threat rather than to fall into a strategically weak position.

Third, China's strategy for promoting the formation of a united front against the Soviet Union and to prevent the United States and the Soviet Union from cooperating or even forming an alliance was the horizontal line strategy. Throughout the 1970s and the early 1980s, China believed that the main danger of war came from the Soviet Union. Opposition to the Soviet threat could be an area for cooperation between the United States and China. However, the United States never fully accepted this way of thinking. China was the weakest of the three countries, and of the three bilateral relationships involving China, the Soviet Union, and the United States, it was China's relationship with the Soviet Union that was the most strained. This put the United States into a comparatively favorable position; it could negotiate with China to establish diplomatic relations, and at the same time it could ease its relationship with the Soviet Union and negotiate an arms control agreement. The United States believed that strengthening its bilateral relationships with both China and the Soviet Union could make those two countries hostile to each other, leaving the United States in a position to play a balancing role between Beijing and Moscow. Both China and the Soviet Union would then seek favors of the United States, and the United States could profit at small expense to itself. Thus, it was the U.S. policy of détente with the Soviet Union that, in large part, checked the development of the Sino-U.S. relationship.

Fourth, because the U.S. policy of détente toward the USSR was ineffective and the Soviet Union was becoming even more aggressively expansionistic, in the late 1970s the United States drastically changed its policy toward China. During the same period, there were significant changes in China's domestic politics. The second generation of leaders, centered on Deng Xiaoping, had dual strategic goals: improving China's external security environment and reforming and opening up China's economy. With these goals as the core of their strategy, they grasped the opportunity to break the deadlock and establish diplomatic relations with the United States. In combination with the changes in U.S. policy toward China, the result was the agreement to establish diplomatic relations.

Fifth, changes in China's policies toward the United States in the late 1960s and the early 1970s transcended ideological differences and reflected a significant strategic adjustment by China's leaders. History has proved undeniably that this strategic adjustment—the relaxation of tensions between China and the United States and the establishment of diplomatic relations—played a significant role in improving China's security environment, maintaining peace and stability both regionally and globally, and furthering China's policy of reform and economic opening.

Finally, although opposition to the Soviet military threat and Soviet global expansion served as the common basis for China and the United States to normalize relations, it was not the only source of Sino-American cooperation. Both Chinese and, increasingly, American strategic analysts realized that the stability and healthy development of relations between China, as the world's greatest developing country, and the United States, as the world's leading developed country, had great significance not only for both countries but also for global peace and development. Thus, even after the end of the cold war and the dissolution of the Soviet Union removed the original foundation for U.S.-China rapprochement and despite some continuing friction, the relationship between the two countries has continued to progress.

SIX

Vietnam and Chinese Policy Toward the United States

LI DANHUI

As relations between China and the Soviet Union deteriorated in the mid-1960s, especially after the Soviet Union sent troops into Czechoslovakia in August 1968, Mao Zedong began to identify the Soviet Union as the primary threat to China's national security. He shifted China's foreign policy from a strategy of resisting both the United States and the Soviet Union to a strategy exerting all efforts against the Soviet Union. The key to this adjustment was to relax tensions between China and the United States. This presented a dilemma, because it simultaneously required China to adjust its relations with Vietnam, the enemy of the United States. China was fully committed to aiding Vietnam in resisting the United States in the late 1960s and early 1970s. Thus, the adjustment of China's diplomatic strategy involved two competing principles: China sought to implement a pragmatic policy to improve relations with the United States, the deadly enemy of Vietnam, even as it sought to adhere to the principle of revolutionary diplomacy, by continuing to aid Vietnam in resisting the United States.

Starting from this historical basis, this chapter examines how Chairman Mao Zedong and other Chinese leaders handled the contradictions between revolution and pragmatism, as they adjusted China's policy toward the United States and sought to adhere to the

principle of revolutionary diplomacy by aiding Vietnam and to
avoid developing relations with the great powers at the expense of
small nations.

Implementing the New Strategy,
November 1968–June 1970

As the Vietnam War grew more intense and as Chinese-Soviet relations turned more hostile, China, the United States, the Soviet
Union, and Vietnam began to implement new foreign policy
strategies. A major element in these new strategies was the peace
talks between Vietnam and the United States.[1] China's evolving
policy from 1968 toward the U.S.-Vietnamese peace talks reflected
its growing confidence in its ability to improve U.S.-China relations.
When Richard Nixon assumed the U.S. presidency in 1969, the
peace talks officially began in Paris, with participation by the Democratic Republic of Vietnam, the National Liberation Front of
South Vietnam, the United States, and the Nguyen Van Thieu regime of southern Vietnam. The Vietnam War then entered into a
phase of talking while fighting, and both China and the United
States saw the necessity to move beyond their previous rigid positions. Nixon's new China policy sought improved U.S.-China relations, Chinese help in solving the Vietnam problem, and cooperation with China against the Soviet Union. China, for its part,
relaxed relations with the United States in response to conciliatory
signals from the United States and concentrated on opposing the
Soviet Union. In the process of adjusting its foreign strategy, China
placed a high priority on not abandoning its principle of revolutionary diplomacy; instead, it sought to exploit the situation in
Vietnam to press the United States to adjust its policy toward
China.

During the period of exploratory talks between Vietnam and the
United States, from early 1965 to early 1968, China maintained the
position that Vietnam had the right to decide when and how to
conduct negotiations, but that Vietnam should not make contact
with the United States if the time was not ripe and not abandon its
principles simply to promote peace talks. On October 20, 1965, for

example, Mao Zedong remarked to a delegation of Vietnamese party and government leaders: "I have not paid attention to what you have talked about with the United States. What I care about is how to fight the United States and drive them out. Someday, you may hold talks, but principles should not be abandoned. You should raise the principle a bit. You should be wary of being fooled by the enemy." On October 5, 1966, Zhou Enlai, in talking with Ion Gheorghe Maurer, the president of Romania's Council of Ministers, pointed out that talks to resolve the Vietnam War were inevitable; the question was who would decide upon the conditions and the timing. This, he said, should be in Hanoi's hands.[2]

When Hanoi declared on April 3, 1968, that it would dispatch a delegation to meet with U.S. representatives at any time, and after talks between Vietnam and the United States began officially on May 13,[3] China interfered, declaring that it opposed surrender and compromise and that Vietnam should not make substantial concessions or lose the initiative in the negotiations. In talks with Vietnamese leaders, Zhou Enlai and Marshal Chen Yi, vice premier and deputy foreign minister, seriously criticized four of Hanoi's decisions: its acceptance of Washington's offer of a partial halt to the bombing of North Vietnam as a precondition of peace talks (rather than a complete halt as Hanoi had previously demanded); its abandonment of the demand that it choose the site of the talks; its lowering of the level of the anti-U.S. struggle and reduction of support for the south; and its acceptance of the Nguyen Van Thieu regime as a participant in the peace talks. They especially criticized the fourth compromise: it gave the "puppet regime" in Saigon legal recognition and deprived the National Liberation Front of its legal standing. Chinese leaders believed that Hanoi had thus strengthened the enemy's stand and weakened China's position. On September 2, 1968, Zhou Enlai, at a reception to celebrate the twenty-third anniversary of Vietnamese independence, openly suggested that if the Vietnamese people simply persisted in fighting a protracted war and refused to surrender, they would be sure to win the final victory in the anti-U.S. struggle to save their nation. This criticism implied that the Vietnamese concessions were in the nature of a surrender and compromise.[4]

But the intensification of the border conflict between China and the Soviet Union, the persistent tensions in their relations, and especially the dispatch of Soviet troops to Czechoslovakia in August 1968 raised Chinese concerns about the threat of war with the Soviet Union and thus the necessity of avoiding simultaneous confrontations with the United States and the Soviet Union. At this time, the military pressure on China's southern borders eased as the United States adjusted its strategy in the Asia-Pacific area, the Vietnam peace talks began, and Washington halted its bombing of North Vietnam on November 1, 1968.[5] Mao Zedong therefore began to adjust China's foreign policy.

China's policy adjustment was first evident in its position on the Vietnam-U.S. peace talks. At this point, Mao Zedong had yet to comment on Vietnam's tendency to make concessions; rather, after listening to Zhou Enlai's report on his talks with Pham Van Dong, on November 14 he developed a new position. Then, on November 17, he commented to Pham Van Dong: "I agree with your policy of fighting while talking. Some of our comrades are afraid you will be fooled, but I don't think you will. Isn't a peace talk the same as fighting? In fighting we may gain experience and lessons. Sometimes, we might be fooled. Just as you have said, the United States is untrustworthy."[6] This represented a great change from his former opinion that Vietnam should not lower its principles and should beware of being fooled. The key change was not his approval of "fighting while talking."[7] Rather, the major changes were his indication that China would not interfere in the U.S.-Vietnamese talks and his acknowledgment that Vietnam might make some concessions or compromises. China had become more flexible on the Vietnam-U.S. peace talks. This shift also signaled Richard Nixon, who was about to become president, that there was some hope of solving the Vietnam problem with China's help.[8]

On November 25, with Mao Zedong's approval, China suggested to the United States that the two sides resume ambassadorial-level talks and that the press release announcing the resumption of the talks mention the Five Principles of Peaceful Coexistence.[9] On the next day, a Chinese Foreign Ministry spokesman, responding to questions about the ambassadorial talks, again suggested that China and the United States sign a treaty based on the Five Principles of Peaceful Coexistence.[10] These statements attracted attention from China specialists in Washington, who noted this was the first time since the beginning of the Cultural Revolution that the Chinese had offered this proposal. They interpreted these statements as messages from Beijing that it was prepared to return to the international stage. President-elect Nixon, on learning of this, immediately directed his foreign policy aides to notify China that his administration would welcome a resumption of the Warsaw talks and would take action as soon as he assumed the presidency.[11]

A few days later, in receiving a Cambodian delegation, Zhou Enlai explained Mao Zedong's strategic thinking about relations with the United States and Vietnam and stressed that in the fight against imperialism and revisionism, it was necessary to consider both policy and tactics. China should have a strategic concept but flexible tactics. It should defeat its enemies one by one; at any time, it should identify the main enemy and that enemy's allies and concentrate its forces to fight them. It should also exploit the contradictions dividing its enemy and that enemy's allies. China should unite the largest possible grouping of all revolutionary people, including revolutionary nationalists, but it should also take any forces that had differences with the main enemy as its indirect allies.[12] In considering the relationship between a relaxation of China-U.S. tensions and the Vietnam War, China viewed its own attitude toward Vietnam-U.S. peace talks as an important factor.

In January 1969, Mao Zedong, after abandoning opposition to Vietnam-U.S. peace talks, offered his first reaction to Nixon's suggestion in his inaugural address that the United States would be more flexible in its relations with China. He directed the publication in *Renmin ribao* (People's daily) and *Hongqi* (Red flag) of a commentary entitled "A No-Way-Out Confession: On Nixon's Inaugural Speech and the Soviet Renegade Group's Flattery." He also directed that the text of Nixon's inaugural speech be published in *People's Daily*.[13] Then, in early February, Nixon directed National Security Advisor Henry Kissinger "to probe the possibility of resuming relations with China" and directed that this should be done secretly. Kissinger asked East Asian experts in the National

Security Council to study U.S. interests and policy options toward China and to prepare a report by March 1, 1969.[14] Although China postponed the ambassadorial-level talks that it had scheduled for February 20, due to the defection to the United States of the Chinese chargé d'affaires *ad interim* in the Netherlands,[15] Mao Zedong had not abandoned his strategic considerations. On February 19, he directed Chen Yi and three other high-ranking generals to study the international situation.[16]

Vietnam had sensed signs of policy changes by both China and the United States. On March 22, Xuan Thuy, director of the International Liaison Office of the Vietnamese Workers Party and Vietnam's chief negotiator at the Paris peace talks, warned the U.S. representative that the United States would get nowhere by trying to exploit the differences between China and the Soviet Union. Although these differences had persisted for nearly ten years, he said, during these years both countries had supported North Vietnam and would continue to do so.[17]

Until April 1969, relations between China and the United States were basically hostile, characterized by misunderstanding and lack of mutual confidence. Despite Nixon's expressed desire to improve relations with China, he had yet to carry out a "revolutionary" policy change. Soon after the armed Sino-Soviet confrontation on Zhenbao Island in early March 1969, at the funeral for former President Eisenhower, Nixon revealed to French President Charles de Gaulle his decision to open a dialogue with China. He asked de Gaulle to pass along a message to that effect to Chinese leaders.[18] At the time, the United States was not fully aware of how much the Sino-Soviet relationship had deteriorated. At a press conference on March 14, Nixon declared that the planned Safeguard anti–ballistic missile plan might reduce U.S. losses to a minimum should China launch a nuclear attack, and he further hinted that the United States and the Soviet Union shared a common interest and purpose in containing and opposing China.[19] His remarks raised serious concerns in Beijing.

Facing pressure from both Vietnam and the United States, China made a short-term tactical adjustment. The Xinhua News Agency accused the United States of "colluding with the Soviet Union," of "joining hands in opposing China militarily," and of "threatening and blackmailing with nuclear weapons" the Chinese people and the people of the entire world.[20] It reminded Vietnam's leaders that they should be alert not to be fooled by U.S. and Soviet policies toward Vietnam and suggested that Vietnam "should not waste its time on the peace talks in Paris." China declared that victory could not be won at the negotiating table; talk was secondary, and its aim was merely to expose one's enemy's plans and disposition. China, it declared, "would spare no effort to help Vietnam win the war." On June 14, China sent a message recognizing and greeting the Provisional Revolutionary Government of South Vietnam at its founding.[21] Lin Biao's political report to the Ninth Party Congress, which had been discussed and approved by Mao Zedong,[22] announced that Chairman Mao had pointed out that "a historical new epoch of anti–U.S. imperialism and anti–Soviet revisionism has begun." China thus drew a clear line separating China from both U.S. imperialism and Soviet revisionism. Lin called on all nations and peoples who had suffered from U.S. imperialism or Soviet revisionism to join in a broad united front to defeat common enemies: "We must not neglect the danger that U.S. imperialism and Soviet revisionism may wage a large-scale war of invasion. We must be fully prepared and ready to fight a large-scale war in the near future, either conventional or nuclear. If others let us alone, we will let them alone; but if we are attacked, we will certainly counterattack."[23]

Nonetheless, Lin's report devoted only one paragraph to U.S. imperialism, which it said was "on the decline." In contrast, it devoted nearly eight paragraphs to Soviet revisionism, emphasizing that "it is desperately practicing social imperialism," has "intensified its fight for the Middle East and other regions with U.S. imperialism, and intensified its threat to invade China." By exaggerating the importance of the conflict on Zhenbao Island, China hoped to make clear to the United States that China and the Soviet Union were on the brink of war. It thus sent a message to the United States that both the Soviet Union and the United States were considered to be threats to China, but the Soviet Union was deemed China's main enemy and China was prepared to avoid war with the United States in Indochina.[24]

The combination of these Chinese signals, the Soviet Union's concern about war with China and its urgent need to know the U.S. position on the Sino-Soviet conflict, and U.S. concern that the Soviet-Chinese alliance might be restored if Moscow compelled Beijing to submit to its military pressure[25] promoted U.S. optimism over the possibility of a triangular diplomacy involving the United States, China, and the Soviet Union. After the Soviet Union rejected Washington's request that it help end the Vietnam war on the grounds that it had little influence on Vietnam, the United States turned to China for assistance. In Nixon's eyes, improved U.S. ties with China might compel the Soviet Union to help the United States extricate itself from Vietnam.[26] Thus, from June 1969 through early 1970, Nixon's strategic thinking gradually formed around the idea of joining with China to contain the Soviet Union, and the United States undertook a series of conciliatory steps toward China.[27] At the same time, Mao Zedong had decided to adjust China's diplomatic policy to concentrate its forces to counter the Soviet Union and thus took the initiative to open ties with the United States.[28]

As the Vietnam-U.S. peace talks began in 1969, China responded to the U.S. signals. Nevertheless, at the request of Vietnam, on October 25 China published the communiqué of a talk between Zhou Enlai and Pham Van Dong, which said that there was only one correct way to solve the Vietnam problem: U.S. imperialism must stop the war of invasion against Vietnam, the invading troops of the United States and its vassals must be withdrawn unconditionally from Vietnam, and the Vietnamese people must be allowed to handle their own internal affairs without foreign interference. The communiqué reiterated that the Chinese people would forever follow the directives of the great leader Mao Zedong, that "700 million Chinese people are powerfully behind the Vietnamese people, and Vietnam can depend upon China's vast territory as its rear base." It declared that China would provide resolute support and assistance to the Vietnamese people in their war.[29]

Simultaneously, however, China shifted the focus of its material support for Vietnam from military to economic aid.[30] China stressed that Hanoi should not rely overly on foreign military assistance and should adopt a principle of self-sufficiency.[31] China also began a gradual withdrawal of support troops. Between February 1969 and July 1970, China repatriated more than 320,000 Chinese troops from Vietnam, where they had engaged in road-building, air defense, defense engineering, and railway maintenance.[32] In a third move, China retreated from its previous suggestion that Vietnam should take the offensive and adjusted its military aid to Vietnam accordingly. China indicated to Vietnamese leaders that, after due consideration, it believed its former advice favoring a large-scale campaign was now impractical.[33] Thus, in 1969, China reduced the amount of its weapons assistance to a level approximately half that of 1968 (see Table 6.1).

China also stated that it would no longer intervene in the Vietnam-U.S. peace talks. In a September 7 meeting with President Ion Gheorghe Maurer of Romania's Council of Ministers, Zhou Enlai said that whether Vietnam continued to fight or instead talked in Paris was the business of the Vietnamese party. He later said, "We have exchanged opinions with our Vietnamese comrades mainly about the war. As to the talks in Paris, we never had any interest, first, because Vietnam was the master, and second, because the Soviet Union had interfered, and therefore we would not: we would pay no attention to it, whether it went smoothly or not."[34]

One of the main reasons for the change in China's aid policy was the suspension of the U.S. bombing of North Vietnam after the peace talks in Paris had begun, which reduced the threat of war against China. In addition, since Vietnam had not tilted toward the Soviet Union, even though the Soviet Union was increasing its aid to Vietnam, China did not feel pressed to maintain its previous level of aid to Vietnam. These factors enabled China to respond to the changes in U.S. policy toward China.

Nevertheless, China remained suspicious of U.S. intentions. Mao Zedong had pointed out emphatically that even though the U.S. imperialistic invasion of Vietnam had failed ignominiously, the United States' aggressive nature would never change. The Nixon administration, he charged, had adopted a dual antirevolutionary

Table 6.1
Chinese Military Aid to Vietnam, 1968–1975

Year	Rifles	Guns	Bullets (000 rounds)	Shells (000 rounds)	Tanks	Ships	Aircraft	Cars
1968	219,899	7,087	247,920	2,082	18			454
1969	139,900	3,906	119,170	1,357				162
1970	101,800	2,212	29,010	397	0			0
1971	143,100	7,898	57,190	2,210	80	24	4	4,011
1972	189,000	9,238	40,000	2,210	220	71	14	8,758
1973	233,500	9,912	40,000	2,210	120	5	36	1,210
1974	164,500	6,406	30,000	1,390	80	6		506
1975	141,800	4,880	20,060	965			20	

SOURCE: Li Ke and Hao Shengzhang, "Wenhua da geming" zhong de Renmin jiefangjun (The PLA in the Cultural Revolution) (Beijing: Zhonggong dangshi ziliao chubanshe, 1989), 416.

strategy: while it talked about peace in high-sounding phrases, it was strengthening its invasion of Vietnam and was attempting to escape failure with the so-called Vietnamization of the Vietnamese war.[35] Moreover, despite the constructive atmosphere of the recent ambassadorial talks, events in Cambodia had heightened tensions. In March, the Lon Nol–Sirik Matak group overthrew the monarchy led by Prince Sihanouk and founded a pro-U.S. regime. The United States then sent Thai forces into Laos and deployed its own troops in Cambodia on April 30. It thus extended its invasion to the whole of Indochina. China responded by declaring its support for the Cambodian National United Front, headed by Sihanouk. It declared that all 700 million Chinese people were sworn to back the people of the three Indochinese countries.[36]

In response to these developments, on May 11, 1970, Mao Zedong assured Le Duan, General Secretary of the Vietnamese Workers Party, that China was the "rear area" of Vietnam and that Vietnamese aircraft could land in China. He said: "We do not fear. If Americans want to attack a 'sanctuary' of the Vietnamese air force, let them come." He also said: "You may hold talks; it is all right to hold talks. But mainly you should fight."[37] On May 16, Zhou Enlai presided over the Politburo meeting that decided to postpone the next round of China-U.S. talks. The Politburo suggested that Mao Zedong should make a public declaration of China's support for the international revolutionary struggle against the United States, for the Summit Conference of the Indochinese People, and for Sihanouk's government. It further suggested that a mass meeting and demonstration should be held in China, at which Mao Zedong and Lin Biao would appear and Sihanouk would speak. Mao Zedong approved the suggestion.[38] On May 18, China officially notified the United States that it would postpone the next meeting of the Warsaw talks.[39] On May 20, the day set for the talks, Mao Zedong published a declaration calling on "all the people of the world to unite and defeat the American aggressor and its lackeys."

The suspension of the China-U.S. talks stalled the relaxation of tension between the two countries. In the May 20 declaration, by not denouncing Soviet revisionism and by stressing the defeat of U.S. imperialism, Mao expressed a strong reaction to the U.S. dispatch of troops to Cambodia, evidently with the aim of exerting pressure on the United States. Mao had three purposes. First, to show that, although China had made a pragmatic choice to relax tensions between the two countries, it would not abandon the people of the three Indochinese countries. The resumption of diplomatic relations between the United States and China was premised on the gradual reduction of U.S. interference in Indochina, and not on an expansion of its aggression and interference. Second, since the late 1960s and early 1970s, the Chinese side had been acutely aware that the Soviet Union had not, since World War II, ever deployed so many troops along the border of any country as the one million now in place near the Soviet-Chinese borders. The objective situation had thus made the Soviet Union the main enemy of China.[40] This strategic context encouraged China to seek improved relations with the United States. But ambassadorial-level talks could not achieve this objective. As Zhou Enlai said later: "There were talks between the two countries, but ambassadorial-level talks could not solve the problems. We talked for sixteen years, but the intensification of the Vietnam War and the U.S. invasion of Cambodia caused us to stop talking. Just as we learned during the period of China's civil war, only talks with Chiang Kai-shek could solve the problem."[41] In other words, the substantial obstacles to relations between the two sides could be solved only by talks at the highest levels. To Mao Zedong, this meant President Nixon.[42] Hence, by suspending the Warsaw talks Mao hoped to press the United States to establish more substantial contacts with China. Third, having signaled its intentions and suspended the talks, China could wait for the U.S. reaction and gauge U.S. sincerity and its determination to relax tension between the United States and China.

Kissinger believed that Mao's May 20 statement had exaggerated China's level of concern.[43] Nixon, however, sensed Chinese pressure. Reacting with great anger, he ordered all U.S. naval ships not needed for the Vietnam War to be sent to the Taiwan Strait within 24 hours. But he soon realized that Mao Zedong had left some space for negotiations within which the United States and China could restore contact and that it served no purpose for Washington to block the road to contact.[44] The result was that Kissinger concluded during the suspension of the ambassadorial talks in Warsaw that the talks were too "restricting."[45] In mid-June, the United States sought renewed contact with China. On June 30 Nixon declared a withdrawal of U.S. troops from Cambodia. In so doing, he met China's objective aims, and the Chinese government began to consider the resumption of contacts with the United States.[46]

Rapprochement and Vietnam, July 1970–December 1971

From July 1970 to December 1971, China and the United States began making high-level contacts in preparation for further relaxation of tensions. Because the two countries had been separated for twenty years, China did not expect to solve all its problems with the United States; rather, contact could enable the two sides to discuss resolution of their problems.[47] In the process, China adhered to its basic diplomatic principles toward Vietnam, renewed its support for Vietnam on a large scale, and refused to exert pressure on Vietnam. By maintaining its Vietnam policy, it hoped to pressure the United States to abandon its stubborn stand on Taiwan and take decisive steps to relax tensions between the two countries.

The Chinese government's declaration on July 10, 1970, that it would release Bishop James Walsh, an American missionary arrested by the Chinese government in 1958, marked the beginning of the period of renewed Chinese and U.S. efforts to establish cooperation. The two sides conveyed messages to each other about holding a high-level meeting. The United States even hinted at a withdrawal of U.S. troops from Taiwan in connection with ending the Vietnam War.[48] There was also a subtle but significant change in China's attitude toward the Vietnam-U.S. peace talks. On September 23, 1970, Mao Zedong said to Pham Van Dong, "I am now sure that you are able to carry out the diplomatic struggle. You have done quite well. At first, we were a bit worried you would be fooled, but now we do not worry any more."[49] China also continued to reduce its military assistance to Vietnam, below the levels of 1969.[50]

In late 1970, as preparations for high-level talks between China and the United States were making progress, the United States escalated the war to force Vietnam to accept its conditions: it invaded Cambodia with several tens of thousands of American and Saigon troops, assaulted Highway 9 in the south, and attacked North Vietnam from air and sea. This time, China did not break off contacts with the United States, but instead adopted a firm, pragmatic attitude that was revolutionary but allowed for limited flexibility in its U.S. policy.

On December 11, China issued a declaration that strongly condemned the risky military action of the United States, thus supporting Vietnam's December 11 "Letter to the People of the State."[51] In March 1971, in his annual report on foreign policy, President Nixon signaled his intention to improve relations with Beijing.[52] In response, China issued a joint communiqué with Vietnam, pointing out that U.S. activities threatened the security not only of Vietnam but also of China. The communiqué reaffirmed support for the people of Indochina and reiterated that war against the United States to save those countries was both the firm and the unswerving principle of China's Communist Party and its government and the international duty of the Chinese people. It emphasized that the Chinese people were wholeheartedly determined to adopt all necessary measures, even the greatest national sacrifices, to support the people of Vietnam and the other Indochinese countries in their efforts to defeat the American aggressors. The communiqué also said that the Vietnamese people strongly supported China's efforts to liberate its own sacred territory, Taiwan province, and stated Vietnam's firm belief that Taiwan would ultimately be liberated.[53] The communiqué in effect warned the United States that China would support the people of the three Indochinese countries, even at the cost of a war with the United States, and alluded to its determination to solve the Taiwan problem by force if necessary. Moreover, the Chinese Politburo, at a meeting on March 3, decided to increase China's aid to Vietnam. At a speech at a rally in Vietnam, Zhou Enlai later said: "Our great leader, Chairman Mao, educates us with the lofty proletarian and international spirit that it would be a betrayal of the revolution if anyone were to say we should not help the Vietnamese people to counter the United States and save the country."[54]

Simultaneously, however, China adopted a flexible position on the China-U.S. talks. On February 4, 1971, Qiao Guanhua, vice minister of foreign affairs, in a discussion with the Norwegian ambassador to China, said that China was aware of the new trends in U.S. policies and expressed the wish to meet with Kissinger; he pointedly reminded the Norwegian ambassador to ask the United States to pay attention to his words.[55]

The American side responded to China by using the formal name "the People's Republic of China" for the first time. It also relaxed trade restrictions.[56] Soon the "table tennis diplomacy" initiated by Mao Zedong made an international sensation. On April 21, Zhou Enlai sent an invitation through Yahya Khan, the president of Pakistan, reiterating the wish of the Chinese government "to receive openly a special envoy of the American president, such as Dr. Kissinger, the American secretary of state, or even the American president himself, to negotiate with China directly in Beijing."[57] American officials advised Nixon to grasp the opportunity by arranging a reception for both the American table tennis team on its return from China and U.S. Marines returning from Vietnam. They also suggested that Nixon make a public declaration of the proportion of troops already withdrawn from Vietnam to underscore that the United States sought peace in Asia and thus diminish the antiwar sentiment of the American people.[58] Taken together, these initiatives established a connection between U.S.-China relations and the Vietnam War, which suggested to China that the United States expected to solve the Vietnam problem with Chinese help. Later, Nixon expressed an intention to visit China and secretly suggested to China that Kissinger should first visit Beijing for a preliminary meeting. This was a breakthrough in China-U.S. relations.

On May 26, 1971, the Politburo met to discuss the upcoming high-level talks between China and the United States. The Politburo stressed that U.S. armed forces should withdraw from Indochina and addressed the question of the impact of the China-U.S. talks on the war against the United States in Indochina and the Vietnam-U.S. peace talks. It concluded that once Chinese intentions were made clear to the United States, the talks might be favorable both to the war of resistance in Indochina and to the Paris peace talks, since

Nixon would realize that the focus of the contention for hegemony between the United States and the Soviet Union lay in the Middle East and Europe, not in the Far East. Thus, progress in the China-U.S. talks would contribute both to the withdrawal of U.S. troops and to the Paris peace talks.[59]

Soon afterward, Zhou Enlai, in a July 5, 1971, discussion with Gough Whitlam, leader of the Australian Labor Party, said that Beijing proposed to convene a conference in Geneva, with participation by non-Asian countries, to solve the problem of Indochina.[60] This shows that China was trying to promote a solution to the Vietnam War by combining high-level China-U.S. contacts with an international conference. Chinese policy was also reflected in the talks between Zhou Enlai and Kissinger several days later. But China was too optimistic about the role it could play, and it underestimated the resentment its efforts would create in Hanoi.

On July 9, 1971, Kissinger flew to Beijing in secret. His mission was to reiterate to the Chinese the strategic basis for the relaxation of tensions between China and the United States and to discuss the Vietnam War. At the beginning of his talks with Chinese leaders, Kissinger drew the connection between the Chinese wish to solve the Taiwan problem and the U.S. wish to end the Vietnam War. He told the Chinese leadership that the United States was ready to withdraw troops from Taiwan, but that withdrawal was linked to the end of the Indochinese war. He said that the end of the war would accelerate the improvement of Sino-U.S. relations, and the continuation of the war would hinder them.[61] He thus attempted to persuade Beijing to pressure Hanoi to accelerate the peace talks. Mao Zedong, in listening to the report by Zhou Enlai on the night of July 9, responded: "The United States should start over. The United States should withdraw troops from Vietnam. We do not need to hurry about Taiwan. There is no war in Taiwan, but there is in Vietnam: people are dying. If we let Nixon come, it is not to solve the problems between us."[62] In talks the next day, therefore, Zhou Enlai told Kissinger unequivocally that the problem of Taiwan was the only question between China and the United States, that China was in no hurry to resolve the Taiwan issue, and that Vietnam was not an issue for U.S.-China discussions: "Although you are occupying Taiwan, there is no war there. But there is fighting in Vietnam; people are being killed and injured. So if there is no relaxation of tension in Indochina, we must continue to support the people of Indochina, and especially the Vietnamese people."[63]

Zhou Enlai objected to Kissinger's characterization of Sino-U.S. relations as having improved. He said that the United States could try to solve the Vietnam problem, based on goodwill and cooperation, but that if the United States wanted to end the war gracefully, the best way would be to withdraw its troops and leave the solutions to all questions to the people of the three Indochinese countries. This would be the most "glorious" way. "There are only two prospects for the Vietnamese people. Either the United States withdraws all its military forces, or they will continue to fight." Zhou Enlai differed with Kissinger over one of the main issues deadlocking the peace talks: Hanoi insisted that the ouster of the South Vietnamese government was a prerequisite for peace, while Washington insisted that Hanoi's recognition of the South Vietnamese government was a prerequisite for the withdrawal of American troops. Zhou maintained that "the Saigon regime would have fallen long ago if there were no support from you. Why should you leave this loose end, and refuse to let it go?" Kissinger explained that even if no talks were held, the United States would withdraw in the end, but it would take much longer, and that the Nguyen Van Thieu regime, with support from the United States, would be strengthened. Zhou responded that the United States hoped that when it withdrew from Vietnam, "the Vietnamese people will agree to retain the Nguyen Van Thieu regime or will [establish] a united government with his participation, while the rule of Lon Nol and Sirik Matak will continue in Cambodia. However, the people of Vietnam and Cambodia will not accept such an outcome. They will continue to fight."[64]

Although China tried to persuade the United States to stop supporting the Thieu regime, it indicated that it would not interfere in the Vietnam-U.S. talks. For example, when Kissinger proposed to discuss the timing of a ceasefire, a schedule for the withdrawal of troops and closing of military bases, and the withdrawal of Vietnamese troops from Laos and Cambodia, Zhou Enlai interrupted:

"We are not Vietnamese. You should discuss them with the Vietnamese. You should not discuss with us questions that concern their interests. We will not interfere."[65] China even objected to including a sentence suggested by the United States in the U.S.-China joint communiqué on Kissinger's visit to China—"The talks will favorably influence peace in Asia and world"—because it would give North Vietnam the impression that China and the United States were bargaining about Vietnam.[66] The United States finally accepted this position. In the first high-level talks in Beijing between China and the United States, China was clear about its position on Vietnam and pointed out that it had not sent a single soldier to fight on Indochinese battlefields.

At the same time, it put forward three positions on the Taiwan problem: the United States must recognize the PRC as the only legal government of China; it must recognize Taiwan as an inseparable part of China and support neither a "Two Chinas" nor a "one China, one Taiwan" policy nor a "Taiwan independence movement"; it should cease stating that the status of Taiwan was undetermined. Zhou challenged Kissinger: if Nixon could not solve these problems during a visit to China, what would be the point of his visit? These were not preconditions for the president's visit; rather, the visit should establish a clear direction for resolving the Taiwan issue.[67]

Three months later, Kissinger made his second trip to China. In talks from October 20 to October 26, 1971, the two sides reached agreement on the main points of the joint China-U.S. communiqué to be released at the end of Nixon's visit. Although serious differences remained, these discussions stressed the two sides' common positions: they opposed Soviet expansionism, and they committed themselves to normalizing relations.[68] On the Taiwan issue, the United States held that its eventual withdrawal of troops from Taiwan could be included in the communiqué only after the discussion of U.S. withdrawal from Vietnam. For its part, China emphasized its commitment to its principles and held that these were nonnegotiable.[69] It maintained that it would not abandon its revolutionary diplomatic principle of providing assistance to Vietnam, nor would it sacrifice the interests of Vietnam to solve the Taiwan problem. Thus, both sides recognized that U.S. troop withdrawal from Vietnam was a key issue in improving China-U.S. relations, although they had different aims.

A second result of the two rounds of talks was that China realized that the United States would not make concessions on its support for the government of Nguyen Van Thieu; subsequently it focused on persuading Vietnam to concentrate on the withdrawal of U.S. troops. China's aims were to realize the withdrawal of U.S. troops, end the Vietnam war, and open the door to China-U.S. relations. On July 13, Zhou Enlai, reporting to Hanoi on the recent China-U.S. talks, urged Vietnam to "exploit every opportunity to solve the problem of the withdrawal of U.S. troops." He observed to Vietnamese leaders that "it will take time to overthrow the puppet regime in Saigon."[70] Zhou thus sought to persuade Vietnam's leaders not to insist that the United States depose Nguyen Van Thieu as part of the withdrawal of U.S. troops.

A third result of the Kissinger visits was the joint recognition of the two sides' shared interest in opposing Soviet hegemony. As part of this recognition, they agreed to support Pakistan against India in the conflict between those two countries.[71] This was the first concrete instance of joint opposition to the Soviet Union, which at that time backed India. The talks also strengthened China's confidence that it could both aid Vietnam in its resistance against the United States and seek reconciliation with the United States in opposition to the Soviet Union, because Kissinger indicated that the United States did not demand an end to Chinese aid to Vietnam. Kissinger also said that the United States would not use the arms control negotiations with the Soviet Union to forge an anti-Chinese alliance with the Soviets and that Washington was ready to discuss the problem of nuclear weapons with China.[72]

A final result of the visits was that Kissinger came to understand that although China would like to see the Vietnam problem solved, Chinese leaders were concerned about greater cooperation between the Soviet Union and Vietnam.[73] Vietnam's reaction to the China-U.S. negotiations was a major worry for China. To dispel Hanoi's suspicions about Chinese intentions, Zhou Enlai, on the day after Kissinger left Beijing, suggested to Vietnamese leaders that he make a secret visit to Hanoi. There, he met with Le Duan and Pham Van

Dong on July 13 and 14 and briefed them on Kissinger's visit. The Vietnamese leaders reacted strongly to the news that Vietnam would be a chief topic of discussion during Nixon's visit to China. Le Duan later recalled that he immediately insisted that "Vietnam is our country, not yours. You have no right to say anything about it; you have no right to discuss this issue with the United States!"[74] Beijing later learned that the *Nanh Dan* (People's newspaper) in Hanoi had published an editorial alluding to the China-U.S. talks, but that it had said nothing about the communiqué on the forthcoming visit to China by President Nixon.[75] Vietnam's opposition to Chinese policy was reflected in its failure to report Nixon's forthcoming visit to Beijing until late 1971.[76] China, however, could not change its principle simply because Vietnam opposed it. Thus, Mao Zedong rejected Pham Van Dong's request on November 22 that China cancel Nixon's visit to China.[77]

Faced with Vietnam's dissatisfaction and its growing closeness to the Soviet Union, China's leaders increasingly focused on solving the contradiction between pragmatism and revolution in their U.S. policy. Zhou Enlai delivered frequent speeches to foreign journalists to explain China's positions, declaring that all the topics discussed by the United States and China had to do with problems between the two countries, not problems involving any third country. China had not betrayed its principles; this, he said, distinguished China from the Soviet Union, which dared not declare its positions openly and made bargains in secret.[78] In November China warmly welcomed a delegation of Vietnamese Workers Party and government leaders led by Pham Van Dong.[79] The joint communiqué issued by China and Vietnam on November 25 reiterated that China's support for Vietnam and the peoples of the three Indochinese countries in their struggle against the United States was "the set policy of the CCP and the Chinese government and also an international responsibility that the Chinese people will not shirk."[80]

In December 1971, after detecting a significant concentration of North Vietnamese troops, the United States bombed Vietnamese supply bases south of the 20th parallel and sent strongly worded notes to Beijing and Moscow, warning that a North Vietnamese attack would lead to serious U.S. retaliation. The Chinese Foreign

Ministry responded with a declaration of China's firm support for Vietnamese policy, as expressed in the declarations issued by the Vietnamese Foreign Ministry on December 18 and December 28, and emphasized once more the Chinese people's firm support of the national struggle of the people of Vietnam and the other Indochinese countries against the United States.[81] China also decided to increase its military support for Vietnam. These actions made it clear that China would not compromise its principles. In 1971, China signed seven economic and military aid agreements with Vietnam, amounting to RMB 3.614 billion. This was 48.67 percent of the total amount of China's foreign assistance agreements for 1971, a ratio that indicates the priority China placed on assistance to Vietnam.[82]

Ending the Vietnam War, *January 1972–May 1973*

Nixon's visit to China and the publication of the Shanghai Communiqué signified the beginning of reconciliation between the two countries. By May 1973, each had set up a liaison office in the other's capital, creating a path for direct official communications and eliminating the need for secret channels. Each worked to develop stable mutual relations in order to realize its own strategies. But the Vietnam War continued, and the United States still hoped that Beijing could influence Hanoi. During the period from January 1972 to May 1973, China's principles toward Vietnam and the United States evolved through two phases.

In the first phase, from January to May 1972, China opposed the United States' attempt to "play the Soviet card" against it on the problem of Vietnam. Instead, China persisted in its principled stand toward the United States: it held to its stance of noninterference in the Vietnam-U.S. peace talks, refused to help Washington by exerting pressure on Vietnam, and continued to assist Vietnam on a large scale. In early January 1972, Deputy National Security Advisor Alexander Haig arrived in Beijing as head of the advance party for President Nixon's visit. In discussions with Zhou Enlai on January 4, Haig conveyed messages from Nixon and Kissinger. The U.S. government, he informed Zhou, had recently decided to resume air attacks on Vietnamese territory, because even though the United

States had made concessions, Vietnam was still attacking. In the U.S. view, the only explanation for Vietnam's acts was that Hanoi was trying to insult the United States, and no great power could tolerate insults. These messages specifically linked the Vietnam War with the Soviet threat to China: the Vietnam War was providing the Soviet Union with opportunities to strengthen its influence in Hanoi and to implement its goal of surrounding the People's Republic of China. Haig also said that the People's Republic of China must continue to exist and suggested that China needed U.S. help in its conflict with the Soviet Union.

Haig's messages were intended to exert pressure on China to push Vietnam to make concessions in the peace talks. Zhou Enlai's immediate response was that Soviet interference in the South Asian continent and in Indochina was prompted by China's and the United States' approaches to one another. He said that this was no surprise to China; it had prepared for such consequences.[83]

After listening to Zhou Enlai's report on the meeting with Haig, Mao Zedong pointed out that the U.S. intention in playing the Soviet card: "They want us to ask them to save China. How could that be!" "It would be very dangerous," Mao said, "for China to depend on American protection for its independence and existence." He approved a draft set of answers to the U.S. messages and said "All right, I think we may say these things. These Americans, if you do not contradict them, would not be comfortable." Mao Zedong thought that the basic issue was that neither the United States nor China could fight on two fronts at the same time.[84] Resisting the Soviet Union was the common goal of both. China should not ask favors from the United States, nor should it repudiate the responsibility of supporting the peoples of Indochina.

When Zhou held his second meeting with Haig and responded to the American's initial presentation, he observed there were basic differences between China and the United States on the problem of Vietnam.

The United States is bombing Vietnam on a large scale, Vietnam is the victim, and China will certainly support Vietnam. It was not Hanoi that insulted the United States, but the United States that insulted Hanoi. How can it be logical to say it is an 'insult' for a small country to defend itself against the invasion of a great power? Such an attitude by the United States cannot shake the will of Vietnam to fight and win the war. It is an obstacle to the withdrawal of American troops and the release of prisoners of war, and it has an unfavorable influence on the proposed visit to China by the U.S. president.

As for Haig's suggestion that China needed U.S. assistance to maintain its independence and existence, Zhou replied that no country could or should rely for its independence and existence on a foreign force, because to do so would make it a mere protectorate or colony of the other country. He insisted that China would not adjust its foreign strategy at the expense of Vietnam's interests and that Nixon should not come to China with the attitude of a protector. But he also said that China would aim for a successful summit and that if both China and the United States were farsighted, relations would ultimately be normalized.[85]

On January 25, 1972, Nixon made a public speech, urging Vietnam to resume the peace talks. At the same time, the Nixon administration contacted both the Soviet Union and China, stating that the United States had gone as far as it would go in making concessions and that if Vietnam should launch a military attack, the United States would react harshly. Zhou Enlai, through a secret channel, sent a letter to the United States, severely criticizing the U.S. efforts to drag China into the Vietnam issue. He said that China knew nothing about the status of the Vietnam-U.S. peace talks and that China had made no promises to the United States on the Vietnam War.[86]

During Nixon's visit to China in February 1972, when Zhou Enlai and Vice Foreign Minister Qiao Guanhua met with Nixon and Kissinger, they maintained China's position of noninterference in the Vietnam-U.S. talks. Zhou Enlai emphasized that the most pressing problem was Indochina: as long as the war continued, China could only support the countries of Indochina. "We have a responsibility to sympathize with them and support them; we have no right to interfere with them, to make suggestions to them, or to speak for them." Mao Zedong, meeting with Nixon, pointed out that "the problem of a U.S. invasion or a Chinese invasion is a comparatively small one, or we may say it is not an important one, because there is no question of fighting between our two countries. You wish to withdraw some of your troops back to the United States; our troops will not go outside our borders."[87] There was only one enemy for both China and the United States, and that was the Soviet Union. To counter this common enemy, the two countries should seek common ground while reserving their differences.

Although the United States was disappointed at the Chinese refusal to pressure Hanoi or interfere in the talks, the United States would have been satisfied if Beijing adopted a stance of noninvolvement and did not encourage Hanoi to fight to the end. Kissinger observed that although China had urged the United States to withdraw its troops from Vietnam, it did not persist in supporting Hanoi's positions and it did not seriously warn the United States against carrying out its plans to retaliate against North Vietnam by escalating military actions. This restrained response created a mutual understanding that the war would not be an obstacle to improvement in relations.[88] Nixon's February 1972 visit to China and the signing of the Shanghai Communiqué led to clarification of each side's position on the Taiwan issue and on the antihegemony issue, paving the way toward improvement of relations.

In early March, shortly after Nixon left China, Zhou Enlai again visited Hanoi to brief North Vietnamese leaders on U.S.-China relations. Zhou observed that "before we thought the time was not ripe to hold Vietnam-U.S. peace talks, but later Chairman Mao approved." But he also warned that "if the problem of Indochina is not solved, it will be impossible to realize the normalization of China-U.S. relations."[89] Zhou thus suggested Beijing's hope that, after China-U.S. relations improved, there would be better results in the Paris peace talks. At the same time, Beijing tried to reassure Vietnamese leaders by expressing China's position on reconciliation with the United States and China's assistance to Vietnam in its anti-U.S. resistance. But to Hanoi, the mere ending of hostilities between China and the United States meant that while one of two brothers continued to fight the enemy, the other one was shaking his hand. As Le Duan explained to Zhou Enlai: "Now that Nixon has talked with you, they will soon hit us even harder."[90] The rift between China and Vietnam had become more serious.

At the end of March 1972, the Vietnamese army launched an all-out attack on southern Vietnam. The Nixon government retaliated by resuming large-scale bombing over northern Vietnam and mining Haiphong harbor. At the same time, Washington exerted diplomatic pressure on the Soviet Union and China, hoping they could force Hanoi to return to the negotiating table. Faced with pressure from the United States and a deepening rift with Vietnam, China continued to express support for Vietnam and refused to interfere in the peace talks. On April 3, Henry Kissinger, in a secret letter to China, said that the Nixon government had to use military action to promote a peaceful solution of the Vietnam War. He argued that it would not benefit China in the long run if the United States suffered further insults in Indochina. China's Foreign Ministry publicly responded by criticizing the U.S. air raids against northern Vietnam. Then, on April 12, Chinese leaders responded to Kissinger's letter through a secret channel. On one hand, they expressed support for Vietnam and warned that the United States should not continue to be "deeply involved" in the Vietnam issue. On the other hand, they reiterated the Chinese intention to normalize relations with the United States.[91] On the same day, Zhou Enlai received Nguyen Tien, chargé d'affaires *ad interim* of the Vietnamese embassy in China, and reassured him that the Chinese government and people resolutely supported the policies of the Vietnamese government and would spare no effort in supporting the Vietnamese people to continue their war of resistance through to the end.[92]

China also increased its support for Vietnam. On May 13 and 14, Zhou Enlai met with Xuan Thuy, Vietnam's foreign minister and head of its delegation to the Paris peace talks. Zhou promised that China would support Vietnam by repairing railways, opening a secret shipping route, increasing military aid, rushing supplies of food and gasoline, and carrying out minesweeping. At a Mobilization Meeting in Support of Vietnam held on May 18–25 by the State Planning Commission and the Industrial Office of the Central Military Commission, Lieutenant General and Vice Premier Yu Qiuli stressed the urgency of increased production in order to assist Vietnam and provide all-out support for the Vietnamese struggle against the United States: "We must try in every way we can to satisfy their needs." The task of assisting Vietnam was "glorious, important, and long-term," he said. China "should not bargain" with Vietnam but must study this task seriously and make all necessary arrangements.

Between May and August, China and Vietnam met frequently to discuss and solve a series of problems in connection with aid to Vietnam.[93] The Chinese government decided to dispatch support troops to northern Vietnam. Under an agreement reached between the Chinese and Vietnamese general staffs, beginning in May the PLA dispatched motor-transport and minesweeping troops to Vietnam.[94] Both the amount of material shipped to Vietnam and that shipped from northern to southern Vietnam with China's help nearly doubled between 1971 and 1972 (Table 6.1). Le Ban, vice minister of Vietnam's External Trade Department and a representative to China regarding aid issues, said that the "various material [aid] may be said to have satisfied our needs 100 percent." Both the Vietnamese party and the government, he said, "are very happy about this."[95]

The acknowledgment of mutual interests by China and the United States and the importance that both attached to strategic cooperation meant that China's firm political stand on Vietnam, including its military support for Hanoi, no longer presented an obstacle to improved U.S.-China relations. When Nixon received a Chinese table tennis team at the White House on April 18, 1972, he said that although Vietnam had launched an attack and the United States had counterattacked by bombing northern Vietnam, China and the United States would continue to make progress toward the restoration of diplomatic relations.[96]

The second phase of adjustment in China's policy took place from June 1972 to May 1973, as both military action in Vietnam and the peace talks became intense and critical. The May 1972 U.S.-Soviet agreement on limiting strategic weapons aroused Chinese fears that the United States and the Soviet Union were moving closer together, to the detriment of China's strategy toward the United States. The Taiwan issue was key to the normalization of China-U.S. relations, and the prerequisite to its solution was ending the Vietnam war; both Beijing and Washington understood this.

China thought not only that withdrawal of U.S. troops from Vietnam would promote China-U.S. relations and cooperation against the Soviet Union, but also that a peace agreement and U.S. withdrawal from Indochina were first steps toward unification of the north and south by military action. Thus, during this period China's policy toward Vietnam underwent subtle changes, especially concerning the Paris peace talks. China protested the U.S. military action in northern Vietnam and satisfied all material demands from Vietnam, laying the foundation for the later war of unification. At the same time, it tried to persuade Vietnam and the United States to negotiate an end to the war even as it maintained contacts with the United States.

On June 19–23, 1972, during another visit to Beijing, Kissinger concluded that although the United States had not succeeded in obtaining substantial Chinese assistance in solving the Vietnam issue, China had nonetheless become more interested in ending the war.[97] Kissinger was right; although China had not changed its principles, Zhou Enlai had adopted a different attitude when speaking to Vietnam. Before the U.S.-Soviet summit, Zhou Enlai told Hanoi that China would not interfere in the Paris peace talks and would support Vietnam to the end, until the government of Nguyen Van Thieu was overthrown.[98] Later, however, China hinted that Vietnam should return to the talks. On July 6, Zhou Enlai met with Xuan Thuy and Le Ban. He pointed out that whether the war continued or the United States stopped prolonging the negotiations, the coming four months would be critical. Several days later, he met with Le Duc Tho, special advisor to Xuan Thuy, and urged him to talk directly with Nguyen Van Thieu and his representatives. He said that Nguyen Van Thieu represented the rightists, and no one would replace him.[99]

In August, Pham Van Dong took a vacation in Kunming in China's Yunnan province. Zhou Enlai made a special trip to see him, and they exchanged views on the Vietnam-U.S. negotiations. Zhou instructed other Chinese diplomats to convey to Pham Van Dong a suggestion from Mao Zedong:

On the Vietnam-U.S. problem, military and political problems should not be solved separately. It is all right to found a government that unites the left, the middle, and the right. First you should ask the United States to withdraw all its troops and exchange prisoners of war. You might [then] discuss the establishment of a united government directly with Nguyen Van Thieu. It will take time. If talk fails, you might fight again, but I think that U.S. troops will not return. Discussions on a united government are just a way to win some time. After rest and reorganization, you can fight again to reach the final victory.

Zhou also met with Le Duc Tho in Beijing on August 18.[100]

When Vietnam undertook large-scale military action instead of focusing on the peace talks, China re-emphasized the importance of negotiations. Beijing opposed Vietnam's insistence that the United States agree to oust Nguyen Van Thieu as one condition for stopping the war. Mao Zedong further explained the tactical justification for such a suggestion: "send away the demon" and let the troops have a good rest, and then achieve unification without foreign interference.[101]

In late August, Le Duc Tho made a new suggestion for the Paris talks: he proposed for the first time that a united government include both the Provisional Revolutionary Government of South Vietnam and the Nguyen Van Thieu regime. This was the first time that Hanoi had indicated it would accept the "puppet" government in Saigon. Vietnamese leaders explained that once U.S. troops were withdrawn, it would be easy to deal with Nguyen Van Thieu.[102] Vietnam's policy shift demonstrates some Chinese influence on Vietnam.

To accelerate its diplomatic strategy, the United States tried to remove the shadow cast on U.S.-China relations by the U.S.-Soviet summit and continued to ask China for help in solving the Vietnam problem. For its part, China, while seeking to persuade Hanoi to seek an early solution to the war, also continued to exert pressure on the United States.

On August 4, 1972, Kissinger met with Huang Hua, China's ambassador to the United Nations. Kissinger said that the United States would oppose Soviet attempts to gain hegemony in Europe and Asia, responding to China's accusations that the SALT I agreement worked against the antihegemony article in the Shanghai Communiqué and to Chinese concerns that U.S.-Soviet cooperation undermined Chinese security. He emphasized the common interests shared by the United States and China and promised that the United States would not sign an agreement to isolate China.[103]

In October, Kissinger again asked Huang Hua for Chinese help in getting Vietnam to resume the Paris peace talks with a sensible attitude. After the talks resumed on October 25, Huang Hua conveyed to the United States both China's condemnation of Saigon for making trouble and its confidence in Washington's sincerity. China advised the United States to exploit this "most favorable chance to put an end to the Vietnam War." When the United States then delayed signing the cease-fire agreement, because of opposition from Saigon, China asked the United States, in the "most indignant language," to "resolutely check" Saigon's obstructionist behavior. It warned the White House that, should the United States prolong the war and postpone the talks, this would undermine confidence in the U.S. declaration of its intention to relax tensions in the Far East. Nonetheless, the peace talks were postponed again because Hanoi sought to exploit the upcoming presidential elections in the United States to press the United States to make more concessions. On November 13, Kissinger met with Vice Foreign Minister Qiao Guanhua and once again suggested that Beijing persuade Hanoi to make concessions. But Qiao advised that it was the United States that should make the concessions. He said that a great power was capable of adopting a tolerant attitude "and should not risk losing the confidence of the whole world for the sake of South Vietnam."[104]

The differences between Washington and Hanoi could not be resolved for the time being. Nixon, meanwhile, decided to launch a final military attack on Vietnam. During the twelve days beginning on December 18, 1972, the United States carried out air attacks of unprecedented scope on Hanoi, Haiphong Harbor, and throughout North Vietnam. Vietnam could not withstand this heavy attack and agreed to resume talks. China tried to keep the situation from deteriorating, advising Vietnam's representative to the Paris talks to bring them to an early and successful conclusion. On December 29, discussing the peace talks in Paris with Nguyen Thi Binh, foreign minister of the Provisional Revolutionary Government of South Vietnam, Mao Zedong predicted that if the peace talks in Paris were successful, both Vietnams would be able to normalize relations with the United States. One day later, Zhou Enlai persuaded Truong Chinh, president of the standing committee of the Vietnamese congress, to hold serious discussions with the United States, maintaining that Nixon did intend to withdraw from Vietnam. Then, on January 3, 1973, Zhou Enlai suggested to Le Duc Tho that ending the war would not prevent the subsequent unification of Vietnam. He pointed out that "there are many international and domestic problems that Nixon must solve, and so, it seems, he would like to withdraw from Vietnam and Indochina. Six months or a year later, therefore, the situation in Vietnam will have changed."[105]

On January 27, 1973, the Paris Peace Agreement was signed, and the U.S. war in Vietnam came to an end. China and the United States were realizing their strategy of uniting to resist the Soviet Union. In early February, Nixon approved the sale to China of eight inertial navigation systems and four aircraft.[106] This was the beginning of military cooperation between China and the United States. Kissinger visited China for a fifth time on February 15. Mao Zedong proposed that "since China and the United States have the same aims," the two countries could "draw a horizontal line," that is, adopt a strategy based on a horizontal line from the United States through Japan, China, Pakistan, Iran, and Turkey to Europe, to counter the expansion of the Soviet Union.[107] In March, U.S. troops began to withdraw from Vietnam. On May 1, both China and the United States set up liaison offices in each other's capital, a major step toward establishing diplomatic relations.

At the same time, however, relations between China and Vietnam were deteriorating. History, nationality, geopolitics, the overseas Chinese presence in Indochina, and relations between China and the Soviet Union nudged Hanoi closer to the Soviet Union and away from China. The rift became wider, until Vietnam fully embraced the Soviet Union. Because the Soviet Union then increased its assistance to Vietnam, Vietnam threw itself into the Soviet embrace, and as Li Shun had warned, the Soviet Union deployed as many as one million troops in Vietnam to counter China.[108] The Soviet Union filled in the gap left by the withdrawal of U.S. troops from Vietnam. The alliance between the Soviet Union and Vietnam left China in a new and unsafe environment.

Conclusion

As this study indicates, in the late 1960s and early 1970s, against the background of the Vietnam War and the threat from the Soviet Union, shared national security interests provided a basis for easing China-U.S. relations. The U.S. retreat from its Asia-Pacific strategy, the beginning of the peace talks between Vietnam and the United States, and the temporary easing of the Vietnam War provided an environment favorable to contact. China adopted a new diplomatic strategy that, on one hand, pragmatically changed its policy toward the United States, while, on the other hand, maintained its revolutionary commitment to aiding Vietnam in its anti-U.S. resistance. Thus China stood firm in aiding Vietnam and did not adjust its relations with the United States at the expense of principle. It was able to develop its relations with the great power while at the same time remaining steadfast in its relations with the smaller nation.

The Soviet Union was the primary factor: China's strategy of joining with the United States to resist the Soviet Union dominated its foreign policy. But in solving the contradiction between pragmatism and revolution, China had to take the Vietnam problem into consideration as it adjusted its U.S. policy. The Vietnam factor persisted throughout the relaxation process. Although some Vietnamese leaders feared that "the bargain between great powers might be made at the expense of the interests of small nations," and although China, in order to avoid adversely affecting China-U.S. tensions, refrained from using force to eliminate the U.S. military pressure on Vietnam, it nevertheless avoided damaging the interests of its ally, Vietnam.[109] In fact, the period of relaxation between China and the United States, between 1971 and 1973, coincided with the years of China's greatest assistance to Vietnam. Economic and military assistance amounted to RMB 900 billion; military matériel shipped to Vietnam in these three years surpassed the combined total for the previous twenty years.[110] The scale of assistance was enormous (see Table 6.1). The Nixon government indicated that it understood China's support and aid for Hanoi, because of its national security priorities in the face of the threat from the Brezhnev government. The United States attached great importance to the understanding reached with China on opposing the expansion of the Soviet Union. Washington also relied on Moscow in its tactics of pressuring Hanoi's allies to solve the problem of the Vietnam War. Thus, the Vietnam War did not prevent the easing of tensions between China and the United States.

In 1972, by the time the Vietnam War was entering its last phase, Sino-Soviet relations had gradually deteriorated from hostility to political and military confrontation. Correspondingly, the problem of Vietnam was linked even more closely to the strategic interests of both China and the Soviet Union. China supported Vietnam in its unfolding strategic offensive, which sought a decisive victory against the United States in the south. In order not to derail strategic cooperation with the United States to counter the Soviet Union, China pursued two goals in increasing its assistance to Vietnam. One was to compete with the Soviet Union in offering assistance, so as to win Vietnam over. In view of the continuing strains between China and the Soviet Union, the Indochinese area was especially important to Chinese national security; China was extremely sensitive to the development of Vietnamese-Soviet relations and hoped that increasing its assistance to Vietnam would prevent Vietnam from being drawn into the Soviet orbit.[111] The second goal was to help Hanoi to rush more armaments and ammunition to the south before the end of the war brought international observers, in preparation for Vietnam's war for unification.[112]

China's foreign policy in this period was substantially and fundamentally revolutionary. To Chinese communists, Vietnam's nationalist and anti-imperialist struggle against the United States was a banner of anti-imperialism and world revolution. Supporting Vietnam fulfilled the spirit of internationalism and world revolution. Moreover, aiding Vietnam wholeheartedly was also a strong counterattack against the betrayals of Soviet revisionism. In the process of improving relations with the United States, China consistently advanced the idea that the substance of imperialism would never change: even though Nixon and his advisors had altered their policy toward China, their attitude toward China remained the same. The

United States wanted to maintain as much as possible of its vested interests and to keep its position of hegemony despite domestic and foreign predicaments. The fundamental principles of Chinese foreign policy were still the avoidance of world war and the promotion of world revolution. But under the new circumstances, Mao Zedong began to emphasize both a highly revolutionary principle and a pragmatic spirit. The purpose of the union of pragmatism and revolution was to exploit contradictions and promote the welfare of the people. The way to conduct world revolution was to exploit contradictions, divide the enemy, make China stronger, and promote revolution.[113] Hence, an important component of Chinese diplomatic strategy was to support Vietnam against the United States and to help Vietnam win its struggle for national unification. Thus, China adhered consistently to the principle of aiding Vietnam. After the end of the Vietnam War, China continued its support and aid to Vietnam to accomplish its unification.[114] China did not agree to the grand plan suggested in June 1973 by Vietnam, asking for RMB 800 billion in aid for 1974, but the total amount of support rendered by China still reached RMB 230 billion, including U.S.$130 million in cash.[115] In spring 1975, southern Vietnam was liberated. Following its victory in the nationalist war of resistance against the United States, Vietnam successfully concluded the war of national unification.

This study of China's policy to deal with its two forms of triangular diplomacy—toward the United States and the Soviet Union, and toward the Soviet Union and Vietnam—from the viewpoint of the international history of the cold war suggests several conclusions.

First, the general focus of Chinese foreign policy changed from revolutionary to pragmatic. China succeeded in realizing its basic goal of improving Sino-U.S. relations, a development that held out the prospect of joining with the United States to counter the Soviet Union, but it was not able to maintain friendly relations with Vietnam and faced a new challenge from a Soviet-Vietnamese alliance.

Second, although the great powers were the main actors in the cold war, small and weak nations also played important roles. When two balls in motion strike one another, the trajectory of the smaller one can cause a significant change in the trajectory of the larger. Sometimes this change can even be decisive. Because of its position in the strategic considerations of the great powers, Vietnam could not be ignored. As the war ended and a new balance of power formed, the independent role of one small nation, Vietnam, became all the more prominent. In the early 1970s, after China began to work with the United States to counter the Soviet Union, Vietnam formed an alliance with the Soviet Union to offset China and the United States.

Third, in the framework of the cold war in Asia, the two alliances or groups headed by the United States and the Soviet Union participated in the conflict. Each emphasized the common interests of its alliance or group. When the interests of the dominant nation conflicted with the interests of the smaller nation, the larger nation usually asked the smaller one to sacrifice its interests for the sake of the common interests of the whole alliance. Hence, differences and contradictions arose. When the smaller, weaker nations no longer acknowledged the interests of the alliance, the principle that the part should be subordinate to the whole no longer held; the result was a split in the alliance. In the socialist group, this process appeared in the relations between China and the Soviet Union, as well as in those between China and Vietnam.

Fourth, just as Chinese diplomatic strategy began to adjust, the cold war in Asia and the rest of the world was beginning to change subtly. In the 1950s, China had made an alliance with the Soviet Union to counter the United States, with China standing on the front lines to fight, face to face, with the United States. In the 1960s, the breakup of the Sino-Soviet alliance led to the collapse of the socialist camp. In the early 1970s, China no longer participated, as a practical matter, in the confrontation between the two camps. The union between China and the United States to oppose the Soviet Union and the U.S. and Soviet positions on the front lines of the cold war caused the international situation to change again.

SEVEN

Taiwan's Policy Toward the United States, 1969–1978

JAW-LING JOANNE CHANG

The Republic of China's relations with the United States in the 1970s were full of setbacks, doubts, and challenges. In 1971, the ROC withdrew from the United Nations. The following year, President Richard Nixon visited Beijing and concluded his eight-day visit to China by signing the Shanghai Communiqué. In February 1973, the United States and the People's Republic of China agreed to establish liaison offices in each other's capital. Although President Nixon won the presidential election by a landslide in 1972, he resigned in 1974 because of the Watergate scandal. Nixon had opened up the China door because he wanted to balance Soviet influences, and he hoped Beijing could help end the Vietnam War. However, South Vietnam fell in 1975, and U.S. troops hastily withdrew.

Chiang Kai-shek, the president of the ROC, died in 1975, followed in 1976 by Zhou Enlai and Mao Zedong. In 1976, President Gerald Ford lost the presidential election to Jimmy Carter. On December 15, 1978, the Carter administration announced its decision to establish diplomatic relations with the PRC. On January 1, 1979, the two countries established official diplomatic relations, and the United States broke off diplomatic relations with its longtime ally— the ROC.

Faced with this series of setbacks and challenges, how did the ROC government react? What are the features of Taipei's dealings

with Washington? This chapter analyzes relations between the
United States and Taiwan from 1969 to 1978, focusing especially on
the termination of the Taiwan Strait patrol in 1969; Taipei's policy
toward dual representation in the United Nations in 1971; and the
normalization of relations between Washington and Beijing. The
principal sources for this paper are memoirs of key decision-
makers,[1] declassified official documents from President Nixon's
tenure in office, declassified official documents of the State Department in the U.S. National Archives, and Archives of the ROC
Ministry of Foreign Affairs.

President Chiang's
Personal Diplomacy, 1969–1970

In 1968, Richard Nixon was elected president of the United States.
Nixon was an old friend of President Chiang Kai-shek of more than
twenty years' standing. When Taipei's relations with Washington
began to change and become uncertain, President Chiang, an experienced leader and negotiator, naturally tried to communicate
with President Nixon directly.

During the six months from November 1969 to May 1970,
Presidents Chiang and Nixon exchanged at least ten letters, the most
important of which were four letters on the termination of regular
U.S. patrols in the Taiwan Strait, and one from President Chiang to
Nixon expressing Taipei's dismay at the resumption of the Warsaw
talks between the United States and Communist China.[2] In July
1971, Henry Kissinger, Nixon's national security advisor, visited
China secretly. Subsequently, the U.S. government made important
changes in its policies toward the PRC, and the number of letters
between Presidents Chiang and Nixon decreased drastically.[3] Since
Nixon was determined to open the China door, Chiang was left to
decide on his own how to deal with the new situation.

On February 3, 1969, only two weeks after Nixon took office,
Kissinger was asked to review U.S. policies toward China, including
alternative approaches to China and their costs and risks.[4] On June
26 of the same year, Nixon decided to modify certain controls on
trade with the PRC and asked the concerned departments to suggest
specific ways of implementation.[5]

On July 21, 1969, the State Department announced new regulations permitting American tourists to purchase limited quantities of goods originating in the PRC and authorizing Americans in six professions to travel to the PRC.[6] On December 29 of that year, the State Department announced changes in the Foreign Assets Control regulations permitting American tourists to make unlimited purchases of PRC goods and relaxing limits on trade in nonstrategic goods by U.S.-owned firms operating abroad.[7]

This series of measures had attracted Taipei's attention, but the real warning was Nixon's decision to discontinue the U.S. 7th Fleet's patrol of the Taiwan Strait.[8] In September 1969, on the pretext that defense budget had been cut, Nixon decided to reduce U.S. naval forces stationed abroad, including the patrol in the Taiwan Strait. Since 1955, two destroyers had conducted the patrol, one stationed in port while the other patrolled the strait.[9]

On November 7, 1969, the Nixon administration notified the ROC that beginning on November 15, the U.S. Navy planned to discontinue its regular patrol of the Taiwan Strait. The Nixon administration believed that this decision did not change the U.S. commitment to defend Taiwan, and that even though Beijing would notice the change, it was unlikely to undertake military provocations. Moreover, Secretary of State William P. Rogers told Chow Shu-kai, the ROC ambassador to the United States, that Washington would not initiate the release of news about this modification. However, Taipei believed that the abrupt withdrawal of the two destroyers would adversely affect Taiwan's security and, accordingly, it wanted to consult with Washington on this issue.[10]

On November 14, after a week of consultation had brought no change, Chiang Kai-shek telegraphed Nixon requesting a delay in implementation of the decision to allow both sides adequate time to exchange views and work out a mutually satisfactory solution. Chiang pointed out that this step was bound to have a serious impact on security in the Taiwan area.[11]

In response to President Chiang's message, U.S. Secretary of Defense Melvin Laird directed that the two ships assigned to continuous patrol in the strait area remain until November 20 to permit time to review the situation. On November 15, 1969, Deputy Secretary of Defense David Packard, accompanied by the commander in chief of the Pacific, Admiral John S. McCain, Jr., called on Chiang to explain the U.S. decision. McCain stated that there was no change in the policy, and that some fifteen U.S. ships would transit the Taiwan Strait monthly for patrol duty. McCain thus assured Chiang that the 7th Fleet would continue to maintain an effective patrol of the Taiwan Strait. Packard pointed out that the deactivation of older U.S. ships was intended to improve the Navy's strength.[12]

Packard reported that Chiang indicated the modified plan was satisfactory to him. Later the U.S. embassy in Taipei sent a telegram saying the ROC government was prepared to "acquiesce" to the modification of the Taiwan Strait patrol. On November 16, 1969, the Nixon administration officially issued orders to proceed immediately with the modification of the patrol as planned.[13]

Nixon hoped to improve relations gradually with the PRC. Relaxing trade restrictions toward the mainland was one element in this program; terminating regular patrols of the Taiwan Strait was another sign of goodwill and was meant to convey an important symbolic message. Henry Kissinger, in his secret talks with Zhou Enlai on July 9, 1971, pointed out that the United States had taken several steps to show its intentions, including the termination of patrols in the Strait and the reduction in the number of U.S. military advisors in Taiwan by 20 percent.[14] When President Nixon met Premier Zhou Enlai in Beijing on February 24, 1972, he told Zhou that there had been opposition in the U.S. bureaucracy to his decisions, but that he had made them anyway.[15] Zhou Enlai replied that Beijing considered the cessation of the continuous Taiwan Strait patrol as one of the first signs of goodwill from the Nixon administration.[16]

Washington's claim that budgetary cutbacks were behind the decision to discontinue the regular patrols did not, however, convince Taipei.[17] Since Chiang Kai-shek was unable to change Nixon's decision, he asked Washington to strengthen Taiwan's military capabilities. On November 19, 1969, President Chiang sent another personal letter to President Nixon, pointing out the disparity between Taiwan's armed forces and those of the PRC. Moreover, he hoped that the United States would strengthen the defensive abilities of the ROC's air and naval forces by providing F-4 aircraft and submarines. For the sake of preventing new hostilities in the Taiwan Strait, Chiang also proposed that Taipei and Washington immediately review the "Rochester Plan," which was designed to implement the Sino-American Mutual Defense Treaty of 1955.[18]

In fact, Taipei had asked for the F-4 aircraft as early as August 1968, but the U.S. Departments of Defense and State had not approved the request, on military and economic grounds. Instead, the United States sold 34 F-100 and 22 F-104 aircraft to Taiwan to strengthen Taiwan's air force.[19] When Secretary of State Rogers visited Taiwan on August 15, 1969, Chiang raised the question of the F-4 aircraft and expressed the hope that President Nixon would consider Taipei's request.[20]

On December 2, 1969, National Security Council staff member John H. Holdridge, in a memorandum to Kissinger, pointed out that the United States did not "owe" President Chiang anything because it had terminated the patrol in the Taiwan Strait. In addition, the model of F-4s Chiang had requested was no longer in production, and the cost would be some $90 million instead of $54.5 million.[21]

On December 15, 1969, Nixon wrote a tactful letter to Chiang but did not directly answer the question of F-4s. As far as he knew, wrote Nixon, the American Defense Command in Taiwan "is presently in contact with your Defense authorities with proposals for the continuing upgrading of the equipment of the Chinese Air Force."[22] Ten days later, the White House announced that the United States was opposed to providing a squadron of F-4s to the Republic of China. The State Department also publicly confirmed the modification of the patrol in the Taiwan Strait on December 25, 1969.[23]

To Chiang, who had a long military career, Nixon's decision to terminate the regular patrol in the Taiwan Strait was, doubtless, a significant turning point. As a document in the State Department pointed out, Taipei had gradually lost its confidence in U.S. intentions toward Beijing.[24]

In December 1969, U.S. Vice President Spiro Agnew visited Taiwan, and Vice Premier Chiang Ching-kuo paid a visit to the United States in April 1970. Although these top-level visits played a positive role in stabilizing relations between the two sides, it did not change Nixon's general orientation of gradually normalizing relations with the PRC.

On February 20, 1970, the United States and the PRC held the 136th ambassadorial talks in Warsaw. Chiang was shocked to learn that the United States had in this meeting announced that it would consider accepting the so-called Five Principles of Peaceful Coexistence and would discuss with the PRC how to settle the Taiwan problem. On March 1, 1970, Chiang wrote another letter to Nixon expressing his concerns and his hope that Washington would "weigh the past so as to be on guard in the future."[25]

Originally, the United States had scheduled the 137th ambassadorial talks for May 20, 1970, but because of a new wave of U.S. military action in Cambodia, Beijing called off the meeting. Later, Nixon decided to communicate with leaders in Beijing through secret channels. Taipei knew nothing of these secret channels and accordingly could make no objection. Although Chiang Kai-shek maintained close, high-level contacts with Washington for the first year after Nixon took office, the role of personal diplomacy was limited because the United States had made fundamental changes in its strategic thinking toward the PRC.

The Dual Representation Issue, 1971

During President Chiang Kai-shek's term of office, the ROC adopted the policy of "no compromise between the Han and the rebels." However, in the 1970s when the international situation deteriorated for the ROC, policymakers in Taipei, facing a new reality, adjusted their tactics and gradually adopted a more pragmatic and flexible response to the situation. One example was Taipei's handling of the Chinese representation issue in the United Nations in 1971.

The Soviet Union raised the issue of Chinese representation in the UN Security Council in January 1950. The Soviet Union did not recognize the legitimacy of the ROC, but Moscow's proposal that the PRC assume the Chinese seat failed with three votes for, six votes against, and two votes abstaining.[26] On June 25, 1950, the Korean War began and the United States dispatched the 7th Fleet to the Taiwan Strait. The Truman administration's policy toward Taiwan shifted from a wait-and-see attitude to a proactive favoring of Taiwan. In October 1950, the PRC intervened in the war against South Korea and the United States. This intervention strengthened U.S. support of the ROC. The Soviet Union and India made separate proposals during the Fifth UN General Assembly meeting in 1950 that the PRC represent China in the UN General Assembly. Neither proposal was accepted.

During the 1950s and 1960s, Taipei responded to proposals concerning the Chinese representation issue by asking friendly states to propose a postponement of all considerations of Chinese representation in the United Nations. At the Sixth UN General Assembly meeting, Thailand raised the postponement proposal on behalf of Taipei. At subsequent UN General Assembly meetings, the postponement proposals were introduced by the United States and passed by a majority of votes.[27]

In 1950, the United Nations had only 59 member-states, but by 1961, the number of members had increased to 104. Most member-states had become impatient with the longstanding practice of postponing consideration of the representation issue. Taipei and Washington then proposed that any resolution to change the status quo of Chinese representation be declared an important one that could be passed only by a two-thirds majority. In 1961, the UN General Assembly passed the Taipei/Washington resolution with 61 votes for, 34 votes against, and seven abstentions. The Soviet Union attempted to pass a resolution that the PRC should take the Chinese seat, but it, too, was defeated in the General Assembly.[28]

From 1965 to 1970, all efforts in Beijing's favor failed in the UN General Assembly. On November 20, 1970, however, the annual Albanian resolution to expel the ROC and accept the PRC gained more than half the votes: 51 for, 49 against, and 25 abstentions.[29] This gave Taipei and Washington notice that they would have to consider new ways to respond to the issue of Chinese representation.

NIXON'S STRATEGIC CONSIDERATION

For Nixon, the issue of Chinese representation was linked to his global strategy. Since Nixon intended to open relations with China gradually, he had to reconsider the U.S. stand on the issue of Chinese representation in the United Nations. On November 19, 1970, a day before the General Assembly vote on Chinese representation, Nixon asked the State Department to review the issue of membership in the UN, including the question of Chinese representation, the mutual effects of bilateral relations between the United States and the PRC, and the impact of the principle of universal membership.[30] Over several months of study, the "dual representation" and "reverse important question" policies gradually took shape.

In a March 20, 1971, memorandum, Henry Kissinger pointed out to Nixon that the tactic of designating the issue of Chinese representation an important question would fail, because the resolution would be blocked if only eight states changed their votes. If the United States persisted in pushing the proposal, Taipei would be driven out of the United Nations and replaced by Beijing in 1971 or, at the latest, 1972. Kissinger suggested the principle of universal membership as an alternative, which would allow both Taipei and Beijing to have UN representatives. Kissinger had reservations about the "dual representation" formula proposed by the State Department. Kissinger pointed out that the then-divided countries of Germany, Korea, and Vietnam might also request membership under the universality principle and that the United States would likely use its Security Council veto to deny their requests on the pretext that these were questions of new membership. In contrast, since the China question was a matter of representation and not of membership, the United States could not exercise its veto powers.[31]

In addition, the old important question tactic might face trouble. The ability of the United States to win the support of two-thirds of the member-states for "dual representation" was in doubt, and Kissinger suggested that the United States might solve the problem by proposing that whereas the support of at least half the member-states would be enough to admit Beijing, that of at least two-thirds of the member-states would be necessary to expel ROC's representation.

At the same time, Kissinger suggested that the United States not continue to guarantee Taipei its seat in the Security Council.[32]

As Washington was discussing new formulas for Chinese representation, the United States, through the channel of President Yahya Khan of Pakistan, contacted leaders in Beijing on the subject of a visit to China by Nixon. On May 31, 1971, the White House received a message from President Khan that Beijing had responded positively to the U.S. request. Kissinger would be invited to visit, and Pakistan would make the travel arrangements.[33] On June 2, the White House received an official letter from Zhou Enlai. President Nixon, now being sure of the invitation, announced at a press conference on June 1 that it might take six weeks to decide the U.S. stand in the next General Assembly of the UN on the Chinese representation issue.[34] Nixon apparently wished to make a final decision in mid-July, after Kissinger had returned from his visit to the PRC.

From July 9 to 11, Henry Kissinger secretly visited Mainland China and stated the U.S. stand on Chinese representation to Zhou Enlai: admittance of the PRC would require only a simple majority, but the expulsion of Taiwan would require a two-thirds. In addition, the Chinese seat on the Security Council would be given to the PRC, and once Beijing won the two-thirds ballot to expel Taiwan from the United Nations, it would be the only Chinese representative.[35] Zhou Enlai explained that China was in no hurry to join the UN—it had waited for 21 years, and it could wait longer. Although China was of the opinion that its legal status should be restored, the U.S. stance meant two Chinas, and China, Zhou Enlai pointed out, was opposed to such a suggestion. Kissinger explained that the United States did not expect Chinese agreement; his suggestion was merely "one China and one Taiwan for the time being." Zhou Enlai expressed his understanding that this was to be a temporary phenomenon; on one hand, the United States recognized Taiwan, but on the other hand, as of July 9, 1971, with Kissinger's arrival in Beijing, the phenomenon of one China and one Taiwan had already begun.[36]

On July 15, 1971, President Nixon announced that he had accepted an invitation from Zhou Enlai and would visit China before May 1972. Twenty minutes before Nixon's announcement, James

C. H. Shen, the Republic of China's ambassador to the United States, received this shocking information in a phone call from Secretary of State William Rogers.[37] Shen met with Kissinger on July 27, 1971, and Kissinger told him that he had not discussed the issue of UN representation at any length with Zhou Enlai, nor had he touched on the ROC's permanent seat on the Security Council. It was, however, Kissinger's impression that the Chinese would insist on Taiwan's expulsion before they would agree to enter the United Nations.[38] In fact, Kissinger had reached a tacit understanding with Zhou Enlai on these issues.

THE EVOLUTION OF
TAIPEI'S UN POLICY

In 1970, the Albanian proposal gained a simple majority of two votes. Among the 25 states abstaining from voting, with one state absent, 16 had diplomatic relations with the ROC. Moreover, two states with diplomatic relations with the ROC voted for the Albanian proposal.[39] Strengthening relations with the states with which it had diplomatic relations became a focus of ROC diplomacy. In April 1971, Chow Shu-kai, the ambassador to the United States, replaced Wei Tao-ming as ROC foreign minister. This may have been regarded as a means of strengthening Taipei's foreign relations, especially its relations with the United States.

The ROC Ministry of Foreign Affairs, in addition to conducting an overall review of how to strengthen its diplomatic relations and its relations with the United States, began to explore whether the Nixon administration would keep its promise to exercise its veto to prevent the PRC from joining the United Nations.

THE PROMISED VETO

On October 16, 1961, President Kennedy privately assured President Chiang Kai-shek that if at any time a U.S. veto was necessary to prevent the PRC from entering the United Nations, the United States would use that veto.[40] Kennedy gave this oral assurance privately, because of the unfavorable impact that public disclosure would have on the United States' position at the United Nations.

Kennedy also explained that any public revelation of this promise would force the United States to issue a denial. The State Department thought Kennedy's aim in making this assurance was to persuade President Chiang not to veto the admission of Outer Mongolia to the United Nations.[41] On April 16, 1964, Secretary of State Dean Rusk, on behalf of the Johnson administration, affirmed this promise during a conversation with Chiang. Rusk pointed out that the policy of the Johnson administration was the same as that of the Kennedy administration.[42]

In the 1960s, the votes concerning Chinese representation had been quite stable, although in 1964, the vote on the Albanian proposal to expel the ROC and to admit the PRC was 47–47. Therefore, the veto had never been necessary. In 1970, when a majority voted for the Albanian resolution, Taipei grew concerned whether the Nixon administration would use the veto, if necessary.

On January 12, 1971, Liu Chieh, the ROC's ambassador to the UN, asked Christopher H. Phillips, the deputy U.S. representative to the UN, whether the U.S. commitment to exercise the veto was still operative. Phillips answered he had never heard of this commitment and was unable to answer the question, but that he would look into it.[43]

On January 22, 1971, Thomas P. Shoesmith, the chief of the Office of the Republic of China Affairs of the State Department, in a brief memorandum, pointed out that the Nixon administration had not reconfirmed this guarantee. In preparing for Secretary of State Rogers's visit to Taiwan in August 1969, the State Department had planned that the United States would avoid reaffirmation of the promise, if the issue came up. Shoesmith believed that the wording of the assurance committed Washington to oppose the entry of the PRC. This would be incompatible with the evolving China policy and would foreclose the option of supporting dual representation. In addition, Shoesmith pointed out that the promise had a built-in escape clause—since there were circumstances in which the veto either would not be available or effective, it was not in U.S. interests to affirm it. Shoesmith suggested that State Department officials take the position that the question would have to be referred to a higher authority for a decision.[44]

On July 10, 1971, ROC Foreign Minister Chow Shu-kai told U.S. Ambassador Walter P. McConaughy in Taipei that the ROC government would consider the vote on the question of the Chinese seat in the Security Council a substantive issue. Chow said the ROC government considered "the exchanges with the Kennedy Administration" as still binding. McConaughy merely responded that he would report Taipei's position.[45]

The U.S. avoidance of responding to Taipei's frequent requests about its veto created some doubt among policymakers in Taipei. However, it was only when Kissinger decided to pay another visit to the PRC, as the UN General Assembly was debating the Chinese representation issue, that Taipei concluded that the situation was taking a decided turn for the worse, prompting it again to inquire about the U.S. exercise of its veto. On October 14, 1971, Foreign Minister Chow met with Secretary of State Rogers to discuss a fallback position should the U.S. proposal fail. Foreign Minister Chow asked whether, if the important question resolution failed and the Albanian resolution passed, the United States would invoke Article 6 of the UN Charter (requiring a two-thirds vote to expel a member-state) to take the issue to the Security Council, where the United States could veto it.

Assistant Secretary Samuel De Palma, who was accompanying Secretary of State Rogers, pointed out that the Albanian resolution referred to exclusion of a representative, rather than expulsion of a member-state. In any event, De Palma believed that the most important question was where to find the votes.[46] Rogers said a U.S. veto could be appealed on the grounds that this was a procedural matter, and the veto would probably be overturned. Rogers added that the United States still expected to win on the important question resolution.

The Department of State thus had no fallback position. At the request of Minister Chow, the State Department on October 21 suggested two basic contingencies: the citing, in the Security Council, of Article 18(a) and Article 6 of the Charter to prevent the Republic of China from being expelled. But, the State Department concluded, if the United States could not muster a simple majority for the important question resolution, neither could it muster majority support for the contingency plan.[47]

Taipei nevertheless again raised the possibility of exercising the veto. However, when President Nixon decided to normalize U.S. relations with the PRC, "dual representation" became at best a temporary arrangement. It was apparent that the United States would not exercise its veto, in order not to jeopardize President Nixon's visit to the PRC, which shocked the world.

THE DUAL REPRESENTATION FORMULA

In 1969, the important question resolution passed 71 to 48, with four abstentions. The Albanian resolution was defeated 48 to 56, with 21 abstentions. Although the State Department favored maintaining the U.S. opposition to Beijing's admission in 1970, Secretary of State Rogers began to consider alternative formulas to handle the representation issue. On June 19, 1970, Rogers sent a memorandum to Nixon, analyzing the possible need to shift tactics, perhaps toward some formula for "dual representation." But Rogers made no specific recommendation; nor did he ask the president to make a decision.[48] On October 25, 1971, Ronald Ziegler, the White House spokesman, stated that the United States opposed the PRC's admission to the United Nations at the ROC's expense. This implied that the United States objected to the expulsion of Taiwan, but not to the admission of the PRC. Kissinger announced that the United States had made a significant shift on the question of Chinese representation.[49]

On November 20, 1971, the important question resolution passed by a vote of 66 to 52, with 7 abstentions, but the Albanian resolution received 51 votes for, 49 against, with 25 abstentions. For the first time, the Albanian resolution had won a simple majority. Although it was still far from a two-thirds majority, the State Department felt that an alternative formula should be considered in order to avoid eventual defeat.

In his memoirs, Kissinger stressed that from the beginning he had been doubtful of the dual representation formula. At a discussion on March 9, 1971, Kissinger stressed that although both Taipei and

Beijing were against dual representation, he thought that Chinese representation was the only piece of action concerning China under State Department control; since the dual representation formula could please both conservative and liberal constituencies in the United States, he did not insist on his view.[50]

On March 25, 1971, the National Security Council held a meeting to discuss the dual representation formula. Both Vice President Spiro Agnew and Secretary of the Treasury John Connally argued that it was better for the United States to maintain a straightforward position and be defeated on it. The existing position of blocking the PRC might fail in the end, but it was at least principled and it avoided legal evasions. Nixon also agreed with this view, but he chose to delay making a decision until the United States had made a breakthrough with the PRC.[51]

In January, April, and June 1971, President Nixon prevented Secretary of State Rogers from making speeches regarding dual representation, on three occasions.[52] At the time, since the State Department did not know of the existence of the secret channel to Beijing, it could not comprehend the impact of the dual representation formula on the sensitive relations between the two sides.

On July 8, 1971, Rogers was informed of Kissinger's trip to Beijing only hours before his departure.[53] After Kissinger had ascertained that Beijing did not consider the UN membership issue central to U.S.-PRC relations, Nixon approved the dual representation formula suggested by the State Department.[54] Rogers then publicly announced on August 2, 1971, that the United States supported the seating of the PRC in the United Nations but would oppose any action to expel the Republic of China.[55] At the time, Taipei had no knowledge of the bureaucratic politics between the White House and the State Department on the issue of Chinese representation, nor of the tacit understanding Kissinger had reached with Beijing.

On March 9, 1971, the State Department, still in the dark about the secret channels between Beijing and Washington, sent Winthrop G. Brown, deputy assistant secretary for East Asian and Pacific Affairs, to Taipei to exchange views on the dual representation formula. According to Vice Foreign Minister Hsi-kun Yang, the Republic of China urgently hoped that the United States would continue to support the important question resolution. As for the dual representation formula, it would effectively maintain the ROC's current status in the United Nations. No doubt, the United States had good intentions, but the ROC was strongly against any "two China" formula. If it were only a tactic, however, to ensure passage of the important question resolution again, and if it could be used to defeat the Albanian resolution, then the ROC would consider the new formula and would like to exchange frank views with the United States.[56]

Ambassador Brown, after returning to the United States, wrote that Vice Minister Yang had strongly urged that President Nixon send a very high level representative, specifically Vice President Agnew, to Taipei to persuade President Chiang to acquiesce to a dual representation formula in the United Nations. But Brown thought that it was just "plain undignified for the United States to send a representative of such a stature" to Taipei. The vice president might be seen as "either an arm-twister, a purchaser, or a suppliant, all postures undesirable from the viewpoint of both governments."[57] Nixon instead decided to send Robert D. Murphy, a former diplomat, as his personal representative to Taipei to see President Chiang.

On April 23, 1971, Murphy talked with Chiang Kai-shek for 90 minutes, along with newly appointed Foreign Minister Chow Shu-kai and James C. H. Shen, ambassador-designate to the United States. Murphy's trip was kept top secret. Nixon had asked Murphy to meet in complete privacy with Chiang Kai-shek, and U.S. Ambassador McConaughy did not attend the meeting.[58]

According to Murphy, Chiang did not really like the dual representation formula, but he did not resist it. Chiang hoped the United States would not be an official sponsor of the new resolution. President Chiang was most concerned about Taipei's seat as China's permanent representative to the Security Council. Murphy stated that the United States had no intention of making it possible for Beijing to get the Security Council seat.[59] Murphy reassured Chiang that any new formula would not involve the ROC's seat on the Security Council. Washington would not permit its proposal to be amended to bring in the question of the Security Council seat.

Chiang warned that "should the ROC one day leave the UN, the world would know that she has been forced out not by the Communists, but by the United States."[60]

Kissinger believed that Murphy had gone beyond his instructions. Murphy, according to Kissinger, had made three mistakes. First, Murphy should not have promised that Taipei would keep the Security Council seat. Second, Murphy failed to present the modified important question resolution (limited to Taipei's expulsion) as a principal element of U.S. thinking. Murphy presented only the existing important question resolution, for keeping Beijing out of the United Nations. Finally, Murphy told Chiang the United States would insist that the new resolution be accepted in toto and not be amended, a stance that would deprive Washington of tactical flexibility.

Taipei was prepared to consider a dual representation strategy, but Chiang said his government would find it impossible to remain in the United Nations if the ROC lost China's seat on the Security Council. Furthermore, he took the position that the important question tactic should remain the principal instrument for keeping the PRC out.[61]

Kissinger felt the United States could not guarantee Taipei's Security Council seat under a dual representation formula. The State Department did not think the United States could effectively exercise a veto in the Security Council, because Chinese representation was likely to be considered as a procedural question—a non-veto matter—by the Council. Besides, the State Department thought there would not be enough votes in the Security Council to prevent Taipei's expulsion. Of the fifteen members of the Security Council, eight recognized the PRC, and six recognized the ROC. Although Belgium had diplomatic relations with Taipei, it had taken a position that the PRC should have the Security Council seat. In addition, the government of Sierra Leone, another friend of Taipei, had also shifted markedly.[62]

As a matter of fact, the U.S. National Security Council had developed a contingency plan concerning the Security Council seat as early as March 1971. In a secret memorandum for Kissinger, National Security Council staff member Marshall Wright predicted that Taipei might offer to accept dual representation on the condition that the United States guarantee its Security Council seat. Wright suggested to Kissinger that should that contingency arise, the United States should use it to put added pressure on Taipei to accept dual representation. Washington should tell Taipei the chances of retaining the Security Council seat were totally dependent on Taipei's continued full participation in the United Nations. If Taipei accepted the dual representation formula and if Beijing refused, then, technically, Taipei and Washington might work together to retain Taipei's seat on the Security Council for the indefinite future. Wright pointed out that the United States should make no further commitment to Taipei, because once the PRC claimed the seat in the Security Council, there would almost literally be no international support for ROC retention of China's Security Council seat.[63]

In the eyes of the White House, Murphy's trip to Taipei was a failure. Kissinger recommended sending another emissary or asking Ambassador McConaughy in Taipei to see Chiang again and tell him that the United States could not guarantee Taipei's Security Council seat. If Chiang maintained his position on this question, then the United States would be prepared to pursue the old policy of seeking to exclude the PRC, with the full realization that it would be defeated in 1971 or 1972. Or the United States could also discuss the problem with newly arrived Ambassador James Shen, who had participated in the Murphy talks.[64]

At the time, however, communication through the secret channel between Washington and Beijing was very sensitive, and President Nixon had no intention of making a decision on Chinese representation; accordingly he did not send another special envoy to Taipei to rescind Ambassador Murphy's promise to President Chiang.

The State Department, on the other hand, had continued discussions with Taipei on the question of Chinese representation in the spring of 1971. After several months of consultations, in early July 1971, Taipei gradually reached a tacit agreement with Washington on the formula of dual representation and the modified important question issue. But Taipei still insisted the ROC's seat in the United Nations and its seat on the Security Council were "inseparable and indivisible."[65] Furthermore, Taipei wished the United States not to mention the Security Council seat in the resolution. The gap between the U.S. State Department and the ROC Foreign Affairs Ministry on the question of Chinese representation gradually narrowed.

But Nixon's announcement that he would visit mainland China posed a new problem for the question of Chinese representation. Kissinger had told Zhou Enlai in Beijing that the United States might support an arrangement under which the admission of the PRC would be settled by a majority vote, but the expulsion of Taiwan would require a two-thirds vote, with the Security Council seat going to the PRC.[66] Under such circumstances, the promise made by Ambassador Murphy to Taipei, of course, could not be realized. On July 18, 1971, Marshall Green, assistant secretary of State for East Asian and Pacific Affairs, and Assistant Secretary of State De Palma, in a memorandum to Secretary of State Rogers, pointed out that the new U.S. policy toward Beijing would undoubtedly reduce the already slim chances of both the dual representation and the important question formulas.[67]

Faced with this new situation, many policymakers in Taipei believed Taiwan should adopt a realistic policy and not assume a passive policy of retreat and surrender. Among them were Secretary-General of the Executive Yuan Y. S. Tsiang, Secretary-General of the National Security Council Huang Shao-ku, Foreign Minister Chow Shu-kai, and Vice Minister Hsi-kun Yang. On July 13, 1971, Vice Minister Yang told Ambassador McConaughy, at a strictly private luncheon, that he was trying to encourage flexibility and realism in the ROC government. Yang was convinced that the withdrawal of the Republic of China from the United Nations would mean isolation and political suicide for Taiwan. But Vice Minister Yang stressed that no outsider could understand how hard it was for President Chiang to accommodate adverse realities.[68] Yang had told his superiors that the traditional policy of walking out rather than "coexisting" was a supine, defeatist policy. Yang told Chang Chun, secretary-general of the Presidential Office, that "better take a bitter pill now than a more bitter pill when it is too late." Yang thought these words had had some influence on Chang Chun and President Chiang. Huang Shao-ku agreed "100 percent" with Yang's thesis. Vice Minister Yang asked Ambassador McConaughy not to leak such extremely sensitive information; to do so would have bad consequences both for the objective he was seeking and for his own position.[69]

On July 22, 1971, Y. S. Tsiang told Ambassador McConaughy that he opposed ROC withdrawal from the United Nations even if it lost its Security Council seat. Tsiang clearly implied that Vice Premier Chiang Ching-kuo shared this view. Tsiang knew that the loss of General Assembly membership would most likely lead very quickly to loss of the ROC's positions in the specialized UN agencies. The ROC would then be driven out of all international organizations by the PRC. But he stressed the ultimate decision had to be made by Chiang Kai-shek.[70] The State Department was rather encouraged to learn from Y. S. Tsiang that Chiang Ching-kuo opposed withdrawal from the United Nations even if the ROC's Security Council seat had to be relinquished.

On July 26, Ambassador McConaughy informed Foreign Minister Chow of U.S. concerns that it would be impossible to maintain the Republic of China's UN membership unless the ROC gave up its seat on the Security Council. Chow responded that to tolerate the U.S. plan for the Security Council seat was one thing but to advocate it was another thing, and that what was most important was for the United States to avoid openly discussing its UN position regarding the Republic of China.[71] McConaughy noted that for the time being, the United States need not articulate its standing on the Security Council issue, but that such a clarification might become necessary in the future.[72]

On July 26, the government of the Republic of China served official notice that Taipei had decided to accept the American proposal to adopt a new approach to the problem of preserving Taipei's UN representation, namely, allowing the United States, Japan, and other states to submit a proposal to defend the ROC position in the UN. Furthermore, Chow Shu-kai made two statements to Ambassador McConaughy on July 27 that were excluded from the "supplement" to the conversational record. First, the government of the

Republic of China would understand if the United States and other friendly nations felt it necessary to submit the so-called dual representation resolution as a tactic to gain approval of the reverse important question procedure and thus to defeat the Albanian resolution. However, the ROC government strongly desired that the issue of its seat on the Security Council be excluded from the dual representation resolution. Second, if other states intended to deprive the Republic of China of its place on the Security Council through amendments or individual proposals, then the Republic of China solemnly asked the American government not to support any such resolution. Even so, as a matter of principle, the ROC government had to make public its opposition to dual representation in any form, because this formula virtually invited the PRC to join the United Nations.[73]

The United States was very concerned whether Taipei would agree to remain in the United Nations in the event the PRC gained the Security Council seat. Chow Shu-kai merely said that the matter required further consideration and that no answer could be given immediately.[74] Meanwhile, Ambassador Shen told Secretary of State Rogers in Washington that the ROC was committed to remaining in the United Nations if at all possible.[75]

To respond to Taipei's multiple requests not to include the question of Security Council representation in the resolution on dual representation, Secretary of State Rogers decided to adopt a two-stage strategy. In the first stage, the issue of Security Council representation would be ignored. However, after consultation with friendly states, the United States would then move to the second stage and inform Taipei that this approach was impractical. If the United States did not include the clause on the transfer of the Security Council seat to Beijing in the dual representation resolution, many states would not support it. Because of domestic public opinion, Rogers considered that the two-stage strategy would be the optimum choice. Taipei had no choice but to accept the decision of the United States.[76]

On August 2, 1972, Secretary of State Rogers officially announced U.S. support for Beijing's admission to the United Nations and its opposition to the ROC's expulsion. As for the question of China's seat on the Security Council, the United States was prepared to let the UN member-states decide this issue. The Foreign Ministry in Taipei also issued a statement on the same day, urging peace-loving member-states to oppose the Albanian proposal. However, Taipei's declaration did not mention the issue of dual representation.

On August 28, 1971, Che Yin-shou, director of the Department of International Organization Affairs of the Ministry of Foreign Affairs, notified the American embassy that, on August 21, the ROC government had directed its ambassadors stationed abroad to take three actions: (1) urge host governments to vote for the simple dual representation proposal; (2) explain that the ROC government, for obvious reasons, could not openly support the dual representation formula in the General Assembly but ask the host state to disregard Taipei's position; and (3) explore the standing of the host state on disposition of Security Council seat but not to voice opposition to its positions.[77]

Just when Taipei thought everything was ready to win over friendly states to support its seat in the United Nations and the Security Council, Secretary of State Rogers, at the suggestion of Assistant Secretaries De Palma and Green, decided to change tactics and move to the second stage. On September 3, 1971, De Palma and Green had pointed out in an action memorandum that the United States must choose between submitting a dual representation resolution that included a recommendation that Beijing hold the Security Council seat and facing the overwhelming defeat of the new initiative.[78] They explained that the United States had made exceptionally intensive efforts to seek support for the version of the dual representation resolution that did not mention the Security Council seat but had been unable to assemble even a minimally acceptable list of co-sponsors. Only two countries—Costa Rica and Guatemala—gave firm assurances of co-sponsorship. More than forty friendly nations had pointed out the omission of the question of the Security Council seat in the resolution. De Palma and Green, therefore, requested Secretary of State Rogers's approval to move to the second stage.[79] On September 8, 1971, Ambassador McConaughy delivered Rogers's message to Foreign Minister Chow, notifying Taipei that Washington had decided it was necessary to amend its draft dual representation resolution to recommend seating the PRC in the Security Council.[80]

Chow was very unhappy. On September 10, 1971, Chow handed McConaughy an official reply, expressing Taipei's regret at the American decision to amend the resolution. Chow stressed that once the revised resolution was submitted, the ROC government would be compelled to issue a public statement voicing its objection in the strongest terms.[81]

On September 16, President Nixon, in a press conference, expressed U.S. support for the PRC's joining the UN and obtaining China's seat in the Security Council.[82] The Foreign Ministry of the ROC, responding to Nixon's statement, announced Taipei's resolute opposition to any arrangement to surrender the ROC seat in the Security Council to Communist China.

Taipei was tired of responding to the frequent U.S. changes on the issue of Chinese representation. Even so, the United States wished Taipei to attempt to persuade friendly states behind the scenes to support the amended U.S. resolution. What Taipei did not expect were the announcements made by Ronald Ziegler on October 5 and 14 that National Security Advisor Kissinger would visit Beijing on October 21 to pave the way for Nixon's subsequent visit to China. On October 18, 1971, the UN General Assembly began to debate the question of Chinese representation. The timing of Kissinger's visit spawned many rumors. The White House's aims were widely perceived to be contradictory or counterproductive and thus caused uncertainty for many states that had not yet made a decision.[83]

On October 21, Zhou Enlai, in another talk with Kissinger in Beijing, expressed China's opposition to the draft resolution. Zhou Enlai pointed out that some felt that the United States wanted the resolution to fail. Zhou did not think that this was completely true.[84] Kissinger, later in his memoirs, concluded that the U.S. opening to Beijing effectively determined the outcome of the UN debate, although the United States did not realize this immediately.[85]

On October 25, the reverse important question resolution was defeated by four votes; the tally was 59 to 55, with fifteen abstentions. Later, George Bush, the U.S. representative to the United Nations, proposed that the expulsion clause of the Albanian resolution be deleted, but the General Assembly president ruled the motion out of order on the grounds that voting on the Albanian resolution had already begun.[86]

Liberia then proposed a separate vote on various provisions of the Albanian resolution—a "vote by division"—and Ambassador Bush seconded Liberia's proposal. But this proposal was defeated 61 to 51, with 19 abstaining. Later, a Saudi Arabian proposal to postpone voting on the Albanian resolution was also defeated.[87]

In the end, the Albanian proposal was passed, 76 to 35, with 17 abstentions. Before the Albanian resolution was put to a vote, Foreign Minister Chow Shu-kai announced the withdrawal of the ROC's delegation: "In view of the frenzied and irrational manners that have been exhibited in this hall, the delegation of the Republic of China has decided not to take part in any further proceedings of this General Assembly."[88] Chow then led Taipei's delegation out of the General Assembly.

The dual representation formula on which the U.S. State Department had labored was not even put to a vote. Taipei had kept a reserved attitude toward the dual representation resolution from the beginning, but under the pressure of Realpolitik, it had tolerated the proposal. However, on October 23, two days before the Chinese representation issue was put to a vote, Ambassador McConaughy was informed by the Ministry of Foreign Affairs in Taipei that the ROC, for reasons of principle, planned to be "absent" from the vote on the dual representation resolution.[89]

Later, Ambassador Shen criticized himself over Taipei's defeat, saying that the reason for the defeat was that states friendly to Taipei did not know what the ROC wished them to do. According to Shen, when the friendly states asked, Taipei did not know how to answer. As a result, many of Taipei's friends were in a quandary.[90] The ambassador, in his memoirs, stated: "I must say that my government's leaders vacillated, when a quick decision was called for."[91] Minister Chow Shu-kai pointed out that the friendly states were not in agreement on the issue. There were two positions: one was firmly anticommunist—these states were against the admission of the PRC; the other states thought that they could not legally consent to one country having two votes. The difference in positions led to the tragic consequence.[92] Several years later, Shen asked Bush what the decisive factors had been. Bush answered: "What was Kissinger doing in Beijing?"[93]

From the declassified official documents, it is clear that even if the dual representation resolution had passed in 1971, Taipei could have remained in the United Nations for, at most, only one year. On July 11, 1971, Kissinger had told Zhou Enlai in Beijing that the U.S. proposal was "temporarily one China and one Taiwan."[94] Kissinger reasoned that as soon as Beijing gained a two-thirds majority for Taiwan's expulsion, the PRC would then be the only representative of China in the United Nations.[95] What Kissinger did not then know was the fact that Beijing would have needed only a simple majority to defeat the important question resolution. In 1971, even if the important question and the dual representation resolutions had passed, Beijing would have refused to join the United Nations until Taipei had been expelled, because the PRC knew U.S. policy had changed and therefore the "dual representation formula" would in the end be ineffective.

On October 26, Secretary of State Rogers sent a telegram to McConaughy directing him to deliver an oral message to President Chiang. If McConaughy were unable to see President Chiang, he was to call on Vice Premier Chiang Ching-kuo as soon as possible. On behalf of the U.S. government, Rogers expressed its sincere and deep regret. He believed the denial of the ROC's representation in the General Assembly was a serious mistake, neither just nor realistic. Rogers stressed that nothing that had happened in the United Nations would in any way affect the ties between the two countries. The U.S. defense commitment to the ROC was in no way affected by these developments. Furthermore, he pointed out that the U.S. representatives who had the honor to work closely on this difficult question with the representatives of the ROC had been greatly impressed with both the adherence to principle and the tactical flexibility reflected in the ROC government's decisions.[96]

Nixon's Normalization Plan

Between 1972 and 1978, although the ROC still maintained diplomatic relations with the United States, relations were rather cool. Although the United States had, on more than 50 different occasions, promised the ROC[97] that their mutual defense treaty would remain in force, in the 1978 negotiations to establish diplomatic relations with the PRC, the Carter administration nevertheless accepted Beijing's demands to break diplomatic relations with the ROC, to withdraw troops from Taiwan, and to terminate the defense treaty. During this seven-year transition period, how did Taipei deal with the situation? What were its responses? What were the steps taken by President Nixon and Kissinger?

After Kissinger's secret visit to Beijing in July 1971, policymakers in Taipei wondered what promises the United States had made on the question of Taiwan. Was there a specific timetable for the establishment of diplomatic relations between Washington and Beijing? What were the conditions for the establishment of diplomatic relations?

Declassified official documents reveal the position of the Nixon administration on the question of Taiwan. On February 22, 1972, Nixon expressed five principles to the leaders in Beijing:

1. There is only one China, and Taiwan is a part of China.

2. The United States has not, and will not support a Taiwan independence movement.

3. The United States will, to the extent it is able, use its influence to discourage Japan from moving into Taiwan as the U.S. presence decreases and also will discourage Japan from supporting a Taiwan independence movement.

4. The United States will support any peaceful resolution of the Taiwan issue that can be worked out. It will not support any military attempts by the government on Taiwan to return to the Mainland.

5. The United States seeks normalization of relations with the PRC.[98]

The Shanghai Communiqué issued in February 1972 mentioned the "normalization of relations" four times. To Beijing, the normal consequence of an improvement of relations between two states was the establishment of diplomatic relations. On July 10, 1971, Zhou Enlai told Kissinger this. But recognizing the PRC as China's sole legitimate government was not a precondition for President Nixon's visit to China.[99] Furthermore, Zhou Enlai stated that the United States must withdraw all its troops and military equipment from Taiwan. Finally, the PRC considered the U.S.-ROC defense treaty of 1954 to be illegal, and the PRC did not recognize it.[100]

As for Zhou Enlai's request that all American troops be withdrawn, President Nixon told Zhou on February 22, 1972, that his goal was to withdraw all remaining forces in Taiwan, but he had to consider Congress and public opinion. Once the Vietnam War ended, the United States would withdraw two-thirds of its troops from Taiwan. It was impossible to withdraw the remaining third until 1973. The withdrawal had to take place over a period of four years. Nixon also told Zhou that if, after he returned to the United States, he were asked whether the United States had made a "deal" with the PRC to withdraw all its troops from Taiwan, he would say "no."[101] Nixon stated that the problem lay not in what the United States would do but in what it would say, and that his record showed that he always did more than he could say.[102] Therefore, Nixon explained, the language of the Shanghai Communiqué should have some "running room"; after he returned to Washington, he had to be able to say that there was no "secret deal" on the question of Taiwan. Indeed, Nixon did not want Taiwan to become a big issue in the coming months or years. Only under such circumstances could he achieve his goal.[103]

As for the timetable and the conditions for the establishment of diplomatic relations, Kissinger, in a talk with Zhou Enlai in February 1973, stated: "We want to work toward full normalization after 1974 and full diplomatic relations before mid-1976." Kissinger mentioned that in the next two years the United States was prepared to move to something like the Japanese solution but had not yet worked this out. Washington wished to keep some form of representation on Taiwan but had not figured out a formula that would be mutually acceptable. At the same time, the United States wished to reach an understanding with Beijing that the final solution of Taiwan would be a peaceful one. In that context, the United States would exercise great restraint in its military supply policy.[104] Kissinger's promises to Zhou Enlai on the timetable and conditions for diplomatic relations were factors contributing to Beijing's consent for establishment of the liaison offices.

Several events worked against Kissinger's timetable, however. Nixon's resignation in August 1974, because of the Watergate scandal, meant that Nixon's goal would not be achieved. In April 1975, Cambodia and South Vietnam fell. President Gerald Ford, beset with difficulties both at home and abroad, could do nothing to normalize relations. The question of the establishment of diplomatic relations was resolved during the succeeding Carter administration.

The ROC Ministry of Foreign Affairs, although uncertain of the development of relations between Washington and Beijing, did correctly analyze the situation on several occasions.

1. After Kissinger's secret visit to China in July 1971 and the subsequent issuance of the "Shanghai Communiqué," the Ministry of Foreign Affairs in Taipei surmised that, although there might not be any written agreement, there "must exist secret, tacit agreements."[105]

2. Nixon's failure to notify Japan before the sudden announcement of his visit to Mainland China caused Japan to lose confidence in the United States. The Ministry of Foreign Affairs correctly estimated that Japan might recognize Communist China before the United States.[106]

3. The Ministry of Foreign Affairs deemed there was only a "slight possibility" that the United States would break off its diplomatic relations with Taiwan and annul the mutual defense treaty.[107]

Taipei's greatest error was to believe that the United States would give the ROC prior notice before it established diplomatic relations with the PRC.[108] It is apparent that the ROC knew the establishment of diplomatic relations between the United States and the

PRC would take place sooner or later. What really concerned Taipei was the way the Carter administration broke off diplomatic relations with the ROC. James C. H. Shen, in his memoirs, pointed out that before France recognized the PRC, President De Gaulle sent a personal envoy to Taipei in January 1964 to explain his decision. Canada, before switching its recognition from Taipei to Beijing in October 1970, also informed Taipei about its talks with Beijing. The Japanese government also sent a top envoy to Taipei in September 1972 to give Taipei advance notice of its establishment of diplomatic relations with Beijing.[109] Taipei was dumbfounded that the United States, which had fought side by side with the ROC in World War II and was its ally during the Korean War and Vietnam War, did not take similar actions. Washington notified Taipei just seven hours before the actual announcement.

Diplomatic analysts in Taipei had long been confused about the meaning of the phrase "normalization of relations." In July 1972, Assistant Secretary Marshall Green, calling on Foreign Minister Shen Chang-huan, explained that the normalization was not tantamount to the establishment of diplomatic relations. On February 9, 1973, Secretary of State Rogers told Shen that the U.S. government did not agree with Shen's view that normalization of relations meant diplomatic recognition, because many countries with diplomatic relations did not have normal relations with each other.[110]

It was not until November 19, 1973, when Ambassador James Shen called on Secretary of State Kissinger, that he comprehended the real meaning of normalization of relations. That meeting was the only time Kissinger received Ambassador Shen in his new capacity as secretary of state. After that, Kissinger referred Ambassador Shen first to his deputy, Kenneth Rush, and later to Robert Ingersoll to handle U.S.-ROC relations.[111] In his meeting with Shen, Kissinger stressed that under no circumstances would the United States abandon its treaty commitments to defend Taiwan. Shen then asked about the diplomatic relations between the countries, but Kissinger did not answer that question.[112] Shen, in his memoirs, reflected that "full normalization of relations" logically meant the establishment of diplomatic relations with Beijing and derecognition of Taipei.[113] Under those circumstances, Taipei had to try its best to respond to the crisis that might result when diplomatic relations ended.

Taipei's Pragmatic Diplomacy
Toward Washington

The ROC's withdrawal from the United Nations was just the beginning of the diplomatic setbacks. From October 1971 to December 1972, 23 states broke off relations with Taipei.[114] In addition, the Republic of China withdrew from various UN specialized organizations. With U.S. support, Taiwan's memberships in the World Bank and the International Monetary Fund were retained, but only until 1980.

Faced with such a significant diplomatic setback, policymakers in Taipei decided that the most important way to respond was to reassure the public and to enhance national strength. A state, it was reasoned, must be able to satisfy its people before it can resist foreign aggression. On June 15, 1971, President Chiang Kai-shek directed his National Security Council to build the nation—"most importantly to make every effort to make improvements, to keep calm in the face of crisis, and to take care to make correct decisions." In this way, "there will be no test that could not be passed, no difficulty that could not be solved, no enemy that could not be defeated."[115] At the time, Chiang sensed that Taipei would experience important diplomatic setbacks. After withdrawing from the United Nations, the ROC would be challenged by normalization of relations between the United States and the PRC. The important principles for the Republic of China, in response to international changes, were to make every effort to improve itself, to keep calm in the face of crisis, to make correct decisions, and to take the initiative.

Taipei recognized that the timing and the means of establishing relations were in the hands of Washington and Beijing, but the initiative for determining the ROC's future and preventing or managing the crisis was in Taipei's hands. Following the UN withdrawal in 1971, Taipei reflected on the situation, examined and criticized itself, and devised several ways to respond to the crisis.

"ALL-OUT DIPLOMACY"

On November 6, 1971, Foreign Minister Chow Shu-kai announced new foreign policy guidelines under which Taipei would actively seek economic, trade, and cultural relations abroad despite the lack of diplomatic ties.[116] The ROC prepared to separate economics from politics, as a response to its deteriorating diplomatic and political position.

After Nixon's visit to the PRC, Taipei embarked on a campaign of "all-out diplomacy" to sustain its international presence. On March 8, 1972, Chow delivered a foreign policy report to the Third Plenary Meeting of the Tenth KMT Central Committee. The report announced the adoption of a "pragmatic" foreign policy encompassing relations of mutual benefit with any "nonhostile" nation, including some Communist countries.

Foreign Minister Chow rejected previous ideological restrictions and indicated that the ROC would consider almost any foreign tie that might benefit it.[117] In February 1972, before Chow delivered his report, the ROC had established a cabinet-level committee to direct a program of "all-out diplomacy." According to then Vice President Yen Chia-kan, "all-out diplomacy" sought to "coordinate culture, economy, and trade into one integrated effort . . . and, under a single command, to closely coordinate and to combine the uses of manpower, materials, and financial resources, both independently and actively, in a feasible mobilization to carry out such a unified, worldwide diplomatic strategy."[118]

To promote bilateral trade, trade offices were established with those countries that did not have diplomatic relations with the ROC. The China External Trade and Development Council (CETRA), a quasi-governmental trading company, and the Central Trust of China, a government-backed private financial institution, as well as a consortium of private companies, served to carry out Taiwan's international economic relations with other countries.[119] In addition, Taipei also sent private industry representatives and government officials all over the world to promote Taiwan's products and investment opportunities. Taipei also increased its participation in international fairs whenever possible, sent missions abroad to expand trade ties, and encouraged foreign investment in Taiwan.[120]

The ROC less frequently voiced—except at home—its claim to be the legitimate government of all of China. At the same time, Premier Chiang Ching-kuo distinguished Taiwan's claim to all of China and the territory it effectively controlled: the ROC was "vested with the sovereignty of the whole of China" yet only "exercise[d] sovereign rights over Taiwan, Penghu, Kinmen and Matsu."[121] In November 1972, Foreign Minister Shen Chang-huan told Ambassador McConaughy that "until last year 'one China' meant the ROC. Now 'one China' means the PRC."[122] According to a State Department analysis, Taipei's "all-out diplomacy" de-emphasized "one China" and implicitly acknowledged "one China–one Taiwan."[123]

THE SOVIET OPTION

After the ROC's withdrawal from the United Nations, there was speculation on the cultivation of relations between Moscow and Taipei. In November 1971, Foreign Minister Chow announced that the ROC would consider trading with Communist countries with the exception of Communist China. On March 8, 1972, Minister Chow stated in a foreign policy report to the KMT Central Committee that because of the sharpening confrontation between Moscow and Beijing, the monolithic Communist bloc of the past had broken into several centers.[124] Taipei was prepared to study the possibility of establishing trade, economic, and other relations with certain Communist countries that were "not sympathetic" to the PRC.[125]

When Minister Chow was interviewed by a group of reporters headed by William Randolph Hearst, Jr., who were touring Asia to gauge the reactions of Asian leaders to Nixon's China trip, he said that he did not envision formal diplomatic relations between the USSR and the ROC, but Taipei would explore what it could do with the Soviet Union. Chow envisioned secret talks between the ROC and the Soviet Union, similar to the U.S.-PRC talks in Warsaw. Chow said, "We are anti-communist. Without affecting our fundamental policy, our philosophy, we will have to try to explore what we could do with countries which are not hostile to us."[126] Were the United States to make important concessions to Communist China or to disengage completely from the Western Pacific, "the free nations of Asia would begin turning toward the Soviet Union."[127] Two days after Chow's interview was published, the Ministry of Foreign Affairs issued a clarification: the ROC "is absolutely against communism and communists and . . . we shall never depart from the family of free nations which uphold principles of freedom and liberty."[128]

Chow's interview immediately revived rumors that the ROC was contemplating a major change in its foreign policy vis-à-vis Communist countries, including the Soviet Union.[129] Chow's remarks apparently had not received clearance from the higher authorities. President Chiang Kai-shek was upset with Chow's view.[130] The Ministry of Foreign Affairs' "clarification" was ordered by the highest authority but drafted by Minister Chow himself.[131] In June 1972, Chow was replaced as foreign minister by Shen Chang-huan and became a minister without portfolio. The State Department believed that Chow "may have been replaced because of his outspoken position on the desirability for relations with Communist countries, and because of the numerous foreign policy reversals suffered during his tenure."[132]

The ROC's top leadership was divided in the early 1970s over the Soviet option. Minister Chow felt that the confrontation between Beijing and Moscow provided room for flexible diplomacy. Signals about possible links between Moscow and Taipei could serve to warn Beijing and Washington not to push too hard.[133] But another group in Taipei believed that contacts with Moscow would undermine U.S. support for Taiwan and becloud the ROC's image of uncompromising anti-communism. Vice Foreign Minister Yang, for example, told Ambassador McConaughy on March 16, 1972, that no Communist country had any use for the ROC and that any one of them would betray the ROC at the first expedient moment.[134] Vice Minister Yang said he had talked at length with Vice Premier Chiang Ching-kuo and had pointed out to him that any supposed benefit from the Soviet option would prove illusory whereas the harm was very tangible.[135] Yang had also mentioned Chiang Ching-kuo's own vulnerability, owing to his early period of residence in the Soviet Union, to charges by unfriendly foreign observers that Chiang was still sympathetic to Soviet communism. Yang had also recalled the Soviet treachery of 1945 and afterward, and he felt Chiang Ching-kuo was fully convinced.[136]

On March 16, 1972, Vice Premier Chiang Ching-kuo stressed to Ambassador McConaughy that it was the ROC's national policy to remain a member of the free world and, within this policy, close relations with Washington were the most fundamental element. The ROC would not change this basic orientation, but it would adopt flexible measures to cope with its international problem.[137]

One reason Minister Chow advocated better ties with Moscow apparently was the U.S.-PRC rapprochement. How did the United States view the ROC's Soviet option? Did Washington feel threatened by Taipei's new Soviet policy?

According to one State Department report on ROC-USSR relations, contacts between Taipei and Moscow ceased after the Nationalists fled to Taiwan in 1949. It was not until the mid-1960s that a few low-level contacts occurred in third countries.[138] In October 1968, Soviet journalist and agent Victor Louis visited Taiwan and had an interview with Chiang Ching-kuo concerning PRC-USSR relations.[139] However, the Louis visit and subsequent contacts in third countries were essentially social in form and unsubstantial in content.[140] In the late 1960s and in 1970, both Chiang Kai-shek and Chiang Ching-kuo had deputed representatives abroad to keep channels to Moscow open. But Chiang Kai-shek seemed to have been more wary of such contacts than Chiang Ching-kuo, because of his fears of alienating the United States.[141] Many PRC leaders had made it clear, privately, that they did not trust Chiang Ching-kuo in the same way they might trust Chiang Kai-shek, because of the younger Chiang's Soviet ties. The PRC feared that Chiang Ching-kuo might come to some arrangement with the USSR.[142]

The United States did not, however, worry about Taipei's Moscow ties. Assistant Secretary of State Marshall Green, for example, pointed out on May 1, 1972, that the Soviets had taken the position that Taiwan was a part of China, and it would be very unlikely that relations between Moscow and Taipei could develop very far.[143] Green believed the occasional rumors about Moscow-Taipei ties were intended to ruffle Beijing.[144] A March 1973 "interim contingency paper" prepared by the State Department predicted that it would be unlikely that Chiang Ching-kuo would seriously pursue a pro-Soviet path after the death of his father, for several reasons:

(a) the Soviets would be unlikely to respond enthusiastically to ROC overtures since to do so would be to give up all hope of friendly relations with the PRC and accept a serious deterioration in the Soviet image in many areas of the world; (b) the ROC might fear that the PRC would be goaded by such an action into a dangerously militant attitude toward Taiwan; (c) the ROC would run the danger of losing such support as it has had around the world in anti-Communist circles.[145]

On May 12, 1973, three to five Soviet warships, including destroyers and submarines, transited the Taiwan Strait during daytime hours at distances ranging from 20 to 40 miles from Mainland China's coast.[146] It was reported by the Taiwan press on May 15, 1973. This transit took place two days before David Bruce, the head of the newly established U.S. Liaison Office in China, was scheduled to assume his post. The ROC military spokesman confirmed that the passage had taken place on the high seas and had been closely watched by the ROC. According to the U.S. Embassy in Taipei's analysis, the ROC's motives in leaking the news probably included a desire to strengthen its argument for a continued, strong U.S. presence in the area in order to counter growing Soviet pressure, and the standard motivation of highlighting increasing Soviet-PRC tensions as means to bolster morale on Taiwan.[147]

Some members of the Taiwanese opposition alleged that the ROC had instigated the Soviet transit because of Chiang Ching-kuo's past Russian ties, but Ambassador McConaughy doubted that anyone in Taiwan would give any real credence to a connection between Chiang Ching-kuo or the ROC and Soviet fleet activities.[148] On June 2, 1973, Premier Chiang Ching-kuo told McConaughy that the ROC would continue to regard the Soviet Union as an "unprincipled and hostile power."[149] The ROC would not consider establishing an understanding or relationship of any sort with the Soviet Union. Chiang also made it clear to McConaughy that the ROC would not now or ever in the future undertake any negotiations, talks, or contacts with the Chinese Communists. Talks with Beijing could only be a prelude to absorption. Chiang predicted to McConaughy, for the first time, that talks with the PRC would precipitate domestic chaos and the fall of the ROC government.[150]

In 1976, the U.S. government learned that Taiwan had begun the secret reprocessing of spent uranium fuel from Canadian and other smaller research reactors.[151] On September 14, 1976, U.S. Ambassador Leonard Unger met with Premier Chiang Ching-kuo to convey a message that continuation of this course would "seriously jeopardize" cooperation in the peaceful uses of nuclear energy.[152] Under U.S. pressure, the ROC government publicly announced in September 1976 that it had no intention of developing nuclear weapons and that all nuclear facilities in the ROC were for peaceful purposes.[153] Chiang Ching-kuo also publicly stated for the first time that the ROC did not plan to acquire a facility for reprocessing spent nuclear fuel.[154] For Taipei, the Soviet and nuclear options apparently were not valid ones. But Taipei's considerations of these two options did send the U.S. government a clear message that if the United States completely abandoned Taiwan, Taipei would be pushed toward more radical options.

During the U.S.-PRC normalization negotiations in 1978, one reason behind the Carter administration's insistence on continuing arms sales to Taiwan was to prevent Taiwan from resorting to radical solutions, such as invoking the Soviet option or reconsidering its nuclear option, both of which would be contrary to U.S. interests. For leaders in Taiwan, on the other hand, continued good relations with the United States had been, and would continue to be, of paramount importance. More important, Taiwan needed to rely on itself, to take the initiative to build its own national strength.

BOOSTING NATIONAL STRENGTH

On June 1, 1972, Chiang Ching-kuo succeeded to the post of premier. Faced with successive diplomatic challenges, Chiang Ching-kuo concluded that the most important ways to safeguard the security of the state were to foster development, plan Taiwan's economy, and maintain a strong military capability.[155] In November

1973, Chiang proposed the so-called Ten Major Development Projects, including a north–south expressway, the Chiang Kai-shek International Airport, railway electrification, an east–west rail line, new harbors, and the construction of capital-intensive industries producing petrochemicals, iron and steel, aluminum, and copper. Of the ten construction projects, seven concerned communications and energy. At the time, Taiwan was in a financially difficult position. Nevertheless, the government resolutely invested a large amount of capital and effort in these projects, and, despite difficulties, they were completed within four years. These basic economic and infrastructure projects fostered large-scale economic development of Taiwan and established the foundation for Taiwan to become a newly developed industrial country.[156]

In December 1977, Premier Chiang proposed twelve more basic projects, including construction of an around-the-island railway, an east–west highway, the second and third engineering phases of the port of Taichung, and the second and third nuclear power plants. During the construction of these projects, Taiwan's average per capita income increased fivefold—from U.S.$257 in 1969 to $1,304 in 1978.[157] Over the same period, Taiwan's per capita foreign exchange reserves increased fourfold—from $361 in 1969 to $1,406 in 1978.[158]

Moreover, Chiang Ching-kuo actively invited native Taiwanese to join the government for the first time. In 1972, Hsu Ch'ing-chung was appointed vice premier; Hsieh Tung-min became the governor of the Taiwan Provincial Government; Henry Kao became minister of communications; and Lee Teng-hui became a minister without portfolio. A State Department memorandum pointed out that previously only people from the mainland had occupied these posts. Chiang Ching-kuo's invitation to the Taiwanese people to join the cabinet might be perceived as a small step, but it was surely a significant step toward "Taiwanizing" the government.[159] The United States had always been concerned about the democratization of Taiwan. More native Taiwanese occupying high-level posts in the government was an important beginning and a positive step in improving long-term relations between Taiwan and the United States. Dr. Lee Teng-hui would later become vice president and then president of the ROC, and he actively promoted the democratization of Taiwan.

EXPANDING COMMERCE AND NONGOVERNMENTAL
EXCHANGES WITH THE UNITED STATES

Since the 1970s, bilateral commerce between Taiwan and the United States has expanded continuously (see Table 7.1). After 1976, shipments from Taiwan to the United States increased significantly. To develop a favorable balance of trade with the United States and to strengthen bilateral economic relations, the Republic of China adopted many measures, including:

1. Sponsoring U.S. commodity exhibitions; contributing financially to setting up the American Trade Center in Taipei.

2. Implementing purchasing limitations. Taiwan designated 785 commodities that U.S. businesses could export to Taiwan with special terms applying to businesses from other states.

3. Visiting the United States to purchase agricultural products.

4. Encouraging ROC-U.S. cooperation in setting up factories in Taiwan to produce heavy industrial and chemical industrial equipment.

5. Establishing, in 1978, a special purchasing delegation that went to the United States three times to purchase agricultural and industrial commodities worth a total of $1.5 billion.

6. Strengthening Taiwan-U.S. communications and encouraging U.S. businesses to increase exports to Taiwan.

7. Lowering customs duties on, and letting in more, U.S. commodities.

8. Inviting high-level officials from various of the 50 states to Taiwan to explore markets for, and promote sales of, commodities from their states in Taiwan.

9. Strengthening measures to ban counterfeit products.[160]

To strengthen commercial and political relations with the United States, the Foreign Affairs Ministry decided to increase the number

Table 7.1
Bilateral Trade Between the United States and Taiwan, 1969–78
(U.S.$100 million)

Year	Taiwan exports to U.S.	U.S. exports to Taiwan	Taiwan's surplus
1969	3.98	3.3	0.65
1970	5.78	4.63	1.155
1971	8.61	4.08	4.534
1972	12.51	5.43	7.079
1973	16.85	9.95	6.894
1974	20.36	16.79	3.567
1975	18.23	16.52	1.71
1976	30.38	17.97	12.41
1977	36.36	19.63	16.72
1978	50.1	23.76	26.34

SOURCES: *Yearbook of the Central Bank* (Taipei, Division of Economic Research, Central Bank), 1969, 56–59; 1970, 54–59; 1971, 55–58; 1972, 53–56; 1973, 58–61; 1974, 63–66; 1975, 58–60; 1976, 59; 1977, 61–62; 1978, 72.

of consulates in the United States. In 1973, the Republic of China set up a consulate general in Atlanta and a consulate in American Samoa. In April 1974, a consulate general was set up in Kansas, and in June of the same year, the consulate in Portland was reopened.[161]

The Republic of China had established a close relationship with the American people over the course of many years. To broaden its contact with the American people, Taipei, in addition to improving commercial relations with various U.S. states, expanded nongovernmental contacts, including increasing visits to the United States by delegations in the fields of culture and education, the arts, science and technology, physical exercise, the media, religion, military veterans, industry and commerce, labor, scholarship, and public opinion. Americans were also invited to visit Taiwan to improve mutual understanding.

Furthermore, Taipei strengthened its close relationships with various state and local governments in the United States. At the end of December 1978, the legislatures of 32 states, 28 municipalities, and seven counties passed resolutions supporting the Republic of China.[162] From 1971 to 1979, 37 U.S. municipalities/counties formed "sister" alliances with corresponding units in Taiwan.[163]

Meanwhile, the number of Taiwan students studying in the United States increased from 3,015 in 1969 to 4,350 in 1978.[164] The ROC government also tried to attract students studying abroad to return to Taiwan and take part in the development of their country. It is worth mentioning that a rather high percentage of high-ranking officials in Taiwan's cabinet studied in the United States, a significant factor in the long-run development of relations with the United States.

WINNING SUPPORT FROM
THE U.S. CONGRESS

Since World War II, Congress's role in foreign policy had always been auxiliary, with the dominant role being in the hands of the executive branch. In the 1970s, influenced by the Vietnam War and the Watergate Scandal, Congress became dissatisfied with the executive branch's dominance of foreign policy and began to take active action to prevent the president from further expanding his power.

In 1970, Congress annulled the Gulf of Tonkin Resolution passed in 1964, thus constraining the president's power to use military force abroad. In 1974, Congress annulled the Formosa Resolution that had authorized the president to use military force, if necessary, to defend Taiwan and Penghu against armed attack. In 1975, Congress's refusal to grant South Vietnam emergency military aid led to the defeat of South Vietnam.

In the 1970s, although Congress had taken an active part in, and had asked to share in, foreign policy decision-making, its role was still limited in influencing policies toward Mainland China. The 1972 Shanghai Communiqué and the 1978 Communiqué on the Establishment of Diplomatic Relations were reached through secret negotiations between Washington and Beijing. Congress had no hand in these decisions. Offended by the lack of security guarantees for Taiwan in the normalization agreement, however, Congress took an active role in drafting the Taiwan Relations Act. Although Congress had annulled the Formosa Resolution, its support for Taipei in the 1970s became multifaceted; for example:

1. In October 1971, before Congress discussed and voted on the Chinese representation proposal, Representatives Joe Waggoner and Robert Sikes sponsored a signature drive resolutely opposing any UN move to deny the Republic of China its seat. They won the support of more than 370 representatives and presented the signed petition to President Nixon and Ambassador Bush.[165] In addition, 70 U.S. senators signed a separate declaration supporting the ROC's retention of its seat in the UN.[166]

2. On July 25, 1975, Representative Dawson Mathis proposed to the House of Representatives that the government avoid damaging the freedom and security of the people of Taiwan in the process of improving U.S. relations with Beijing. This proposal passed with support from 218 representatives (more than half the total).[167] On November 19, Senator Barry Goldwater presented a letter signed by 29 senators to President Ford, appealing to the administration not to damage the ROC and the freedom of its people in the process of improving relations with the PRC.[168]

3. On July 25, 1978, the House of Representatives passed with a margin of 94 votes the Dole-Stone Amendment, asking the American government to consult with the Senate before making any policy changes that would affect the ROC-U.S. Mutual Defense Treaty.[169]

4. On October 10, 1978, 25 senators from both the Republican and the Democratic parties, under the leadership of Senator Goldwater, proposed a congressional resolution stipulating that the president could not unilaterally annul or influence the effectiveness of any multilateral or bilateral security defense treaties signed by the United States and its allies since World War II, without the approval of both houses of Congress.[170]

These congressional resolutions supporting Taiwan, however, did not prevent the Carter administration from terminating the Mutual Defense Treaty with the Republic of China. After diplomatic relations between the United States and the ROC were ended in January 1979, forces friendly to Taiwan in Congress drafted the Taiwan Relations Act to maintain continuing political, economic, and defense relations between the United States and Taiwan.

Table 7.2
U.S. Arms Sales to Taiwan, FY 1974–78
($ millions)

Fiscal year	Foreign military sales	Commercial export licenses
1974		
Orders	88.7	
Deliveries	93.3	8.1
1975		
Orders	144.8	
Deliveries	115.0	45.0
1976		
Orders	324.0	
Deliveries	136.5	42.5
1977		
Orders	153.0	
Deliveries	142.4	46.1
1978		
Orders	346.3	
Deliveries	131.1	174.5

SOURCE: Bureau of Public Affairs, Department of State, January 1979.

Congress was also very concerned about the balance of military power in the Taiwan Strait. In March, the House Armed Services Committee proposed a bill (H.R. 15728) to lend three United States submarines to the ROC.[171] The bill passed in the House with a vote of 281 to 66, but not in the Senate because the Nixon administration opposed it.[172] In 1969, the House of Representatives appropriated $54.5 million to Taiwan to buy a squadron of jet fighters, but the Senate did not pass the bill.[173] Even so, the attention paid by the U.S. Congress to military sales to the ROC played an active and positive part in maintaining the balance of military power between the two sides of the Taiwan Strait. Table 7.2 details the amount of U.S. arms sales to Taiwan from 1974 to 1978.

In the early 1970s, faced with a series of diplomatic setbacks, the emphasis of Taipei's public relations was on the "tyranny of the communist gangster clique" and the ROC's determination to counterattack and to preserve its state.[174] Corresponding to Beijing's

Table 7.3
Diplomatic Ties with the PRC and Taiwan (ROC)
(percent)

Date	Establish ties with PRC		Continue ties with Taiwan		Derecognize Taiwan in favor of normalization with PRC	
	Yes	No	Yes	No	Yes	No
1966	43%	33%				
1967	41	34				
1968	39	44				
1971	55	20				
1975	61	23	70%	14%	10%	70%
1976	64	18			26	51
Apr. 1977(a)			68	19	33	53
Apr. 1977(b)	62	21	61	22	28	47
Aug. 1977	56	23	64	12	8	65
1978	66	25				
Jan. 1979	60	27				

SOURCES: 1966–71, 1978–79, Harris Poll; 1975, Aug. 1977, Gallup Poll; 1976, Apr. 1977(a), Foreign Policy Association poll; Apr. 1977(b), Potomac Associates poll; table modified from Michael Y. M. Kau et al., "Public Opinion and Our China Policy," *Asian Affairs* 5, no. 3 (Jan.–Feb. 1978), 136; and Connie De Boer, "The Polls: Changing Attitudes and Policies Toward China," *Public Opinion Quarterly* 44, no. 2 (Summer 1980), 271.

practice of "smiling diplomacy" in the international realm, Taiwan's international posture focused on its domestic political stability and economic prosperity, in order to enhance American support for Taiwan.[175]

Besides winning the support of Congress, Taipei paid much attention to public support of Taiwan. Since the mid-1970s, although a majority of the American people supported the establishment of diplomatic relations with the PRC, a majority also opposed breaking off diplomatic relations with Taiwan (see Table 7.3). But congressional and public support of Taiwan did not prevent secret talks between the United States and the PRC on the establishment of diplomatic relations. Nevertheless, Taiwan's efforts to make friends in the United States in the past certainly influenced and even improved relations in the long run.

Conclusion

The Republic of China was founded in 1911, but the United States did not officially recognize the new government until May 2, 1913. In April 1914, the Republic of China sent Hsia Chia-fu to Washington with the rank of minister. But it was only in May 1935 that the United States and the Republic of China raised the status of their diplomatic envoys to the rank of ambassadors.[176]

International politics constantly change. The story of the development of relations between the United States and the ROC since the 1970s is troubling. At the same time, it was not easy for the United States to support the ROC during the difficult times of the 1950s, nor for the two countries to mutually support each other during the cold war.

Although the reality of international politics is changing, the world cannot ignore a long existing fact: in 1979, Washington established diplomatic relations with the PRC by turning from one extreme of ignoring the existence of Beijing to the other extreme of officially neglecting the ROC's existence. The question of the development of relations between the two sides of the Taiwan Strait and the evolution of triangular relations among the United States, China, and Taiwan can be resolved peacefully only on the basis of honestly facing this reality.

EIGHT

Soviet Policy Toward the United States and China, 1969–1979

VITALY KOZYREV

In the history of international relations, the decade between 1969 and 1979 was an era of unprecedented changes induced by the emergence of strategic parity between the Soviet Union and the United States, by dramatic developments in the Vietnam War, by instability in third world countries in search of developmental alternatives, and especially by the advance of China into the international arena after its years of Maoist "socialist reconstruction" and autarky.

The U.S.-Soviet confrontation in the 1960s demonstrated the "globalist" intentions of each country's leadership and its interpretation of its country's role in world affairs. For the United States, the idea of the "universal humanism of America's mission" became prevalent during the presidency of John F. Kennedy.[1] The internationalism of the "Brezhnev era" substantiated Moscow's certainty, by the end of that decade, of its new and growing global role. In this competitive context, the early 1970s marked the beginning of détente and of a new cooperation between the two adversaries.

But the 1970s were also characterized by both superpowers' tendency to go outside the boundaries of their respective "playground," and by the formation of triangular and even multipolar arrangements in the international system. The era of negotiations initiated by President Nixon precipitated the disintegration of the existing bipolar structure, and the next two decades witnessed a decline in the two superpowers' international leadership. Indeed, those changes led to an unprecedented interdependence between the leading powers, which laid the foundation for the post–cold war evolution to multipolarity.

The triangular international relations of the United States, China, and the Soviet Union in the 1970s have attracted great interest in recent historical and political literature. Scholars of international relations have begun to acknowledge imperfections in both realist interpretations, which emphasize the balance of power,[2] and liberal interpretations, which focus on the role of ideas, domestic institutions, and the nonsecurity aspects of international politics in state behavior.[3] In the search for rigor in analyzing triangular relations, empirical regional studies have been combined with theoretical analysis, based on a comprehensive examination of various causal factors.[4]

In addition to traditional studies of the influence of domestic politics on a country's foreign policy or of the politics of bilateral relationships, there has been a remarkable shift toward examination of the impact of the structural characteristics of the international system, particularly the evolution of the structure of the global and regional orders, on state behavior.[5] The exploration of the structure of the Asia-Pacific region has been based on the view that the evolution of this structure was not determined merely by the establishment or decay of bilateral or multilateral alliances. Rather, it reflected changes in the general configuration of long-stable relationships in the region, irrespective of the mode of their formal relationship. Professor Alexei D. Bogatourov, in an examination of the patterns of evolution of the structure of the regional order (from a typical "leadership" model to a "spatial" order in the 1970s and 1980s, because of the growing influence of the other countries in the Pacific area), has pointed to the importance of observing the whole picture, including nationalist components of regional processes, rather than assessing regional politics within the framework of a binary "totalitarian-liberal" analysis.[6]

This chapter studies the influence of both doctrine and international events on the evolution of Soviet foreign policy. It deliberately eschews the customary Soviet approach of imposing a chronology based on the conventions and strategic political programs of the Communist Party of the Soviet Union (CPSU). That approach to studying Soviet foreign policy decision-making once had a logical justification. The 1970s were a period of striking internal political stability and political consensus. The highest power was concentrated in the Politburo, which consisted of fifteen members starting in April 1971, and General Secretary of the CPSU Leonid Brezhnev shared power only with his closest supporters, such as Mikhail Suslov, the main ideologist in the Soviet Union. By the end of the decade, however, as Brezhnev's health was weakening, Minister of Defense Dmitri Ustinov, KGB Director Yuri Andropov, and Minister of Foreign Affairs Andrei Gromyko became more important.

Nevertheless, Soviet policy toward the United States and China was to a great extent determined by developments outside the Soviet Union, such as the East–West dialogue, the various U.S. presidents and their strategic objectives, the significant changes in Chinese-American relations, and major shifts in China's domestic situation. The structure of triangular diplomacy and the main guidelines that determined relationships for the rest of the decade were formed between 1969 and 1972. From 1972 to 1976, key policymakers in Moscow, Washington, and Beijing assessed the implications of the new pattern of Chinese-American and Soviet-American relations. The U.S. debacle in Indochina and domestic turbulence in the United States, as well as the oil crisis, led to diminished U.S. activity around the world. This change was reflected in Richard Nixon's "Guam Doctrine" and in the 1975 "Ford Doctrine."

The U.S. retrenchment, the emerging stalemate in U.S.-China relations, the progress of U.S.-Soviet détente, and Moscow's successful expansion into the third world combined to produce a tension in Soviet foreign policy between reactivism and radicalism. But by 1976, when the Soviet Union formulated the "Brezhnev Doctrine" based on the "geo-ideological" paradigm, the United States had started to depart from the Ford Doctrine and enter a new, active phase of constraining the Soviet Union by playing the "China card." During this period there were also changes in the Chinese leadership following the deaths of Zhou Enlai and Mao Zedong, the downfall of the "Gang of Four," and the ascendance of Deng Xiaoping. These developments in U.S. policy and Chinese politics marked a new stage in the U.S.-China dialogue, which eventually led to normalization of relations in 1978, and created new challenges for the Soviet Union.

Recently, few documents from the Chinese and Soviet governmental archives have been published; in contrast, there is broad access to relevant documents in the United States,[7] as well as a rich memoir literature of high-ranking U.S. politicians, diplomats, and statesmen.[8] As a result, the principal sources on Soviet foreign policy are works by western political scientists specializing in the triangular diplomacy of the 1970s, patterns of development of Soviet-U.S. and China-U.S. relations, and their bilateral and international dimensions.[9]

In post-Soviet Russia, there has not as yet been a comprehensive analysis of Soviet foreign policy during the 1970s. Theoretical works written before 1991 were constrained by Soviet-era ideological evaluations and party rhetoric, although one may still trace the sources of Soviet foreign policy in some of these works.[10]

The analytical works of Russian authors, including those by many former party analysts and officials and influential scholars, have begun to shed light on the reasoning behind Soviet actions and the changes in the international context and domestic circumstances that affected Soviet foreign policy–making. For example, recent works by A. Bogatourov, K. Pleshakov, and A. Voskressenski have sought to break with the old Soviet models of scholarship to re-examine international relations in East Asia.[11] Useful Chinese evaluations of Soviet foreign policy can be found in the publications of, among others, Gu Mingyi, Hu Lizhong, Pei Jianzhang, Xia Yishan, and Yu Zhengliang.[12]

A detailed description of Soviet policy toward the United States and China during the years of détente is beyond the scope of this chapter. Rather, the focus here is the impact on Moscow's international behavior of the leadership's conceptions of Soviet foreign-policy objectives and systemic changes in the triangular relationship. How did the Soviet Union face the challenges of the transition from stability based on the "dual leadership" of the Soviet Union and the

United States to new models of regional order? To what extent did the alterations in the system arising from shifts in the roles of the United States and China affect the evolution of Soviet position and political activities?

In this chapter, descriptions of the characteristics of Soviet foreign policy are based primarily on openly published documents on the history of Soviet foreign policy.[13] Of particular importance are the documents of the Twenty-Fourth and Twenty-Fifth Congresses of the CPSU, the resolutions of the CPSU Central Committee's plenary meetings, and materials from the archives, such as the protocols of the party's plenary meetings through the 1970s, including reports of discussions by the Central Committee members about the international activities of the CPSU and the drafts of resolutions. Also useful are documents from "Fond no. 89," the unclassified materials of the Politburo and the Central Committee, materials from the Russian State Archive of Contemporary History (originally the CPSU Central Committee's archive), as well as reference materials from the Department of the Far East of the Ministry of Foreign Affairs in the Archive of Russia's Foreign Policy (AVP). In addition, memoirs published in Russia have become an excellent source for research materials on détente and on Soviet-American and Soviet-China relations.[14]

Formation of the Triangular
Regional Structure, 1969–1972

In the 1960s, the Soviet Union and the United States began working out a "code of conduct" to regulate and restrain their political competition. However, the escalation of the Soviet-Chinese border conflict in 1969 had a crucial effect on the situation in East Asia. China had become an independent actor in world politics; it began to oppose its former "elder brother," while moving toward rapprochement with the rest of the world.[15] The Soviet-Chinese conflict also revealed the scope of the U.S. strategic doctrine of "flexible response": war between China and the Soviet Union could draw the United States into a regional clash, if Washington feared that such a war infringed on vital U.S. interests in the maintenance of a stable correlation of forces in Eurasia.

In contrast with the European system of stability, which was based on formal agreements between the United States and its allies, there were no formal commitments in the U.S. relationship with China. On the contrary, at the time the United States and China remained at odds. Nevertheless, the Nixon administration did not exclude the possibility of limited cooperation with China. This factor seriously constrained Moscow's search for solutions to its conflict with Beijing.

Nixon's China policy reflected his understanding that rigid adherence to the postwar U.S. policy of relying on global superiority to intervene unilaterally throughout the world would undermine U.S. security. Nixon, as Raymond Garthoff puts it, "believed that while the United States was entering a new era of strategic parity, in which it could not again restore the military superiority it had enjoyed in the 1950s and 1960s, it retained considerable strength that could be brought to good advantage in negotiating with the Soviet Union."[16] The U.S. interest in détente reflected Nixon's acceptance of strategic parity with the Soviet Union, his understanding of the cost of an uncontrolled arms race, and his confidence that the superpower competition could be channeled into political, economic, and cultural spheres, in which western and communist values could compete for the minds of people worldwide.

Thus, while trying to prevent Soviet dominance, the United States moved away from the classical mode of bipolarity and toward multipolarity, in which the resources of several partners could be joined together to oppose domination by the remaining power. Thus, "by strengthening American relations with Europe and Japan as well as building new relations with China and the Soviet Union," Nixon and National Security Advisor Henry Kissinger sought "to enhance the political leverage of the United States in the world."[17]

In the logic of multipolarity, as China established its independence from the Soviet camp, it possessed sufficient power to resist subservience to Washington in a U.S.-controlled "diocese." Thus, rather than seek a formal alliance with China,[18] Washington looked forward to a rapprochement with Beijing that aimed to contain the Soviet attempt to fill the vacuum of power following the retrenchment of the American presence in Asia. This was the substance of Nixon's Guam Doctrine. The United States also needed improved relations with both Moscow and Beijing to help it manage the "Vietnam factor."[19] More generally, the emergence of an additional pole in Asia created auspicious conditions for maintaining regional stability and for the future resurgence of Washington's influence.[20]

Despite newly elected President Nixon's willingness to consider changes in U.S. policy toward China, initially he regarded the improvement of relations as "a matter of theory"; he had even considered China the "more aggressive of the Communist powers."[21] It was the bloody Soviet-Chinese military conflict in spring 1969 that prompted the White House to take concrete action. After the Soviet invasion of Czechoslovakia the year before, the United States became more alert to Soviet actions under the banner of "proletarian internationalism." Ambassador Anatoly Dobrynin's repeated attempts in spring 1969 to convince Kissinger that China was provoking the border incidents had absolutely the opposite effect— Nixon and Kissinger suspected that Moscow might use the same method of punitive action to resolve its problems with China that it had used against Czechoslovakia.[22]

Later, in the 1980s, western scholars found that, notwithstanding the substantial Soviet military buildup near the Chinese borders in the late 1960s, it was Beijing that initiated the clash on Zhenbao (Damanski) Island. Peter Zwick has argued that the Soviets were in a generally reactive mode during the height of the conflict and exhibited restraint in responding to what they saw as Chinese provocations.[23] Michael Yahuda has suggested that the border clashes might be "regarded as a typical example of Mao's approach of using a limited force in a pre-emptive strike to diffuse a larger strategic threat." He wrote that "Mao presumably was content that by having displayed a readiness to fight a small-scale border war he had stood up for Chinese sovereignty; he had refused to be coerced by superior firepower and he had perhaps averted a larger war later." It was "an exercise in brinkmanship." Yahuda nevertheless concludes that the "high crisis paved the way ultimately for the Sino-American rapprochement."[24]

It is well known that the possibility of a normalization of relations with the United States was hotly debated by Chinese leaders. Their decision-making reflected both geostrategic perceptions and domestic factors. It is also generally acknowledged that ultimately it was the Soviet threat, which was widely discussed in China, that prompted China to turn to the West for help in opposing the Soviet Union's "social-imperialism."[25]

But China's pursuit of normalization of relations with the United States cannot be explained solely by Beijing's fear of the Soviet threat. China's evaluation of other geopolitical changes at the end of the 1960s, such as Beijing's assessments of changes in U.S. policy, Washington's turn toward a more defensive stance in superpower relations, and Mao's conviction that U.S. expansionism would come to an end after its experience in Vietnam, should also be taken into consideration. China also recognized that European affairs could constrain America's international activities in Asia. Mao's conviction that the balance between the superpowers had changed in favor of the Soviet Union made China tilt toward the weaker party. Washington's opening toward China was, in Mao's eyes, nothing less than a desperate maneuver to adjust to the new reality. In Zhou Enlai's words, "the U.S. imperialists cannot but improve their relations with China to combat the Soviet revisionists."[26]

Mao's decision to improve relations with the United States created domestic political problems. The Chinese Communist Party (CCP) leadership had to explain to thousands of party cadres, as well as to the masses, the meaning of these dramatic policy changes. In a special informational circular distributed by the CCP Central Committee shortly after arrangements were made for Kissinger's secret visit to Beijing in July 1971, Chinese leaders assured party cadres that the decision to respond positively to Nixon's request to visit China had been made by Mao and that it was unanimously supported by the central party authorities. The new policy was presented as a continuation of the anti-imperialist struggle in a new and different way. It was portrayed as a new mode of support for the anti-American fight in the third world, in Vietnam in particular, and as a new opportunity for all revolutionaries. It would give revolutionaries the opportunity "to use U.S. difficulties, while its will power is weakened at the negotiating table, to force the Americans out and to gain victories."[27] The circular argued that Nixon's visit was also a very important strategic maneuver, for it might help to isolate Soviet social-imperialism, prevent a dangerous Soviet-American collision, and make the United States withdraw its troops from Taiwan. The new strategy was interpreted as a repeat of the famous tactics of the Chongqing talks, which had enabled the Chinese to "pull the wool over the imperialists' eyes."[28]

On the surface, the Chinese explanations for U.S-China rapprochement resembled those of Soviet leaders, who regarded détente, or peaceful coexistence, as simply a different mode of struggle against world imperialism. Both sides were bound by ideological paradigms in their policymaking. But the Soviet posture was more rigid and overt. Moscow constantly viewed its contradictions with the capitalist world as dominant, and the pursuit of détente was justified as a possible opportunity to dislodge the United States from the Soviet Union's zones of interest throughout the world. In contrast, Chinese leaders, while declaring their adherence to ideological principles, managed to implement a more flexible course, allowing China both to keep its distance from the superpowers and to avoid direct clashes with them. Beijing used the conflict between the strongest powers to offset China's relative weakness and to secure compromises from the West that would help China modernize. China sought a partnership that could bring it the external support it needed during the socioeconomic recovery from the turmoil of the Cultural Revolution.[29] It clearly could no longer expect such a relationship with the Soviet Union.[30] Thus, its geostrategic assessments and theoretical thinking, based on its strategic weakness, reflected pragmatic domestic and international premises.

The leaders of the Soviet Communist Party could hardly follow this logic. For Moscow, the Chinese concepts of "intermediary zones" and the subsequent "three worlds theory," developed by Beijing by 1974, were challenges to Soviet ideological leadership. What most irritated the Soviets was that China had deviated sharply from the unified ideological approach to world affairs. China's pragmatic reticence regarding the ultimate objectives of the world communist movement drew relentless criticism from the "socialist camp" headed by the Soviet Union. Moscow considered Chinese attempts to revise the concepts of class struggle, solidarity, and support for revolutionary movements as intolerable errors. Therefore, Soviet policy toward China after the late 1960s was built on two fundamentals tenets: distrust of Mao's leadership and an ideologically justified "active" political course that conformed to the principles of proletarian internationalism and the unity of the socialist camp.

After the meeting between Alexei Kosygin and Zhou Enlai at the Beijing airport in September 1969, following the Zhenbao (Damanski) Island clashes, Sino-Soviet talks failed to make any progress.[31] The parties proposed different approaches to settlement of the border problems. The Soviet Union insisted on the principles of "the right of historical precedence" and of "the right of de facto possession," whereas the Chinese side cited the principle of border demarcations with tsarist Russia and the norms of international law. On the other hand, the Soviet Union did not fulfill Kosygin's promise to Zhou Enlai to remove Soviet troops from the Chinese border area.[32] The arguments the Soviet premier brought back to Moscow from the Beijing airport were apparently not strong enough to convince the central authorities to start the process of troop withdrawal. Kremlin leaders were still concerned about the possibility of a large-scale Chinese invasion of Soviet territories.

At the same time, Moscow's diplomatic efforts demonstrated a determination to destroy the myth of the "Soviet threat" and to propagate the concept of divergence between the interests of the Chinese people and the "Maoist leadership." The Soviet leadership repeatedly proclaimed its principled position on the "China problem." At a Central Committee plenum in June 1969, it was proposed to re-establish intergovernmental relations and to revive friendship between the peoples of the Soviet Union and the PRC. Moscow's main objective was for China to "return to the way of friendship and cooperation with the Soviet Union and the other socialist countries," because of a "coincidence of the vital interests of the Soviet and Chinese peoples."[33]

In December 1969, Brezhnev responded to China's proposal for interim agreements, including an agreement on mutual military nonaggression. The Soviet leadership suggested that a nonaggression treaty should be signed in tandem with a new border agreement. But the Chinese side did not accept this.[34] In subsequent initiatives, the Soviet Union proposed a series of agreements on mutual nonaggression (July 1970) and on nonutilization of military force (January 1971); these might have raised the level of mutual confidence in both countries. However, Beijing rejected these proposals.[35]

Official talks between Soviet leaders and Chinese Ambassador Liu Xinquan at the end of 1970 reflected the stalemate in relations. On December 10, Soviet Deputy Minister of Defense Admiral of the Fleet S. Gorshkov said to Ambassador Liu that it was very difficult for the Soviet government to understand China's fears of a Soviet invasion. He emphasized that the Soviet Union had "never planned to attack China [and] considered the Chinese people to be the friends of the Soviet people." Responding to the Chinese ambassador's claim that there had been little progress on the border problem, the Soviet admiral referred to the Soviet-China treaty of 1950 as a basis for state-to-state relations. Gorshkov tried to convince Liu Xinquan that it was because of their two countries' "common enemy—the imperialist states"—that the Soviet Union needed a strong fleet; Liu replied that China, too, supported all actions against imperialism, but it possessed only a defensive fleet.[36]

The Soviet interest in improving relations with China was also reflected in the decisions of the Twenty-Fourth Congress of the CPSU in March–April 1971. Nonetheless, the rationale for improved Soviet-Chinese relations was still the Soviet concept of unification of all anti-imperialist and revolutionary forces worldwide.[37] It was only in March 1972 that Brezhnev deviated for the first time from this posture, when he argued that maintaining the "ideological closeness of the 'camp'" would pressure China to change its policies. Following that, Moscow held that the relationship between the two countries should be developed on the basis of the Five Principles of Peaceful Coexistence.[38]

The U.S.-China Rapprochement
and Moscow's Response

In July 1971, during his secret mission to Beijing, Henry Kissinger reached an agreement with Chinese leaders on the terms of U.S.-China rapprochement. In October 1971, China joined the United Nations, in accordance with Albania's "one China" proposal. During President Nixon's visit to Beijing in 1972, the principles of the U.S.-China rapprochement were embodied in the joint communiqué signed in Shanghai on February 27. In the communiqué, the United States and China declared their positions on major international problems: on a negotiated solution in Vietnam, on peace in South Asia, and on the maintenance of peace on the Korean Peninsula. They accepted the fundamental principles of national self-determination and agreed to exert their efforts to avert conflicts and exercise peaceful competition between states with different social systems and ideologies. They conceded that although there were essential differences between the two countries, they would apply the Five Principles of Peaceful Coexistence to their relationship: nonaggression, respect for the sovereignty and territorial integrity of all states, noninterference in the internal affairs of other states, equality and mutual benefit, and peaceful coexistence in their relationship. The communiqué expressed the two countries' agreement that progress toward normalization of their relations was "in the interests of all countries." Both sides expressed the wish to reduce the danger of international military conflict. The two sides' desire to develop relations in the spheres of trade, scientific, technological, and cultural exchanges, sports, and journalism was also significant.[39]

One of the most important articles in the Shanghai Communiqué was directed at the Soviet Union. It held that "neither [side] should seek hegemony in the Asia-Pacific region and each is opposed to efforts by any other country or group of countries to establish such hegemony." Beijing and Washington also stated that neither was "prepared . . . to enter into agreements or understandings with the other directed at other states." They expressed their opposition to any kind of collusion by "any major country" with another state against other countries and to the efforts of "major countries" to divide the world into spheres of interest.[40] Implicitly, the United States thus confirmed its intention to support China in the event of an increased Soviet threat. China promised to continue its policy of keeping its distance from Moscow. The U.S. commitments marked the abandonment of the U.S. policy of "double containment" of both China and the Soviet Union, in favor of containment directed at the Soviet Union in concert with China.

The Shanghai Communiqué revealed that Taiwan remained the primary obstacle to normalization of relations. The United States acknowledged its "one China" position while reaffirming its interest in the "peaceful settlement of the Taiwan question by the Chinese themselves." It affirmed the ultimate objective of the withdrawal of all U.S. forces and promised to reduce its forces and military installations on Taiwan "as the tension in the area diminishes."[41]

Soviet concern over the Chinese-American rapprochement was a critical factor in Soviet leaders' decision to reach arms control agreements with the United States. Despite intensive U.S. bombing of northern Vietnam in the spring of 1972, Brezhnev invited President Nixon to Moscow. He countered doubts of this policy by arguing that reducing tensions with the United States would simply be a different way of struggling against imperialism. He stressed that the improvement of Soviet-American relations was a matter of long-term strategy and that constant dialogue with Washington would prevent a U.S.-Chinese rapprochement based on anti-Soviet postures.[42] Brezhnev's position was reconfirmed in a series of subsequent party statements.[43] Thus, despite overall Soviet satisfaction with Nixon's assertion that his Moscow visit was of major significance in comparison with his visit to China, there was suspicion in the Kremlin that Washington and Beijing might reach secret agreements behind Moscow's back.[44]

Unlike China, which had shifted toward a more pragmatic approach to structural changes since the late 1960s, and the United States, which had started the process of transforming bipolar diplomacy into a triangular strategy, the Soviet party leadership adhered to its dogmatic perception of "globalization." Constrained by ideological imperatives and a belief in the final worldwide victory of socialism, it held a very particular understanding of internationalization. Soviet leaders believed that world development would eventually proceed along one line as part of an inevitable revolutionary process.

The universalism of Marxist thought concerning the global victory of communism was a legacy of party doctrine. Since strategic objectives and political ideals were regarded as tasks common to all mankind, the national objectives of Soviet foreign policy were considered part of international and historical progress. The Soviet Union pursued détente in order to secure favorable terms for the settlement of global problems; attention to the problems of mankind was, in turn, essential for putting the principles of peaceful coexistence into practice. In the solution of global problems, "internationalists" should proceed on the basis of the interrelationship between human nature and the nature of social classes; they should thus oppose western ideas of "global humanism" and "the unity of world consciousness," which promoted concepts of "de-ideologization" and the "convergence" of capitalism and socialism. To the Soviet Union, such concepts served as evidence of the mounting global crisis of capitalism.[45]

The concept of a deepening world crisis of capitalism in the 1970s inspired Moscow's ideologues to seize the opportunity to mobilize a coalition of forces consisting of the socialist camp, the international labor movement in the capitalist countries, and the national liberation movements in the third world.[46] Brezhnev had been calling for support of national liberation movements from the beginning of his rule in 1964.[47] In the late 1960s, the problem of unity of the communist parties had been emphasized, and in 1969, the International Conference of Communist and Workers' Parties was convened in Moscow. There, Brezhnev suggested that proletarian internationalism remained the most effective instrument in the struggle for the unity of the communist movement.[48]

A class approach to international politics kept the Politburo of the CPSU Central Committee from moving beyond the bipolar principle of "he who is not with us is against us." Every political event, for example, the U.S. initiative to start an "era of negotiations," was interpreted through the prism of loyalty to the socialist camp and the struggle against imperialism. At the December 1969 Plenary Meeting of the Twenty-Third Central Committee, party leaders argued that although the United States sought to undermine socialism and to oppose the influence of the Soviet Union and other socialist countries in international affairs, it was the U.S. fear of an armed clash with the Soviet Union that had forced the United States to seek improved relations with the Soviet Union.[49]

Much has been written about the Soviet Union's attitude toward détente and its relations with the United States. Apart from domestic reasons, Moscow's acceptance of détente generally resulted from changes in the international environment.[50] Moscow's overall assessment of the balance of power and theoretical conclusions regarding global trends were the decisive factors behind the emergence of détente and peaceful coexistence as the general line of the Soviet party and government in international affairs at the Twenty-Fourth Party Congress in 1971. Although there were debates over how to characterize the achievements of détente, throughout the 1970s such debates never led to radical changes in policy.[51] Talks with the United States were interpreted as a creative approach to the task of opposing imperialism by using contradictions among the imperialists.

Differences in U.S. and Soviet understandings of the objectives of détente did not interfere with the disarmament talks in the early years. By the end of 1972, notwithstanding China's opening to the United States, progress toward superpower détente had, in Kissinger's view, became the dominant trend.[52] Having played the China card, the United States placed priority on the Soviet-American dialogue and strove primarily for mutual understanding on European and global matters. There were some achievements, despite the contradictions in the Soviet Union's simultaneous pursuit of revolutionary superpower status and improvement of relations with the West. A series of Soviet-German agreements on the status of Berlin were signed in 1970–72. Brezhnev's plan to resolve other postwar problems resulted in the convening of the Conference on Security and Cooperation in Europe (CSCE) in 1973. Negotiations with the United States led to the 1972 Strategic Arms Limitation Treaty (SALT I), a breakthrough in Soviet-U.S. relations.[53] The Anti–Ballistic Missile (ABM) Treaty between Moscow and Washington was concluded in the same year.

Although the United States valued détente as an opportunity to restrain Soviet behavior in Europe, the reduction of tensions between the superpowers made the Soviet Union more secure as it pursued its ambitious global plans. However, Kremlin leaders could not ignore the persistent U.S. pursuit of multipolarity in East Asia. In the opinion of the Soviet leadership, the ambivalence of their U.S. counterparts regarding the centrality of superpower relations injected uncertainty into Soviet-American cooperation; for Moscow, this was a constant irritant and cause of distrust.

Thus, 1972 was an important milestone in the history of international relations. As a result of the Chinese-U.S. and Soviet-U.S. summits, the contours of triangular diplomacy were shaped, and the character of the intricate great power game became clearer. In subsequent years, the development of this great power arrangement was crucial in the formulation of the final version of Brezhnev's geo-ideological doctrine and encouraged Soviet adventurism in many regions, including Asia.

Brezhnev's Geo-ideological Doctrine, 1972–1976

On the face of it, Moscow reacted with less alarm to the 1972 Sino-American summit than it had to the early stages of the U.S.-China dialogue. Ilya Gaiduk, analyzing Soviet Foreign Ministry documents, points out that the reports from China reassured Soviet leaders to some extent. They noted with satisfaction that the Shanghai Communiqué was a result of tough bargaining between the two sides, which were "divided by disagreements" that were "difficult to overcome." The Kremlin may also have decided to counter the summit in China by improving Soviet-American relations.[54]

The Soviet attitude toward the China-U.S. rapprochement and the results of the Sino-American summit in particular was reflected in the internal analysis used in policymaking. On March 1, 1972, Professor Mikhail Sladkovsky, director of the influential Institute of

Far Eastern Affairs of the Soviet Academy of Sciences, submitted a
report to Soviet Foreign Minister Andrei Gromyko. The authors of
the report acknowledged that although there were differences in the
Chinese and U.S. positions, both countries sought improved relations and that, by signing the Shanghai Communiqué, they had
reached agreement on many major international issues. The report
expressed puzzlement that the Chinese portion of the communiqué
ignored "the existence of the socialist world" and that the Chinese
failed to mention that China "was a socialist country and would
protect the interests of socialism." Pointing to the Chinese declaration that China would "never be a superpower," the report emphasized that the Chinese thus confirmed that they had rejected the
"class approach to the characterization of the world powers."[55]

Because the Chinese statement did not refer to the relaxation
of international tensions, the Soviet analysts harshly criticized
"China's line aimed at aggravation of tensions," especially in regional conflicts, including the struggle over self-determination in
Kashmir. In Sladkovsky's view, the antihegemony declarations of
the China-U.S. communiqué were directed against both the Soviet
Union and Japan. Even the statement regarding the Taiwan problem in the communiqué was interpreted as a threat to the Soviet
Union. Although the United States had made concessions on this
issue, the Soviet experts concluded that Washington was moving
toward a settlement only because of "its intent to use this problem
to push Beijing further toward a final reorientation favorable to the
United States." The report concluded that the United States counted
on "the blurring of differences between the nationalists in Beijing
and Taipei," which eventually could allow the United States to reward Beijing with Taiwan in exchange for "China's deviation from
socialism."[56]

Lev Delusin, a former Andropov advisor and head of the Soviet
sinology think tank in the 1960–70s, argues that after the Shanghai
Communiqué was signed, the competition between Moscow and
Beijing to influence Washington intensified. Soviet policy aimed to
convince the United States of the falseness and duplicity of the
Maoist leadership.[57] In their discussions with Chinese leaders, how-

ever, Soviet leaders sought to drive a wedge between Beijing and Washington by using the Soviet-American détente to reveal "the real face" of American imperialism. Despite progress in its own negotiations with the United States, Moscow apparently remained anxious about the possibility of a secret arrangement between Washington and Beijing. Soviet leaders focused on Nixon's statement in Shanghai promising that no part of China would ever be occupied by a foreign power. Kremlin strategists interpreted Nixon's wording as "an American promise to support China in a certain situation."[58]

Soviet fears of U.S.-China collusion laid the foundation for an exaggeration of the "China threat" and acceleration of Soviet military preparations along the Soviet-Chinese border. Most decision-makers in the CPSU Central Committee were sure that the "China threat" was real; they were the "hawks" in Soviet policymaking. Despite protests from some in party headquarters, hard-line views of Chinese strategy, supported by influential experts and politicians such as Mikhail Sladkovsky and Deputy Minister of Foreign Affairs Mikhail Kapitsa, encouraged decision-makers to launch an unprecedented military buildup in the Soviet Far East, which diverted enormous resources from civil reconstruction in major Soviet cities.[59]

Similarly, the concept of a growing alliance between "reactionary imperialists" and Maoist leaders had taken hold in the minds of Soviet leaders.[60] This view laid the foundation for a national security strategy that required Moscow to confront any combination of adversaries simultaneously. This strategy required an unprecedented level of military preparations. Belief in a "growing alliance" also encouraged Moscow to pursue détente with Washington to create opportunities to use the "American card" against China. It also fueled Moscow's propaganda activities in the socialist camp and the third world, as it tried to persuade countries to turn away from China.

The Kremlin's aversion to Chinese perceptions of the world order, as well as the Soviet struggle to enforce ideological conformity on China, pushed Moscow to oppose China's new role in the international arena. Beginning in the early 1970s, China's brisk activity in the third world as "a developing country" challenged the Soviet role as "a locomotive of history" in the world revolutionary process and contributed to an unprecedented Soviet push for influence in third world countries.[61] Moscow's anti-U.S., anti-imperialist doctrine and its China policy now overlapped, and this confluence intensified the Soviet push for influence in the third world.

While opposing Chinese influence in Asia and Africa, Moscow also sought to strengthen its position in areas vitally important to the United States. In 1972 the American scholar Robert Scalapino emphasized that, despite some complementary interests, Soviet and U.S. priorities might not coincide. Scalapino predicted that if revolution or internal cataclysms in other countries could help the Soviet Union increase its influence and enhance its prestige, Moscow would use them without hesitation, justifying its activities by reference to proletarian internationalism.[62]

Scalapino's observation was true: during the rise of détente, Brezhnev repeatedly revealed the true meaning of peaceful coexistence with the West. He explained in April 1973 that "although the United States has by no means become our ally," détente was necessary for "successful socialist and communist reconstruction." By pursuing such a course, the Soviet Union "made a contribution to the communist parties in the western countries and to the peoples of South America, Africa, and Asia, because this created a barrier against use of military force or intervention against progressive nations."[63] Marxist coups d'état, supported by the Soviet Union and Cuba in former colonies of Portugal after its 1974 revolution, were typical implementations of Brezhnev's policies.

Moscow was wary of Chinese efforts to "pervert" the meaning of détente, which it feared could encourage opposition to Soviet policies in Africa and Asia.[64] As early as 1971, while supporting China's bid to join the United Nations, Soviet party leaders cast doubts on the consequences of Chinese membership. They feared that UN membership would give Beijing new opportunities to undermine Soviet ties with the developing world or even with other socialist countries.[65]

The Soviet strategy of strengthening relations with third world countries resulted in treaties of friendship and cooperation with India on August 9, 1971; with Iraq on April 9, 1972; and with Somalia on July 11, 1974. Moscow focused great attention on relations with Syria, South Yemen, Afghanistan, Palestinian leaders, and many African countries, especially Angola. The Kremlin's extreme position on the question of Bangladesh was not merely a sign of goodwill toward the people of east Bengal or toward India in general; it was also aimed at blocking U.S.-China cooperation on a critical international issue.[66]

The USSR actively used the "Vietnam factor" in its competition with Beijing for influence in the third world. Brezhnev feared a secret agreement between the United States and China regarding the Vietnam War. Moscow interpreted Beijing's willingness to meet with the U.S. president to discuss the resolution of the war as a Chinese attempt to secure influence in Southeast Asia. Moscow felt that it had to demonstrate China's true intent to the United States and reveal the Sino-American collusion to the Vietnamese people.[67] Kremlin strategists were thus pleased when, in early February 1972, Hanoi rejected China's proposal for direct high-level talks with the Americans.[68]

The end of the Vietnam War in 1975 eventually undermined U.S. and Chinese influence in Southeast Asia, and the Soviet Union gained a strong foothold in the region. Moscow's resultant conviction that the failure of imperialism would inevitably lead to the success of the socialist camp gave rise to incorrect assumptions and further excessive ambition.

Meanwhile, during 1973 and 1974, Chinese-American rapprochement stalled. According to Harry Harding, the main reasons for the stagnation in U.S.-China relations were differences over strategy toward the Soviet Union, the inability to find a mutually acceptable solution to the Taiwan issue, and the mounting domestic political difficulties of both the Chinese and the U.S. governments.[69] Indeed, the U.S. détente with the Soviet Union suggested to some Chinese leaders that progress could be made in Soviet-Chinese talks on the mutual withdrawal of forces from disputed territories. But

Brezhnev's disregard of Chinese feelers in 1974 and 1975 strengthened the Chinese leaders' view that a more conciliatory policy toward Moscow would be counterproductive.[70]

In April 1974, the Chinese delegation at the Sixth Special Session of the UN General Assembly proclaimed the fundamentals of China's foreign policy based on the "theory of the three worlds." China argued that the "socialist camp" did not exist, and it placed itself in opposition, together with other developing countries (the "third world"), to the United States and the Soviet Union (the "first world").[71] Moscow regarded China's declaration as a serious attempt to establish a united front against the Soviet Union under the banner of "struggle against the hegemony of the two superpowers."[72] China's declaration provoked a Soviet counterpolicy, which has been described as the encirclement of China.

Soviet strategy attempted to prevent China from dividing the "Soviet-tutelary" socialist movement by creating an anti-Chinese coalition of Soviet allies and developing countries. To unify the international communist movement against Beijing and its criticism of the Soviet Union's "revisionist" policy, Moscow had convened the Conference of Communist and Workers' Parties in 1969.

Soviet suggestions that the socialist camp support the separatist East Turkestan movement in Xinjiang were raised during a discussion of the "China problem" at a June 1969 plenum of the CPSU. Rather than support a separatist movement in China, Moscow argued that there was a divergence between the narrow nationalist goals of China's ruling elite and the objective interests of the Chinese people. Thus, support for the East Turkestan movement coincided with the position of proletarian internationalism pursued by all socialist countries. Because CPSU plenary meetings were political shows at which decisions made beforehand would be publicized and legitimated, the East Turkestan issue was introduced at the plenum by the First Secretary of the Communist Party of Kazakhstan, Dinmuhammed Kunaev, during the so-called discussions. According to reports of the Moscow 1969 International Congress of Communist and Workers' Parties, the participants in the plenum considered ways to facilitate the victory of "healthy" forces in China. In this context, Kunaev called for consideration of "the establishment of an independent socialist state of East Turkestan." This proposal might be considered a response to the destructive domestic policies of the Chinese leadership.[73] But it can also be interpreted as the beginning of Moscow's effort to establish an anti-Chinese coalition.[74]

Concerned since the late 1960s over the growth of Chinese influence in Asia, Soviet leaders made great efforts to establish a regional anti-Chinese coalition, although other countries that bordered China had never been able to join together in a united front against China since the end of World War II. In 1969, at the International Congress of Communist and Workers' Parties, Brezhnev proposed the idea of a collective security system for Asia. This scheme was based on the alleged China threat. However, other countries in Asia did not share Moscow's view of China. Furthermore, most Asian countries were trying to avoid commitments that would subject them to great power manipulation. They had long considered the great powers' interference in regional politics as the catalyst that transformed local conflicts into long and costly wars. Therefore, the Soviet Union's potential partners for its collective security program, including those close to the Soviet Union, such as North Vietnam, were reluctant to accept its proposal.[75] Nevertheless, Moscow never abandoned this concept. It persisted as a basic concept of Soviet policy in the Asian-Pacific region, although it was ineffective in shaping actual politics in the region and was sometimes even a hindrance to Soviet objectives.

Thus, although the Soviet Union was very concerned about the situation in the Far East, it developed an inflexible response to China's challenge to Soviet policy. Containment of the PRC along the Chinese periphery remained a high priority throughout the 1970s.[76] But Moscow failed to develop a basis for cooperation with China's neighbors. It could not overcome the fact that many Asian nations perceived the Soviet Union not as "one of them" but as a rather aggressive power with only a limited ability to provide economic support.[77]

By the mid-1970s, Moscow's inflexible Asia policy had produced a deadlock in relations with Japan. In the first half of the decade, the Soviet Union could have responded to messages from Tokyo rooted in the concept of multipolar diplomacy elaborated by Japanese

Prime Minister Kakuei Tanaka.[78] In a series of discussions during Gromyko's visit to Japan in January 1972 and Premier Tanaka's return visit to Moscow in 1973, the Soviet Union refused to disavow its unilateral refusal in 1960 to adhere to the terms of the Joint Declaration with Japan of 1956 and rejected Tanaka's proposals for improved relations. A more positive Soviet policy could have offset the harm to Soviet interests from the China-U.S. containment of the Soviet Union. At a minimum, a more flexible Japan policy could have reduced the diplomatic isolation of the Soviet Union caused by Beijing's struggle against "hegemony" and gained the Soviet Union significant economic benefits. Soviet-Japanese relations worsened following the hijacking of a MiG-23 fighter to Japan in September 1976 and subsequent Soviet-Japanese tensions over the Soviet Union's claim to territorial waters out to 200 miles.

In considering Soviet policy of the mid-1970s, one may reasonably ask why, despite such favorable factors as diminished tension with China by 1974 and the stalemate in U.S.-China relations, Moscow increased its pressure on China and confronted China in the third world. The answer can be found in the auspicious conditions for Soviet political maneuvering. Favorable international factors reinforced the Kremlin's fundamental belief in the correctness of Brezhnev's geo-ideological doctrine. Indirectly, these potentially positive factors eventually doomed U.S.-Soviet détente.

The reasons for the failure of détente are in dispute. One of the weak points of Soviet détente policy was that it was based on an implicit double standard with respect to waging the ideological struggle under peaceful coexistence. As Garthoff has characterized it, "That approach assumes that it is all right and consistent with détente for the Soviet Union to carry on such a struggle in the capitalist and Third World, but that the same does not apply to the United States or others within the socialist world." Moreover, "waging a political and ideological struggle tends to undermine, if it does not contradict, declared desires for increasing trust and confidence, and ultimately even the ability to conduct a policy of détente."[79]

There are various interpretations of Soviet policy in Asia. Some scholars point to the inherent aggressiveness of the Soviet Union as an explanation for its failure to take a positive approach to relations with the United States. Adam Ulam, for example, assumed that the Soviet Union, after failing to involve the United States in its anti-China activity, lost interest in détente by the mid-1970s and began pursuing expansion in the third world.[80]

Another persuasive interpretation is proposed by Bogatourov. He argues that in the 1970s the Soviet leadership was dominated by aging politicians with a conservative *Weltanschauung*. Given their confidence in the Soviet Union's global superiority, corroborated by strategic parity with the United States, the U.S. fiasco in Vietnam, and the panic in the West during the oil shocks of the 1970s, Moscow could not accurately assess the potential for U.S. resurgence. The Politburo was not capable of abandoning its belief in the "world crisis of capitalism." Thus, the CPSU Central Committee could not forcefully convey the possibility of a reversal in trends in the United States to Soviet party leaders, who were tempted to use short-term U.S. weaknesses for their own purposes, in a reflection of the tenets of proletarian internationalism.[81]

The Soviet Union's confrontational approach and its reliance on Brezhnev's geo-ideological paradigm deepened in response to the Asia strategy proposed by President Gerald Ford. In December 1975 in Hawaii, President Ford proclaimed the so-called Ford Doctrine for Asia. The principle of "multilateral containment" in the Pacific region, developed by the Nixon administration, remained dominant, and Washington continued to argue that the "quadrilateral" balance of power in Asia served the vital interests of the United States.[82] Thus, while Washington's adherence to détente remained solid, its pursuit of an "anti-bipolar" structure intensified.

The priority given to global issues and, to a lesser extent, to regional affairs in U.S. statements did not escape the attention of Soviet leaders. But most important was Washington's re-evaluation of the United States' strategic posture in Asia. After its defeat in Vietnam, the United States seemed to reshuffle the roles of its Asian allies to favor Japan. President Ford's statement that "shock diplomacy" toward Japan had ended revealed the importance of Japan to the United States.[83] In addition, Soviet analysts regarded the emergence in 1974 of the "Schlesinger Doctrine," which was based on a nuclear strategy of flexible response minimizing collateral damage from nuclear assured destruction, as a sign of U.S. doubts about the efficacy of Sino-American rapprochement.[84]

A thorough analysis of President Ford's visit to China in December 1975 strengthened Moscow's belief that the United States would not sacrifice the achievements of détente to deepen relations with China. Moscow also realized that Beijing was exhibiting some nervousness about Soviet-U.S. relations and that China's call to "surround" the Soviet Union had become louder. At that time, Vladimir Lukin, a prominent Soviet expert on international relations, concluded that Washington clearly acknowledged the priority of its relations with the Soviet Union over those with China. He noted that the United States was led by its national interests, not by Chinese advice.[85]

Perhaps it was Moscow's analysis of the Ford doctrine and of Ford's visits to China, Japan, the Philippines, and Indonesia that encouraged Moscow to maintain its course in international politics. The Soviets concluded that the United States had made concessions because of détente and that there were visible limits to the Chinese-U.S. alliance. These conclusions filled Kremlin ideologists with confidence about the direction of Soviet foreign policy.

Thus, by 1976 a convergence of factors in the international environment enabled Moscow to use the achievements of détente in favor of its revolutionary objectives in world affairs and in its competition with China. These spurred Soviet leaders to greater efforts to implement Brezhnev's global doctrine, which was developed and elaborated at the Twenty-Fifth Congress of the CPSU in February and March 1976.

New Challenges After 1976 and the Soviet Response

During the Twenty-Fifth Congress of the CPSU, the principal Soviet international course developed in the early 1970s was reconfirmed and theoretically justified. The proceedings of the congress reveal that Moscow's understanding of détente had reached its final form and peaceful coexistence had gained a well-defined focus: the responsibility and highest priority of Soviet foreign policy was securing the victory of international communism. One year later, this formulation was legitimized in the new constitution of the Soviet Union, which held that the precondition for friendship and cooperation with other countries was their commitment to socialist internationalism (not proletarian internationalism).[86]

The party congress also reconfirmed the idea of a system of collective security for Asia composed of all the states in the region. Brezhnev called for a search for ways to strengthen peace in Asia, rejecting the western assertion that a collective security system could not be established because of conflicts between the nationalism of the powerful and the nationalism of the powerless. In addition, the Soviet Union agreed with the proposal of the Association of Southeast Asian Nations (ASEAN) to establish a Zone of Peace, Freedom, and Neutrality in Southeast Asia. Brezhnev generally welcomed the PRC's participation in measures aimed at strengthening security in Asia, but he noted that China had been the first to oppose this idea.[87] There was no indication that the United States could participate in Moscow's plan. Moscow remained determined to divide its adversaries by any and all means.

The year 1976 was a landmark in terms of domestic changes in China. After Mao's death in September, China's foreign policy remained unclear until the summer of 1977. But Beijing's assessment of the prospects for its relationship with the superpowers appeared to be influenced less by Mao's death than by changes in the international environment. After 1975, the Soviet Union extended its military power to distant areas in several African countries. Moreover, the American debacle in Vietnam suggested opportunities for increased Soviet influence throughout Indochina. In this context, China began to warn that the Soviet Union presented the "most dangerous" threat of war.[88] Similarly, although Mao's successors did not adhere to his view that a new world war was inevitable, they concurred with Mao that there would not be a war between China and the Soviet Union and that superpower contention was the most likely source of world war. They also concurred that the pursuit of détente with Moscow was a dangerous illusion.[89] Thus, those in Moscow who expected radical changes in China's policy were disappointed. Moscow's continuing opposition to

Chinese policy led it to intensify Soviet expansionism to secure a strategic advantage in regional affairs.

Although advocating the concept of the two-power condominium with regulated competition with the United States, in practice Moscow more than once challenged this approach in its activities in Asia, Africa, and South America. The dogmatic presumption of a deepening crisis in the capitalist countries encouraged Kremlin strategists to greater efforts to develop a "global revolutionary process." Although the Soviet leadership was well aware of western accusations that it was "undermining détente" by supporting liberation struggles, it ignored such criticisms. After gaining access to ports in Ethiopia and South Yemen in the second half of the 1970s, the Soviet military developed a greater ability to project power along the strategic oil transportation routes from the Middle East to the United States, and Moscow enjoyed greater political influence throughout the Persian Gulf and Middle East. These provocative measures, although unimportant in enhancing Soviet security vis-à-vis the United States, were of great concern in Washington, especially in the context of U.S.-Iranian tensions after the Islamic revolution in Iran in 1979.

The sources of Soviet expansion in the Persian Gulf and the Middle East have yet to be closely analyzed. The available evidence does not allow a definitive statement whether Moscow undertook these policies merely to pressure the United States regarding Chinese-U.S. strategic cooperation. It is more persuasive to argue that Soviet activity in this area was a part of its overall program of fighting imperialism on a global scale.[90]

The post-Mao continuity in China's foreign policy was reflected in Beijing's response to the expansion of Soviet and Vietnamese influence in Southeast Asia. Chinese leaders assessed Vietnamese and Soviet efforts in Indochina as part of Moscow's objective of "encircling" China. They were concerned that Vietnamese success, with Soviet help, in building a formal or tacit "Indochinese federation" could revive the concept of an Asian collective security system, which Beijing continued to regard as a transparent vehicle to legitimate a Soviet strategic presence on China's periphery.[91]

China exaggerated Moscow's role in the political changes in Indochina and underestimated Vietnam's concern for Chinese power. In 1977–78, Vietnam demonstrated its own intent to dominate Indochina; its expansionism was not just a result of its relationship with Moscow. Some scholars have found evidence for Vietnamese ambitions in the declarations of high-level Vietnamese politicians.[92] Nevertheless, Vietnam's entry into the Council for Mutual Economic Assistance in June 1978 and the signing of the Soviet-Vietnamese Treaty of Peace and Friendship in November of that same year underscored the degree of cooperation between the Soviet Union and Vietnam in Indochina. Harry Gelman has argued that the treaty was instrumental in Vietnam's incursion into Cambodia a month after the treaty was signed.[93]

Although the 1976 CPSU congress demonstrated the continuity of the Soviet interest in maintaining bipolarity, the new Carter administration was strengthening the tendency toward multipolarity. Unlike more pragmatic Republicans, the Democratic party and President Carter could not accept the Soviet model of dual superpower hegemony. The new administration's approach to foreign affairs stressed opposition to restrictions on freedom of choice and attempts to subjugate smaller nations to global-scale strategies.

After years of Chinese criticism of U.S.-Soviet détente and disarmament agreements, in 1977 President Carter started to develop a new China policy and was determined to revive U.S.-China cooperation. Considerable efforts were needed, however, to convince Beijing of the United States' good faith. From the spring of 1978, Zbigniew Brzezinski, as Carter's advisor for national security affairs, became the most influential policymaker in the development of the United States' Asia policy. Well known as an advocate of a tough posture toward the Soviet Union, Brzezinski argued that Washington could use Chinese-Soviet tensions to draw Soviet attention away from events in Poland, thus reducing Soviet pressure in Europe. This new assessment of China's potential contribution to containment accelerated U.S.-China contacts in the last years of the Carter administration. By advancing the normalization of relations, Washington played a pivotal role in triangular politics.

Coincidentally, beginning in 1977 the "pragmatists" in Beijing gained the upper hand and sought a Chinese role in the U.S. strategic system in East Asia. This objective promoted greater Chinese cooperation with Japan. The Sino-Japanese Treaty of Peace and Friendship of 1978, which included a joint commitment to oppose "hegemonism," was a result of those efforts.[94] Thus, Chinese leaders continued to use an "antihegemony" front to contain the Soviet Union.[95]

The United States' playing of the "China card" was generally successful. In May 1978, President Carter confirmed that he would not object to sales by Western European countries of weapons to China. At the end of the year, Washington restored diplomatic relations with China and thereafter maintained only unofficial, nongovernmental relations with Taiwan. In January 1979, Deng Xiaoping paid his historic visit to the United States. The visit coincided with the deterioration of Chinese-Vietnamese relations, following Hanoi's dispatch of troops to Cambodia against the Pol Pot regime. When Deng returned from the United States and launched China's punitive invasion of Vietnam, there was an implicit understanding that the attack had been sanctioned by the United States.[96] Over the course of the next year, Washington withdrew U.S. troops from Taiwan and abrogated the U.S.-Taiwan Mutual Defense Treaty of 1954.

Chinese participation in the U.S. strategic system led to Soviet concerns about a Sino-American alliance.[97] But Moscow's policy remained ambivalent. After 1976, as China continued to adhere to its three worlds concept, Moscow characterized this theory as "evidence of a class betrayal by the Chinese leadership."[98] Soviet leaders also persisted in trying to pressure China to return to "socialism." But there were also new developments in Soviet policy. First, Moscow used the phrase "socialist internationalism" more often than "proletarian internationalism" to describe the basis for relations with China. Second, in its opposition to U.S. use of the "Chinese card," Moscow appealed to Chinese nationalism. Soviet leaders stressed to China the duplicity of U.S. policy and pointed out that, for Washington, China was an object, not a subject, of international relations.[99]

In this context, in 1978 Moscow launched a series of important initiatives toward China, including the Supreme Soviet's appeal to the Standing Committee of China's National People's Congress (CNPC) on February 24. Because of their concern about the U.S.-China interactions, the Soviets were trying to resume talks in any form, to respond in a timely fashion to new developments, and, possibly, to start a deeper dialogue with China's new leaders. In a special letter addressed to the delegates of the CNPC, Moscow stated that Sino-Soviet tensions could undermine peace and stability in Asia and proposed to jointly formulate some key principles of the relationship between the two nations.

Two days later, in a report to the CNPC session, Hua Guofeng asked the Soviet Union to prove its intent with concrete practical actions. The Chinese leader suggested that the two sides should sign an agreement on the maintenance of the status quo along the Soviet-Chinese border, on mutual withdrawal of armed forces from disputed areas, and on Soviet withdrawal of troops from other areas near the Chinese border and also from Mongolia. Officially, in a memo dated March 9, 1978, Beijing characterized Moscow's appeal as "unable to settle any practical issue." The Chinese side reconfirmed its position in an official diplomatic note of July 9, 1978, addressed to Moscow. China needed additional Soviet commitments to guarantee China's security and eliminate the "Soviet threat."

For the Soviet side, these were unacceptable and unreasonable requirements. Moscow was wounded by China's cool response and its unwillingness to extend the famous 1950 Sino-Soviet friendship treaty, although it had signed a peace treaty with Japan on August 12, 1978. At a Politburo meeting in August, Kremlin leaders harshly criticized Beijing's policy of military cooperation and alignment with imperialist countries. China's official declarations in August-October 1978 of termination of the Sino-Soviet treaty aggravated the situation. China-NATO relations became one of the hottest issues at the Warsaw Treaty Political Consulting Committee's meeting in November that year, which evaluated China's attachment to the western military through the prism of strategic concerns.

Nevertheless, the Chinese posture as it was formulated at the CNPC, despite its requirements and terms, laid the foundation for concrete talks. Besides, the 1979 China-Vietnam border war demonstrated the limits of China-U.S. cooperation. The United States seemed cautious about becoming involved in this war against the Soviet camp, especially after Russia's adventurism in Afghanistan at the end of 1979.[100] Likewise, the China-Vietnam conflict demonstrated an important change in the Soviet posture toward China. Moscow revealed its caution about using its military to help its socialist ally resist aggression. It is widely assumed that, after the revival of U.S.-China relations in 1978, the Soviet Union had to take into account the possibility of an American military response if it invaded China in support of Vietnam, as suggested by the terms of the Soviet-Vietnamese treaty.

In Bogatourov's view, the moderate Soviet position on the Chinese-Vietnamese war reflected the nature of the treaty, which stipulated consultative measures in cases of aggression and did not obligate Moscow to respond militarily to all external threats to Vietnam. The treaty with Vietnam contained a weaker commitment of Soviet support than those found in Soviet agreements with the Warsaw Pact countries, Mongolia, and North Korea. By omitting a clear obligation to assist Vietnam militarily, Moscow diminished the strategic significance of this treaty, thus signaling to China and the United States its reluctance to increase tensions in Southeast Asia. Although the Chinese leadership remained intent on underscoring the danger of the Soviet-Vietnamese alliance to Washington, its understanding of Soviet restraint was an important factor in facilitating the Moscow-Beijing dialogue in 1979.[101] In April 1979 Moscow proposed a resumption of talks with China on intergovernmental issues, and Beijing responded positively.

The Chinese-Soviet talks started in September 1979. There may have been a real opportunity at this time for the Soviet leadership to improve relations with Beijing, due to the increased post-normalization tensions between Beijing and Washington over Taiwan. It was the first opportunity for Moscow and Beijing to talk about state-to-state relations, putting aside ideological, party-to-party, and even border issues. The Chinese side advanced conditions for ending the "cold war" between the two countries, but the Soviet Union could not take advantage of the situation.[102] Moscow was unable to overcome the inertia in its strategic thinking and therefore considered the Chinese demands one-sided, rather than as serving mutual interests.[103] Then, after the first round of negotiations in November, they were never resumed, because of the Soviet invasion in Afghanistan.[104] Although little was achieved at these early talks, the initial Chinese proposals were advanced without the usual insistence on prior conditions unacceptable to Moscow, such as demanding Soviet troop withdrawals from Mongolia and disputed areas along the border.

The Soviet invasion of Afghanistan was the last major expression of the Soviet Union's decade-long approach to world politics. The invasion caused great damage to the Soviet position in the third world and to U.S.-Soviet détente. In addition, it accelerated China's military rapprochement with the United States to contain Soviet power. Despite progress in talks with President Carter on the SALT II agreement in June 1979, Soviet policy was becoming more unpredictable, because of the growing role of force in Soviet foreign policy. By 1980 the Soviet Union found itself isolated in world affairs.

Conclusion

Soviet foreign policy in the 1970s toward the United States and China had both active and reactive aspects. The active aspect was determined by the ideological imperative of world revolutionary struggle against imperialism, as Leninist thinking from the beginning of the twentieth century was applied to a new era. However, the practical evolution of Moscow's foreign policy was not consistent with the formal logic of the party's conventions and theories. Since Soviet foreign policy combined competing elements, it often appeared to be contradictory. In the "reactive" dimension, Soviet policymakers tried—unsuccessfully—to adapt doctrine to changes in the structure of relations in the Asia-Pacific region, including intergovernmental and systemic dimensions. The predominance of ideological dogmatism led the Soviet Union to develop an idealistic approach to world affairs. Hence, Moscow failed to grasp the character of the changes in international politics and was slow in developing an adequate response.

The changes in Soviet geostrategic interests and international behavior in the 1960s determined the historic turn in China's foreign policy. The Soviet Union's striving for peaceful coexistence with capitalist powers, its efforts to consolidate the socialist camp after its 1968 invasion of Czechoslovakia, and its increased political and military pressure directed at internationally isolated and domestically devastated China inspired Beijing's search for a new relationship with the outer world. In response to the Nixon administration's interest in using the "China card" to settle the Vietnam War, U.S. détente and arms control negotiations with the Kremlin, and its own fears of the "Soviet threat," the Chinese leadership ended China's global isolation. They turned to U.S.-China rapprochement to build a political bulwark to contain Soviet expansion.

Significant changes in Asian political configurations, brought about by the Sino-Soviet border conflict and the Chinese-American rapprochement, dramatically affected Soviet policy in Asia (in both its active and reactive dimensions) and the Soviet posture in its negotiations with the United States in the first half of the 1970s. The emergence of a "China factor" was extremely significant in both global and regional affairs.

Throughout the 1970s, the Chinese-American rapprochement did not mean that Washington ignored the Soviet role in world affairs. Even as U.S. policies rejected the regional bipolar structure in Asia, U.S.-Soviet relations remained the basis for the global balance of power and the international order until 1991. Washington's policy was a very effective effort by the United States to further its national interests by developing a multipolar balance of power in Asia.

However, the Soviet Union adhered firmly to its perception of bipolarity and opposed the growing trend toward regional multipolarity. Thus, it resisted U.S. abandonment of the logic of bipolarity. In addition, a well-grounded anxiety about the gradual encirclement of the Soviet Union from the east by the armed forces of China, the United States, and its allies in East Asia became a decisive factor in Soviet policymaking. Soviet leaders responded to these new challenges by seeking military-strategic parity with this anti-Soviet coalition. Thus, well before the 1980s, Moscow engaged in a self-defeating arms race as it sought the capability to conduct "two and a half wars" simultaneously and to establish an equilibrium of power with the aggregate potential of the United States, China, and Western Europe.

Throughout most of the 1970s, the Soviet Union made great efforts to press Washington to resist explicit cooperation with China against the Soviet Union. At times it even promoted active anti-Chinese cooperation with the United States. In general, the United States responded positively to Soviet concerns, even as it developed closer relations with Beijing. Only at the end of the decade, following the Soviet invasion of Afghanistan, did the Soviet Union and the United States demonstrate a serious divergence in their approaches to China.

During the 1970s, the Asian aspects of Soviet foreign policy never took priority over the European ones. The failure of détente can by no means be attributed solely to the Soviet response to U.S.-China cooperation, but the Chinese policy toward developing countries clearly pressured Moscow to be more aggressive in the struggle for the allegiance of third world countries, and this obviously undermined détente. Thus, China played an indirect role in the decline of détente. Chinese policy, in turn, reflected the dogmatic Soviet attachment to "proletarian internationalism" and Moscow's expansionism in the third world. Chinese leaders' perception of both a specific Soviet military threat and a serious Soviet geopolitical threat reflected their view of the Soviet Union as a "social-imperialist" power.

Soviet policy toward China was based primarily on a continuous evaluation of the degree of China's conformity to the tenets of proletarian internationalism and the class struggle. Throughout the 1970s, Soviet leaders persistently tried to convince their Chinese counterparts that a small group of leaders in Beijing was acting under a great delusion; they persisted in the effort to draw the Chinese Communist Party back to the "socialist camp" under the banner of the anti-imperialist struggle. Even at the end of the decade, when Moscow began to take China's national interests into account, the Soviet Union mechanically adhered to its guiding geo-ideological premises and continued to increase its overall military potential.

Reference Matter

Notes

Introduction

1. Two books were published in China: Jiang Changbin and Robert S. Ross, eds., *1955–1971 nian de Zhong Mei guanxi—Huanhe zhiqian: lengzhan chongtu yu kezhi de cai tantao* (U.S.-China relations, 1955–71—Before détente: an examination of cold war conflict and restraint) (Beijing: Shijie zhishi chubanshe, 1998); and Jiang Changbin and Robert S. Ross, eds., *Zong duizhi zouxiang huanhe: lengzhan shiqi zhong Zhong Mei guanxi zai tantao* (From confrontation to détente: a re-examination of cold war U.S.-China relations) (Beijing: Shijie zhishi chubanshe, 2000). The second volume included papers from the first volume as well as from the second stage of the project. The American volume covered the papers from both stages of the project: Robert S. Ross and Jiang Changbin, eds., *Re-examining the Cold War: U.S.-China Diplomacy, 1954–1973* (Cambridge, MA: Harvard University Asia Center, 2001). The Chinese-language edition of the current volume was published in China as Gong Li, William C. Kirby, and Robert S. Ross, eds., *Zong jiedong zouxiang jianjiao: Zhong Mei guanxi zhengchanghua jincheng zai tantuo* (From thaw to normalization: a re-examination of the normalization of U.S.-China relations) (Beijing: Zhongyang wenxian chubanshe, 2004).

Chapter 1

1. Henry Kissinger, *White House Years* (Boston: Little, Brown, 1979), 1062, 1092.

2. Robert J. McMahon, "Credibility and World Power: Exploring the Psychological Dimension in Postwar Diplomacy," *Diplomatic History* 15 (Fall 1991): 455–72; Walter Isaacson, *Kissinger, A Biography* (New York: Simon and Schuster, 1992), 115.

3. Memorandum of conversation, Feb. 22, 1972, box 848, For the President's Files (Winston Lord)-China Trip/Vietnam (FPF-China Trip/Vietnam), National Security Council Files (NSC), Richard M. Nixon Presidential Materials (NPM), National Archives, Washington, DC (NA).

4. Department of State Briefing Paper, "Modification of the Taiwan Strait Patrol," Feb. 17, 1972, in ibid.

5. Memorandum, Kissinger to the President, Oct. 16, 1969, box 1031, For the President's Files-China/Vietnam Negotiations (FPF-China/Vietnam Negotiations), NSC, NPM.

6. "Modification of the Taiwan Strait Patrol," Feb. 1972, box 848, FPF-China Trip/Vietnam, NSC, NPM.

7. Kissinger, *White House Years*, 189–90, 684–93.

8. "Paul Kreisberg Oral Interview," Apr. 18, 1989, in *Frontline Diplomacy: The U.S. Foreign Affairs Oral History Collection*, CD-ROM (Arlington, VA: Association for Diplomatic Studies and Training, 2000). Kreisberg was the director of the Office of Asian Communist Affairs at the time of the Warsaw talks.

9. Cable, Rogers to U.S. Embassy Warsaw, Jan. 17, 1970, *China and the United States: From Hostility to Engagement*, Microfiche Collection (Alexandria, VA: Chadwyck-Healey, 1999), microfiche 00115.

10. Cable, Stoessel to State Department, Jan. 20, 1970, microfiche 00118, in ibid.; cable, Stoessel to State Department, Jan. 21, 1970, microfiche 00122, in ibid.

11. Memorandum, Kissinger to the President, Jan. 21, 1970, box 700, Country Files-Poland Warsaw Talks, NSC, NPM.

12. Memorandum, Rogers to the President, Feb. 7, 1970, box 2188, POL CHICOM-US, Subject-Numeric File, 1970–73, Department of State Record Files, Record Group (RG) 59, NA; State Department Paper, "U.S. Strategy in Current Sino-U.S. Talks," [Feb. 1970], ibid.

13. Memorandum, Kissinger to the Acting Secretary of State, Feb. 18, 1970, ibid.

14. Cable, State Department to U.S. Embassy Warsaw, Feb. 18, 1970, ibid.

15. Cable, Stoessel to State Department, Feb. 20, 1970, box 1031, FPF-China/Vietnam Negotiations, NSC, NPM.

16. Kissinger, *White House Years*, 690–91; memorandum, Rogers to the President, Mar. 10, 1970, box 2188, POL CHICOM-US, Subject-Numeric File, 1970–73, RG 59, NA; Kissinger to Rogers, Mar. 20, 1970, box 913, NSC, VIP Visits, NPM.

17. Cable, State Department to U.S. Embassy Warsaw, May 7, 1970, *China and the United States, 1960–1998*, microfiche 00172.

18. Kissinger, *White House Years*, 693.

19. Ibid., 686.

20. Message from the Chinese Government, Dec. 9, 1970, box 1031, FPF-China/Vietnam Negotiations, NSC, NPM.

21. Excerpt from memorandum of conversation, Oct. 26, 1970, ibid.

22. Kissinger, *White House Years*, 701.

23. Attachment to memorandum of conversation, Dec. 16, 1970, box 1031, FPF-China/Vietnam Negotiations, NSC, NPM.

24. Record of a discussion, Dec. 16, 1970, ibid.

25. Memorandum, Kissinger to the President, Jan. 11, 1971, box 1025, Presidential/HAK Memcons, NSC, NPM.

26. Kissinger, *White House Years*, 714–16.

27. Transcript of a Telephone Conversation, Apr. 27, 1971, box 1031, FPF-China Trip/Vietnam Negotiations, NSC, NPM.

28. Message to the Chinese, May 10, 1971, ibid.

29. Message from Chou En Lai (Zhou Enlai), no date, ibid.

30. NSSM 106, "United States China Policy," Feb. 16, 1971, *China and the United States, 1960–1998*, microfiche 00194; Department of State Issues Paper (NSSM 106) on U.S. China Policy, Mar. 6, 1971, microfiche 00122, ibid.

31. NSSM 124, "Next Steps Toward the People's Republic of China," May 27, 1971, microfiche 00211, ibid.

32. Memorandum, Kissinger to the Acting Secretary of State, May 15, 1969, box 1985, POL CHINAT-US, Subject-Numeric File, 1967–69, RG 59, NA.

33. Memorandum, Theodore Eliot, Jr., to Kissinger, Aug. 5, 1969, box 1986, POL 17 CHINAT-US, ibid.; memorandum, Kissinger to the Vice President, Dec. 17, 1969, box 81, NSC, HAK Office Files, Country Files-Far East-General, NPM; "Republic of China Objectives Paper," August 1970, box 74, Briefing Books, 1958–1976, RG 59, NA.

34. Nixon to Chiang Kai-shek, Mar. 27, 1970, box 751, Presidential Correspondence, 1969–72, Name Files, NSC, NPM.

35. Cable, State Department to U.S. Embassy Taipei, Apr. 24, 1970, box 913, FPF-China Trip/Vietnam, VIP Visits, NSC, NPM; James C. H. Shen, *The U.S. and Free China: How the U.S. Sold Out Its Ally* (Washington, DC: Acropolis Books, 1983), 51.

36. Leonard A. Kusnitz, *Public Opinion and Foreign Policy: America's China Policy, 1949–1979* (Westport, CT: Greenwood Press, 1984), 120, 138, 143–44; Rosemary Foot, *The Practice of Power: U.S. Relations with China Since 1949* (Oxford: Clarendon Press, 1995), 101–8.

37. Mary C. Brennan, *Turning Right in the Sixties: The Conservative Capture of the GOP* (Chapel Hill: University of North Carolina Press, 1995), 122–24, 135; James Mann, *About Face: A History of America's Curious Relationship with China from Nixon to Clinton* (New York, Knopf, 1999), 22.

38. "[Briefing Paper] Summit," Briefing Book July 1971 Trip to China, box 850, FPF-China Trip/Vietnam, NSC, NPM.

39. "[Briefing Paper] Taiwan," ibid.

40. Kissinger, *White House Years*, 749.

41. Memorandum of conversation, July 9, 1971, box 846, FPF-China Trip/Vietnam, NSC, NPM.

42. Memorandum of conversation, July 10, 1971, ibid.

43. Memorandum of conversation, July 9, 1971, ibid.

44. Memorandum, Winston Lord to Kissinger, Nov. 23, 1971, box 330, Director's Files (Winston Lord), 1969–77, RG 59, NA. A paper on Taiwan in a briefing book later prepared for the president by the State Department for his China trip described the Taiwan independence movement as a "collection of uncoordinated expatriate factions resident primarily in Japan and the United States." The paper stated that the United States had never given official support or encouragement to Taiwan independence groups in the United States, Japan, or Taiwan. "[Briefing Paper] Taiwan," [Feb. 1972]. Briefing Book for February 1972 China Trip, box 848, FPF-China Trip/Vietnam, NSC, NPM.

45. Memorandum of conversation, July 9, 1971, box 846, FPF-China Trip/Vietnam, NSC, NPM. For China's involvement in the Vietnam conflict, see Qiang Zhai, *China and the Vietnam Wars, 1950–1975* (Chapel Hill: University of North Carolina Press, 2000).

46. Memorandum of conversation, July 10, 1971, box 846, FPF-China Trip/Vietnam, NSC, NPM.

47. "U.S-China: Renunciation of Force," attached to Eliot to Kissinger, Mar. 24, 1971, *China and the U.S., 1960–1998*, microfiche 00206.

48. Memorandum of conversation, July 11, 1971, box 846, FPF-China Trip/Vietnam, NSC, NPM.

49. Memorandum, Kissinger to the President, July 14, 1971, box 1032, ibid.; Kissinger, *White House Years*, 751–53.

50. Memorandum, Kissinger to the President, July 14, 1971, box 1032, FPF-China Trip/Vietnam, NSC, NPM.

51. "Remarks to the Nation Announcing Acceptance of an Invitation to Visit the People's Republic of China," July 15, 1971, *Public Papers of the Presidents of the United States, Richard Nixon, 1971* (Washington, DC: U.S. Government Printing Office, 1972), 819–20.

52. Seymour M. Hersh, *The Price of Power: Kissinger in the Nixon White House* (New York: Summit Books, 1983), 372.

53. Memorandum, John Richardson, Jr., to the Secretary of State, Oct. 4, 1971, box 52, Office of Public Opinion Studies, 1943–1975, RG 59, NA.

54. Richard Nixon, *The Memoirs of Richard Nixon* (New York: Grosset and Dunlap, 1978), 554; Mann, *About Face*, 37–38.

55. Following his visit to Taipei, Reagan informed the president that the situation on the island was "understandably unsettled" as a result of the China initiative "but that in the final analysis he felt that the people of Taiwan understand the reasons for the President's trip to Peking." Memorandum for the President's File, Nov. 17, 1971, box 86, President's Office Files, Memoranda for the President, NSC, NPM.

56. Cable, U.S. Embassy Taipei to State Department, July 16, 1971, box 2205, POL CHINAT-US, Subject-Numeric File, 1970–73, RG 59, NA; telegram, U.S. Embassy Taipei to State Department, July 17, 1971, ibid.

57. Cable, State Department to U.S. Embassy Taipei, July 19, 1971, ibid.; Shen, *U.S. and Free China*, 72–74.

58. Telegram, State Department to U.S. Embassy Taipei, July 16, 1971, box 751, Presidential Correspondence, 1969–74, NSC, NPM.

59. Memorandum, Rogers to the President, July 21, 1971, box 2191, POL 1 CHICOM-US, Subject-Numeric File, 1970–73, RG 59, NA.

60. Foot, *Practice of Power*, 22–45.

61. NSSM 107, "Study of the Entire UN Membership Question: U.S./China Policy," January 25, 1971, *China and the U.S., 1960–1998*, microfiche 00199.

62. *New York Times*, Aug. 3, 1971.

63. Kissinger, *White House Years*, 772–74.

64. Memorandum, Kissinger to the President, Mar. 20, 1971, box 86, HAK Office Files, Country Files-Far East, NSC, NPM.

65. Memorandum, Kissinger to the President, Apr. 9, 1971, box 1025, Presidential/HAK Memcons, NSC, NPM.

66. Memorandum of conversation, Mar. 31, 1971, box 321, UN 6 CHICOM, Subject-Numeric File, 1970–73, NA; cable, Marshall Green to Walter McConaughy, Apr. 19, 1971, box 86, HAK Office Files, Country Files-Far East, NSC, NPM.

67. "Summary Record of Conversation Between President Chiang Kai-shek and Mr. Robert D. Murphy," Apr. 23, 1971, box 1031, FPF-China/Vietnam Negotiations, NSC, NPM.

68. Memorandum, Kissinger to the President, May 13, 1971, ibid.; Memorandum for the President's File, May 21, 1971, box 85, President's Office Files, Memoranda for the President, NPM.

69. Briefing Paper [Taiwan], Briefing Book July 1971 Trip to China, box 850, FPF-China Trip/Vietnam, NSC, NPM.

70. Memorandum of conversation, July 10, 1971, box 846, ibid.; memorandum of conversation, July 11, 1971, ibid.

71. Briefing Paper, Briefing Book for Kissinger's October 1971 Trip to China, Oct. 12, 1971, box 851, ibid.

72. Memorandum, Rogers to the President, May 28, 1971, box 85, Briefing Books, 1958–76, RG 59, NA; memorandum of conversation, May 28, 1971, UN 6 CHICOM, box 3210, Subject-Numeric File, 1970–73, RG 59, NA.

73. Memorandum, Rogers to the President, July 3, 1971, UN 6 CHICOM, box 3211, Subject-Numeric File, 1970–73, RG 59, NA.

74. Cable, U.S. Embassy Taipei to State Department, July 27, 1971, ibid.

75. H. R. Haldeman, *The Haldeman Diaries: Inside the Nixon White House* (New York: G. P. Putnam's Sons, 1994), 318.

76. *New York Times,* Aug. 3, 1971; cable, U.S. Embassy Taipei to State Department, July 31, 1971, UN 6 CHICOM, box 3211, Subject-Numeric File, 1970–73, RG 59, NA.

77. Memorandum, Rogers to the President, Sept. 5, 1971, UN 6 CHICOM, box 3212, Subject-Numeric File, 1970–73, RG 59, NA.

78. Cable, U.S. Embassy Taipei to State Department, Sept. 10, 1971, POL CHINAT-US, box 2205, ibid.; memorandum, Rogers to the President, Sept. 11, 1971, UN 6 CHICOM, box 3213, ibid.; circular cable, State Department to Various U.S. Embassies, Sept. 17, 1971, POL 7 CHINAT, box 2202, ibid.

79. Foot, *Practice of Power*, 45–46; John W. Garver, *The Sino-American Alliance: Nationalist China and American Cold War Strategy in Asia* (Armonk, NY: M. E. Sharpe, 1997), 253–62.

80. Kissinger, *White House Years*, 775–76; cable, USUN Mission to State Department, Oct. 7, 1971, POL 7 CHINAT, box 2202, Subject-Numeric File, 1970–73, RG 59, NA.

81. Memorandum, Rogers to the President, Oct. 12, 1971, UN 6 CHICOM, box 3214, Subject-Numeric File, 1970–73, RG 59, NA.

82. Kissinger, *White House Years*, 775–76, 784.

83. George Bush, *Looking Forward* (Garden City, NY: Doubleday, 1987), 115; telegram, State Department to U.S. Embassy Taipei, Oct. 27, 1971, UN 6 CHICOM, box 3216, Subject-Numeric File, 1970–73, RG 59, NA; Nancy Bernkopf Tucker, ed., *China Confidential: American Diplomats and Sino-American Relations, 1945–1996* (New York: Columbia University Press, 2001), 262–63.

84. Memorandum, Rogers to the President, Nov. 10, 1971, UN 6 CHICOM, box 3216, Subject-Numeric File, 1970–73, RG 59, NA.

85. Rogers told Nationalist officials that "the President had been deeply involved in the effort to assure continued ROC representation in the United Nations." Memorandum of conversation, Oct. 29, 1971, ibid. Nixon personally called the presidents of several Latin American countries in a last-ditch attempt

to gain their support on the UN votes. Haig to Kissinger, Oct. 22, 1971, box 1035, FPF-China Trip/Vietnam, NSC, NPM.

86. Memorandum of conversation, Oct. 21, 1971, box 846, ibid. This new evidence contradicts the view of some authors that Kissinger wanted U.S. efforts to prevent Taiwan's ouster to fail in order to eliminate an obstruction to improved U.S.-PRC relations. See, e.g., Patrick Tyler, *A Great Wall: Six Presidents and China, an Investigative History* (New York: Public Affairs, 1999), 112. A fine new study of Kissinger echoes Tyler in stressing Kissinger's lack of interest in safeguarding Taiwan's membership in the United Nations but does not take into account the evidence presented here. See Jussi Hanhimaki, *The Flawed Architect: Henry Kissinger and American Foreign Policy* (New York: Oxford University Press, 2004), 145, 174–75.

87. Kissinger, *White House Years*, 785.

88. Haldeman, *Haldeman Diaries*, 386.

89. Briefing Book for Under Secretary Johnson's East Asian Trip, Nov. 9–23, 1971, Nov. 5, 1971, box 92, Briefing Books, 1958–76, RG 59, NA.

90. Bureau of Intelligence and Research, "Republic of China: Post-UN Priorities," Oct. 29, 1971, UN 6–2 CHINAT, box 3217, Subject-Numeric Files, 1970–73, RG 59, NA.

91. Briefing Paper [Taiwan], Briefing Book for October 1971 Trip to China, Oct. 12, 1971, box 851, FPF-China Trip/Vietnam, NSC, NPM.

92. Memorandum of conversation, Oct. 21, 1971 [10:30 A.M.–1:45 P.M.], box 846, ibid.

93. Ibid.

94. Memorandum, "My October China Visit: Drafting the Communiqué," Kissinger to the President [Nov. 1971], ibid.

95. Memorandum of conversation, Oct. 20, 1971 [4:40–7:10 P.M.], ibid.

96. Memorandum of conversation, Oct. 26, 1971 [5:30–8:10 P.M.], ibid.

97. First Chinese Draft, Oct. 24, 1971 [9:30 P.M.], China Visit, Record of Previous Visits, Arranged by Subject Matter, Book II [Feb. 1972], ibid.

98. Final Draft, Oct. 26, 1971 [8:00 A.M.], ibid.; First U.S. Draft, Oct. 22, 1971 [8:00 P.M.], ibid.

99. First U.S. Draft, Oct. 22, 1971 [8:00 P.M.], ibid.

100. Memorandum of conversation, Oct. 26, 1971 [5:30 A.M.–8:10 P.M.], ibid.

101. Memorandum, "My October China Visit: Discussions of the Issues," Kissinger to the President, Nov. 11, 1971, box 847, ibid.

102. "[Briefing Paper] Taiwan" [Feb. 1972], Briefing Book for February 1972 China Trip, ibid.

103. "[Briefing Paper] Taiwan" [Feb. 1972], State Department Briefing Book for Nixon's China Trip, box 848, ibid.

104. William Bundy, *A Tangled Web: The Making of Foreign Policy in the Nixon Presidency* (New York: Hill and Wang, 1998), 305; memorandum for the President, Dec. 31, 1971, box 92, HAK Office Files, Country Files-Far East, NSC, NPM; memorandum of conversation, Feb. 21, 1972 [4:15–5:30 P.M.], ibid.

105. "The Future of Taiwan: Proposal for a 'Policy of Peaceful Settlement," Feb. 2, 1972, box 1036, FPF-China/Vietnam Negotiations, NSC, NPM. Rogers's paper was not drafted by the same group that prepared the State Department briefing book but rather by the Republic of China desk. Memorandum, Holdridge and Lord to Kissinger, Feb. 3, 1972, box 88, HAK Office Files, Country Files-Far East, NSC, NPM.

106. Memorandum, Kissinger to the President, Mar. 8, 1972, box 1036, FPF-China/Vietnam Negotiations, NSC, NPM. The date of this memorandum indicates that Rogers's paper was not forwarded to Nixon until after his return from Beijing.

107. Stephen E. Ambrose, *Nixon: The Triumph of a Politician, 1962–1972* (New York: Simon and Schuster, 1989), 512–18.

108. William Burr, ed., *The Kissinger Transcripts: The Top Secret Talks with Beijing and Moscow* (New York: New Press, 1998), 59–65.

109. Excerpts from memorandum of conversation, Feb. 22, 1972 [2:10–6:10 P.M.], box 848, FPF-China Trip/Vietnam, NSC, NPM.

110. Excerpts from memorandum of conversation, Feb. 24, 1972, ibid.

111. Memorandum of conversation, Jan. 3, 1972, box 1037, FPF-China/Vietnam Negotiations, NSC, NPM; memorandum of conversation, Feb. 22, 1972 [10:15–11:55 A.M.], box 92, HAK Office Files, Country Files-Far East, NSC, NPM.

112. The memoranda of conversations between Kissinger and Qiao Guanhua, together with American and Chinese draft formulations, are in box 92, HAK Office Files, Country Files-Far East, NSC, NPM. The text of the Shanghai Communiqué is in John H. Holdridge, *Crossing the Divide: An Insider's Account of Normalization of U.S.-China Relations* (Lanham, MD: Rowman and Little-field, 1997), app. A.

113. Remarks by Ambassador Winston Lord, Conference on China–United States Relations, 1969–1979, Beijing, Jan. 18–19, 2002.

114. Marshall Green, "Evolution of U.S.-China Policy, 1956–1973: Memoirs of an Insider," in *Frontline Diplomacy,* CD-ROM; Tucker, *China Confidential,* 273–75; Kissinger, *White House Years,* 1083–84.

115. Memorandum of conversation, Feb. 27, 1972 [10:20 A.M.–1:40 P.M.], box 92, HAK Office Files, Country Files-Far East, NSC, NPM; memorandum for the President's File, Mar. 8, 1972, box 87, President's Office Files, Memoranda for the President, NPM; Haldeman, *Haldeman Diaries,* 422.

116. "Remarks at Andrews Air Force Base," Feb. 28, 1972, *Public Papers of the Presidents of the United States: Richard Nixon, 1972* (Washington, DC: U.S. Government Printing Office, 1974), 381–83.

117. Memorandum for the President's File [Cabinet meeting], Feb. 29, 1972, box 88, President's Office files, Memoranda for the President, NPM; "Briefing Given by Dr. Kissinger in the Family Theater of the White House," Mar. 7, 1972, box 1026, Presidential/HAK Memcons, NSC, NPM; memorandum for the President's File [Meeting with Bipartisan Leadership], Feb. 29, 1972, box 88, President's Office Files, Memoranda for the President, NPM; Transcript of Background Press Briefing [Mar. 1972], box 49, White House Special Files, Staff Members and Office Files, Alexander M. Haig, Jr., Files, Speech Files, 1969–73, NPM.

118. Kissinger, *White House Years*, 1093.

119. Robert G. Sutter, *The China Quandary: Domestic Determinants of U.S.-China Policy, 1972–1985* (Boulder, CO: Westview, 1983), 19; Kusnitz, *America's China Policy*, 138; Tucker, *China Confidential*, 279–80; memorandum, John Richardson, Jr., to the Secretary [of State], Mar. 1, 1972, box 52, Office of Public Opinion Studies, 1943–75, RG 59, NA; News Summary, Mar. 9, 1972, box 39, President's Office Files, Annotated News Summaries, NPM.

120. Memorandum for the President's Files, Mar. 23, 1972, box 88, President's Office Files, Memoranda for the President, NPM.

121. Holdridge, *Crossing the Divide*, 97–102; Green, "Memoirs of an Insider," chap. 7.

122. Shen, *U.S. and Free China*, 95–98, 107–11. In addition to conferring with Shen separately, Kissinger was present at the ambassador's meeting with the president. At both meetings, he advised the Taiwan government to maintain a steady course because of the possibility of domestic upheaval on the mainland following the death of Mao and Zhou Enlai. He apparently believed that presenting such a prospect might help induce Taipei to moderate its reaction to Nixon's trip.

123. Memorandum, Haig to the President, Mar. 23, 1972, box 1036, FPF-China/Vietnam Negotiations, NSC, NPM.

124. Memorandum, Kissinger to the President, Jan. 5, 1973, box 1026, Presidential/HAK Memcons, NSC, NPM.

125. Message, State Department to U.S. Embassy Taipei, Oct. 17, 1972, POL CHINAT-US, box 2206, Subject-Numeric File, 1970–73, RG 59, NA; memorandum of conversation, June 19, 1972, box 851, FPF-China Trip/Vietnam, NSC, NPM.

126. Briefing Book for Kissinger's China Trip, Feb. 1973, box 98, HAK Office Files, Country Files-Far East, NSC, NPM.

127. Bureau of Intelligence and Research Intelligence Note, "Republic of China: 'All-Out Diplomacy,'" Apr. 12, 1972, POL CHINAT, box 2202, Subject-Numeric File, 1970–73, RG 59, NA; Bureau of Intelligence and Research Intelligence Note, "Republic of China: Riding Out the Storms," Nov. 8, 1972, ibid.; Chiao Chiao Hsieh, *Strategy for Survival: The Foreign Policy and External Relations of the Republic of China on Taiwan* (London: Sherwood Press, 1985), chap. 6; Jay Taylor, *The Generalissimo's Son: Chiang Ching-kuo and the Revolutions in China and Taiwan* (Cambridge, MA: Harvard University Press, 2000), 315.

128. Memorandum, Kissinger to the President, box 1026, Presidential/HAK Memcons, NSC, NPM, Jan. 5, 1973.

129. Briefing Book for Kissinger's China Visit, Feb. 1973, box 98, HAK Office Files, Country Files-Far East, NSC, NPM.

130. Memorandum of conversation, Feb. 15, 1973, ibid.; Henry Kissinger, *Years of Upheaval* (Boston: Little, Brown, 1982), 60–63.

131. Particularly important were the assurances given by Kissinger at the start of his July 1971 talks with Zhou Enlai that the United States did not seek an independent Taiwan or either a "two China" or "one China, one Taiwan" solution. John Holdridge, who prepared Kissinger's opening statement, felt that "it was essential to make these points about Taiwan at the very outset, in order to allay any Chinese suspicions about U.S. intentions in seeking rapprochement with China" (Holdridge, *Crossing the Divide*, 46).

Chapter 2

1. The Gang of Four was formed by Mao Zedong's wife, Jiang Qing (1913–91), the Shanghai Propaganda Department official Zhang Chunqiao (1917–91), the literary critic Yao Wenyuan (b. 1931), and the Shanghai security guard Wang Hongwen (1935–92). They rose to power during the Cultural Revolution (1966–76) and dominated Chinese politics during the early 1970s.

2. On April 1, 1969; Lin Biao, in his political report on the Ninth Congress, quoting Mao Zedong; reported in *Renmin ribao*, Apr. 28, 1969.

3. Minutes of talk by Mao Zedong at the First Plenary Session of the Ninth Congress.

4. The revised draft of "The Slogans Celebrating the Twentieth Anniversary of the Founding of the People's Republic of China," review by Mao Zedong, Apr. 28, 1969.

5. Minutes of conversation by Mao Zedong at the First Plenary Session of the Ninth Congress.

6. Mao Zedong's instructions on a report by Zhou Enlai, March 1969.

7. Minutes of a conversation between Mao Zedong and members of the Brief Meeting of the Central Cultural Revolution Team, Feb. 19, 1969.

8. *Nie Rongzhen nianpu* (Chronicle of the life of Nie Rongzhen) (Beijing: Renmin chubanshe, 1999), 2: 1107.

9. Zhonggong, Zhongyang wenxian yanjiushi, ed., *Zhou Enlai nianpu* (Chronicle of the life of Zhou Enlai), *1949–1976* (Beijing: Zhongyang wenxian chubanshe, 1997), 2: 306; Zhonggong, Zhongyang dangshi yanjiushi, ed., *Zhongguo gongchandang lishi dashiji* (Chronicle of historical events of the Chinese Communist Party) (Beijing: Renmin chubanshe, 1989), 302.

10. Zhonggong, Zhongyang wenxian yanjiushi, ed., *Zhou Enlai nianpu*, 2: 329; Zhang Hua and Su Caiqing, eds., *Huishou "Wen'ge"* (Recollections of the Cultural Revolution) (Beijing: Zhongdang dangshi chubanshe, 2000), 2: 1011–12.

11. Minutes of talks between Mao Zedong and Nixon, Feb. 21, 1972.

12. Fu Hao, *Feng yu cang sang ji: Fu Hao wenxuan* (Storms and upheavals: selected essays by Fu Hao) (Beijing: Shijie zhishi chubanshe, 2001), 169.

13. Zhonggong, Zhongyang wenxian yanjiushi, ed., *Zhou Enlai nianpu*, 2: 505–6.

14. Ibid., 2: 506.

15. Minutes of Mao Zedong's talk with the prime minister of Sri Lanka, June 28, 1972.

16. Zhonggong, Zhongyang wenxian yanjiushi, ed., *Zhou Enlai nianpu*, 2: 541–42, 565, 566.

17. *Renmin ribao*, Feb. 23, 1973.

18. Minutes of Mao Zedong's talk with Kissinger, Feb. 17, 1973; William Burr, ed., *The Kissinger Transcripts: The Top Secret Talks with Beijing and Moscow* (New York: New Press, 1998), 94.

19. Zhonggong, Zhongyang wenxian yanjiushi, ed., *Zhou Enlai nianpu*, 2: 585–86.

20. Ibid., 2: 600.

21. Minutes of Zhou Enlai's talk with David Bruce, June 25, 1973.

22. Mao Zedong's instruction on Zhou Enlai's report, June 26, 1973.

23. Foreign Ministry, ed., *The New Information*, no. 153 (June 28, 1973).

24. Zhou Enlai's letter to the party group and the America-Pacific group of the Foreign Ministry, July 3, 1973.

25. Minutes of Mao Zedong's talk with Zhang Chunjiao and Wang Hongwen, July 4, 1973.

26. Mao Zedong's comment on Zhou Enlai's letter to the party group and the America-Pacific group of the Foreign Ministry, July 5, 1973.

27. Mao Zedong's comment on Zhou Enlai's letter, July 15, 1973.

28. In 1973, Mao Zedong indicated that the criticism of Lin Biao and his followers should be combined with a thorough criticism of Confucius. In the following months, Mao's remarks gave rise to a spate of articles, and historical al-

legories were used to support the Gang of Four and oppose Zhou Enlai. In January 1974, the struggle became a large-scale, national movement.

29. *Renmin ribao,* Nov. 15, 1973.

30. Minutes of Mao Zedong's talk with Zhou Enlai and others, Nov. 17, 1973.

31. Minutes of Mao Zedong's talk with Deng Xiaoping, Nov. 28, 1973.

32. Zhonggong, Zhongyang wenxian yanjiushi, ed., *Zhou Enlai nianpu,* 2: 634.

33. Ibid.

34. Zhou Enlai's directive to the *Bulletin of Foreign Affairs Activities,* Nov. 13, 1973.

35. Zhonggong, Zhongyang wenxian yanjiushi, ed., *Zhou Enlai nianpu,* 2: 634.

36. Ibid.

37. Ibid., 2: 634–35.

38. Ibid., 2: 636.

39. Ibid., 2: 636–37.

40. Shi Shi, " 'Woniu shijian' shimou" (The story of the "Snail Incident"), in *Xin Zhongguo waijiao fengyu* (Storm over the diplomacy of New China), no. 2 (Beijing: Shijie zhishi chubanshe, 1991), 176–80; Zhonggong, Zhongyang wenxian yanjiushi, ed., *Zhou Enlai nianpu,* 2: 650.

41. Mao Zedong, letter to Jiang Qing, Mar. 27, 1974.

42. For the second and third points, see minutes of Deng Xiaoping's talk with Premier Bhutto of Pakistan, May 14, 1974.

43. After the Lushan Plenum in 1959, Lin replaced Peng Dehuai as minister of defense.

44. Zhonggong, Zhongyang wenxian yanjiushi, ed., *Zhou Enlai nianpu,* 2: 679.

45. Ibid., 680.

46. Ibid.

47. Ibid., 682.

48. Ibid., 685–87.

49. Minutes of Mao Zedong's talk with Deng Xiaoping, Nov. 12, 1974.

50. See Fu Hao and Li Tongcheng, eds., *Lusi shui shou? Zhongguo waijiaoguan zai Meiguo* (Who will win the game? Chinese diplomats in the United States) (Beijing: Huaqiao chubanshe, 1995), 18–20, 25–37.

51. Zhonggong, Zhongyang wenxian yanjiushi, ed., *Deng Xiaoping sixiang nianpu (1975–1979)* (Chronological record of Deng Xiaoping thought) (Beijing: Zhongyang wenxian chubanshe, 1998), 26–27.

52. Ibid., 40.

53. Ibid., 43–44.

54. Minutes of Deng Xiaoping's meeting with the foreign minister of Norway, Mar. 25, 1978.

55. *Chronicle of Deng Xiaoping (1975–1997)* (Beijing: Party Literature of the Central Committee Publishing House, July 2004), 279.

56. Gu Mu's recollection; see *The Full-Length TV Documentary Film "Deng Xiaoping"* (Beijing: Zhongyang wenxian chubanshe, 1997), 191.

57. See Zhonggong, Zhongyang dangshi yanjiushi, Disan yanjiubu, ed., *Zhongguo gaige kaifang 20 nian shi* (Twenty years of the history of China's reform and opening up) (Shenyang: Liaoning renmin chubanshe, 1998), 29.

58. See Cheng Zhongyuan, Wang Zhengxiang, and Li Zhenghua, *1976–1981 nian de Zhongguo* (China in 1976–81) (Beijing: Zhongyang wenxian chubanshe, 1998), 186–87.

59. Deng Xiaoping's talk with a press delegation from the Federal Republic of Germany, Oct. 10, 1978, in *Deng Xiaoping wenxuan* (Selected works of Deng Xiaoping), 2nd ed. (Beijing: Renmin chubanshe, 1994), 2: 132.

60. Yu Guangyuan, *Wo qinli de naci lishi zhuanzhe* (My personal history of historical turning points) (Beijing: Zhongyang wenxian chubanshe, 1998), 69–70.

61. *Li Xiannian wenxuan* (Selected works of Li Xiannian) (Beijing: Renmin chubanshe, 1989), 331.

62. Fang Weizhong, ed., *Zhonghua renmin gongheguo jing ji dashiji (1949–1980)* (Chronicle of economic events in the People's Republic of China, 1949–80) (Beijing: Zhongguo shehui kexue chubanshe, 1984), 605–6.

63. The flexible policy on the Taiwan problem, as suggested by Deng Xiaoping, is summed up by the phrase "one country, two systems." In a January 24, 1979, meeting with Hedley Donovan, editor-in-chief of Time Inc., and Marsh Clark, director of *Time* magazine's Hong Kong bureau, Deng Xiaoping said: "We respect the reality in Taiwan. The Taiwan authority, as a local government, has its own power; that means it can maintain a certain size of army and can continue its commercial and trade relations and its nongovernmental intercourse with foreign countries. Their way of life can be maintained, but it can only be maintained under the principle that there is only one China. It will take a long time to solve the problem. The main part of China, that is, the mainland, will also undergo changes and will also develop" (Zhonggong, Zhongyang wenxian yanjiushi, ed., *Deng Xiaoping sixiang nianpu*, 109). This is the embryonic form of "one country, two systems."

64. See Wang Taiping, ed., *Zhonghua renmin gongheguo waijiaoshi* (History of the diplomacy of the People's Republic of China), vol. 3 *(1970–1978)* (Beijing: Shijie Zhishi chubanshe, 1999), 375; Zhonggong, Zhongyang wenxian yanjiushi, ed., *Deng Xiaoping sixiang nianpu*, 36–37.

65. Minutes of talk between Deng Xiaoping and the delegation of the AP Board of Directors, Sept. 6, 1977.

66. Zhonggong, Zhongyang wenxian yanjiushi, ed., *Deng Xiaoping sixiang nianpu*, 53.

67. Minutes of talk between Deng Xiaoping and Senator Henry Jackson, Feb. 16, 1978.

68. Quoted in *Xin Zhongguo waijiao* (The diplomacy of New China) (Beijing: Jiefangjun wenyi chubanshe, 1999), 242.

69. Ibid., 242–43.

70. See Wang Taiping, ed., *Zhonghua renmin gongheguo waijiaoshi*, 378.

71. Ibid.

72. Minutes of talk between Deng Xiaoping and Japanese visitors, Nov. 29, 1978.

73. *Chronicle of Deng Xiaoping (1975–1997)*, 442.

Chapter 3

1. See, e.g., Henry Kissinger, *Years of Upheaval* (London: Weidenfeld and Nicolson, 1982), together with other volumes of memoirs produced by Kissinger covering his time in office; Zbigniew Brzezinski, *Power and Principle* (New York: Farrar, Straus, and Giroux, 1983); Cyrus Vance, *Hard Choices* (New York: Simon and Schuster, 1983); John Holdridge, *Crossing the Divide: An Insider's Account of Normalization of U.S.-China Relations* (Lanham, MD: Rowman and Littlefield, 1997); and James Lilley, with Jeffrey Lilley, *China Hands: Nine Decades of Adventure, Espionage, and Diplomacy in Asia* (New York: Public Affairs, 2004).

2. Of particular note are Robert S. Ross, *Negotiating Cooperation: The United States and China, 1969–1989* (Stanford: Stanford University Press, 1995); Yufan Hao, *Dilemma and Decision* (Berkeley: University of California Press, 1997); Richard Solomon, *Chinese Negotiating Behavior* (Washington, DC: United States Institute of Peace Press, 1999); James H. Mann, *About Face* (New York: Vintage, 1998); Patrick Tyler, *A Great Wall: Six Presidents and China* (New York: Public Affairs, 1999); and Alan D. Romberg, *Rein In at the Brink of the Precipice: American Policy Toward Taiwan and U.S.-PRC Relations* (Washington, DC: Henry L. Stimson Center, 2003). The invaluable compilation edited by William Burr, *The Kissinger Transcripts: The Top Secret Talks with Beijing and Moscow* (New York: New Press, 1998), also has added greatly to our knowledge and proved helpful to this chapter too. I thank Dr. Burr for answering my queries about some of the material in this compilation and for sharing some documentary material from the Ford era. Dr. Evelyn Goh has also been extremely generous in sharing some of her materials from the Nixon and Kissinger eras,

some of which she has now utilized in Goh, *Constructing the U.S. Rapprochement with China, 1961–1974: From "Red Menace" to "Tacit Ally"* (Cambridge, Eng.: Cambridge University Press, 2005).

3. After perusing the documentary record, Michel Oksenberg (at the time, the China specialist on the National Security staff) stated that the "Chinese humiliated [Kissinger] in a series of very tough sessions" on that October 1975 trip. Memorandum from Michel Oksenberg to Zbigniew Brzezinski, Feb. 4, 1977, China Vertical File, Jimmy Carter Library (JCL), Atlanta, GA.

4. Memo from Kissinger to the President, Nov. 11, 1971, "My October Visit," Pol 7/US/Kiss, National Security Archive, Washington, DC.

5. Note Nixon's remarks on Feb. 22, 1972, in Beijing, which suggest some of the reasons for the ambiguities in the language adopted in official public statements: "Our problem is to be clever enough to find language which will meet your need yet does not stir up the animals so much that they gang up on Taiwan and thereby torpedo our initiative." Nixon-Chou, Box 87, President's Office Files (POF), Nixon Presidential Materials (NPM), National Archives (NA). The analysis in Romberg's *Rein In at the Brink* basically supports my summary of these negotiations, although it detects more nuance in the U.S. position; see especially chaps. 3 and 4.

6. Thomas Schelling, *The Strategy of Conflict* (New York: Oxford University Press, 1963), *passim*.

7. Zhou-Kissinger Memcon Feb. 22, 1972, Box 87, POF, NPM, NA.

8. Although, as should become clear, I do not believe that they were connected in the negotiations firmly enough.

9. These kinds of points obtain in many different kinds of negotiations. See the discussion in Howard Raiffa, *The Art and Science of Negotiation* (Cambridge, MA: Harvard University Press, 1982), esp. chap. 1.

10. As Kissinger told Zhou on June 19, 1972: "We believe that the future of our relationship with Peking is infinitely more important for the future of Asia than what happens in Phnom Penh, in Hanoi or in Saigon." Memcon, National Security Files (NSF), NPM, Box 851, NA. Occasionally, Kissinger's staff spelled out the reasons in internal policy documents: the value of normalization related to the strategic benefits of a "non-confrontation posture with the PRC, the impetus it has given the diplomacy of 'detente' with the Soviets, and the long-term benefits to the U.S. of having eleminated [*sic*] one front of the Cold War battle lines of the 1950s and '60s." There was also the matter of "preventing American isolation on the China issue in multilateral forums (such as the U.N.) and in our bilateral diplomacy; and maximizing the possibility of sustaining if not enhancing parallel foreign policy moves with Peking in a number of third-country areas." Memorandum for Secretary Kissinger from Philip Habib, William

Gleysteen, Winston Lord, Richard H. Solomon, "U.S.-PRC Relations and Approaches to the President's Peking Trip: Tasks for the Rest of 1975," July 3, 1975, in National Security Adviser, Temporary Parallel File, "Kissinger-Scowcroft West Wing Office File," Box A1, Gerald R. Ford Library (GRFL), Ann Arbor, MI.

11. Steven M. Goldstein, *The United States and the Republic of China, 1949–1978: Suspicious Allies* (Stanford: Institute for International Studies, Asia/Pacific Research Center, Stanford University, Feb. 2000), 26.

12. Zhou-Kissinger Memcon, Nov. 13, 1973, in Burr, *Kissinger Transcripts*, 203–4.

13. Burr, *Kissinger Transcripts*, 205.

14. As early as February 1973, Zhou said to Kissinger, "You want to reach out to the Soviet Union by standing on Chinese shoulders." Memcon, Chou-Kissinger, Feb. 15, 1973, Kissinger Office Files, NSF, Box 98, NA. Kissinger thought, on the other hand, that much had been accomplished. As he reported to Nixon, "in plain terms we have now become tacit allies." Memo for the President from HAK, "My Trip to China," Mar. 2, 1973, Box 6, President's Personal Files (PPF), NPM, NA.

15. Goldstein, *Suspicious Allies*, 34–35.

16. Robert Hartmann (Ford's speechwriter), oral history interview, Dec. 8, 1977, GRFL.

17. Ross, *Negotiating Cooperation*, 80–81.

18. Memcon, Ford-Kissinger, Oct. 31, 1975, National Security Adviser (NSA), Box 16, GRFL. As Kissinger put it to the president: "The Chinese turned down our statement but accepted the cut-down version of the trip. . . . There are two options: cancel, or else go but get the word out that we don't expect anything of substance but that it is important to exchange views." Ford assented to the latter suggestion.

19. Memcon, Ford with Republican Congressional Leadership, Dec. 10, 1975, NSA, Box 17, GRFL.

20. See *Public Papers of the Presidents of the United States, Gerald R. Ford*, 1975, Book II, July 21–Dec. 31, 1975 (Washington, DC: U.S. Government Printing Office, 1977), 707.

21. Memcon, Mao-Ford, Dec. 2, 1975, "President Ford's Trip to China 1–5 Dec. 1975," Lord Files, Box 373, NA.

22. Memcon, Teng–Ford, Dec. 3, 1975, "President Ford's Trip to China 1–5 Dec. 1975," Lord Files, Box 373, NA. Also in Burr, *Kissinger Transcripts*, 402–3.

23. All former U.S. officials who attended the workshop that was held in Beijing, January 2002, to review drafts of the chapters contained in this edited

volume testified to the constraints that were imposed on U.S. policy formulation in the 1970s by the evident political instabilities in Beijing.

24. Memcon, Ford-Fraser, July 27, 1976, "President's Meeting with Prime Minister Fraser," NSA, '73–'77, Box 20, GRFL.

25. Burr, *Kissinger Transcripts*, 372.

26. Memorandum for the President from Zbigniew Brzezinski, NSC Weekly Report 75, Oct. 13, 1978, Brzezinski collection, Subject file, Box 42, JCL (President's handwritten comment).

27. Memcon, Carter-Huang, Feb. 8, 1977, China vertical file, JCL.

28. Memcon, Vance–Huang Hua, Aug. 24, 1977, China vertical file, JCL. Vance was not disappointed that little progress was made during the visit since his preference was to secure the SALT agreement with the Soviet Union first before moving on the China issue.

29. Vance-Woodcock, June 28, 1978, Brzezinski Collection, geographic File, China PRC, Box 9, JCL.

30. Note, too, Robert Accinelli's chapter in this volume, which significantly advances our understanding of the negotiations leading to this landmark communiqué.

31. Starr to Brown, "US Legal Position on the Status of Taiwan and the 1954 US-ROC Mutual Defense Treaty," Mar. 2, 1972, Box 1698, SNF [1970–73], RG 59, NA.

32. President's Personal Files, Name/Subj files, Box 7, Feb. 22, 1972, NA.

33. Memcon, Nixon-Zhou, Feb. 22, 1972, Box 87, POF/Memos for Pres, NPM, NA. Also referred to in Oksenberg to Brzezinski, Feb. 4, 1977, China vertical file, JCL. Many of these issues came up on Kissinger's first visit in July 1971. For example, he confirmed that the United States would not support a Taiwan independence movement. Zhou replied: "I attach great importance to what you have just now said: the U.S. government and the President do not support, and will not support, the so-called Independence Movement of Taiwan." Memcon, Zhou-Kissinger, July 9, 1971, NSF, NPM, Box 851, NA. James Lilley, a former deputy chief in the China division of the CIA and ambassador at the time of the 1989 Tiananmen crisis, has described Nixon's promise to establish full relations in his second term as a "severe blow to Taiwan" (Lilley, *China Hands*, 159).

34. Memcon, Chou-Kissinger, Feb. 6, 1973, Kissinger Office Files, NSF, Box 98, NA.

35. There were a number of occasions when influential Americans tried to get the Chinese to be more imaginative with regard to the "Japan formula." For example, Senator Mike Mansfield, during a visit to China in October 1976, reminded Vice Foreign Minister Wang Hairong that there were elements of pre-

tence associated with this formula, hinting that perhaps the Chinese government could be more flexible on the matter: Taiwan and Japan did "have trade organizations established in both Tokyo and Taipei and it is a subterfuge and the one in Taipei, I believe, is headed by a former Japanese ambassador." Office of Staff Secretary, Handwriting File, Confidential 11/76–1/77, Box 1, Oct. 7, 1976, JCL.

36. Kissinger-Nixon, "My Talks with Chou En Lai," July 17, 1971, Pol 7, US/Kissinger, National Security Archive, Washington, DC; and Memcon, Chou-Kissinger, July 9, 1971, Kissinger Office Files, NSF, Box 851, NA. As Zhou put it in July: "In recognizing China the U.S. must do so unreservedly. It must recognize the PRC as the sole legitimate government of China and not make any exceptions. . . . Taiwan is a Chinese province. . . . The U.S. must withdraw all its armed forces and dismantle all its military installations on Taiwan and in the Taiwan Straits within a limited period." The 1954 defense treaty "is considered to be illegal." Ibid. Kissinger offered the perspective that "if the Korean War hadn't occurred, a war which we did not seek and you did not seek, Taiwan would probably be today a part of the PRC." Zhou repeated several times that Taiwan was "the crucial issue." For developments in 1973, see Lord Files, Box 371, Summaries Feb. 1972–Nov. 1973, NA, where he records Mao as stating: "As long as the US severs the diplomatic relations with Taiwan, then it is possible for the two of us to solve the issue of diplomatic relations. That is to say, like China did with Japan." See also Burr, *Kissinger Transcripts*, 186.

37. "Secretary's Conversations in Peking, Nov. 1973," Lord Files, Box 372, Nov. 12, 1973, NA.

38. This latter suggestion regarding the consulate was made in a memo for Kissinger from Richard Solomon, "Confirming the Principle of One China," Jan. 19, 1974, China-Sec. Kissinger, Lord Files, Box 371, NA.

39. Kissinger to Scowcroft for the President, NSC/HAK 41, Nov. 16, 1973, National Security Archive; Memcon, Chou-Kissinger, Nov. 14, 1973, Secretary's Conversations in Peking, Lord Files, Box 372, NA.

40. See both memoranda for Kissinger from Solomon, " 'Confirming the Principle of One China': Next Steps," Jan. 19, 1974, Lord Files, Box 371, and memo to the secretary from Hummel, Lord, and Solomon, "Imperatives for Planning and Action on the China Issue," May 24, 1974, China-Sec. Kissinger, Lord Files, Box 371, NA, which begins "Our China policy is drifting without a clear sense of how we will move toward normalization, or indeed what the shape of a future normalized relationship with the PRC will look like—particularly as it affects Taiwan."

41. Memcon, Teng-Ch'iao-Kissinger, April 14, 1974, "China Sensitive," Lord Files, Box 374, NA.

42. Burr, *Kissinger Transcripts*, 294–97.

43. Memcon, Teng-Ford, Dec. 4, 1975, "President Ford's Trip to China," Lord Files, Box 373, NA.

44. Memo from Oksenberg to Brzezinski, Feb. 4, 1977, China vertical file, JCL.

45. Letter from the President to Cyrus Vance (no date), National Security Affairs Staff Material (NSASM), Far East, Box 4, Armacost 8/16–25/77, JCL.

46. Vance–Huang Hua, Aug. 23, 1977, China vertical file; Vance–Deng Xiaoping, Aug. 24, 1977, China vertical file, both at JCL.

47. Reading from China's record of a discussion with Kissinger in Nov. 1974, Deng claimed that Kissinger had said: "We do not ask you to take any reciprocal measures." Kissinger went on: "I understand this issue [of Taiwan] and I believe it can be solved in conformity with these three principles. I appreciate the Chinese side which gives me the opportunity to reconsider this question. I realize for the Chinese side to adopt this position is an expression of great wisdom, generosity and self-restraint. I also recognize due to the nature of this issue and our previous discussions we indeed owe you a debt." If this Chinese record is reasonably accurate, then the report reinforces the general argument that I am making in this chapter. Deng also reminded Vance that Ford in Dec. 1975 had said that, after the 1976 presidential elections, he would be able to adopt the Japanese formula. Vance-Deng, Aug. 24, 1977, China vertical file, JCL.

48. Brzezinski-Carter, Aug. 25, 1977, NSASM, Far East, Armacost, Box 4, JCL.

49. Habib, Gleysteen, Lord, Solomon to Secretary Kissinger, July 3, 1975, National Security Affairs Temporary Parallel File, Kissinger-Scowcroft West Wing Office File, Box A1, GRFL.

50. Oksenberg to Brzezinski, Feb. 4, 1977, China vertical file, JCL. See also Hummel/Lord to the Secretary, Jan. 29, 1974, "Normalization of Relations with the PRC and the Issue of Taiwan," Lord Files, Box 380, NA, which asserted that "under most scenarios we see no significant problems of continued U.S. military sales to the G[overnment of the] R[epublic of] C[hina]."

51. Letter, Carter-Vance [no date], NSASM, Far East, Armacost, Box 4, JCL.

52. Memcon, Vance–Huang Hua, Aug. 23, 1977, China vertical file, JCL.

53. Memcon, Vance–Huang Hua, Aug. 24, 1977, China vertical file, JCL.

54. Brzezinski to the President, Aug. 25, 1977, NSASM, Far East, Armacost, Box 4, JCL.

55. Armacost/Oksenberg-Brzezinski, Mar. 24, 1978, NSASM, Far East, Box 6, JCL.

56. Memcon, Brzezinski-Deng, May 21, 1978, China vertical file; and Memcon, Brzezinski-Hua, May 22, 1978, China vertical file, JCL.

57. Memcon, Han-Brzezinski, June 19, 1978, China vertical file, JCL.

58. Holbrooke report of conversation to Ambassador Woodcock, Sept. 7, 1978, Brzezinski collection, geographic file, Box 9, JCL.

59. Memcon, Hsu-Holbrooke, Sept. 12, 1978, China vertical file, JCL; Memcon, Carter-Ch'ai, Sept. 19, 1978, China vertical File, JCL.

60. Memcon, Vance-Huang, Oct. 3, 1978, China vertical file, JCL.

61. Brzezinski collection, geographic file, Nov. 13, 1978, Box 9, JCL.

62. Ibid., Nov. 14, 1978, Box 9, JCL.

63. Ibid., Dec. 4, 1978, Box 9, JCL.

64. Brzezinski to the President, Dec. 5, 1978, China vertical file, JCL.

65. Woodcock to Vance and Brzezinski, Dec. 13 and 14, 1978, China vertical file, JCL. This issue is also discussed in Ross, *Negotiating Cooperation*, 136–38. Note Ross's argument (p. 136): "The PRC's leaders were now fully aware of . . . U.S. insistence on continuing to sell weaponry to Taiwan after normalization," but his acknowledgment (p. 138) that "China had yet to acquiesce directly to Washington's insistence that it would continue to sell defensive weapons to Taiwan after normalization, albeit now subject to the one-year moratorium. Moreover, Chai Zemin seemed to think that the United States had agreed to terminate arms sales to Taiwan." These points tend to support my argument that the matter was subject to confusion.

66. Vance and Brzezinski to Woodcock, Dec. 15, 1978, China vertical file, JCL.

67. Woodcock to Vance and Brzezinski, Dec. 15, 1978; Memcon, Brzezinski-Chai, Dec. 15, 1978; both in China vertical file, JCL.

68. Woodcock to Vance and Brzezinski, Dec. 15, 1978, China vertical file, JCL.

69. Ibid.

70. Rogers to Nixon, "The Scope for Agreement in Peking," Feb. 9, 1971, Box 184, Haldeman Files, NPM, NA.

71. Memcon, Zhou-Kissinger, July 11, 1971, NSF, NPM, Box 851, NA. In October, Zhou said: "We will try to bring about a peaceful settlement." Ibid, Oct. 21, 1971.

72. "Private Statements Made by PRC leaders to Secretary Kissinger or President Nixon Regarding the Peaceful Liberation of Taiwan" [no date], Box 371, Lord Files, NA.

73. Burr, *Kissinger Transcripts*, 186.

74. "Private Statements" [no date], Box 371, Lord Files, NA. U.S. officials recognized a distinct hardening of the line on Taiwan in 1974. See, e.g., Bureau of Intelligence and Research, Intelligence Note, Apr. 2, 1974, Lord Files, Box 371,

NA. Using Mao's statements was a useful and effective way for the Chinese to signal that they had reached their minimum position in the negotiations.

75. Memcon, Teng-Ford, Dec. 4, 1975, Lord Files, Box 373, NA.

76. Mansfield-Wang, Office of Staff Secretary, Handwriting File, Confidential, Box 1, Oct. 7, 1976, JCL. Not to be outdone, the Senate minority leader, Hugh Scott, had been told during his trip to Beijing: "It is more reliable to settle this question [of Taiwan] through a war." Taiwan was a "noose around the neck of the U.S." and if the United States did not remove it, China's PLA would "cut it off." Meeting with Senator Hugh Scott, July 27, 1976, National Security Affairs Presidential Name File, 1974–77, Hugh Scott, Box 3, GRFL.

77. Memcon, Carter-Huang, Feb. 8, 1977, China vertical file, JCL.

78. These figures were given by Vance to Huang Hua during discussions in Beijing on Aug. 23, 1977, China vertical file, JCL.

79. Carter-Vance [no date], NSASM, Far East, Armacost, Box 4, JCL.

80. Memcon, Vance-Deng, Aug. 24, 1977, China vertical file, JCL.

81. Memcon, Brzezinski-Deng, meeting May 21, 1978, China vertical file, JCL.

82. Woodcock to Vance and Brzezinski, Dec. 4, 1978, Brzezinski Collection, geographic file, Box 9, JCL.

83. Admittedly, some of the congressional anger came from the Carter administration's failure to consult. James Lilley records that prominent Republicans such as Ronald Reagan and George H. W. Bush thought it either a "betrayal" (Reagan) or a "sell-out" (Bush). Lilley (*China Hands*, 210–11) himself saw it as "a bungled, compromised agreement." For an analysis of the creation of the Taiwan Relations Act and its consequences, see Steven M. Goldstein and Randall Schriver, "An Uncertain Relationship: The United States, Taiwan and the Taiwan Relations Act," *China Quarterly*, no. 165 (Mar. 2001), 147–72.

84. Rosemary Foot, *The Practice of Power: US Relations with China Since 1949* (Oxford: Oxford University Press, 1995), esp. the conclusion.

Chapter 4

1. On December 31, 1953, Premier Zhou Enlai first put forward the Five Principles of Peaceful Coexistence in a meeting with Indian representatives: mutual respect for territorial integrity and sovereignty, mutual nonaggression, noninterference in internal affairs, equality and mutual benefits, and peaceful coexistence (Ministry of Foreign Affairs of the People's Republic of China website, www.fmprc.gov.cn/eng/ziliao/3602/3604/t18053.htm).

2. "A Summary of Zhou Enlai's Exposition of the Joint Communiqué," Mar. 3, 1972, in Zhonggong, Zhongyang wenxian yanjiushi, ed., *Zhou Enlai zhuan* (Biography of Zhou Enlai) (Beijing: Zhongyang wenxian chubanshe, 1998), 2: 1109.

3. The draft circular of the Foreign Ministry stated that "President Nixon's visit to China and the publication of the China-U.S. Joint Communiqué have caused strong repercussions in the United States and also in the rest of the world. Generally speaking, the reaction to the communiqué is positive; most think it symbolizes a new beginning of relations between China and America, and that the international situation will undergo significant changes. This is a turning point in international relations, and the influence will be far-reaching. But we must also recognize these agreements are on paper only; whether they can be realized depends upon the practical actions of the United States. We must be prepared for twists and turns" (Zhonggong, Zhongyang wenxian yanjiushi, ed., *Mao Zedong jianguo yilai wen'gao* [Mao Zedong's manuscripts since the founding of the republic] [Beijing: Zhongyang wenxian chubanshe, 1998], 13: 291*n*).

4. On March 6, 1972, Mao Zedong responded to a request for instructions submitted by four organizations, including the Xinhua News Agency and *People's Daily*, on how to report the international reaction to Nixon's visit to China and the joint communiqué: "It seems unnecessary to compile such document. This [request] seems too exaggerated" (Zhonggong, Zhongyang wenxian yanjiushi, *Mao Zedong jianguo yilai wen'gao*, 13: 292).

5. "Circular by the Foreign Ministry on the China-U.S. Joint Communiqué," Mar. 6, 1972, in Zhonggong, Zhongyang wenxian yanjiushi, *Mao Zedong jianguo yilai wen'gao*, 13: 291.

6. "Notice by the Central Committee of the Communist Party of China (CPC) on the China-U.S. Joint Communiqué," Mar. 7, 1972.

7. In July 1971, during a secret visit to China, Henry Kissinger had reached an agreement with Zhou Enlai that the Paris secret channel would be the new path for contacts between China and the United States. At that time, the Chinese representative was Huang Zhen, Chinese ambassador to France, and the U.S. representative was Vernon A. Walters, military attaché of the U.S. Embassy in France. The two sides held 45 talks through this channel. During this period, as Kissinger took part in the Paris peace talks on the Vietnam war, he met secretly with Huang Zhen three times.

8. After that, both China and the United States set up a liaison office in the other's capital.

9. On June 19, 1972, Kissinger made his fourth visit to China, sharing with Chinese leaders the results of the summit meeting between the United States and the Soviet Union and his assessment of the first U.S.-Soviet arms control agreement (SALT I).

10. Contacts between China and the United States in New York began in November 1971. Kissinger opened this channel by meeting with Huang Hua, Chinese representative to the United Nations (William Burr, ed., *The Kissinger*

Transcripts: The Top Secret Talks with Beijing and Moscow [New York: New Press, 1998], 48–57).

11. Zhuang had performed with outstanding success in table-tennis diplomacy and had been world champion three times. Initially Chinese authorities had appointed Li Menghua head of the delegation, but Zhou Enlai decided to appoint Zhuang Zedong instead.

12. The Shanghai Communiqué clearly states that both sides saw bilateral commerce as a field of benefit to both sides, and that equal and mutually beneficial economic relations correspond to the interests of the people of both countries. They agreed to facilitate the gradual development of commerce between the two countries. For details, see Dong Mei, ed., *Zhong-Mei guanxi ziliao xuanbian* (Selected materials on Sino-American relations) (Beijing: Shishi chubanshe, 1982), 7.

13. The figures are from President Nixon's report to the Congress, "American Foreign Policy in the 1970s: Creating Lasting Peace," May 3, 1973; cited in Dong Mei, *Zhong-Mei guanxi ziliao xuanbian*, 106.

14. In 1971 and 1972, China viewed the Indochina War as the primary obstacle to the improvement of relations between the two countries, and the Taiwan problem as only a secondary obstacle. Mao Zedong had said, "The United States should start a new life. . . . The United States must withdraw its troops from Vietnam. There is no hurry for Taiwan, there is no war in Taiwan. But there is a war in Vietnam, people are dying! If we let Nixon come, it is not for ourselves" (Wei Shiyan, "Jixingge miji fang Hua neimu" [The inside story of Kissinger's secret visit], in Waijiaobu, Waijiaoshi bianjishi, ed., *Xin Zhongguo waijiao fengyun* [Storms over the diplomacy of New China] [Beijing: Shijie zhishi chubanshe, 1991], 41–42).

15. "Minutes of the Fourth Limited Talk Held Between Zhou Enlai and Nixon," Feb. 22–25, 1972; in Zhonggong, Zhongyang wenxian yanjiushi, *Zhou Enlai zhuan*, 2: 1107.

16. Zhonggong, Zhongyang wenxian yanjiushi, ed., *Zhou Enlai nianpu, 1949–1976* (Chronicle of Zhou Enlai) (Beijing: Zhongyang wenxian chubanshe, 1997), 579.

17. "The Shanghai Communiqué," Feb. 22, 1973, in Dong Mei, *Zhong-Mei guanxi ziliao xuanbian*, 9.

18. In fact, the Chinese side had anticipated the task of setting up liaison institutions. On May 25, 1971, Zhou Enlai convened leading members of the Foreign Ministry to discuss relations between China and the United States. On May 26, he convened and presided over a meeting of the Central Politburo to discuss the principles guiding the Sino-U.S. talks. The expectations were that it would take time for the United States to change its attitude on the Taiwan issue and

that the United States would not consent to all the conditions suggested by the Chinese side. However, the relaxation of tensions between China and the United States would need a channel of communication, and therefore, under the leadership of Zhou Enlai, the conference suggested that if the U.S. side could not satisfy all the conditions posed by the Chinese side, and as a result "China and the United States could not establish diplomatic relations, [then] each side could set up a liaison organization in the capital of the other side" (Zhou Enlai, "Zhongyang zhengzhiju guanyu Zhong-Mei huitan de baogao, 1971 nian 5 yue 29 ri" [Report by the Politburo on the China-U.S. Talk, May 29, 1971], *Zhongfa* 1971, no. 40).

19. Waijiaobu, *Waijiao tongbao*, no. 12, Feb. 24, 1973.

20. For China's estimate of the increase in Soviet troops, see ibid. See also the chapter by Wang Zhongchun in this volume.

21. Excerpt from "Mao Zedong huijian Jixingge shi de huitan, 1973 nian 2 yue 17 ri" (Mao Zedong's talk with Kissinger, Feb. 17, 1973), Waijiaobu Special Briefing File, no. 1. On Jan. 5, 1974, Mao Zedong met with Japanese Foreign Minister Ōhira Masayoshi and suggested the idea of "a cordon of land," meaning the countries along the line that Mao had specified. His aim was to unite all the countries along the line, including the United States, Japan, and all other forces in the world that could be used to counter Soviet expansion.

22. Waijiaobu, *Waijiao tongbao*, no. 12, Feb. 24, 1973.

23. Huang Zhen, who was then the Chinese ambassador to France, had taken part in the Long March, had been a general, and was one of the exclusive group of members of the CCP Central Committee. Han Xu was then the chief of the Department of Protocol in the Foreign Ministry and also an experienced diplomat; between 1985 and 1989, he served as Chinese ambassador to the United States.

24. Geng Biao, Ji Pengfei, Wang Youping, and Han Nianlong, "In Commemoration of Old Comrade-in-Arms Comrade Huang Zhen," *Renmin ribao*, May 3, 1990.

25. Wang Yongqin, ed., "1966–1976 nian Zhong-Mei-Su guanxi dashiji" (A chronicle of events in the relations among China, the United States, and the Soviet Union), *Dangdai Zhongguoshi yanjiu* 1998, no. 1, pt. 4: 105.

26. "Mao Zedong yu Wang Hongwen, Zhang Chunqiao de tanhua jiyao" (Minutes of Mao Zedong's talk with Wang Hongwen and Zhang Chunqiao), Waijiaobu Special Briefing File no. 17, July 4, 1973; Gong Li, *Kuayue: 1969–1979 nian Zhong-Mei guanxi de yanbian* (Across the chasm: the evolution of relations between China and the United States, 1969–79) (Zhengzhou: Henan renmin chubanshe, 1992), 213.

27. *Renmin ribao*, Sept. 1, 1973.

28. Ibid.

29. This epithet, frequently applied to the Soviet Union at this time, meant that the Soviet Union was "socialist" in name but "imperialist" in substance.

30. The Japanese established diplomatic relations with China in 1973 and ended all official ties with Taiwan; Japanese contracts with the Taiwan government were limited to nongovernmental personnel and organizations.

31. See Wang Yongqin, "Mao Zedong and Kissinger," *Dang de wenxian* (Party documents), 1997, no. 1: 93–94.

32. Wang Taiping, ed., *Zhonghua renmin gongheguo waijiaoshi* (History of the diplomacy of the People's Republic of China), vol. 3, *1970–1978* (Beijing: Shijie zhishi chubanshe, 1999), 368; Xue Mouhong and Pei Jianzhang, eds., *Dangdai Zhongguo waijiao* (The diplomacy of contemporary China) (Beijing: Zhongguo shehui kexue chubanshe, 1987), 225.

33. Waijiaobu, Dang'an guan, ed., *Weiren de zuji: Deng Xiaoping waijiao huodong dashiji* (The footprints of a great man: chronicle of Deng Xiaoping's diplomatic activities) (Beijing: Shijie zhishi chubanshe, 1998), 91.

34. "President Ford's Speech to the Joint Session of the Senate and House of Representatives," Aug. 12, 1974; reprinted in Dong Mei, *Zhong-Mei guanxi ziliao xuanbian*, 265.

35. Waijiaobu, Dang'an guan, ed., *Weiren de zuji*, 106.

36. Agence France Presse, Beijing, Oct. 21, 1974, in *Cankao xiaoxi*, Oct. 23, 1974.

37. Waijiaobu, Dang'an guan, ed., *Weiren de zuji*, 113.

38. The act rescinded the Resolution on the Defense of Taiwan passed by the U.S. Congress in January 1955; see Dong Mei, *Zhong-Mei guanxi ziliao xuanbian*, 265.

39. This referred to the plan to set up an embassy in Beijing and a liaison office in Taibei.

40. Xue Mouhong and Pei Jianzhang, *Dangdai Zhongguo waijiao*, 226.

41. Gong Li, *Kuayue*, 217.

42. U.S. Information Agency, May 6, 1975, in *Cankao xiaoxi*, May 10, 1975.

43. Ibid.

44. Zhonggong, Zhongyang wenxian yanjiushi, ed., *Deng Xiaoping sixiang nianpu (1975–1997)* (Chronicle of Deng Xiaoping's thought) (Beijing: Zhongyang wenxian chubanshe, 1998). For a recollection of Deng's meeting with the delegation of the American Society of Newspaper Editors by an American participant, see http://oakridger.com/stories/022797/smyser.html.

45. Wang Taiping, *Zhonghua renmin gongheguo waijiaoshi*, 3: 368.

46. Zhonggong, Zhongyang wenxian yanjiushi, *Deng Xiaoping sixiang nianpu*, 22.

47. Mao Zedong's talk with Deng Xiaoping, Nov. 12, 1974 (unpublished).

48. Wang Taiping, *Zhonghua renmin gongheguo waijiaoshi*, 3: 368.

49. Ibid.

50. Zhonggong, Zhongyang wenxian yanjiushi, *Deng Xiaoping sixiang nianpu*, 23.

51. Dong Mei, *Zhong-Mei guanxi ziliao xuanbian*, 275.

52. Cyrus Vance, *Hard Choices: Critical Views in American Foreign Policy* (New York: Simon and Schuster, 1983), 82–83.

53. Waijiaobu, Dang'an guan, ed., *Weiren Zuji*, 105–6.

54. Robert Ross, *Negotiating Cooperation: The United States and China, 1969–1989* (Stanford: Stanford University Press, 1995), 104.

55. Deng Xiaoping's talk with the AP Delegation of Board of Directors to China, Sept. 6, 1977; in Zhongyang wenxian yanjiushi, ed., *Deng Xiaoping nianpu* (Chronicle of Deng Xiaoping) (Beijing: Zhongyang wenxian chubanshe, 2004), 1: 196–97.

56. Deng Xiaoping's talk with the Delegation of U.S. Congressmen to China, Jan. 7, 1978; in Zhonggong, Zhongyang wenxian yanjiushi, ed., *Deng Xiaoping sixiang nianpu*, 53.

57. Dong Mei, *Zhong-Mei guanxi ziliao xuanbian*, 276.

58. Zbigniew Brzezinski, *Power and Principle* (New York: Farrar, Straus and Giroux, 1983), 207–9, appendix 1.

59. Ibid., 211–12; Xue Mouhong and Pei Jianzhang, *Dangdai Zhongguo waijiao*, 228.

60. Zhonggong, Zhongyang wenxian yanjiushi, *Deng Xiaoping sixiang nianpu*, 65.

61. In late November 1978, Foreign Minister Huang Hua was hospitalized; China appointed Han Nianlong as acting foreign minister to negotiate with the United States.

62. Hao Yufan, *Meiguo dui Hua zhengce neimu* (The inside story of U.S. policy toward China) (Beijing: Taihai chubanshe, 1998), 228–29.

63. Wang Taiping, *Zhonghua renmin gongheguo waijiaoshi*, 3: 377.

64. Deng Xiaoping's talk with the Delegation of U.S. Congressmen to China, July 9, 1978; in Zhongyang wenxian yanjiushi, ed., *Deng Xiaoping nianpu*, 1: 338–39.

65. Xue Mouhong and Pei Jianzhang, *Dangdai Zhongguo waijiao*, 229.

66. Wang Taiping, *Zhonghua renmin gongheguo waijiaoshi*, 3: 377; Alan D. Romberg, *Rein in at the Brink of the Precipice: American Foreign Policy Toward Taiwan and U.S.-PRC Relations* (Washington, DC: Henry L. Stimson Center, 2003), 90.

67. Deng Xiaoping's talk on the meeting of the Central Politburo, Nov. 2, 1978 (unpublished).

68. Zhonggong, Zhongyang wenxian yanjiushi, *Deng Xiaoping sixiang nian-pu*, 441.

69. Ibid., 97.

70. Deng Xiaoping's talk with Li Xiannian, Xu Shiyou, Li Desheng, and other leaders, Dec. 1, 1978 (unpublished).

71. Wang Taiping, *Zhonghua renmin gongheguo waijiaoshi*, 3: 378–79.

72. Zhonggong, Zhongyang wenxian yanjiushi, *Deng Xiaoping sixiang nian-pu*, 449–50.

73. Wang Li, *Bolan qifu: Zhong-Mei guanxi yanbian de quzhe licheng* (Tumultuous waves: the tortuous history of the Sino-US relations) (Beijing: Shijie zhishi chubanshe, 1998), 212.

74. Deng Xiaoping's talk with Woodcock, Dec. 13. 1978 (unpublished).

75. Deng Xiaoping's talk with Woodcock, Dec. 15, 1978 (unpublished). In addition, Zhu Qizhen recalled, "In the last phase of negotiations between China and the United States on the establishment of diplomatic relations, one problem blocked the negotiations, and that was the sale of weapons to Taiwan by the United States. We adhered to the three principles, which had been accepted by the United States. But the United States would make no concessions on the sale of weapons to Taiwan. At the time, if we had insisted that the United States had to stop selling weapons to Taiwan, we might have lost the chance to establish diplomatic relations with the United States. But if we let go of the problem of the selling of weapons, so as to establish diplomatic relations with the United States, the problem would be left unresolved for a long time. So when Deng Xiaoping talked about this problem with U.S. representatives in the last phase, he suggested, 'Why don't we agree to publish a communiqué on the establishment of diplomatic relations and leave the weapons problem to be negotiated by the two governments after the establishment of diplomatic relations?' It was due to these words that the 'August 17 communiqué' could be published" (Zhonggong, Zhongyang wenxian yanjiushi, and Zhongguo zhongyang dianshitai, eds., *Deng Xiaoping* [Beijing: Zhongyang wenxian chubanshe, 1997], 220–21).

76. Zhonggong, Zhongyang wenxian yanjiushi, *Deng Xiaoping sixiang nian-pu*, 102.

77. "Statement by the Government of the People's Republic of China," Dec. 16, 1978; in Dong Mei, *Zhong-Mei guanxi ziliao xuanbian*, 30.

78. On January 5, 1979, Deng Xiaoping mentioned this problem to some American reporters: "At the time when both sides reached the agreement to establish diplomatic relations, President Carter expressed his wish that the

Taiwan issue could be solved peacefully. We took note of the wish, but we expressed at the same time that it was a problem of Chinese internal affairs. We, of course, will try our best to solve the problem of the return of Taiwan to the motherland peacefully, but are not sure whether this is possible, because it is a complicated problem" (Dong Mei, *Zhong-Mei guanxi ziliao xuanbian*, 35).

79. Ibid., 9–10.

80. Deng Xiaoping, during his visit to the United States, said to President Carter, "China, the United States, Japan, West Europe and the Third World should unite to counter the strategic plan of the Soviet Union" ("Deng Xiaoping's talk with U.S. President Carter," Jan. 29, 1979; unpublished).

81. "Deng Xiaoping's Comments at the Welcoming Party Held in the White House," Jan. 29, 1979, in Renmin chubanshe, ed., *Lishixing de dashi: Zhong-Mei jianjiao he Deng Xiaoping fu zongli fang Mei* (A historic event: the establishment of diplomatic relations between China and the United States, and Vice Premier Deng Xiaoping's visit to the United States) (Beijing: Renmin chubanshe, 1979), 54.

Chapter 5

1. In the year after the Central Committee of the Soviet Communist Party repudiated the agreement, the USSR withdrew all its specialists from China, terminated its aid projects, and removed all blueprints and materials.

2. From October 1964 to February 1969, Soviet frontier forces initiated 4,160 border incidents along the border region of China and the USSR; see Han Huaizhi, ed., *Dangdai Zhongguo jundui de junshi gongzuo* (The military work of the contemporary Chinese military) (Beijing: Zhongguo shehui kexue chubanshe, 1989), 1: 635.

3. Zhongguo renmin jiefangjun, Kexueyuan, ed., *Zhongguo renmin jiefang-jun dashiji* (Chronicle of events of the Chinese People's Liberation Army) (Beijing: Junshi kexue chubanshe, 1983), 351.

4. Wang Taiping, ed., *Zhonghua renmin gongheguo waijiaoshi* (Diplomatic history of the People's Republic of China) (Beijing: Shijie zhishi chubanshe, 1999), 3: 201, 272.

5. In an October 22 directive of the same year, Mao Zedong wrote: "We must be prepared to fight a war, a big war and an early war, and to prepare for war actively. We must be prepared for an early war, a big war, and an atomic war" (Liao Guoliang et al., *Mao Zedong junshi sixiang fazhanshi* [History of the development of Mao Zedong's military thought] [Beijing: Jiefangjun chubanshe, 1991], 539).

6. Li Deng et al., *Jianguo yilai junshi baizhuang dashi* (One hundred important events in military history since the founding of the republic) (Beijing: Zhishi chubanshe, 1992), 203.

7. Han Huaizhi, *Dangdai Zhongguo jundui de junshi gongzuo*, 54–55.

8. In the early 1980s, the Chinese military believed that the USSR had deployed, in the region east of the Ural Mountains, 54 army divisions consisting of 44 motorized infantry divisions, 8 tank divisions, 2 airborne divisions, more than 15,000 tanks, and more than 10,000 guns, as well as approximately 630,000 troops. In addition, there were 1,900 fighter aircraft, supported by approximately 125,000 personnel, 1,140 military aircraft, and 3,000 surface-to-air guided missiles, with approximately 124,000 troops. Naval forces in the area included 162 main fighting ships of the Soviet Pacific Fleet, totaling 540,000 tons, plus 345 navy aircraft and approximately 130,000 military personnel. Soviet strategic nuclear forces in the area included 550 intercontinental guided missiles, 135 medium-range ballistic missiles, and approximately 121,000 military personnel. In all, Soviet forces in the Soviet Far East were believed to total 1,180,000 troops.

9. Since the start of the Cold War, the military forces of the USSR stationed in the Asian areas of Soviet territory, especially in the Far Eastern area, had been directed mainly at the U.S. military forces stationed in East Asia. But, starting in the mid-1960s, as Sino-Soviet relations deteriorated, the USSR increased its military forces stationed in its Far Eastern area significantly, especially motorized forces in the territory of Mongolia. This buildup was apparently directed at China.

10. Shen Weilie and Chen Li, *Zhongguo zhoubian guojia junshi dili* (The military geography of China's surrounding countries) (Beijing: Jiefang jun chubanshe, 1989), 190.

11. From the late 1960s to the early 1970s, I was assigned to a unit of the PLA in the northeast; during that period, I often heard high-ranking officers quote this metaphor and attribute it to Mao Zedong. Although I have found no published evidence that Mao Zedong actually said these words, they do seem to reflect worries by top Chinese policymakers about the strategic intention behind the stationing of the Soviet army in Mongolia.

12. Wang Taiping, *Zhonghua renmin gongheguo waijiaoshi*, 2: 276–77.

13. Han Huaizhi, *Dangdai Zhongguo jundui de junshi gongzuo*, 1: 635–45. On August 13 of the same year, the Soviet frontier force moved 2 km into the Tilekti region along the western part of the Sino-Soviet border and made a surprise attack on the Chinese frontier patrol, resulting in a fierce fight.

14. Li Danhui, "1969 nian Zhong-Su bianjie chongtu: yuanqi he jieguo" (The Sino-Soviet border conflict of 1969: origins and consequences), *Dangdai Zhongguo shi yanjiu* 1996, no. 3: 48.

15. Mao Zedong, speech at the First Session of the Ninth Central Committee of the Chinese Communist Party, Apr. 28, 1969 (unpublished).

16. Zhonggong, Zhongyang wenxian yanjiushi, ed., *Zhou Enlai nianpu, 1949–1976* (Chronicle of the life of Zhou Enlai) (Beijing: Zhongyang wenxian chubanshe, 1997), 2: 286; Li Lianqing, *Lengnuan suiyue: yibo sanzhe de Zhong-Su guanxi* (Twists and turns in Sino-Soviet relations: hot and cold years) (Beijing: Shijie zhishi chubanshe, 1999), 354–57.

17. Arkady N. Shevchenko, *Breaking with Moscow*, trans. from Russian into Chinese by Wang Guanshen et al. (Beijing: Shijie zhishi chubanshe, 1986), 194.

18. One of the articles was by American strategic analysts Donald C. Daniel and Harlan W. Jencks. They wrote that China would doubtless be worried that the USSR expected to destroy China's nuclear capability even if there were no overall war between the United States and the USSR. After the Zhenbao Island incident, the USSR apparently considered the possibility of destroying China's nuclear arsenal. See Donald C. Daniel and Harlan W. Jencks, "Soviet Military Confrontation with China: Options for the USSR, the PRC, and the USA," *Conflict* 5, no. 1 (1983): 57–87; trans. Wang Tianchen.

19. Wang Taiping, *Zhonghua renmin gongheguo waijiaoshi*, 2: 275.

20. Wang Taiping, ed., *Xin Zhongguo waijiao wushinian* (50 years of diplomacy of the New China) (Beijing: Beijing chubanshe, 1999), 936. By the end of the 1960s, Chinese mass media were openly calling the USSR "our most dangerous enemy."

21. Wei Shiyang, "Heige shuai xianqian wei Nikesong fang Hua anpai de jingguo" (The experience of the advance team led by Alexander Haig for Nixon's visit to China), in Waijiaobu, Waijiaoshi bianjishi, ed., *Xin Zhongguo waijiao fengyun* (Storms over the diplomacy of New China) (Beijing: Shijie zhishi chubanshe, 1994), 3: 78–79.

22. Richard M. Nixon, "Asia After Vietnam," *Foreign Affairs*, no. 46 (Oct. 1967).

23. Wang Taiping, *Xin Zhongguo waijiao wushinian*, 1329–30.

24. Henry Kissinger, *Baigong suiyue: Jixingge huiyilu*, trans. Chen Yaohua et al. of *White House Years* (Beijing: Shijie zhishi chubanshe, 1980), 223.

25. Zhonggong, Zhongyang wenxian yanjiushi, *Zhou Enlai nianpu*, 2: 304; Xiong Xianghui, *Lishi de zhujiao* (Footnote to history) (Beijing: Zhonggong, Zhongyang dangxiao chubanshe, 1995), 177.

26. For details of Mao Zedong's request to Chen Yi and the other three marshals to analyze international questions, see Xiong Xianghui, *Lishi de zhujiao*, 173–204.

27. Wang Taiping, *Zhonghua renmin gongheguo waijiaoshi*, 3: 346.

28. Han Huaizhi, *Dangdai Zhongguo junduidejunshi gongzuo*, 1: 635–45.

29. *Zhou Enlai waijiao wenxuan* (Selected writings on foreign affairs by Zhou Enlai) (Beijing: Zhongyang wenxian chubanshe, 1990), 462.

30. Mao Zedong's talk with Edward Snow, Dec. 18, 1970; reported in *Mao Zedong waijiao wenxuan* (Selected writings on foreign affairs by Mao Zedong) (Beijing: Zhongyang wenxian chubanshe and Shijie zhishi chubanshe, 1994), 592–93.

31. The Shanghai Communiqué declared that neither party would seek hegemony in the Asia-Pacific region and that both parties opposed efforts by any other state or bloc to establish such a hegemony. This is clearly an expression by both China and the United States of an intention to oppose any attempt by the Soviet Union or the Soviet bloc to seek hegemony in the Asia-Pacific region.

32. Mao Zedong, discussion with Zhou Enlai, Ji Pengfei, and others, on July 24, 1972 (unpublished).

33. Mao Zedong, discussion of the reassignment of the posts of commanders of the main military districts, Dec. 1973 (unpublished).

34. Henry Kissinger, *Da waijiao* (Diplomacy) (Hainan: Hainan chubanshe, 1998), 672.

35. Wang Shuzhong, ed., *Mei-Su zhengba zhanlue wenti* (The question of contention for hegemony between the United States and the Soviet Union) (Beijing: Guofang daxue chubanshe, 1988), 361.

36. Mao Zedong, discussion with Henry Kissinger, Feb. 17, 1973 (unpublished).

37. Mao Zedong, discussion with Henry Kissinger, Nov. 12, 1973 (unpublished); also in William Burr, ed., *Kissinger Transcripts: The Top Secret Talks with Beijing and Moscow* (New York: New Press, 1998), 184.

38. Ibid. Mao Zedong, in "Directive on the Foreign Ministry's Request for Instruction on the Plan for Interviewing Kissinger," suggested repeatedly that "we should invite the U.S. Secretary of Defense to visit China" (*Mao Zedong jianguo yilai wen'gao* [Mao Zedong's manuscripts since the founding of the republic] [Beijing: Zhongyang wenxian chubanshe, 1998], 13: 406).

39. Mao Zedong, discussion with the president of Zambia, Feb. 22, 1974, in *Mao Zedong waijiao wenxuan*, 600–601.

40. Burr, *The Kissinger Transcripts*, 85.

41. Mao Zedong, discussion with Henry Kissinger, Feb. 17, 1973, in ibid., 94.

42. Mao Zedong, discussion with Henry Kissinger, Nov. 12, 1973 (unpublished).

43. Summary of Mao Zedong, discussions with Wang Hongwen and Zhang Chunjiao, July 4, 1973 (unpublished).

44. Mao Zedong, discussion with members of the Central Military Commission, Dec. 21, 1973 (unpublished).

45. The phrase "Gang of Four" refers to Jiang Qing, Zhang Chunjiao, Wang Hongwen, and Yao Wenyuan.

46. See letter of the National People's Congress dated March 9, 1979, answering a letter from the Soviet Union (unpublished).

47. On this, Deng Xiaoping, in an interview with the editor in chief of the *Christian Science Monitor*, declared that China and the United States should make a real effort to check the expansion of the USSR. Relations between China and the USSR could not be improved if the USSR did not change its strategy of expansion and hegemony. Deng stated that China wished relations between the United States and China to continue to improve, and that this was required by global strategy.

48. Xu Xiangqian, "Tigao jingti, junbei dazhang" (Raise the warning, prepare for war), *Hongqi* 1978, no. 8: 46.

49. Cyrus R. Vance, *Hard Choices: Critical Years in American Foreign Policy* (New York: Simon and Schuster, 1983), 44, 76–78.

50. Han Nianlong and Xue Mouhong, eds., *Dangdai Zhongguo waijiao* (Contemporary Chinese diplomacy) (Beijing: Zhongguo shehui kexue chubanshe, 1990), 226.

51. Deng Xiaoping, discussions with delegation of the Board of Directors, United Press International. Jimmy Carter Presidential Library, National Security Council documents, Zbigniew Brzezinski Material, country file, Box 4-8, China 7-9, 77.

52. Zbigniew Brzezinski, *Power and Principle: Memoirs of the National Security Adviser, 1977–1981* (New York: Farrar, Straus, and Giroux, 1983), 204–5.

53. Deng Xiaoping, talk with George Bush, chief of the U.S. Liaison Office in Beijing, Sept. 27, 1977. Qian Jiang, "Deng Xiaoping yu Zhong-Mei jianjiao" (Deng Xiaoping and the establishment of diplomatic relations between China and the United States), *Huanqiu shibao*, Jan. 12, 2001, 11.

54. Brzezinski, *Power and Principle*, 201.

55. Ibid., 207–9.

56. Wang Taiping, *Zhonghua renmin gongheguo waijiaoshi*, 3: 1336.

57. Qian Jiang, "Deng Xiaoping yu Zhong-Mei jianjiao," Feb. 16, 2001, 11.

58. Waijiaobu, Dang'an guan, ed., *Weiren de zuji: Deng Xiaoping waijiao huodong tashiji* (Footprints of a great man: chronicle of Deng Xiaoping's diplomatic activities) (Beijing: Shijie zhishi chubanshe, 1998).

59. Qian Jiang, "Deng Xiaoping yu Zhong-Mei jianjiao," Feb. 16, 2001, 11.

60. In early 1979, China concentrated troops in the Sino-Vietnam border area in preparation for war with Vietnam; at the same time, some combat divisions in the Three Norths area were moved to a staging area to guard against

potential Soviet military attack and to contain aggressive actions by the Soviet Union.

61. *Renmin ribao*, Jan. 7, 1980.

62. Zhang Jingyi, "Zhong-Mei guanxi zhong de anquan yinsu: huigu yu zhanwang" (The security factor in Sino-U.S. relations: retrospect and prospects), in Zhongguo shehui kexueyuan, Meiguo yanjiusuo, and Zhonghua Meiguo xuehui, eds., *Zhong-Mei guanxi shinian* (Ten years of Sino-U.S. relations) (Beijing: Shangwu yinshuguan, 1989), 43.

Chapter 6

1. There has been little research on Vietnam as a factor in the adjustment of China's policy toward the United States. Recent works of importance include Niu Jun, "Liushi niandai mo Zhongguo dui Mei zhengce zhuanbian de lishi beijing" (The historical background of the change in China's policy toward the United States in the late 1960s); Shen Zhihua, "Zhong-Mei hejie yu Zhongguo dui Yue waijiao (1968–1973)" (The China-U.S. reconciliation and China's diplomacy toward Vietnam, 1968–73), both in *Zhongguo yu Yinduzhina zhanzheng* (China and the Indochina War), ed. Li Danhui (Hong Kong: Tiandi tushu, 2000), 192–220, 221–50, respectively; Shen Zhihua and Li Danhui, "Zhong-Mei hejie yu Zhongguo dui Yue waijiao (1971–1973)" (The China-U.S. reconciliation and China's diplomacy toward Vietnam, 1971–73), *American Studies* 1 (2000): 98–116; Qiang Zhai, *China and the Vietnam Wars, 1950–1975* (Chapel Hill, NC: University of North Carolina Press, 2000). Niu Jun's article suggests the important thesis that the change in North Vietnamese–Chinese relations had an extremely important impact on China's policy toward the United States. To China, national security and support for the Vietnamese national revolution were the main considerations behind its support for North Vietnam. The peace talks were essential elements in the strategic considerations of both sides. I agree with this point, but Niu's article stresses the peace talks, whereas this chapter seeks to explain Chinese leaders' attitudes toward the peace talks at various stages and their relationship to adjustments in China's policies toward the United States. Neither Zhai's book nor Shen's article touches on the changes in China's attitude toward the peace talks.

2. See Zhonghua renmin gongheguo, Waijiaobu, and Zhonggong, Zhongyang wenxian yanjiushi, eds., *Mao Zedong waijiao wenxuan* (Selected writings on foreign policy by Mao Zedong) (Beijing: Zhongyang wenxian chubanshe and Shijie zhishi chubanshe, 1994), 572; Zhonggong, Zhongyang wenxian yanjiushi, ed., *Zhou Enlai nianpu, 1949–1976* (Chronicle of Zhou Enlai) (Beijing: Zhongyang wenxian chubanshe, 1997), 74. Hereafter both of these publications are cited by title only.

3. Wang Taiping, ed., *Zhonghua renmin gongheguo waijiaoshi* (History of the diplomacy of the People's Republic of China), 3 vols. (Beijing: Shijie zhishi chubanshe, 1998–99), 2: 41.

4. See minutes of talk between Zhou Enlai and Pham Van Dong on April 13 and 19, 1968; minutes of talk between Chen Yi and Le Duc Tho, in Odd Arne Westad, Chen Jian, Stein Tonnesson, Nguyen Vu Tung, and James G. Hershberg, eds., "77 Conversations Between Chinese and Foreign Leaders on the Wars in Indochina, 1964–1977," Working Paper no. 22, Cold War International History Project (CWIHP), Woodrow Wilson International Center for Scholars, Washington, DC (hereafter cited as CWIHP, "77 Conversations"), 123–29, 138, 140; *Zhou Enlai nianpu*, 2: 256. In addition, on China's attitude toward the Vietnam-U.S. peace talks, see Li Danhui, "Zhongguo dui Yue Mei hetan de lichang, fangzhen, jiqi bianhua (1965–1968)" (China's position, principles, and adjustments toward the Vietnam-U.S. peace talks, 1965–68), *Dangdai Zhongguo shi yanjiu*, special issue, 2001.

5. See Wang Taiping, *Zhonghua renmin gongheguo waijiaoshi*, 2: 42.

6. *Zhou Enlai nianpu*, 2: 266; *Mao Zedong waijiao wenxuan*, 580–83.

7. In fact, Chinese leaders did not oppose the principle of fighting while talking. When speaking with Pham Van Dong on April 7–11, 1967, Zhou Enlai suggested that it was all right for Vietnam to adopt the principle of fighting while talking, but that China had a different understanding of the political struggle. What China emphasized was time and more propaganda in the world in order to win sympathy, to split the enemy, and to exploit contradictions among enemies, rather than concessions. See Wang Taiping, *Zhonghua renmin gongheguo waijiaoshi*, 2: 40; *Zhou Enlai nianpu*, 2: 143.

8. In self-criticism, some Chinese leaders said that "sometimes we did not understand the situation; we did not grasp Chairman Mao's ideas about the talks. We did not understand why our Vietnamese comrades held the talks in Paris." See Qiao Guanhua, "Guanyu dangqian guoji xingshi jige wenti de jianghua" (On some questions in the current international situation), Mar. 23, 1972, Fujian Archive, series no. 244, catalog 1, no. 77, 115.

9. On China's initial suggestion and Mao Zedong's approval for resumption of the China-U.S. talks, see Gong Li, "Mao Zedong zenyang dakai Zhong-Mei guanxi de damen" (How Mao Zedong opened up the gate of China-U.S. relations), in *All the World Has the Same Feeling: International Strategic Thoughts of Leaders of the First Generation*, ed. International Strategic Studies Fund (Beijing: Zhongyang wenxian chubanshe, 1993), 272; Wang Taiping, *Zhonghua renmin gongheguo waijiaoshi*, 2: 451. According to U.S. sources, China accepted the U.S. suggestion to resume talks on Feb. 20, 1969, and also mentioned the Five Principles of Peaceful Coexistence. This was new evidence of flexibility in China's

policies (see Alfred Jenkins to Rostow, memorandum, Dec. 2, 1968; the collection number of this declassified document is unavailable; copy in possession of the author).

10. See Wang Taiping, *Zhonghua renmin gongheguo waijiaoshi*, 2: 450–51.

11. See Tad Szulc, *Heping de huanxiang: Nikesong waijiao neimu*, trans. Deng Xin of *The Illusion of Peace: Foreign Policy in the Nixon Years* (Beijing: Shangwu yinshuguan, 1982), 1: 148–49.

12. Comments by Zhou Enlai while receiving Pol Pot, leading cadre of People's Revolutionary Party of Cambodia, on Nov. 30, 1968; *Zhou Enlai nianpu*, 2: 267.

13. From Mao Zedong's directives and corrections on telegrams by the Central Office, the Office of the Military Commission, the Ministry of Central Liaison, and the Ministry of Foreign Affairs; Changchun archives, file 1, catalogue 1–3, folder 21, 65–66. The article was published in the *People's Daily*; the full text of Nixon's inaugural speech on January 20, 1969, was also published.

14. President Nixon to Henry Kissinger, Feb. 1, 1969; National Security Study Memorandum (NSSM) 14, Henry Kissinger to the Secretary of State, the Secretary of Defense, the Director of Central Intelligence, Feb. 5, 1969.

15. Luo Yisu, "Zai Bolan de suiyue" (Days in Poland), in *Dangdai Zhongguo shijie waijiao shengya* (Lives of contemporary diplomatic envoys) (Beijing: Shijie zhishi chubanshe, 1996), 4: 178–79.

16. *Zhou Enlai nianpu*, 2: 281.

17. Henry Kissinger, *White House Years* (Toronto: Little Brown, 1979), 173.

18. Zi Zhongyun, ed., *Zhanhou Meiguo waijiaoshi* (History of U.S. diplomacy after the war), 19th ed. (Beijing: Shijie zhishi chubanshe, 1994), 2: 628.

19. *Renmin ribao*, Mar. 17, 1969; Kissinger, *White House Years*, 170.

20. *Renmin ribao*, Mar. 17, 1969.

21. See minutes of talk between Zhou Enlai, Kang Shen, Pham Van Dong, Hoang Van Thai, Pham Hung, etc., on Apr. 20, 1969; and minutes of talk between Li Xiannian and Le Duc Tho on Apr. 29, in CWIHP, "77 Conversations," 158–60; conversation between Zhou Enlai and Wang Youping, Chinese ambassador to Vietnam, on June 4, 1969; Yun Shui, *Chushi qiguo jishi: jiangjun dashi Wang Youping* (Missions to seven countries: General and Ambassador Wang Youping) (Beijing: Shijie zhishi chubanshe, 1996), 102; *Zhou Enlai nianpu*, 2: 304.

22. *Zhou Enlai nianpu*, 2: 286, 288–89.

23. *Renmin ribao*, Apr. 28, 1969.

24. Lin Biao's report was entitled "On the Relations Between China and Foreign Countries." On the U.S. evaluation of Lin Biao's report, see Kissinger, *White House Years*, 176.

25. On the communications to the United States by Soviet Ambassador Anatoly Dobrynin regarding the Zhenbao Island Incident, and the U.S. analysis, see Kissinger, *White House Years*, 172–73; idem, *Diplomacy* (New York: Simon and Schuster, 1994), trans. Gu Shuxin as *Da waijiao* (Hainan: Hainan chubanshe, 1998), 667–68; and Dobrynin, *Xinlai: Duoboleining huiyilu* (Trust: memoirs of Anatoly Dobrynin), trans. Xiao Ming et al. (Beijing: Shijie zhishi chubanshe, 1997), 232 [published in English as *In Confidence: Moscow's Ambassador to America's Six Cold War Presidents (1962–1968)* (New York: Times Books, 1997)].

26. See Kissinger, *White House Years*, 266, 264.

27. On various measures adopted by the United States, see National Security Decision Memorandum (NSDM) 17, Henry Kissinger to Secretary of State, Secretary of Defense, Director of Central Intelligence, and Chairman of the Joint Chiefs of Staff, June 26, 1969; Kissinger, *Da waijiao*, 667–70; Szulc, *Heping de huanxiang*, 1: 149–64; Wang Taiping, *Zhonghua renmin gongheguo waijiaoshi*, 3: 348–49.

28. Zhou Enlai, commenting on Chen Yi's report on the activities of the International Problems Study Team, emphasized the importance of the three tasks assigned by Mao Zedong: "To read, to discuss collectively, and to submit suggestions." Zhou Enlai had previously told Chen Yi and the others that "Chairman Mao assigned you the task of studying international problems because he saw the necessity to continue the study. It was the chairman's consistent thought that subjective knowledge should seek to correspond with objective reality. The objective situation is changing and developing continuously, and thus the subjective knowledge should change and develop accordingly. You should not be restricted by former views and conclusions, but should correct part or even the whole of them." When Mao Zedong was contemplating further adjustments to diplomatic strategy, the four generals submitted to Zhou Enlai "A Written Report on the Preliminary Estimate of the War Situation" in July, and "Views on the Present Situation" in September. Chen Yi suggested that China should take advantage of the contradictions between the United States and the Soviet Union to break the deadlock in relations between China and the United States. China subsequently responded actively to indications of adjustments in U.S. policy toward China. See *Zhou Enlai nianpu*, 2: 301–2; Xiong Xianghui, *Lishi de zhujiao; huiyi Mao Zedong, Zhou Enlai ji si laoshuai* (Footnote to History: recollecting Mao Zedong, Zhou Enlai, and the four generalissimos) (Beijing: Zhonggong, Zhongyang dangxiao chubanshe, 1995), 184–200; and Wang Taiping, *Zhonghua renmin gongheguo waijiaoshi*, 3: 346–49.

29. *Renmin ribao*, Oct. 26, 1969.

30. Mao Zedong, in discussions with the party and state delegation from Vietnam led by Pham Van Dong, said that China might permit use of Guang-

dong, Guangxi, Yunnan, and Hunan as supporting bases for Vietnam. These provinces and autonomous regions later organized "assistance to Vietnam teams," and negotiated assistance with recipient Vietnamese provinces in the areas of agriculture, animal husbandry, aquatics, water conservancy, soil testing, and the like. See Yun Shui, *Chushi qiguo jishi*, 127–28.

31. See minutes of the talk between Zhou Enlai, Kang Shen, and Pham Van Dong on April 12, CWIHP, "77 Conversations," 156–57.

32. Between June 1965 and March 1969, 23 detachments, 95 regiments, and 83 battalions, totaling more than 320,000 Chinese troops, entered Vietnam. The troop numbers peaked at 170,000. All road-building troops (which had been sent to Vietnam in September 1965) were withdrawn in February 1969. All air defense forces (which had entered Vietnam in August 1965) were withdrawn in March 1969. Five groups of anti-aircraft troops, totaling 15,000, were stationed in Vietnam from February 1966 to March 1969. All national defense engineering troops (three detachments and one regiment, which had entered Vietnam in June 1965) were withdrawn in November 1969. All railroad troops (totaling 30,000 troops, which had entered Vietnam in June 1965) were withdrawn in June 1970. After negotiations between China and Vietnam, all Chinese support troops in Vietnam, having accomplished their missions, were withdrawn to China by July 1970. Qiu Aiguo, "Zhongguo zhiyuan budui zai Yuenan zhan-chang de junshi xingdong" (The military actions of Chinese support troops on Vietnam's battlefields), in *Zhongguo yu Yinduzhina zhanzheng*, 91–97.

33. See minutes of talks between Zhou Enlai, Pham Van Dong, Hoang Van Thai, and Phan Hung on Apr. 12, 1969, CWIHP, "77 Conversations," 157; talk between Zhou Enlai, Phan Hung, and Hoang Van Thai on Apr. 21, Zhongguo renmin gongheguo, Waijiaobu, Waijiaoshi yanjiu shi, ed., *Zhou Enlai waijiao huodong dashiji* (Chronicle of Zhou Enlai's diplomatic activities) (Beijing: Shijie zhishi chubanshe, 1993), 535.

34. *Zhou Enlai waijiao huodong dashiji*, 538–39.

35. Telegrams from Mao Zedong and others with congratulations on the twenty-fourth anniversary of the independence of the People's Republic of Vietnam (Sept. 1, 1969); telegram from Mao Zedong and others, with congratulations on the ninth anniversary of the founding of South Vietnam's National Liberation Front (Dec. 19, 1969); *Mao Zedong jianguo yilai wen'gao* (Mao Zedong's manuscripts since the founding of the People's Republic) (Beijing: Zhongyang wenxian chubanshe, 1998), 13: 63–65, 70–72.

36. *Renmin ribao*, Mar. 24 and May 5, 1970.

37. Minutes of conversation between Mao Zedong and Le Duan on May 11, 1970, in CWIHP, "77 Conversations," 163–69.

38. *Zhou Enlai nianpu*, 2: 366–67.

39. *Renmin ribao*, May 19, 1970.

40. See Qiao Guanhua, "Guanyu dangqian guoji xingshi jige wenti de jiang-hua," Mar. 23, 1972, Fujian archives, file 24, catalogue 1, 77: 155.

41. See minutes of Premier Zhou's talk with British writer and correspondent Neville Maxwell, in Waijiaobu, ed., *Dangqian zhongda guoji wenti he woguo dui-wai zhengce* (Current important international problems and China's foreign policy), Fujian Archive, vol. 244, catalog 1, no. 77, 53.

42. "If Nixon comes, I would like to talk with him" (*Mao Zedong waijiao wenxuan*, 593).

43. Kissinger took it as an empty statement, not really raising any threat, and having no bearing on the bilateral problems that were in dispute between the two sides. See Kissinger, *White House Years*, 695.

44. Ibid., 695–96.

45. John Holdridge, *Crossing the Divide: An Insider's Account of the Normalization of U.S.-China Relations* (Lanham, MD: Rowman and Littlefield, 1997), trans. Yang Liyi et al., *1945 nian yilai Mei-Zhong guanxi zhengchanghua* (The normalization of U.S.-China relations since 1945) (Shanghai: Shanghai Translation Press, 1997), 48–49.

46. On contacts between China and the United States, see Wang Taiping, *Zhonghua renmin gongheguo waijiaoshi*, 3: 350; and Kissinger, *White House Years*, 696.

47. See Premier Zhou's talk with James Reston, vice president of the *New York Times*, in Waijiaobu, *Dangqian zhongda guoji wenti he woguo duiwai zhengce*, 52.

48. On contacts between China and the United States, see Wang Taiping, *Zhonghua renmin gongheguo waijiaoshi*, 3: 350–51; and Kissinger, *White House Years*, 597–703.

49. Minutes of conversation between Mao Zedong and Pham Van Dong, Sept. 23, 1970, in CWIHP, "77 Conversations," 178.

50. See Table 6.1 for the amount of China's military aid to Vietnam in 1970.

51. Wang Taiping, *Zhonghua renmin gongheguo waijiaoshi*, 3: 49.

52. General Alexander Haig to Tom Charles Huston, memorandum, Feb. 25, 1971.

53. Joint communiqué by the CCP Central Committee, the Government of the People's Republic of China, the Central Committee of the Vietnamese Workers Party, and the Government of the Democratic Republic of Vietnam, issued on Mar. 8, 1971, and published in the *Renmin ribao*, Mar. 11, 1971.

54. Speech by Zhou Enlai at the meeting held by the people of Hanoi to welcome the party and state delegation of China on Mar. 6, 1971, in Waijiaobu, *Dangqian zhongda guoji wenti he woguo duiwai zhengce*, 19.

55. Kissinger, *White House Years*, 706.

56. See ibid., 706–7.

57. *Zhou Enlai nianpu*, 2: 453.

58. John A. Scali to Dwight Chapin, memorandum, Apr. 12, 1971 (unpublished).

59. Report of the Political Bureau of the Central Committee of the Chinese Communist Party on the China-U.S. talks, May 29, 1971 (unpublished).

60. More than a year earlier, China had adamantly refused similar suggestions by the Soviet Union; see Zhai, *China and the Vietnam Wars, 1950–1975*, 197–98; and *Zhou Enlai nianpu*, 2: 467.

61. See Memorandum of Conversation, July 9, 1971, 4:35 P.M.–11:20 P.M., 20, 25 (unpublished). In June 2001, the Cold War International History Project (CWIHP) of the Woodrow Wilson International Center for Scholars in Washington, DC, East China Normal University in Shanghai, and the Modern History Research Center and Archives of Peking University held a symposium entitled "The Evolution of Sino-U.S.-Soviet Relations and the Transformation of the Cold War." Christian Ostermann, director of the CWIHP, attended the symposium and provided copies of documents from U.S. archives, such as the Memorandum of Conversation between Kissinger and Zhou Enlai in July 1971, which had recently been declassified.

62. Wei Shiyan, "Jixingge miji fang Hua neimu" (The inside story of Kissinger's secret visit), in Waijiaobu, Waijiaoshi bianjishi, *Xin Zhongguo waijiao fengyun* (Storms over the diplomacy of New China) (Beijing: Shijie zhishi chubanshe, 1991), 41–42.

63. See Memorandum of Conversation, July 10, 1971, 12:10 P.M.–11:20 P.M., 13, 25 (see note 61 to this chapter for this source).

64. See ibid., July 9, 1971, 4:35 P.M.–11:20 P.M., 28, 29, 32, 33.

65. See ibid., 34; and ibid., July 10, 1971, 12:10 P.M.–11:20 P.M., 22–23, 25.

66. See ibid., July 11, 1971, 12:00 midnight–1:40 A.M.; 9:50 A.M.–10:35 A.M., 2.

67. See ibid., July 9, 1971, 4:35 P.M.–11:20 P.M., 24; and ibid., July 10, 1971, 12:10 P.M.–11:20 P.M., 5.

68. See Kissinger, *White House Years*, 783.

69. The "Diplomatic Circular" sent by the Ministry of Foreign Affairs to all institutions outside China in August 1971, in explaining principles toward the United States, emphasized this one especially; see *Zhou Enlai nianpu*, 2: 469.

70. Vietnamese sources; see S. J. Ball, *The Cold War: An International History, 1947–1991* (New York and London: Arnold Press, 1997), 140.

71. Memorandum of Conversation, July 11, 1971, 12:00 midnight–1:40 A.M.; 9:50 A.M.–10:35 A.M., 17 (see note 61 to this chapter on this source).

72. Ibid., July 10, 1971, 12:10 P.M.–11:20 P.M., 26, 29.

73. See William Burr, ed., *The Kissinger Transcripts: The Top Secret Talks with Beijing and Moscow* (New York: New Press, 1998), 41.

74. Comrade B, "The Plot of the Reactionary Chinese Clique against Vietnam," quoted in CWIHP, "77 Conversations." According to Chinese sources, Vietnam's leaders were greatly surprised when they learned that Kissinger had visited China secretly and that Nixon would visit China the next year, but they expressed no opposition; see Wang Taiping, *Zhonghua renmin gongheguo waijiaoshi,* 3: 54.

75. On the *Nahn dan* editorial hinting at the China-U.S. talks, Zhou Enlai, in instructions to Zhang Chunqiao and Yao Wenyuan, said: "The article expresses our Vietnamese comrades' worries and estimates. . . . I think we should publish the whole article, and not just an abstract, to show we are open and aboveboard." He added: "Events will show that China, under the leadership of Chairman Mao, supports the fight of the people of the three Indochinese countries to the end" (*Zhou Enlai nianpu,* 2: 469–70). The article was not published, however, because of opposition from Zhang Chunqiao.

76. See Zhai, *China and the Vietnam Wars, 1950–1975,* 197.

77. See memorandum of August 1979 interview by Seymour Hersh with Nguyen Co Thach, vice minister of Vietnam's Foreign Ministry; he had visited Beijing with Pham Van Dong in November 1971 (quoted in Zhai, *China and the Vietnam Wars, 1950–1975,* 198).

78. See Zhou Enlai's interviews with James Reston, vice president of the *New York Times,* on Aug. 5, 1971; with Gotō Motoo, chief of the editorial board of *Asahi shinbun,* Japan, on Oct. 28; and with Neville Maxwell on Nov. 20, in Waijiaobu, ed., *Dangqian zhongda guoji wenti he woguo duiwai zhengce,* 48, 52–54.

79. On Nov. 20–27, 1971, during the visit of Pham Van Dong and the Vietnamese delegation to China, the front page of the *People's Daily* carried a large photo of Pham Van Dong, and that issue contained a special editorial. Zhou Enlai accompanied the delegation during the whole trip, and hundreds of thousands of people lined the streets to welcome the delegation; see *Renmin ribao* for these dates; and *Zhou Enlai nianpu,* 2: 497.

80. *Renmin ribao,* Nov. 27, 1971.

81. Ibid.

82. Percentage calculated from data in Fang Weizhong, ed., *Zhonghua renmin gongheguo jingji da shiji, 1949–1980* (Chronicle of important economic affairs in the PRC) (Beijing: Zhongguo shehui kexue chubanshe, 1984), 484. See Table 6.1 for details of Chinese military aid to Vietnam in 1971.

83. Wei Shiyan, "Heige shuaixian qianzu wei Nikesong fang Hua anpai de jingguo" (The course of arrangements for Nixon's visit by the Haig advance

party), in Waijiaobu, Waijiaoshi bianjishi, *Xin Zhongguo waijiao fengyun*, 3: 73–74.

84. See ibid., 3: 78–79.

85. See Ibid., 3: 79–81; *Zhou Enlai nianpu*, 2: 506–7; and Wang Taiping, *Zhonghua renmin gongheguo waijiaoshi*, 3: 359–60.

86. See Kissinger, *White House Years*, 1102–3, 1052, 1104.

87. Wang Taiping, *Zhongguo renmin gongheguo waijiaoshi*, 3: 364; for the quotation, see *Mao Zedong wiajiao wenxuan*, 595.

88. See Kissinger, *White House Years*, 1052, 1086, 1073, 1087.

89. See Yun Shui, *Chushi qiguo jishi*, 138–39.

90. Ibid., 138; and Comrade B, "The Plot of the Reactionary Chinese Clique Against Vietnam," in CWIHP, "77 Conversations."

91. See Kissinger, *White House Years*, 1113–15, 1118–19, 1123.

92. *Zhou Enlai nianpu*, 2: 519; CWIHP, "77 Conversations," 181–82.

93. See minutes of talk between Zhou Enlai and Xuan Thuy on May 13 and 14, Archive General Office, Department of Railways, office 1972, no. 53, 2–10; Yu Qiuli's speech on the mobilization meeting to support Vietnam on May 19, 1972, Archive of State Planning Commission, 20–0149. On assistance during this period, see Shen Zhihua and Li Danhui, "Zhong-Mei hejie yu Zhongguo dui Yue waijiao (1971–1973)," 108–10.

94. See Qiu Aiguo, "Zhongguo zhiyuan budui zai Yuenan zhanchang de junshi xingdong," 101.

95. See Vietnam, Ministry of Defense, Army History Research Institute, ed., *Yuenan renminjun lishi* (History of the Vietnamese People's Army), trans. Miao Xianchun et al. (Nanning: Guangxi renmin chubanshe, 1991), 2: 292; minutes of conversation of Ye Jianying and Li Xiannian with Le Ban, Archive General Office, Department of Railways, office 1972, no. 53, 73–79. The Soviet Union estimated Chinese aid to Vietnam at U.S.$500 million. See the Soviet Union Foreign Ministry Memorandum, "Vietnam-China Relations," July 4, 1973, quoted in Ilya V. Gaiduk, *The Soviet Union and the Vietnam War* (Chicago: Ivan R. Dee, 1996), 231. See Table 6.1 for the amount of China's military aid to Vietnam in 1972.

96. See Zhai, *China and the Vietnam Wars, 1950–1975*, 203.

97. See Kissinger, *White House Years*, 1304; Dobrynin, *Xinlai*, 296–97.

98. See minutes of conversation between Zhou Enlai and Le Duc Tho on June 18, 1972, Archive, General Office, Department of Railways, office 1972, no. 52, 19–36.

99. *Zhou Enlai nianpu*, 2: 534; minutes of conversation between Zhou Enlai and Le Duc Tho on July 12, 1972, in CWIHP, "77 Conversations," 182–84.

100. Wang Taiping, *Zhonghua renmin gongheguo waijiaoshi*, 3: 56; *Zhou Enlai waijiao huodong dashiji*, 2: 642.

101. Zhou Enlai had made similar suggestions to Vietnam on July 13 the year before, but not firmly enough to convince Hanoi; to diminish Hanoi's resentment over the China-U.S. dialogue, China soon stopped attempting to press Vietnam on this issue.

102. See Zhai, *China and the Vietnam Wars, 1950–1975*, 204, 263.

103. See Burr, *The Kissinger Transcripts*, 70–73.

104. See Kissinger, *White House Years*, 1396, 1402, 1413.

105. Minutes of conversation between Mao Zedong and Nguyen Thi Binh, in CWIHP, "77 Conversations," 185; *Zhou Enlai nianpu*, 2: 569, 571.

106. National Security Decision Memorandum 204, Henry Kissinger to Secretaries of State, Defense, and Commerce, Feb. 6, 1973. This document was declassified in May 1995, but references to aircraft models and technical equipment standards were blacked out.

107. Wang Taiping, *Zhonghua renmin gongheguo waijiaoshi*, 3: 367.

108. See *Cold War International History Project Bulletin*, Fall/Winter 2001: 282.

109. Quotation from memorandum of conversation between Li Xiannian and Pham Van Dong, quoted in Zhai, *China and the Vietnam Wars, 1950–1975*, 201.

110. See Xue Mouhong and Pei Jianchang, eds., *Dangdai Zhongguo waijiao* (Contemporary Chinese diplomacy) (Beijing: China Academy of Social Sciences, 1988), 162; Wang Taiping, *Zhonghua renmin gongheguo waijiaoshi*, 3: 51.

111. On the impact of Sino-Soviet relations on China's relationship with Vietnam and the principles that guided China's assistance to Vietnam, see Li Danhui, "Zhong-Su zai yuan Yue kang Mei wenti shang de fenqi he chongtu" (Differences and confrontations between China and the Soviet Union on assistance to Vietnam against the United States), in *Zhongguo yu Yinduzhina zhanzheng*, 126–91.

112. On October 16, 1972, Vice Minister of Foreign Trade Li Qiang, in answer to a request from Vietnam's Le Ban on delivery of military matériel, Le Ban said that China would transport materials intended for southern Vietnam as soon as possible but asked to delay the transport of the rest. On November 13, Le Ban relayed the hope of Le Thanh Nghi, vice premier of Vietnam, that China would deliver the heavy weapons. Because the production of new heavy weapons would take time, it was suggested that the Chinese side take heavy weapons from various units and send them to Vietnam, replacing them with new weapons as they were produced. Once the war came to an end and there was international supervision, it would be difficult to transport heavy weapons to

the south. Because there was as yet no international supervision and it was the dry season, it was suggested that China should try to transport more heavy weapons to the south soon. Li Qiang pointed out that much military matériel was still held back in China and could not be handed to the Vietnamese side; thus, he suggested, China should transport more ammunition to the south, before international supervision made this difficult, according to Comrade Le Ban's suggestion. See minutes of conversation between Li Qiang and Le Ban on Oct. 16 and Nov. 13, 1972, archive of the general office, Military Railway, office 1972, 53: 144, 147, 149–50.

113. See Qiao Guanhua, "Guanyu dangqian guoji xingshi jige wenti de jianghua," Mar. 23, 1972, Archive Fujian Province, Archive no. 244, catalog no. 1, no. 77, 112–13, 117.

114. See Table 6.1 for the amount of Chinese military aid to Vietnam in this period.

115. Fang Weizhong, *Zhonghua renmin gongheguo jingji da shiji*, 512; *Zhou Enlai nianpu*, 2: 598.

Chapter 7

1. Richard Nixon, *The Memoirs of Richard Nixon*, 2 vols., paperback edition (New York: Warner Books, 1979); Alexander M. Haig, Jr., *Caveat: Realism, Reagan, and Foreign Policy* (New York: Macmillan, 1984); Cyrus Vance, *Hard Choices: Critical Years in America's Foreign Policy* (New York: Simon and Schuster, 1983); George Bush, *Looking Forward* (Garden City, NY: Doubleday, 1987); Gerald Ford, *A Time to Heal* (New York: Harper and Row, 1979); Henry Kissinger, *The White House Years* (Boston: Little, Brown, 1979); Henry Kissinger, *Years of Upheaval* (Boston: Little, Brown, 1982); Jimmy Carter, *Keeping Faith: Memoirs of a President* (Toronto: Bantam Books, 1982); John H. Holdridge, *Crossing the Divide: An Insider's Account of Normalization of U.S.-China Relations* (Lanham, MD: Rowman and Littlefield, 1997); Marshall Green, *Pacific Encounters* (Lawrence, NJ: Princeton Academic Press, 1997); U. Alexis Johnson, *The Right Hand of Power* (Englewood Cliffs, NJ: Prentice-Hall, 1984); William Burr, ed., *The Kissinger Transcripts* (New York: New Press, 1998); Zbigniew Brzezinski, *Power and Principle: Memoirs of the National Security Adviser, 1977–1981* (New York: Farrar, Straus, and Giroux, 1983); Richard H. Soloman, *Chinese Political Negotiating Behavior, 1967–1984* (Santa Monica, CA: Rand Corporation, 1995); James C. H. Shen, *The U.S. and Free China* (Washington, DC: Acropolis, 1983); Yen Chia-kan, *National Construction Collections* (Taipei: Editorial Board of the National Construction Collections, 1971); Priscilla Roberts, ed., *Window on the Forbidden City: The Beijing Diaries of David Bruce, 1973–1974* (Hong Kong: Centre of Asian Studies, University of Hong Kong, 2001).

2. The ten letters are: (1) package concerning letter from Chiang Kai-shek to Nixon dealing with modification of Taiwan Strait patrol, dated Nov. 14, 1969; (2) reply from Nixon to Chiang Kai-shek responding to Chiang's letter dated Nov. 14, 1969; (3) letter from Chiang Kai-shek to Nixon containing birthday congratulations; (4) Taiwan Strait patrol package—letter from Chiang Kai-shek dated Nov. 19, 1969, and reply by Nixon on Dec. 15, 1969; (5) Nixon's Mar. 20, 1970, reply to Chiang's letter of March 1, 1970; (6) letter from Nixon, dated Apr. 13, 1969, to Chiang Kai-shek wishing Madame Chiang an early recovery from her accident; (7) July 23, 1969, message from Nixon expressing regrets that he would be unable to visit the Republic of China on his trip; (8) Mar. 1, 1970, letter from Chiang expressing his dismay at the resumption of the Warsaw talks; (9) Apr. 17, 1970, letter from Chiang Kai-shek concerning Vice Premier Chiang Ching-kuo's visit to the United States; (10) May 5, 1970, letter from Chiang to Nixon expressing support and satisfaction concerning U.S. actions in Cambodia. All of these are contained in Republic of China corres. President Chiang Kai-shek, Presidential Correspondence 1969–1974, Box 751, Nixon Presidential Materials (hereafter cited as NPM), National Archives, College Park, MD.

3. On July 16, 1971, Nixon sent a letter to Chiang Kai-shek, expressing no change in his promise to defend Taiwan jointly. On Oct. 18, 1971, Chiang sent a letter to Nixon, expressing his gratitude for Nixon's dispatching of Ronald Reagan, governor of California, to attend the sixtieth anniversary of the founding of the Republic of China. The date of the last letter from Chiang to Nixon collected by the U.S. National Archives is Jan. 6, 1972. In the letter, Chiang pointed out he was convinced Nixon knew thoroughly the nature of the Chinese Communist regime and "would never be fooled." See "Letter from President Chiang to President Nixon, January 6, 1972," "Letter from President Chiang to President Nixon, October 18, 1971," and From SECSTATE to AMEMBASSY TAIPEI, secret telegram, "Letter to President Chiang from President Nixon," July 16, 1971; all in Republic of China corres. President Chiang Kai-shek, President Correspondence 1969–1974, Box 751, NPM.

4. From Henry Kissinger to Secretary of State, Secretary of Defense, and Director of Central Intelligence, "National Security Study Memorandum 14," Feb. 5, 1969, US China Policy 1969–1972 (1 of 2), Far East, Box 86, NPM.

5. From Henry Kissinger to Secretary of State, Secretary of Treasury, and Secretary of Commerce, "National Security Decision Memorandum 17," June 26, 1969, US China Policy 1969–1972 (1 of 2), Far East, Box 86, NPM.

6. The six categories were congressmen; correspondents; teachers; scholars or students; scientists or doctors; and representatives of the Red Cross (U.S. Department of State, Press Releases no. 211, July 21, 1969, and no. 378, Dec. 19, 1969).

7. U.S. Department of State, Press Release no. 378, Dec. 19, 1969.

8. Shen, *The U.S. and Free China*, 2–3.

9. "Modification of the Taiwan Strait Patrol," Secret BP-12, Dec. 8, 1969, V.P. Agnew's Trip December 1969–January 1970, Republic of China, FOR THE VICE PRESIDENT, Far East–General, Box 81, NPM.

10. "The Foreign Ministry's Telegram to the Delegation in the UN," secret telegram no. 604, Nov. 13, 1969; "Wei Tao-ming to the Foreign Ministry," Top Secret Telegram no. 9778, Nov. 13, 1969, "Le Cheng Program," Department of North American Affairs, Ministry of Foreign Affairs, MOFA Beitou Archives.

11. From AMEMBASSY TAIPEI to SECSTATE, secret telegram, "Modification of Taiwan Strait Patrol," Nov. 14, 1969, Republic of China corres. President Chiang Kai-shek, Presidential Correspondence 1969–1974, Box 751, NPM.

12. From AMEMBASSY TAIPEI to SECSTATE, secret telegram, "Modification Taiwan Strait Patrol," Nov. 16, 1969, Republic of China corres. President Chiang Kai-shek, Presidential Correspondence 1969–1974, Box 751, NPM.

13. From William P. Rogers to the President, "Memorandum," Response to President Chiang's Message concerning Modification of the Taiwan Strait Patrol, Nov. 19, 1969, Republic of China corres. President Chiang Kai-shek, Presidential Correspondence 1969–1974, Box 751, NPM.

14. "Memorandum of Conversation: July 9, 1972," China Visit Record of Previous Visits Arranged by Subject Matter, Book 1, Far East, Box 90, NPM.

15. "Memorandum of Conversation, July 22, 1972," Presidential Conversation in the PRC February 1972, arranged by Subject Matter, for the President's Files (Winston Lord–China Trip/Vietnam), Box 848, NPM.

16. Ibid.

17. Shen, *The U.S. and Free China*, 3.

18. From President Chiang Kai-shek to President Richard M. Nixon, Nov. 19, 1969, Republic of China corres. President Chiang Kai-shek, Presidential Correspondence 1969–1974, Box 751, NPM.

19. "Modification of the Taiwan Strait Patrol," Secret BP-12, Dec. 8, 1969, V.P. Agnew's Trip, December 1969–January 1970, Republic of China, FOR THE VICE PRESIDENT, Far East–General, Box 81, NPM.

20. Ibid.

21. From John H. Holdridge to Dr. Kissinger, secret memorandum, "Proposed Presidential Letter to Chiang Kai-shek—the Issue of F-4s," Dec. 1, 1969, Republic of China corres. President Chiang Kai-shek, Presidential Correspondence 1969–1974, Box 751, NPM.

22. "Reply Letter from President Nixon to Chiang Kai-shek responding to Chiang's Letter dated November 14, 1969," Dec. 15, 1969, Republic of China

corres. President Chiang Kai-shek, Presidential Correspondence 1969–1974, Box 751, NPM.

23. Shen, *The U.S. and Free China*, 67.

24. "Modification of the Taiwan Strait Patrol," Secret BP-12, Dec. 8, 1969, V.P. Agnew's Trip December 1969–January 1970, Republic of China, FOR THE VICE PRESIDENT, Far East–General, Box 81, NPM.

25. "Letter from President Chiang Kai-shek to President Richard Nixon, March 1, 1970," Republic of China corres. President Chiang Kai-shek, Presidential Correspondence 1969–1974, Box 751, NPM.

26. United Nations, *Yearbook of the United Nations* (Lake Success, NY: Department of Public Information, United Nations, 1950), 423.

27. Yen, *National Construction Collections*, 186.

28. The Soviet proposal was voted down with 48 against, 36 for, and 30 abstaining (ibid).

29. Ibid., 188.

30. National Security Study Memorandum 107, Nov. 19, 1970, National Security Council to the Secretary of State and Director of Central Intelligence, "Study of Entire UN Membership Question: US-China Policy," US-China Policy, 1969–1972 (1 of 2), Far East, Box 86, NPM.

31. From Henry Kissinger to the President, memorandum, "Chinese Representation at the United Nations," Mar. 20, 1971, China–United Nations, Far East, Box 86, NPM.

32. Ibid.

33. Nixon, *The Memoirs of Richard Nixon*, 2: 17.

34. "The President's News Conference of June 1, 1971," US-China Policy, 1969–1972 (1 of 2), Far East, Box 86, NPM.

35. "Memorandum of Conversation, July 11, 1971, 10:35 A.M.–11:55 A.M.," China Visit Record of Previous Visits, arranged by Subject Matter, February 1972, Book I (1 of 2), Far East, Box 90, NPM.

36. Ibid.

37. "James C. H. Shen to the Ministry of Foreign Affairs," Urgent Top Secret Telegram no. 8005, July 15, 1971, 405–22 (Nixon Visit to Communist Region 3), Department of North American Affairs, Ministry of Foreign Affairs, MOFA Beitou Archives (hereafter DNAA); Shen, *The U.S. and Free China*, 69.

38. Shen, *The U.S. and Free China*, 74.

39. Gao Lang, *Zhonghua minguo waijiao guanxi zhi yanbian, 1950–1972* (The evolution of the diplomatic relations of the Republic of China) (Taipei: Wu Nan tushu chuban, 1993), 203.

40. Ibid.

41. From Thomas P. Shoesmith to Green and De Palma, briefing memorandum, "Your Meeting with Ambassadors Chow and Liu—Response to GRC Queries on Our Use of the Veto in the Security Council," Jan. 22, 1972, POL 17, Ambassador Chow's Consultation with White House and Department Officials, 1969–1971, Box 9, The Office of Republic of China Affairs, RG59, General Records of the Department of State, National Archives, College Park, Maryland (hereafter GRDS).

42. From US Mission USUN to SECSTATE, "CHIREP–Phillips/Liu Meeting January 12," POL 17, Ambassador Chow's Consultation with White House and Department Officials, 1969–1971, Box 9, The Office of Republic of China Affairs, RG59, GRDS.

43. From Shoesmith to Green and De Palma, "Your Meeting with Ambassadors Chow and Liu" (see note 41 to this chapter).

44. Ibid.

45. From AMEMBASSY TAIPEI to SECSTATE, secret telegram, "CHIREP," July 12, 1971, UN 6 CHICOM, 7/1/71–8/6/71, Box 3211, Central Foreign Policy Files, 1970–1973, RG59, GRDS.

46. From USMISSION UNUS to SECSTATE, secret telegram, "Memorandum of Conversation: FM Chow, October 14, 1971," October 15, 1971, UN 6 CHICOM, 7/1/71–8/6/71, Box 3211, Central Foreign Policy Files, 1970–1973, RG 59, GRDS.

47. From USUN to TAIPEI, "Chirep–Contingency Planning," October 21, 1971, UN 6 CHICOM, 10/14/71–10/23/71, Box 3215, Central Foreign Policy Files, 1970–1973, RG 59, GRDS.

48. Kissinger, *White House Years*, 771.

49. Ibid.

50. Ibid., 772.

51. Ibid., 773.

52. Ibid.

53. Nixon did not tell Rogers the details; he said Kissinger had received an invitation when he was in Pakistan, and the visit was a last-minute decision (ibid., 739).

54. Ibid., 773.

55. William P. Rogers, "Chinese Representation in the United Nations," Aug. 2, 1971, US-China Policy, 1969–1972 (1 of 2), Far East, Box 86, NPM.

56. "A Brief Record of the Conference between Ambassador Brown and This Ministry on the Chinese Representation in the UN," Mar. 9, 1971, 414–18 (Chinese Representation in the UN, Vol. 1), DNAA.

57. Thomas P. Shoesmith to Ambassador Brown, "CHIREP Proposed VP Visit to Taipei," Mar. 19, 1971, POL 36 Chinese Recognition, 1971–1972, Box 9, Subject Files of the Office of Republic of China Affairs, RG 59, GRDS.

58. From Secretary of State to AMEMBASSY TAIPEI, top secret telegram, Apr. 19, 1971, China UN Sensitive, Far East, Box 86, NPM.

59. Shen, *The U.S. and Free China*, 58.

60. Murphy was then chair of the Board of Directors of Corning Glass International. For the record of the meeting, see "Summary Record of a Conversation Between President Chiang Kai-shek and Mr. Robert D. Murphy" and from Henry A. Kissinger to the President, "Bob Murphy's Meeting with Chiang," not dated, China–United Nations Sensitive, Far East, Box 86, NPM.

61. Ibid.

62. From Theodore L. Eliot, Jr., executive secretary of Department of State, memorandum for Mr. Henry A. Kissinger, "Chinese Representation in Security Council," May 5, 1971, China–United Nations Sensitive, Far East, Box 86, NPM.

63. From Marshall Wright to Henry Kissinger, "NSSM–the UN Membership question," March 3, 1971, China–United Nations Sensitive, Far East, Box 86, NPM.

64. From Henry A. Kissinger to the President, "Chinese Representation in the UN," May 19, 1971. China–United Nations Sensitive, Far East, Box 86, NPM.

65. From AMEMBASSY TAIPEI to SECSTATE, secret telegram, "CHIREP," July 12, 1971, UN 6 CHICOM 7/1/71–8/6/71, Box 3211, Central Foreign Policy Files, 1970–1973, RG 59, GRDS; from Marshall Green and Samuel De Palma to Acting Secretary, "CHIREP: ROC Acceptance of a Dual Representation Formula," July 12, 1971, UN 6 CHICOM 7/1/71–8/6/71, Box 3211, Central Foreign Policy Files, 1970–1973, RG 59, GRDS.

66. Memorandum of conversation, "China Visit," July 9, 1971, China Visit Record of Previous Visits Arranged by Subject Matter, Book I, Far East, Box 90, NPM.

67. From Marshall Green and Samuel De Palma to Secretary, "CHIREP-Scenario," July 18, 1971, UN 6 CHICOM, 7/1/71–8/6/71, Box 3211, Central Foreign Policy Files, 1970–1973, RG 59, GRDS.

68. From AMEMBASSY TAIPEI to SECSTATE, secret telegram, "VICE-MIN Yang's Effort Toward GRC Flexibility on CHIREP and CHIREC," July 20, 1971, UN 6 CHICOM 7/1/71–8/6/71, Box 3211, Central Foreign Policy Files, 1970–1973, RG 59, GRDS.

69. Ibid.

70. From AMEMBASSY TAIPEI to SECSTATE, secret telegram, "GRC Response to President's Announcement on CHIREP," July 22, 1971, UN 6

CHICOM 7/1/71–8/6/71, Box 3211, Central Foreign Policy Files, 1970–1973, RG 59, GRDS.

71. From AMEMBASSY TAIPEI to SECSTATE, secret telegram, "Ambassador's Conversation with FONMIN Chow on CHIREP," July 26, 1971, UN 6 CHICOM 7/1/71–8/6/71, Box 3211, Central Foreign Policy Files, 1970–1972, RG 59, GRDS.

72. Ibid.

73. From AMEMBASSY TAIPEI to SECSTATE, secret telegram, "CHIREP: GRC Partial Decision," July 27, 1971, UN 6 CHICOM 7/1/71–8/6/71, Box 3211, Central Foreign Policy Files, 1970–1973, RG 59, GRDS.

74. Ibid.

75. From Department of State to AMEMBASSY TAIPEI, secret telegram, "Secretary's Meeting with Ambassador Shen and Liu," July 26, 1971, UN 6 CHICOM 7/1/71–8/6/71, Box 3211, Central Foreign Policy Files, 1970–1973, RG 59, GRDS.

76. From William Rogers to the President, Memorandum, "Chinese Representation in the United Nations," UN 6 CHICOM, 9/1/71–9/24/71, Box 3213, Central Foreign Policy Files, 1970–1973, RG 59, GRDS.

77. From AMEMBASSY TAIPEI to SECSTATE, secret telegram, "CHIREP," August 28, 1971, UN 6 CHICOM 8/1/71–9/4/71, Box 3212, Central Foreign Policy Files, 1970–1973, RG 59, GRDS.

78. From Samuel De Palma and Marshall Green to the Secretary, Action Memorandum, "CHIREP–Message to ROC Foreign Ministry on Need to Table Dual Representation which includes Security Council Recommendation," Department of State, September 3, 1971, UN 6 CHICOM 8/1/71–9/4/71, Box 3212, Central Foreign Policy Files, 1970–1973, RG 59, GRDS.

79. Ibid.

80. From the Secretary to AMEMBASSY TAIPEI, secret telegram, "CHIREP: Delivery of Secretary's Message to ROC FONMIN," Sept. 8, 1971, UN 6 CHICOM 8/1/71–9/4/71, Box 3212, Central Foreign Policy Files, 1970–1973, RG 59, GRDS.

81. From AMEMBASSY TAIPEI to SECSTATE, secret telegram, "CHIREP: Text of FONMIN Chow's Reply to Secretary's Message of September 8," Sept. 10, 1971, UN 6 CHICOM 8/1/71–9/4/71, Box 3212, Central Foreign Policy Files, 1970–1973, RG 59, GRDS.

82. "The President's News Conference of September 16, 1971," US China Policy, 1969–1972 (1 of 2), Far East, Box 86, NPM.

83. From USMISSION USUN to SECSTATE, "Memorandum of Conversation: FM Chow, October 14, 1971," October 15, 1971, UN 6 CHICOM

10/14/71–10/23/71, Box 3215, Central Foreign Policy Files, 1970–1973, RG 59, GRDS.

84. Memorandum of conversation, "UN and IndoChina," Oct. 21, 1971, China Visit Record of Previous Visits Arranged by Subject Matter, Book I, Far East, Box 90, NPM.

85. Kissinger, *White House Years*, 770.

86. John W. Garver, *The Sino-American Alliance* (Armonk, NY: M. E. Sharpe, 1997), 259.

87. Ibid.

88. "Premier Yang's Report on the Current Diplomatic Situation," *Bulletin of the Legislative Yuan* 60, no. 80 (Oct. 30, 1971): 4; Wang Jinghong (James C. Wang), *Caifang lishi: cong Hua fu dang'an kan Taiwan* (In search of history: Taiwan as seen in Washington's classified files) (Taipei: Yuanliu chuban, 2000), 388–89; "The Annual Report of the Chinese Delegation to the 26th Session of the UN General Assembly" (Taipei: Ministry of Foreign Affairs, 1971), 108; Garver, *Sino-American Alliance*, 259.

89. TAIPEI to SECSTATE, Confidential Telegram, "CHIREP, ROC," Oct. 23, 1971, UN 6 CHICOM 10/14/71–10/23/71, Box 3215, Central Foreign Policy Files, 1970–1973, RG 59, GRDS.

90. Shen, *The U.S. and Free China*, 62.

91. Ibid., 60.

92. Foreign Minister Chow Shu-kai, "The Course of Our Withdrawal from the UN and the Diplomacy in the Future," Legislative Yuan Meeting no. 48, Record of the 4th Meeting of the Foreign Relations Committee, Nov. 6, 1971.

93. Shen, *The U.S. and Free China*, 63.

94. Memorandum of conversation, "China Visit," July 11, 1971, China Visit Record of Previous Visits Arranged by Subject Matter, Book I, Far East, Box 90, NPM.

95. Memorandum of conversation, "China Visit," July 9, 1971, China Visit Record of Previous Visits Arranged by Subject Matter, Book I, Far East, Box 90, NPM.

96. From the Secretary to AMEMBASSY TAIPEI, secret telegram, "CHIREP," Oct. 26, 1971, UN 6 CHICOM, 10/24/71–11/25/71, Box 3216, Central Foreign Policy Files, 1970–1973, RG 59, GRDS.

97. Before the end of 1974, the United States repeatedly reiterated its intent to keep the Mutual Defense Treaty with the ROC; see "An Analysis of U.S. Policy Toward China Since the Issuance of the Shanghai Communiqué by the U.S. and Communist China," Jan. 1, 1972, to Dec. 31, 1974, 411–2, DNAA.

98. Memorandum of conversation, Feb. 22, 1972, 2:10 P.M.–6:00 P.M., Presidential Conversations in the PRC, February 1972 Arranged by Subject Matter, for the President's Files (Winston Lord)–China Trip / Vietnam, Box 848, NPM.

99. Memorandum of conversation, July 10, 1971, 12:10 P.M.–6:00 P.M., "Taiwan," China Visit Record of Previous Visits arranged by Subject Matter, Book I, Box 90, Far East, NPM.

100. Memorandum of conversation, July 9, 1971, 4:35 P.M.–11:20 P.M., "Taiwan," China Visit Record of Previous Visits Arranged by Subject Matter, Book I, Box 90, Far East, NPM.

101. Memorandum of conversation, Feb. 24, 1972, "Taiwan," Presidential Conversation in the PRC, February 1972 Arranged by Subject Matter, for the Presidential Files (Winston Lord)–China Trip / Vietnam, Box 848, NPM.

102. Memorandum of conversation, Feb. 22, 1972, "Taiwan," ibid.

103. Memorandum of conversation, Feb. 24, 1972, "Taiwan," ibid.

104. Memorandum, "Taiwan, February talks, 1973," China Visit Record of Previous Visits Arranged by Subject Matter, Book I, Far East, Box 90, NPM.

105. "An Analysis of U.S. Policy Toward China Since the Issuance of the Shanghai Communiqué by the U.S. and Communist China," Jan. 1, 1972, to Dec. 31, 1974, 411-2, DNAA; "President Nixon Declared He Would Visit Mao and Communist China Soon" (Report on Nixon's visit to Communist Region), Aug. 4–11, 1971, 401-1, DNAA.

106. "Influence of Nixon's Visit to Communist Region and Our Countermeasures" (Report on Nixon's visit to Communist Region, various reactions), July 1971 to April 1972, 405-22, DNAA.

107. "Foreign Minister Shen Chang-huan's Letter to Premier Chiang," Nov. 13, 1975 (President Ford's Visit to Communist Region, Vol. 1), Oct. 1 to November 1975, 405-22, DNAA.

108. Ibid.

109. Shen, *The U.S. and Free China*, 18.

110. "An Analysis of U.S. Policy Toward China Since the Issuance of the Shanghai Communiqué by the U.S. and Communist China," Jan. 1, 1972, to Dec. 31, 1974, 411-2, DNAA.

111. Shen, *The U.S. and Free China*, 167.

112. Ibid., 171.

113. Ibid., 173.

114. U.S. Congress, House, Committee on Foreign Affairs, *The New Era in East Asia*, Hearings, 97th Congress, 1st Session, May 19, 20, 28; June 3, 10; and July 16, 1981 (Washington, DC: GPO, 1981), 39.

115. "An Analysis of the Statement by U.S. President Nixon to Visit Communist Region and Our Standing," Aug. 28, 1971, Foreign (60), North America 1, no. 017090, "Nixon's Visit to Communist Region," vol. 4, 405–22, DNAA.

116. From AMEMBASSY TAIPEI to SECSTATE, telegram, "FONMIN Announces ROC Foreign Policy Guidelines," Nov. 17, 1971, from POL CHINA to POL 7 CHINAT, Subject Numeric Files, 1970–73, Box 2202, RG59, GRDS.

117. From American Embassy TAIPEI to Department of State, airgram, "ROC Foreign Minister Announces 'Pragmatic' Foreign Policy," Apr. 3, 1972, from POL CHINA to POL 7 CHINAT, Subject Numeric Files, 1970–73, Box 2202, RG59, GRDS.

118. "Republic of China: 'All-Out Diplomacy,'" intelligence note, secret, Apr. 12, 1972, 3, from POL CHINA to POL 7 CHINAT, Subject Numeric Files, 1970–73, Box 2202, RG59, GRDS.

119. Ibid.

120. Ibid.; from AMEMBASSY TAIPEI to Department of State, airgram, confidential, "The ROC's International Position," Mar. 6, 1973, 8, from POL CHINA to POL 7 CHINAT, Subject Numeric Files, 1970–73, Box 2202, RG59, GRDS.

121. On Aug. 8, 1972, Premier Chiang delineated the territory of the ROC in a formal attack on Japan's China policy; see "The ROC's International Position," Mar. 6, 1973, 5.

122. Ibid., 3.

123. "Republic of China: 'All-out Diplomacy,'" intelligence note, secret, from POL CHINA to POL 7 CHINAT, Subject Numeric Files, 1970–73, Box 2202, RG59, GRDS.

124. "Foreign Minister Cho[w] Shu-kai's Foreign Policy Report," Mar. 8, 1972, 6, from POL CHINA to POL 7 CHINAT, Subject Numeric Files, 1970–73, Box 2202, RG59, GRDS.

125. From AMEMBASSY TAIPEI to Department of State, airgram, confidential, "The ROC's International Position," Mar. 6, 1973, 6, from POL CHINA to POL 7 CHINAT, Subject Numeric Files, 1970–73, Box 2202, RG59, GRDS.

126. *China News*, Mar. 9, 1972, 1; John W. Garver, "Taiwan's Russian Option: Image and Reality," *Asian Survey* 17, no. 7 (July 1978): 765.

127. Garver, "Taiwan's Russian Option," 765.

128. *China Yearbook, 1972–1973* (Taipei: China Publishing, 1973), 151; Garver, "Taiwan's Russian Option," 766.

129. Shen, *The U.S. and Free China*, 114.

130. Ibid.

131. From AMEMBASSY TAIPEI to Department of State, airgram, secret, "Conversation of Vice Foreign Minister H. K. Yang with Ambassador," Mar. 24, 1972, 3, from POL CHINA to POL 7 CHINAT, Subject Numeric Files, 1970–73, Box 2202, RG59, GRDS.

132. From Marshall Green to the Secretary of State, action memorandum, confidential, "Letter to Former Foreign Minister Chow Shu-kai," June 1, 1972, from POL 7 CHINAT to POL 15-2 CHINAT, Subject Numeric Files, 1970–73, Box 2203, RG59, GRDS.

133. Garver, *Sino-American Alliance*, 278.

134. "ROC Political Matters," memorandum of conversation, secret, Mar. 16, 1972, 3, from POL CHINAT-US to POL 17 CHINAT-US, Subject Numeric Files, 1970–1973, Box 2206, RG59, GRDS.

135. Ibid., 4.

136. Ibid.

137. From AMEMBASSY TAIPEI to SECSTATE, secret telegram, "Sensitivities in ROC over Adjustments in ROC–East European Relations," Mar. 16, 1972, 1, 3, from POL CHINA to POL 7 CHINAT, Subject Numeric Files, 1970–73, Box 2202, RG59, GRDS.

138. "The Republic of China and the USSR: Fishing Around," intelligence note, secret, July 11, 1972, from POL 17-1 CHINAT-US to POL 2 COL, Subject Numeric Files, 1970–73, Box 2207, RG59, GRDS.

139. Ibid.

140. Ibid.

141. Ibid.

142. "After the Gimo: Interim Contingency Paper," secret, Mar. 30, 1973, 5, NSC EA/IG Contingency Study: Succession in the Republic of China, 1972, from POL 7 CHINAT to POL 15-2 CHINAT, Subject Numeric Files, 1970–73, Box 2203, RG59, GRDS.

143. "China, Taiwan, and the Soviet Union," memorandum of conversation, confidential, May 1, 1972, from POL 17-1 CHINA-US to POL 2 COL, Subject Numeric Files, 1970–73, Box 2207, RG59, GRDS.

144. Ibid.

145. "After the Gimo: Interim Contingency Paper," secret, Mar. 30, 1973, 6, NSC EA/IG Contingency Study: Succession in the Republic of China, 1972, from POL 7 CHINAT to POL 15-2 CHINAT, Subject Numeric Files, 1970–1973, Box 2203, RG59, GRDS.

146. From AMEMBASSY TAIPEI to SECSTATE, confidential telegram, "ROC Leaks Information on Soviet Warship Transit of Taiwan Straits," May 16, 1973, 1, from POL 18 CHINA to POL A CHINAT, Subject Numeric Files, 1970–1973, Box 2204, RG59, GRDS.

147. Ibid., 2.

148. From AMEMBASSY TAIPEI to SECSTATE, telegram, "Reaction to Soviet Warships Transiting Taiwan," May 29, 1973, 2, from POL 18 CHINA to POL A CHINAT, Subject Numeric Files, 1970–1973, Box 2204, RG59, GRDS.

149. From AMEMBASSY TAIPEI to SECSTATE WASHDC, secret telegram, "Ambassador's June 4 Conversation with Premier Chiang Ching-kuo: Latter's Enumeration of Cardinal Points in ROC Foreign Policy," June 8, 1973, from POL CHINA to POL 7 CHINAT, Subject Numeric Files, 1970–1973, Box 2204, RG59, GRDS.

150. Ibid.

151. Garver, *Sino-American Alliance*, 279.

152. Testimony by Assistant Secretary for East Asian and Pacific Affairs Arthur W. Hummel, Jr., before Subcommittee on Arms Control, Senate Foreign Relations Committee, Sept. 22, 1976, in *Department of State Bulletin* 75, no. 1946 (Oct. 11, 1976): 455.

153. Ibid., 455–56.

154. Ibid., 456.

155. "Premier's Administrative Report," *Bulletin of the Legislative Yuan* 66, no. 77 (Sept. 24, 1977): 97.

156. "Yu Guohua fayin, Ma Shuli fanyin" (Statements of Yu Kuo-hua and Ma Shu-li), in Zhongguo guomindang, Zhongyang dangshi weiyuanhui, ed., *Zhuisi yu huainian: Jinian Jiang Jingguo xiansheng shishi shizhounian koushu lishi zuotanhui jishi* (Memories and remembrances: records of an oral history symposium on the tenth anniversary of Chiang Ching-kuo's death) (Taipei: Jindai Zhongguo chubanshe, 1999), 6, 35, 36.

157. *Yearbook of the Central Bank* (Taipei: Division of Economic Research, Central Bank), 1969, 18; 1970, 17; 1971, 27; 1972, 25; 1973, 21; 1974, 24; 1975, 22; 1976, 23; 1977, 23; 1978, 28.

158. International Monetary Fund, *International Financial Statistics Yearbook* (Washington, DC: International Monetary Fund, 1979), 138–39.

159. Leo J. Moser, "Is CCK 'Taiwanizing' the ROC?" memorandum, political, general, 1972, Box 8, Bureau of East Asian Affairs, Subject Files of the Office of the Republic of China Affairs, RG59, GRDS.

160. "Administrative Report of the Board of Foreign Trade by Minister of Economic Affairs and Director of the Board of Foreign Trade," *Bulletin of the Legislative Yuan* 68, no. 58 (July 1, 1979): 51, 52; "Executive Yuan's Administrative Report—September, 67th Year," *Bulletin of the Legislative Yuan* 67, no. 76 (Sept. 23, 1978): 108.

161. "An Analysis of U.S. Policy Toward the ROC Since the Issuance of the Shanghai Communiqué by the U.S. and Communist China," Jan. 1, 1972, to

Dec. 31, 1974, 411-2, DNAA; from Winthrop G. Brown to the Secretary of State, action memorandum, "ROC Request to Open New Consulates," Mar. 1, 1972, POL 17 Diplomatic and Consular Representation, 1972, Box 10, Subject Files of the Office of Republic of China Affairs, 1951–1978, RG59, GRDS.

162. "Premier's Administrative Report," February 1979, *Bulletin of the Legislative Yuan* 68, no. 15 (Feb. 21, 1979): 103.

163. Compiled by Chang Chongyan, Department of the North American Affairs, Ministry of Foreign Affairs.

164. Department of Statistics, Executive Yuan, "Abstract of Statistics, 59th year of the ROC," 1971, 518; "Abstract of Statistics, 66th year of the ROC," 1978, 742; Ministry of Education, "Statistics of Education in the ROC," 1971, 144; 1972, 144; 1973, 155; 1974, 168; 1975, 42; 1976, 60; 1977, 36; 1979, 34.

165. "Telegram from the Embassy in Washington to the Foreign Ministry," no. 12775, Oct. 7, 1971 (American congressmen's proposal against expelling the ROC from the UN), Aug. 1 to Dec. 31, 1971, 414–28, DNAA.

166. "Telegram from the Embassy in Washington to the Foreign Ministry," no. 13428, Oct. 22, 1971 (American congressmen's proposal against expelling the ROC from the UN), Aug. 1 to Dec. 31, 1971, 414–28, Department of North America, Ministry of Foreign Affairs, MOFA Beitou Archives.

167. "Telegram from Shen Chien-hung to the Foreign Ministry," no. 008028, Nov. 15, 1975 (Resolution of the House of Representatives to befriend the ROC), Oct. 1 to Dec. 31, 1975, 400–32, DNAA.

168. "Telegram from James Shen to the Foreign Ministry," no. 15351, Nov. 21, 1975 (Resolution of the House of Representatives to befriend the ROC), Oct. 1 to Dec. 31, 1975, 400–32, DNAA.

169. "Telegram from the Embassy in Washington to the Foreign Ministry," urgent secret, no. 11670, July 25, 1978 (U.S. Senators Dole and Stone's amendment concerning the ROC-US Mutual Defense Treaty), and (Goldwater: signed with others to prevent Carter from annulling the treaty unilaterally), July 1 to Oct. 31, 1978, 400–31, DNAA.

170. "Telegram from James Shen to the Foreign Ministry," top secret, no. 16678, Oct. 12, 1978, July 1 to Oct. 31, 1978, 400-31, DNAA.

171. "Telegram from Chow Shu-kai to the Foreign Ministry," no. 1987, Mar. 14, 1970 (Renting submarines from the U.S.), Jan. 1, 1970, to Jan. 31, 1972, 422-2, DNAA.

172. "Secret Telegram from Chow Shu-kai to the Foreign Ministry," no. 11832, Dec. 5, 1970 (Renting submarines from the U.S.), Jan. 1, 1970, to Jan. 31, 1972, 42-2, DNAA.

173. "Representative Rivers Defends the Act to Lend Submarines to the ROC," Mar. 19, 1970, *yangmichai* (59), no. 0527 (Renting submarines from the U.S.), Jan. 1, 1970, to Jan. 31, 1972, 42-2, DNAA.

174. "An Analysis of Nixon's Visit to Communist China and Our Countermeasures in Propaganda Work" (Statements by the ministry against Nixon's visit to Communist China), Feb. 17 to Dec. 31, 1972, DNAA.

175. "A Letter from the Government Information Office, the Executive Yuan to Guanghua Committee, the Executive Yuan on May 5, the 61nd year of the Republic," (61) *jiujing jijia*, no. 2763 (Propaganda to the US), May 10, 1971, to Oct. 31, 1872, 403, DNAA.

176. Shen, *The U.S. and Free China*, 1.

Chapter 8

1. In 1970, Zbigniew Brzezinski characterized President John F. Kennedy as the first "globalist" U.S. president; see Zbigniew Brzezinski, *Between Two Ages: America's Role in the Technotronic Era* (New York: Viking Press, 1970), citation from the Russian translation (Moscow: Progress Publishers, 1970), 291.

2. See, e.g., Barry Buzan, Charles Jones, and Richard Little, *The Logic of Anarchy: Neorealism to Structural Realism* (New York: Columbia University Press, 1993).

3. Scott Burchill et al., *Theories of International Relations* (London: Macmillan; New York: St. Martin's Press, 1996).

4. An example is the attempt by Alexei Voskressenski to paint a coherent picture of past and present Russian-Chinese relations by using the concept of a multifactor equilibrium of the system (the separate political entities or national states); see A. D. Voskressenski, *Rossiya i Kitai: teoriya i istoriya mezhgosudarstvennikh otnoshenii* (Russia and China: theory and history of intergovernmental relations) (Moscow: Moskovskii obshestvennii nauchny fond, 1999).

5. See, e.g., the excellent monographs by Robert S. Ross, ed., *China, the United States, and the Soviet Union: Tripolarity and Policy Making in the Cold War* (Armonk, NY: M. E. Sharpe, 1993); Thomas W. Robinson and David Shambaugh, eds., *Chinese Foreign Policy: Theory and Practice* (Oxford: Clarendon Press, 1995); and Michael B. Yahuda, *The International Politics of the Asia-Pacific, 1945–1995* (London and New York: Routledge, 1996).

6. See A. D. Bogatourov, *Velikie derzhavi na Tikhom okeane: istoriya i teoriya mezhdunarodnikh otnoshenii v Voscochnoi Azii posle Vtoroi mirovoi voini* (Great powers in the Pacific Ocean: history and theory of international relations in East Asia after World War II [1945–95]) (Moscow: Voskovskii obshestvenni nauchnyi fond, 1997), 10.

7. For example, documents of the U.S. National Security Council, the Joint Chiefs of Staff (up to 1953), and hearings of the U.S. House and Senate subcommittees responsible for East Asia have been published.

8. Zbigniew Brzezinski, *Power and Principle: Memoirs of the National Security Adviser* (New York: Farrar, Straus and Giroux, 1983); Henry A. Kissinger, *White House Years* (Boston and Toronto: Little, Brown, 1979); Henry A. Kissinger, *Years of Upheaval* (Boston and Toronto: Little, Brown, 1982).

9. Soviet foreign policy has been thoroughly examined by many analysts, and a huge volume of special literature has been published, primarily in western countries. See, e.g., Gordon H. Chang, *Friends and Enemies: The United States, China, and the Soviet Union, 1948–1972* (Stanford: Stanford University Press, 1990); Ross, *China, the United States, and the Soviet Union*; Lowell Dittmer, *Sino-Soviet Normalization and Its International Implications, 1945–1990* (Seattle: University of Washington Press, 1992); Raymond L. Garthoff, *Perspectives on the Strategic Balance* (Washington, DC: Brookings Institution, 1983); Raymond L. Garthoff, *Détente and Confrontation: American-Soviet Relations from Nixon to Reagan* (Washington, DC: Brookings Institution, 1985); Harry Harding, *A Fragile Relationship: The United States and China Since 1972* (Washington, DC: Brookings Institution, 1992); Drew Middleton, *The Duel of the Giants: China and Russia in Asia* (New York: Scribners, 1978); Nicolai N. Petro and Alvin Z. Rubinstein, *Russian Foreign Policy: From Empire to Nation-State* (New York: Longman, 1997); Robert S. Ross, *Negotiating Cooperation: The United States and China, 1969–1989* (Stanford: Stanford University Press, 1995); Robert A. Scalapino, *Asia and the Major Powers: Implications for International Order* (Washington, DC: American Enterprise Institute for Public Policy Research, 1972); Richard Wich, *Sino-Soviet Crisis Politics: A Study of Political Change and Communication* (Cambridge, MA: Harvard University Press, 1980); Michael B. Yahuda, *Towards the End of Isolationism: China's Foreign Policy After Mao* (New York: St. Martin's Press, 1983).

10. It seems unlikely that the subject could be adequately understood without a thorough review of the materials contained in classical Soviet studies. See, e.g., S. L. Tikhvinsky et al., eds., *Vneshniaya politika Sovetskogo Soyuza* (Foreign policy of the Soviet Union) (Moscow: Politizdat, 1985); *Vneshniaya politika Sovetskogo Soyuza i mezhdunarodnie otnosheniya, 1961–1985* (Foreign policy of the Soviet Union and international relations) (Moscow: Mezhdunarodnie otnosheniya, 1988); O. B. Borisov and B. T. Koloskov, *Sovetsko-kitaiskiye otnosheniya, 1945–1980* (Soviet-Chinese relations, 1945–1980), 3rd ed. (Moscow: Mysl, 1980); A. M. Dubinsky, *Vneshniaya politika i mezhdunarodniye otnosheniya Kitaiskoi Narodnoi Respubliki* (Foreign policy and international relations of the People's Republic of China) (Moscow: Nauka, 1974); E. M. Zhukov, M. I. Sladkovsky,

G. V. Astafiev, and M. S. Kapitsa, eds., *Mezhdunarodniye otnosheniya na Dalnem Vostoke v poslevoyenniye godi* (International relations in the Far East in the years after the war), 2 vols. (Moscow: Mysl, 1978); M. S. Kapitsa, D. V. Petrov, and B. N. Slavinsky, *Istoriya mezhdunarodnikh otnoshenii na Dalnem Vostoke, 1945–1977* (The history of international relations in the Far East) (Khabarovsk: Khabarovskoye knizhnoye izdatelstvo, 1978); B. N. Slavinsky, *Vneshnyaya politika SSSR na Dalnem Vostoke, 1945–1986* (Foreign policy of the Soviet Union in the Far East) (Moscow: Mezhdunarodniye otnosheniya, 1988); G. V. Fokeev, ed., *Istoriya mezhdunarodnykh otnoshenii i vneshney politiki SSSR, 1917–1987* (The history of international relations and the Soviet Union's foreign policy) (Moscow: Mezhdunarodnyie otnosheniya, 1987).

11. For an example of Pleshakov's scholarship available in English, see Vladislav Zubok and Constantine Pleshakov, *Inside the Kremlin's Cold War: From Stalin to Khrushchev* (Cambridge, MA: Harvard University Press, 1996). For representative examples of old Soviet models of scholarship, see A. Arbatov, *Voenno-strategicheski paritet i politika SShA* (Military-strategic parity and U.S. policy) (Moscow: Politizdat, 1984); E. Bazhanov, *Dvizhushiye sily politici SShA v otnoshenii Kitaya* (The United States moving forces toward China) (Moscow: Nauka, 1982); Borisov and Koloskov, *Sovetsko-kitaiskiye otnosheniya*; M. S. Kapitsa, *KNR: tri desyatiletiya-tri politiki* (The PRC: three decades, three policies) (Moscow: Izdatelstvo politicheskoi literaturi, 1979); A. A. Kokoshin, *V poiskah vikhoda: voenno-politicheskiye aspecti mezhdunarodnoi bezopasnosti* (Military-political aspects of international security: the search for alternatives) (Moscow: Politizdat, 1989); V. P. Lukin, *Tzentry sili: kontzeptzii i realnost* (The centers of power: concepts and reality) (Moscow: Mezhdunarodniye otnosheniya, 1983); *Mesto Kitaya v globalnoi politike SShA* (China's place in U.S. global policy) (Moscow: Nauka, 1987); O. B. Rakhmanin, *K istorii otnoshenii RSFSR, SSSR, RF s Kitayem, 1917–1997 (obzor osnovnikh sobitiy, otzenki expertov)* (The history of the relationship between the RSFSR, the Soviet Union, the Russian Federation, and China, 1917–97 [review of major events, experts' appraisals]) (Moscow: Institut Dalnego Vostoka, 1999); S. M. Rogov, *Sovetskii Soyuz i SShA: poisk balansa interesov* (The Soviet Union and the United States: a search for the balance of interests) (Moscow: Mezhdunarodniye otnosheniya, 1989); B. N. Slavinski, *Vneshniaya politika SSSR na Dalnem Vostoke, 1945–1986* (Foreign policy of the Soviet Union in the Far East) (Moscow: Mezhdunarodniye otnosheniya, 1988); G. A. Trofimenko, ed., *Sovremennaya vneshniaya politika SShA* (Contemporary foreign policy of the United States), vols. 1–2 (Moscow: Nauka, 1984); G. A. Trofimenko, *SShA: politika, voina, ideologiya* (The United States: policy, war, ideology) (Moscow: Mysl, 1976); A. G. Yakovlev, *KNR i sotsiali-*

stichesky mir, 1949–1979 (The PRC and the socialist world), 2 vols. (Moscow: Institut Dalnego Vostoka, 1981).

12. Gu Mingyi, ed., *Zhongguo jindai waijiao shilue* (Essay on the history of contemporary Chinese diplomacy) (Changchun: Jilin wanshi chubanshe, 1987); Hu Lizhong, Jin Guangyao, and Chen Jishi, *Cong Nibuchu tiaoyue dao Eliqin fang Hua—Zhong-E Zhong-Su guanxi 300 nian* (From the Treaty of Nerchinsk to Yeltsin's visit to China: 300 years of Sino-Russian and Sino-Soviet relations) (Fuzhou: Fujian renmin chubanshe, 1994); Pei Jianzhang, ed., *Zhonghua renmin gongheguo waijiaoshi* (Diplomatic history of the People's Republic of China) (Beijing: Shijie zhishi chubanshe, 1994); Xia Yishan, ed., *Sulian waijiao liushiwu nian jishi* (History of Soviet foreign policy during the past 65 years) (Beijing: Shijie zhishi chubanshe, 1987); Yu Zhengliang, Yan Shengyi, and Wang Hongxiang, *Zhanhou guoji guanxi shigang* (History of international relations after World War II) (Beijing: Shijie zhishi chubanshe, 1987).

13. A. A. Gromyko, ed., *Dokumenti vneshnei politiki SSSR* (Documents of the Soviet Union's foreign policy), vols. 9–21 (Moscow: Gospolitizdat, 1957–77); *Vneshniaya politika Sovetskogo Soyuza i mezhdunarodniye otnosheniya: sbornik dokumentov, 1961–1985* (Foreign policy of the Soviet Union and international relations: collected documents, 1961–85) (Moscow: Mezhdunarodniye otnosheniya, 1962–86); *SSSR-KNR (1949–1983): dokumenty i materiali* (The USSR and the PRC [1949–83]: documents and materials) (Moscow: Ministry of Foreign Affairs of the Soviet Union, various dates).

14. G. A. Arbatov, *Zatyanuvsheesia vizdorovleniye (1953–1985): svidetelstvo sovremennika* (Long-drawn-out recovery [1953–85]: testimony of contemporaries) (Moscow: Mezhdunarodniye otnosheniya, 1991); A. A. Gromyko, *Pamyatnoye* (Unforgettable), vols. 1–2 (Moscow: Politizdat, 1990); A. F. Dobrynin, *Sugubo doveritelno: posol v Vashingtone pri shecti presidentah* (1962–1986) (Doubly confident: ambassador to Washington through six presidencies) (Moscow: Avtor, 1997); M. S. Kapitsa, *Na raznykh parallelyakh* (On different parallels) (Moscow: Kniga i Biznes, 1996); G. M. Korniyenko, *Holodnaya voina: svidetelstvo ee uchastnika* (The cold war: testimony of a participant) (Moscow: Mezhdunarodniye otnosheniya, 1995).

15. Shih Chih-yu, *China's Just World: The Morality of Chinese Foreign Policy* (Boulder, CO: Lynne Rienner, 1993), 123.

16. Garthoff, *Détente and Confrontation*, 26.

17. Ibid., 26. For an extrapolation of this approach to U.S.-Japanese cooperation, see Chalmers Johnson, "History Restarted: Japan-American Relations at the End of the Century," in *Pacific Economic Relations in the 1990s: Cooperation or Conflict?* ed. Richard Higgott, Richard Leaver, and John Ravenhill (St. Leonards, Australia: Allen and Unwin, 1993), 132–54.

18. Harry Harding, "China's Co-operative Behaviour," in Robinson and Shambaugh, *Chinese Foreign Policy*, 378.

19. The Nixon administration worked out the concept of "linkage" of the political settlement of the Vietnam problem with U.S. readiness to start arms control talks with the Soviets. Moscow's intractability about such linkage, and its relatively limited political influence over the intransigent North Vietnamese leaders, had by the end of the 1960s inspired Nixon to think of the trump card in the game with Moscow: a U.S.-China rapprochement. See Ilya Gaiduk, *The Soviet Union and the Vietnam War* (Chicago: Ivan R. Dee, 1996), 202–22.

20. See the profound analysis of the U.S. attitude toward its relations with China in Harding, *A Fragile Relationship*, 30–47.

21. Kissinger, *White House Years*, 172.

22. At the height of the Soviet-Chinese confrontation in 1969, Moscow was extremely sensitive to any sign of possible Sino-American collusion. In his memoirs, Nixon recalled Moscow's diplomatic offensive, starting as early as October 1969, toward the United States. Based on some information, probably from intelligence sources, about U.S. attitudes toward relations with China, the Soviet authorities charged Ambassador Dobrynin with the mission of delivering a strong message from Soviet leaders. They warned the American side that "to make a profit from Soviet-Chinese relations at the Soviet Union's expense" could "lead to very grave miscalculations" and would not be consistent with the goal of better relations between the United States and the Soviet Union. See Richard M. Nixon, *The Memoirs of Richard Nixon* (London: Sidgwick and Jackson, 1978), 405.

23. Peter Zwick, *Soviet Foreign Relations: Process and Policy* (Englewood Cliffs, NJ: Prentice-Hall, 1990), 205.

24. Yahuda, *Towards the End of Isolationism*, 117, 119.

25. See Ross, *Negotiating Cooperation*, 26–27, 30–31. Zhou Enlai admitted in August 1971 that for China the Soviet threat had, to a certain extent, become even more dangerous than the U.S. threat; quoted in O. B. Borisov, *Kitaiskaya problema, 70-e godi* (The Chinese problem, 1970s) (Moscow: Institut Dalnego Vostoka, 1978), 1: 20.

26. See Yahuda, *Towards the End of Isolationism*, 38.

27. "The CCP Central Committee Letter of Instruction on Nixon's visit to Beijing," July 20, 1971, Russian Archive of Foreign Policy (AVP), Reference materials on China (Mar. 6–Aug. 31, 1972), Inventory 59, Box 7, File 253, KI-040, 2: 53.

28. Ibid., 53–54.

29. See Harold C. Hinton, *The Bear at the Gate: Chinese Policymaking Under Soviet Pressure* (Washington, DC: American Enterprise Institute for Public Pol-

icy Research, 1971), 2–3; Ross, *Negotiating Cooperation*, 27; and Donald Zagoria, "Kremlinology: A Second Reply," *China Quarterly*, no. 50 (April–June 1872), 343–50.

30. Scalapino, *Asia and the Major Powers*, 28.

31. See A. I. Elizavetin, "Peregovori A. N. Kozygina s Zhou Enlaem v pekinskom aeroportu" (Talks between A. N. Kosygin and Zhou Enlai at the Beijing airport), *Problemi Dalnego Vostoka*, no. 5 (1992): 39–63.

32. Malcolm McIntosh, "Soviet Attitudes Toward East Asia," in *The Soviet Policy in East Asia: Predicaments of Power*, ed. Gerald Segal (London: Heineman, 1983), 24. In January 1975, Zhou accused the Soviet Union of bad faith because it had failed to adhere to the agreement that he claimed he had reached with Kosygin at their September 1969 meeting; see Michael B. Yahuda, "The Significance of Tripolarity in China's Policy Toward the United States Since 1972," in Ross, *China, the United States, and the Soviet Union*, 19.

33. See Leonid Brezhnev, report to the plenum, "On the Results of the International Conference of Communist and Workers' Parties," Russian State Archive of Contemporary History, Fond 2, Inventory 3, File no. 161, 3.

34. See Leonid Brezhnev, "On the CPSU Central Committee International Activity . . . ," 73.

35. Borisov and Koloskov, *Sovetsko-kitaiskie otnosheniya*, 466–67.

36. See AVP, Reference materials on China, Fond 57, Box 3, File no. 242, 13–18.

37. *Materiali XXIV siezda KPSS* (Materials of the Twenty-Fourth Congress of the CPSU) (Moscow: Politizdat, 1971), 11.

38. L. I. Brezhnev, *Leninskim kursom: rechi i statyi* (On the Leninist way: speeches and articles) (Moscow: Politizdat, 1973), 3: 495.

39. "Joint Communiqué Between the People's Republic of China and the United States of America, February 27, 1972," in Harding, *A Fragile Relationship*, 375.

40. Ibid., 376.

41. Ibid.

42. L. I. Brezhnev, "Report on the International Situation to the Plenary Meeting of the Central Committee of the CPSU," May 19, 1972, Russian State Archive of Contemporary History, Fond 2, Inventory 3, File no. 270, 65–67.

43. See, e.g., "Protocols of the Proceedings of the Plenary Meeting of the Central Committee of the CPSU, Apr. 26–27, 1973," Russian State Archive of Contemporary History, Fond 2, Inventory 3, File no. 292, 33.

44. See "Documents of the CPSU Central Committee Plenum in November 1971," Russian State Archive of Contemporary History, Fond 2, Inventory 3, File no. 245, 104.

45. See, e.g., the slashing criticisms of the ideas of Daniel Bell, *The Cultural Contradictions of Capitalism* (New York: Basic Books, 1976), by leading party ideologists V. Zagladin and I. Frolov, "Globalniye problemi sovremennosti: sotzialno-politicheskiye i ideino-teoreticheskiye aspecty" (Contemporary global problems: socio-political and ideological-theoretical aspects), *Kommunist* 1976, no. 16 (Nov.): 93–104.

46. For an assessment of the situation in the capitalist countries from the angle of Lenin's characterization of imperialism, see N. Inozemtzev, "O leninskoi metodologii analiza mirovogo obshestvennogo razvitiya" (On the Leninist methodology of the analysis of world social development), *Kommunist* 1976, no. 12 (Aug.), 66–77.

47. Garthoff, *Détente and Confrontation*, 41. Perhaps it was a reaction to Zhou Enlai's visits to countries in Asia and Africa in 1964; see Borisov, *Kitaiskaya problema*, 88.

48. *International Conference of Communist and Workers' Parties: Materials* (Moscow: Politizdat, 1969), 64.

49. See L. Brezhnev's report to the plenum in December 1969, "On the Practical Activity of the CPSU Central Committee's Politburo in the Spheres of Foreign and Domestic Policy," Protocol no. 12 of the CPSU Central Committee Plenary Meeting, Dec. 15, 1969, Russian State Archive of Contemporary History, Fond 2, Inventory 3, File no. 168, 79–80.

50. Garthoff (*Détente and Confrontation*, 13) points out that between 1969 and 1972, as Brezhnev was establishing his pre-eminence in foreign relations, a shift to new policies was required. Perhaps the need to develop economic ties was also essential.

51. Garthoff's (ibid., 14) suggestion that some Politburo members opposed Brezhnev's course is not supported by the facts. The members who left the Politburo in the 1970s, including P. Shelest, G. Voronov, A. Shelepin, and N. Podgorny, had nothing to do with international matters and were highly dependent on Brezhnev or Suslov. There were some debates on the lower level, but they never spread to the highest level. See Arbatov, *Zatyanuvsheesia vizdorovleniye*, 192–94. A high degree of consensus existed among Politburo members concerning the problems of foreign policy, according to Professor Lev Delusin, a former member of the CPSU Central Committee's think tank, a former assistant to Yuri Andropov, and an expert on China issues (pers. comm.).

52. Kissinger considered détente to be a new mode of containment, based on a balance of incentives and penalties depending on Moscow's behavior; see Kissinger, *Years of Upheaval*, 250–54.

53. Thomas W. Wolfe, "Concluding Reflections on the SALT Experience," in *The Conduct of Soviet Foreign Policy*, ed. Erik P. Hoffmann and Frederic J. Fleron (New York: Aldine, 1980), 407.

54. Gaiduk, *The Soviet Union and the Vietnam War*, 232.

55. AVP, Reference materials on China, Fond 59, Box 19, File no. 255, 1972, Doc. no. 276-kc, 28.

56. Ibid., 30.

57. Personal interview with Professor Delusin.

58. AVP, Reference materials on China, Fond 59, Box 19, File no. 255, 1972, Doc. no. 276-kc, 30.

59. Personal interview with Professor Delusin.

60. See details in the report of Soviet Minister of Foreign Affairs Andrei Gromyko to the party plenum in April 1975, Russian State Archive of Contemporary History, Fond 2, Inventory 3, File no. 353, 25.

61. Borisov and Koloskov, *Sovetsko-kitaiskiye otnosheniya*, 457–58.

62. Scalapino, *Asia and the Major Powers*, 60.

63. L. I. Brezhnev, "On the CPSU Central Committee International Activity in Realization of the Decisions of the Twenty-Fourth Party Congress," report to the plenary meeting of the Central Committee of the CPSU, Apr. 26, 1973, Russian State Archive of Contemporary History, Fond 2, Inventory 3, File no. 292, 33–35.

64. See N. I. Lebedev and N. M. Nikolsky, eds., *Vneshniaya politica Sovetskogo Soyuza: aktualnie problemi* (Foreign policy of the Soviet Union: actual problems) (Moscow: Mezhdunarodniye otnosheniya, 1976), 103–4.

65. See Materials of the CPSU Central Committee Plenum in November 1971, Russian State Archive of Contemporary History, Fond 2, Inventory 3, File no. 245, 105.

66. L. I. Brezhnev, "Report on the International Situation to the Plenary Meeting of the Central Committee of the CPSU," May 19, 1972, Russian State Archive of Contemporary History, Fond 2, Inventory 3, File no. 270, 14.

67. Materials of the CPSU Central Committee Plenum in November 1971, Russian State Archive of Contemporary History, Fond 2, Inventory 3, File no. 245, 72.

68. North Vietnamese officials, in talks with Soviet diplomats, expressed concern over the possibility of a future U.S.-Chinese agreement; see Gaiduk, *The Soviet Union and the Vietnam War*, 232.

69. Harding, *A Fragile Relationship*, 48.

70. Ibid., 50.

71. *Renmin ribao*, Apr. 11, 1974.

72. See Borisov and Koloskov, *Sovetsko-kitaiskiye otnosheniya*, 459.

73. "Protocols of the Proceedings of the Plenary Meeting of the Central Committee of the CPSU," June 26, 1969, Russian State Archive of Contemporary History, Fond 2, Inventory 3, File no. 156, 100–101.

74. See the speech of the first secretary of the Uzbek Central Committee of the CPSU, Dinmuhammed Kunaev, at the Plenary Meeting of the Twenty-Third Central Committee of the CPSU, June 26, 1969, during the discussion of the International Conference of Communist and Workers' Parties, Russian State Archive of Contemporary History, Fond 2, Inventory 3, File no. 156, 101.

75. For example, even the leaders of North Vietnam, although very close to the Soviet Union, admitted that in the search for a solution to the Vietnam problem, they had to take "the Chinese factor" into serious consideration. See Materials of the CPSU Central Committee Plenum in November 1971, Russian State Archive of Contemporary History, Fond 2, Inventory 3, File no. 245, 72. That is why in recent years scholars have begun to pay more attention to the "political and psychological context," which they had underestimated as factors in great power policies; see Voskressenski, *Rossiya i Kitai*, 241.

76. As early as 1970, Zbigniew Brzezinski (*Between Two Ages*, 271) pointed out that Moscow's concern about the China threat was stimulating Soviet military preparations along the border.

77. Moreover, the Soviet leaders themselves had doubts about the USSR's status as an Asian power and hence excluded the United States and China from participation in the suggested system of collective security. Even after the Soviets changed their position in 1973 and agreed that all Asian nations could join the system, China was still not invited directly and the United States, as a non-Asian nation, was still regarded as unqualified. Thus, because the Soviets were limited by old stereotypes and the class-struggle approach, they began to lose the initiative in regional affairs.

78. See details in A. Bogatourov, *Yaponskaya diplomatiya v borbe za istochniki energeticheskogo siria (70-e godi)* (Japanese diplomacy in the struggle for the sources of energy raw material in the 1970s) (Moscow: Nauka, 1988).

79. Garthoff, *Détente and Confrontation*, 52.

80. In negotiating with their American counterparts, Soviet leaders tried to impose their own political "linkage" on Washington by pledging Moscow's help with Vietnam on the condition of reaching an understanding with the United States concerning China; see Adam Ulam, *Dangerous Relations: The Soviet Union in World Politics, 1970–1982* (New York: Oxford University Press, 1983), 75–76.

81. Bogatourov, *Velikie derzhavi na Tikhom okeane*, 168.

82. See A. Doak Barnett, "The Changing Strategic Balance in Asia," in *Sino-American Détente and Its Policy Implications*, ed. Gene T. Hsiao (New York: Praeger, 1974), 22.

83. *New York Times*, Dec. 8, 1975.

84. See, e.g., V. P. Lukin, *O nekotorikh aspectah amerikanskogo podhoda v Asii* (On several aspects of the American approach toward Asia), *SShA* 1976, no. 5 (May): 43.

85. Ibid., 46.

86. V. Sobakin, *Konstitutzionniye osnovi vneshnei politiki SSSR* (Constitutional basis for the Soviet Union's foreign policy), *Kommunist* 1977, no. 17 (Nov.): 110.

87. *Materiali XXV siezda KPSS* (Materials of the Twenty-Fifth Congress of the CPSU) (Moscow: Politizdat, 1976), 25; L. Koutakov, "Mir i bezopasnost v Azii: uroki istorii i sovremennost" (Peace and security in Asia: lessons of history and the present), *Kommunist* 1976, no. 11 (July): 107–17.

88. Yahuda, *Towards the End of Isolationism*, 200.

89. Ibid., 174.

90. "Soviet geopolitical activism was a result of a massive buildup of strategic and conventional weapons, the capability to deploy power in support of clients to distant points on the globe, and the will to do so, all, it must be said, under the rubric of détente" (Richard C. Thornton, "Recalculating the Strategic Triangle: America, Russia and China in the New World Order," in *The Study of Modern China*, ed. Eberhard Sandschneider [London: Hurst, 1999], 122).

91. Harry Gelman, "Outlook for Sino-Soviet Relations," in Hoffmann and Fleron, *The Conduct of Soviet Foreign Policy*, 617.

92. Yahuda, *Towards the End of Isolationism*, 169.

93. Gelman, "Outlook for Sino-Soviet Relations," 616.

94. The Soviets were sure that Beijing had foisted this thesis on Tokyo, although in general the treaty inspired great concern in Moscow; see, e.g., the interview with Yuri Tavrovsky, senior official of the CPSU Central Committee, in *USSR-China in the Changing World: Soviet Sinologists on the History and Prospects of Soviet-Chinese Relations* (Moscow: Novosty Press Agency Publishing House, 1989), 77.

95. See Robert A. Scalapino, *Major Power Relations in North East Asia* (Lanham, MD: University Press of America, 1987), 31.

96. See interview with Tavrovsky in *USSR-China in the Changing World*, 78.

97. For China, such policies were also related to the needs of the broad economic reform initiated at the Third Plenum of the CCP's Eleventh Central Committee. On the reasoning behind Chinese policy, see Kenneth Lieberthal, "China and the Soviet Union: The Background of Chinese Politics," in *The*

Sino-Soviet Conflict: A Global Perspective, ed. Herbert Ellison (Seattle: University of Washington Press, 1982), 3–28.

98. See Borisov and Koloskov, *Sovetsko-kitaiskiye otnosheniya*, 581.

99. For example, in Soviet appeals and statements to China, Moscow expressed the hope of seeing China friendly and prosperous. References to China as a socialist country are seldom found in those documents. See, e.g., TASS Statement on Soviet-China relations, *Pravda*, Mar. 21, 1978.

100. In a special statement, the USSR assured China that it would fulfill all the obligations stipulated by the Soviet-Vietnamese Treaty of Friendship and Cooperation; *Vneshniaya politika Sovetskogo Soyuza i mezhdunaridniye otnosheniya: cbornik dokumentov, 1979* (Foreign policy of the Soviet Union and international relations, collected documents) (Moscow: Mezhdunarodniye otnosheniya, 1980), 16–17.

101. Bogatourov, *Velikie derzhavi na Tikhom okeane*, 194–95.

102. See Zwick, *Soviet Foreign Relations*, 207.

103. Voskressenski, *Rossiya i Kitai*, 243.

104. See Borisov and Koloskov, *Sovetsko-kitaiskiye otnosheniya*, 601–2. See also Soviet statement in *Pravda*, Apr. 18, 1979.

Index

258, 261, 268–69, 317n11; military buildup of, 149–53, 157–58, 161–62, 169, 277–78, 285–86, 312n20, 317nn8–9; missiles of, 152, 157–59, 166, 267; new constitution of (1977), 277; and normalization, 145, 147–74, 255; nuclear weapons of, 58, 98, 153, 157, 163, 167, 172, 181, 193, 317n8; Pacific Fleet of, 150, 152, 157–58, 166, 262, 317n8; and Paris peace talks, 180, 183, 189–90; and PRC's U.S. policy, 122, 124, 154, 156, 205–6; and Sino-Japanese relations, 353n94; and Sino-U.S. relations, 2, 7, 9–10, 23, 25, 90–91, 93–94, 115, 158–61, 172, 176, 182, 192–93, 201, 209, 263–67, 269, 271, 278; and Sino-Vietnamese relations, 204–5; threat of war from, 58, 60, 62, 74, 151, 158, 316n5; and UN representation issue, 214–15; and Warsaw talks, 15
Soviet-Vietnamese relations: and PRC foreign policy, 278–79; and Sino-Soviet relations, 3–4, 166, 196–97, 206, 271, 273, 330n111, 352n80, 354n100; and Sino-U.S. relations, 115, 207, 351n68; and Sino-Vietnamese relations, 97, 166, 171, 204–5, 271, 352n75; and Soviet aid, 183, 204, 206, 282; and U.S.-Soviet relations, 162, 197, 199, 348n19, 352n80; and Vietnam War, 254, 271, 275, 277
Soviet-Vietnamese Treaty of Peace and Friendship (1978), 279, 354n100
Sri Lanka, 64
Stapleton, Roy, 3

State Council (PRC), 62, 66, 74–76, 80–81
State Department, U.S.: and Kissinger, 18, 28; and Nixon, 30, 43–44; and Shanghai Communiqué, 48–49; and Soviet-Taiwanese relations, 240–42; and Taiwan issue, 11–12, 27, 110, 213, 292n44; and UN representation issue, 32, 34–37, 216, 219–22, 224–27, 231; and Warsaw talks, 13–18
Steele, A. T., 87, 140
Stoessel, Walter, 13–14, 17
Supreme Soviet (USSR), 281
Suslov, Mikhail, 254, 350n51
Switzerland, 80
Syria, 271

Table-tennis diplomacy, 19, 119–20, 156, 189, 200, 311n11
Taiwan (Republic of China; ROC): anti-Americanism in, 30–31, 38; and communist countries, 238–43; and death of Mao, 297n122; democratization of, 244–45; diplomatic recognition of, 51, 224, 237, 250–51; economic development in, 22, 31, 38, 51–52, 83, 238–39, 243–44, 250; fears of instability in, 29–31, 38, 44, 51–53; foreign policy of, 51–52, 218, 238–40, 242; independence for, 21–22, 44, 115; independence movement on, 21–22, 27, 39, 42, 44–45, 100, 192, 233, 305n33; international status of, 38, 40, 51, 237, 250–51; legal status of, 25, 39; legitimacy of, 10, 21; media in, 64; military of, 13, 22, 45–46, 212,

Harvard East Asian Monographs
(*out-of-print)

Harvard East Asian Monographs

Harvard East Asian Monographs

Harvard East Asian Monographs

Harvard East Asian Monographs

Harvard East Asian Monographs

Harvard East Asian Monographs